THE MONEY MANAGER FOR CANADIANS

THE PRACTICAL GUIDE TO MAKING YOUR MONEY GROW

HENRY B. CIMMER

THE MONEY MANAGER FOR CANADIANS

HENRY B. CIMMER

First published in 1984 by Totem Books
and by Collins Publishers in 1989
This updated edition published 1993
by Springbank Publishing
5425 Elbow Drive SW, Calgary, Alberta T2V 1H7

Fourth edition
Formerly titled Making Your Money Grow and Henry B. Zimmer's Money Manager for Canadians.

Canadian Cataloguing in Publication Data

Cimmer, Henry B., 1943-
The money manager for Canadians

First-2nd eds. published under title: Henry B. Zimmer's money manager for Canadians ; 3rd ed. has title: Making your money grow.
ISBN 1-895653-10-X

1. Investments--Canada. 2. Finance, Personal. 3. Interest--Canada. I. Title. II. Title: Making your money grow.
HG4537.Z55 1993 332.6'78'0971 093-091743-X

Printed and bound in Canada

Contents

ACKNOWLEDGEMENTS

I would like to thank Doug Takahashi, computer consultant, for providing me with the math tables contained in this book. Great care has been taken in the preparation of these tables, although there is no warranty of their complete accuracy.

A special thank you to Sue Blanchard, my partner in Springbank Publishing for her encouragement and to Denton and Harold Pendergast, designers extraordinaire. My appreciation is also extended to Sherry Willetts who typed her heart out until all hours of the night!

This book is dedicated to everyone who needs
just that little bit of extra motivation to save
money and invest wisely.

For a ship that has no port, no wind is the right one.
Seneca

At present,
the prospects for real interest rates
are uncertain even over the near term.
Beyond 1986, this uncertainty increases enormously.
(Former) Finance Minister Michael H. Wilson

May 23, 1985

ON
ON/C
CE

ONE

You Don't Have to Be a Mathematical Genius

I failed algebra in my first term in grade eight. So, why, you might ask, am I writing this book? Well, eventually I caught on and did reasonably well in my high school math courses. In fact, when I finally realized (at the age of sixteen) that I'd never be a professional baseball player, I even decided to become a chartered accountant. A chartered accountant uses the initials "C.A.". In my case, C.A. stands for "Can't Add" and if I can't add, I can't do much better when it comes to subtraction, multiplication or division. Of course, that's without the benefit of a pocket calculator. In 1964, when I started in the accounting program as a junior audit clerk, my boss forced me to add columns of figures in my head for the first year to sharpen my skills.

In the last thirty years, the advances in mathematical technology have been nothing less than astounding, although I'm just starting to enter the computer age. The picture on the opposite page is a humorous but fairly accurate drawing of the *only calculator* I've used in the last eight years. It adds, subtracts, multiplies and divides quite accurately. It has square root and percentage keys, but I've never used them. The error correction key I use often.

The book you're now starting to read will never be obsolete – even when practically every home in North America has a home computer and the software necessary to do all kinds of practical math calculations. When that day comes, what you'll learn from this book will be even more relevant. Some day, you'll be able to call up a program which will allow you to verify the daily interest on your savings account at the touch of a button. For the time being, however, *a simple calculator and this book are all you'll need to painlessly do virtually any mathematical calculations you require in business and investment decision-making.* Once you learn how to use the tables at the end of this book, the rest is easy. All you really have to do is be careful to use the *right* table at the *right* time.

There are actually many books of math tables available at your local bookstore. These books, however (at least the ones I've seen), are downright intimidating since they provide calculations to ten decimal places. This is perfectly acceptable if you're doing complex scientific calculations requiring accuracy to the nth degree. However, in order to make an intelligent business or investment decision, tables to three or four places are more than adequate. For example, they will enable you to check, within a few pennies, whether or not a lending institution is charging you the correct monthly payments on your mortgage, or calculate, within a few dollars, how much you'll have at the end of ten years if you save $100 a month.

Moreover, the table headings in the other books tend to confuse as well. The authors, generally being mathematicians, use terminology with which the average business person or investor is unfamiliar, such as "sinking fund factors payable at the end of each period" or "annuity whose accumulation at compound interest is $1". What often happens is that people are afraid to use these tables because they don't always know *which table to use and when to use it.*

Take a moment and flip through the thirteen tables which make up the last *hundred* pages or so of this book. You'll see each one is accompanied by a summary page that tells you immediately what its uses are and which chapters in this book explain or use each particular table. For example, Table 1 shows you how much you'll have at the end of one to fifty years if you invest $1 now at various interest rates and simply leave your money to grow. If you're presently sitting with $640 in your bank account, you need only multiply the factor in the table for $1 by 640 and there's your answer. What could be simpler?

Most of the other books I've looked at also contain not more than ten to twenty pages of explanation. These explanations deal with money but they don't give you a practical situation to which you can relate. With a little bit of effort, almost anyone can understand the concept of compound interest which is explained in Chapter Two. Also, it's not that hard to understand annuities, which are just income flows. For example, in Chapter Three you'll find out how to calculate what you'll have at the end of, say, ten years if you're capable of saving $100 each month and can earn 10% on your money. This, however, is only the beginning. **Practical business and investment mathematics has many much broader applications; and this is really what this book is all about.**

In the chapters which follow, you'll learn how to use tables in deciding whether you can afford to borrow money and how much. If you're thinking about buying a house, the tables will help you make up your mind whether you should own or rent. How do you evaluate a home as an investment? Sure, if you buy, you expect to sell at a profit at some future time. But what is that profit worth in *today's* dollars?

If you're considering real estate as an investment, you'll be shown technical approaches used by "sophisticated" investors and traders. You'll see how to compare the potential returns on this kind of an investment to the benefits of leaving your money in a term deposit or savings bond.

Chapter Sixteen is called "Understanding Life Insurance Policies". You'll see that pure life insurance is not an investment. Life insurance has a *cost.* How can you determine this cost? It's simply a matter of figuring out what you can be expected to pay over a period of time (perhaps the rest of your life) and comparing the cost of these payments to the value of what your estate will get at the end. When you finish reading this chapter, you'll be able to compare different types of policies issued by different companies and you'll be able to calculate your cost in each case.

Chapter Seventeen deals with the option of either leasing property or buying it. Whether you are considering an automobile, an airplane or a personal computer, the rules are the same. You'll learn how to determine the interest cost built into a lease and, at the same time, be introduced to various non-financial considerations.

But why am *I* writing this book? I've already told you I'm not a mathematician, and have just barely learned how to operate a personal computer. Those of you who've read any of my previous books know my field of expertise, as it were, lies in taxation, financial planning techniques and related matters—not in mathematics.

This book is, however, a very natural extension of everything I've previously written and intend to write in the future. This is because it's impossible to make any "real life" business or investment decisions without a basic knowledge of the income tax rules and a bit of mathematical analysis. Earlier, I told you that one of the simple things the tables in this book will help you do is calculate how much you'll have at the end of ten years if you can save $100 a month and earn 10% interest on your money. But can you really earn 10%? If your employment income puts you in a 40% tax bracket, the government will then take almost half of your annual investment income. Thus, your real rate of return may be as little as 6%, not 10% . If you use the tables for 10% in order to get your answer, you'll be hopelessly misled.

On the other hand, Chapter Fifteen deals with registered retirement savings plans. You are probably already aware that income earned in such plans is *not* taxable until you take it out. Thus, if you deposit $100 a month for 10 years and earn, on average, 10%, it's quite appropriate to use the table for a 10% yield in order to determine what you'll have at the end.

Previously, I suggested using this book to help you evaluate home ownership as an investment. Anyone who buys a home expects to sell it at a profit at some point in the future. But what is that profit *after* tax? As you probably know, if the home is a "principal residence" the before-tax and after-tax return are both the same. But what if the property is a vacation cottage or a "second" home? Under such circumstances, your profit may be reduced by a related capital gains tax. There's no sense in trying to determine the present value of this future profit unless you take income taxes into account.

I don't mean to scare you, however. It's not necessary for you to be a tax expert. Nor is it necessary for you to buy all of my other books—although I hope you have or eventually will. This book will contain enough basic income tax information so you can make proper business and investment decisions.

For example, Chapter Thirteen deals with stock market investments. You'll become adept at making valid after-tax comparisons of dividends from Canadian stocks to interest from savings accounts, bonds and term deposits. You'll also find it easier to answer questions such as this: If I borrow for stock market investments, what rate of capital growth do I need to break even, taking into account a dividend yield?

The topic of borrowing money is dealt with in Chapter Six. You must realize from the outset you can't possibly calculate your true cost without knowing whether your interest expense is tax-deductible. If I borrow at 11% to acquire real estate or invest in the stock market, my actual cost is only 6.6% if I'm in a 40% bracket. On the other hand, if I borrow for personal purposes, such as to buy a home, all my calculations must take the full 11% rate into account.

A Few Words About the Tables

In concluding these introductory thoughts, it would be appropriate to examine some of the specifications I've adopted for the tables in this book. Tables 1 to 5 and 8 to 12 are all based on calculations for one year to fifty years. All of them deal with whole number percentages between 3% and 18%, except Tables 5 and 11, which are designed to show you how much you have to pay periodically to pay off a loan over various periods of time. These tables provide calculations ranging from 5% to 20%.

I've chosen to deal with whole numbers only since my major objective is to present a practical approach. If you're interested in precision and pinpoint accuracy, you can always buy the more detailed and sophisticated tables. Alternatively, a friend with a home computer and the necessary programs can provide you with any printout you need—as long as you know what to ask for. Assuming, however, you're only seeking reasonable accuracy to make intelligent decisions, the ranges provided in this book should suffice. For example, what if you're dealing with an interest factor of 10½%? You might consider making calculations at both 10% and 11% and simply averaging your results. Granted, the larger your numbers, or the longer the period over which your calculations are being made, the more significant the variance. Nevertheless, in percentage terms these differences should be quite negligible. This is explained further in Chapter Two.

In two cases, I've compiled figures which provide you with greater accuracy. Table 6 provides the monthly payments required to repay a mortgage loan of $1000 over various periods of time. The conventional Canadian mortgage requires payments to be made monthly, although interest is calculated semi-annually. This is in contrast to normal loans made by lending institutions where payments are ordinarily made on a monthly basis with interest *also* calculated on the monthly balance outstanding from time to time. Table 6, the Canadian Mortgage Amortization Table, deals with a range from 5% to 16⅞%, increasing by one-eighth of one per cent each time. The payback periods range from one to forty years. Most mortgages today are calculated on the basis of twenty-five or thirty-year payouts (although they are usually renewed at current prevailing rates every few years). From a practical standpoint, therefore, the range of one to forty years should provide you with enough information.

Table 7 contains calculations based on interest rates from 5% to 16¾%, increasing by one-quarter of one per cent each time. This table shows the principal balance outstanding on a twenty-five-year mortgage loan of $1000 at the end of each year from year one to the end of year twenty-five. Of all the tables in this book, Table 7 is the only one with an extremely narrow application. It's designed simply as an aid to the material contained in Chapter Eleven, which deals with borrowing money to buy a home. This table will also reinforce one of my major suggestions—a home mortgage should be paid off as soon as possible, especially in Canada where your interest is non-deductible.

Finally, Table 13 deals with life expectancy for both males and females ages ten to eighty-five. This table will be of use to you in understanding life insurance policies and annuity yields (Chapters Fifteen and Sixteen). The range corresponds to the ages of the people to whom this book is addressed! (There are no tables more recent than 1970-72.)

What About Interest Rates?

Over the last twelve years, interest rates have fluctuated rather widely. When you read this book, current market rates may be quite different from the examples contained in the various chapters. Don't let this bother you. Remember, I'm only trying to give you an *approach* to solving your business and investment mathematics problems. *The rates of interest are really only secondary.*

The Lifetime Capital Gains Exemption

In May 1985, the Canadian government introduced a $500,000 cumulative lifetime capital gains exemption for individuals which was to be phased-in over a five-year period. However, in 1987, the exemption was frozen at $100,000 except for farmers and small business owners. Moreover, the exemption doesn't apply to gains on real estate sales attributable to the period after February 1992. The examples in this book therefore generally assume the exemption does *not* apply. You'll see that this is the most conservative approach in evaluating investment alternatives, especially if you're considering relatively long-term holding periods. If the exemption *does* apply to you, your return on investment can only be better!

So, here it is. Go slowly. You don't have to read every chapter, although you should at least skim the next nine chapters. If real estate investing isn't for you, skip Chapter Twelve. Similarly, if you find the stock market has no appeal to you, don't bother with Chapter Thirteen. In other words, this isn't a novel. I hope, however, you'll quickly agree it really isn't all that difficult to take the mystery out of ordinary business and investment mathematics.

TWO

Compound Interest Calculations

What Will $1 Today Be Worth at Some Time in the Future?

If you've ever dealt with a bank, trust company or any other financial institution, you are certainly familiar with the concept of compound interest. You know if you deposit money into a savings account, the amount will increase, or compound, as time goes on. In order to determine exactly what you'll have at some future time you basically need to know three things:

1. The amount of money originally deposited (this is called the "present value");
2. The number of periods (or term) that your money will be left in the account; and
3. The interest rate per period.

Once these three variables are determined, Table 1 (pages 126-34) will tell you how to calculate the future value.

From the very beginning, it's important that you understand the concept of an *interest rate per period*—the third variable mentioned above. The length of a "period" can be a day, month or year, or, in fact, any amount of time, but whatever the period's length, we always assume that the compounding of interest takes place only *once during each period.*

Years ago, banks generally calculated interest on your savings account twice a year. Eventually, they began to make quarterly calculations, and now, with computers available to do the work, many institutions give credit for interest daily. In the tables at the back of this book, all calculations are presented assuming interest is calculated monthly, quarterly, semi-annually or annually. Again, as I indicated in the introduction, the purpose of this book is to teach you the proper techniques for making business and investment decisions by using mathematical analysis and tables. If you're ever faced with the need to prepare calculations where interest is compounded daily, you can probably obtain access to a computer program that will do the work for you.

Any time you make calculations, the *number of periods* and the *interest rate per period* must be consistent. This means if interest periods are designated quarterly, the interest rate must be a quarterly rate as well.

For example, suppose you deposit $1000 into a bank account that pays 8% interest per year compounded quarterly and you decide to leave the money in your account for three years. You would like to know what you'll have in your account at the end of this period. Because the bank calculates interest quarterly, picture the whole problem in terms of quarters. Since there are twelve quarters in three years, a time diagram of this example would have twelve divisions, as Figure 1 illustrates.

Figure 1
Time diagram for a $1000 bank deposit which earns 8% interest compounded quarterly for three years

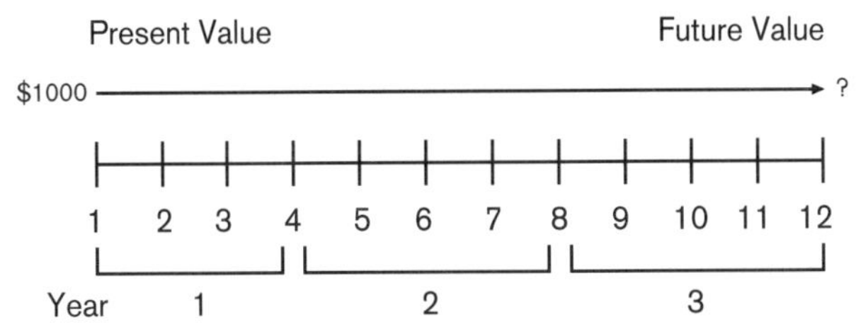

To find the interest rate per quarter, divide the annual interest (8%) by four and you get the quarterly interest rate of 2%. You now have sufficient information to calculate what your money will be worth at the end of three years if you want to make your calculations "longhand". This is illustrated in Figure 2. The first line of numbers shows that you've deposited $1000 at the beginning of the first quarter. Interest of $20 is earned during that first quarter and $1020 (your original $1000 plus $20 interest) is in your account at the end of this quarter. The amount on deposit at the end of the first quarter becomes the amount on deposit at the beginning of the second quarter, and line 2 of the table is computed in the same way as line 1.

Figure 2
Value of $1000 after three years with interest at 8% compounded quarterly

Quarters	*Amount on Deposit Beginning of Quarter*	*Interest for the Quarter*	*Amount on Deposit End of Quarter*
1	$1,000.00	$ 20.00	$1,020.00
2	1,020.00	20.40	1,040.40
3	1,040.40	20.81	1,061.21
4	1,061.21	21.22	1,082.43
5	1,082.43	21.65	1,104.08
6	1,104.08	22.08	1,126.16
7	1,126.16	22.52	1,148.68
8	1,148.68	22.97	1,171.65
9	1,171.65	23.43	1,195.08
10	1,195.08	23.90	1,218.98
11	1,218.98	24.38	1,243.36
12	1,243.36	24.87	1,268.23
Total Interest		$268.23	

You'll notice the interest in the second quarter is greater than the interest in the first and the interest each quarter continues to increase as long as your money stays in the account. This is because the bank will pay interest not only on your original deposit of $1000 but also on the accumulated interest from previous quarters. This method of computing interest is called "compound interest" and it certainly is to your advantage. The other type of interest you may run into from time to time is "simple interest". Under simple interest calculations, interest is paid on your *deposit only.* If you were to earn 8% simple interest only on $1000 for three years, you would have $1240 at the end instead of $1268.23.

Obviously, calculations such as the ones in Figure 2 can be quite tedious, especially over extended periods of time. Also, the more numbers you play with, the greater the chance of error. And here we come to the first application of the tables in this book. Table 1 gives you the compound value of $1 after one to 50 years at interest rates ranging from 3% to 18% . *This table takes into account the possibilities of interest being calculated monthly, quarterly, semi-annually or annually.* In fact, if you use this table, you don't even have to calculate an interest rate per period. The table does this for you. All you need is the *annual* rate.

Turn to Figure 3, which provides you with the calculations for interest at 7% and 8%. At the end of three years, a $1 initial deposit will amount to $1.268 if interest is calculated at 8% compounded quarterly.

Figure 3
The compound amount of $1 after three years

	7% interest compounded				8% interest compounded			
End of Year	Monthly	Quarterly	Semi-Annually	Annually	Monthly	Quarterly	Semi-Annually	Annually
3	1.233	1.231	1.229	1.225	1.270	1.268	1.265	1.260

Common sense and, if necessary, a small hand-held calculator will now tell you that if $1 will amount to $1.268 after three years with interest calculated at 8% compounded quarterly, then $1000 will amount to $1268. Actually, this isn't quite correct since the actual accumulation is $1268.23. In other words, there is a 23¢ discrepancy. This is because the tables in this book are only accurate to three or four decimal places. If, for some reason, you need greater accuracy, tables to ten places are, as I've indicated, available. However, out of total interest of $268.23, how significant is 23¢?

Take a few moments and study the extract from Table 1 which appears in Figure 3. Try to get familiar with the various ways of compounding interest. For example, how much difference does it make if interest is compounded annually instead of quarterly? After three years, your $1000 deposit would amount to $1260 instead of $1268. In other words, you'd lose $8 over this three-year period. How significant is this? It may not be all that important if you have $1000 to invest, but what if your initial investment capital was $10,000, $100,000 or even $1,000,000?

Would it really matter if you earn, say, 1% less? What if the bank were only paying you 7% interest compounded quarterly? At the end of three years, you'd have $1231 instead of $1268. The difference here is $37.

Clearly, the higher the rate, the more you will have at the end of any given number of periods. Also, the more often interest is calculated, the better off you are. What becomes astounding, however, is the effect of compound interest on an original investment after *many* years have elapsed. Figure 4 is another extract from Table 1, using the same interest rates, but in this case the original deposit of $1 is left to compound for thirty years instead of three years.

After thirty years, $1 invested at 8%, with interest calculated quarterly, comes to $10.76. Thus, $1000 left to earn interest at this same rate will amount to $10,760. Mind-boggling, isn't it? Now ask yourself if it matters whether interest is calculated quarterly or annually. On a $1000 initial deposit the difference is $702 ($10,765 minus $10,063).

Figure 4
The compound amount of $1 after thirty years

	7% interest compounded				8% interest compounded			
End of Year	Monthly	Quarterly	Semi-Annually	Annually	Monthly	Quarterly	Semi-Annually	Annually
30	8.116	8.019	7.878	7.612	10.936	10.765	10.520	10.063

Does it really matter whether you earn 7% or 8% compounded quarterly over that same thirty-year period? Yes, it does. On $1000, the difference is $2746 ($10,765 minus $8,019)! This simple exercise shows you *it always pays to shop around for the best available interest rates.*

The GIGO Principle

The advent of the age of computers has created a brand new terminology. However, anyone who learns to use a computer quickly discovers that the output is only as good as the input. In other words, if the wrong information is fed into a computer, the answer to any question which is then asked will be incorrect as well. In computer shorthand, this concept is known as the "GIGO principle"—garbage in, garbage out.

The same principle applies equally to the use of the math tables in this or any other book. If you use the *wrong* tables, your answer will be meaningless at best, or, at worst, harmfully misleading.

Making Reasonable Estimates

What if you want to know, from Table 1, how much you'd have if you deposit $1000 to earn 8% compounded quarterly and you left your money for, say, fifteen-and-a-half years? Obviously, this table won't give you an accurate answer. However, you can make reasonable *approximate* calculations. After fifteen years, $1 left to compound interest quarterly at 8% will amount to $3.281. After sixteen years, this same $1 will amount to $3.551. Therefore, after fifteen-and-a-half years, you might expect to have the following:

$$\frac{3.551 + 3.281}{2} = 3.416$$

Thus, $1000 will amount to approximately $3416. The real answer is $3413.55. From a practical standpoint, the discrepancy isn't particularly significant. However, what if your original deposit was $1,000,000? Clearly, in some cases, greater accuracy is warranted and you should use the more sophisticated tables, which are readily available. From these, you can make calculations for periods ranging from months to years and fractions of years. Often these tables are constructed to give you results from one to a hundred periods or even more. *If you use such a table, you must make sure that the number of periods and the interest rate per period are consistent*; that is, you have divided the annual rate by the number of periods. Figure 5 is an extract from such a table with calculations at 3% for fifty-nine to sixty-three *periods*.

Figure 5
The compound amount of $1

Periods	*Interest Rate, 3%*
59	5.720
60	5.892
61	6.068
62	6.250
63	6.430

The table in Figure 5 can tell you many things. For example:

- $1 invested for sixty years at 3% compounded annually will amount to $5.892
- $1 invested for thirty years at 6% compounded semi-annually (3% twice a year) will also amount to $5.892, and
- $1 invested for fifteen years at 12% compounded quarterly (3% per quarter) will also amount to $5.892 at the end.

The last two points can be verified using Table 1 in this book:

- $1 @ 6% compounded semi-annually after thirty years = $5.892 (page 128)
- $1 @ 12% compounded quarterly after fifteen years = $5.892 (page 131)

For purposes of this book, I've traded some degree of accuracy and precision (such as the opportunity to calculate results for periods of time other than whole years) for the major advantage of simplicity. It will not be necessary for you to make any conversions in using this book. In other words, if you're told interest is calculated at 8% compounded quarterly for fifteen years, you don't have to look for a 2% table with sixty periods. Instead, simply use the table for 8% and the column which gives the results assuming interest is computed quarterly. Thus, the figures on page 129 for interest at 8% are equivalent to: 8\12 of 1% calculated monthly, 2% per quarter, 4% semi-annually or 8% annually. When it comes to part-year calculations, use the method described on page 9, and you'll have a good approximation of the actual answer.

Realities—Taxes and Inflation

No business or investment decision should be made in a vacuum. It's well and good to assume that $1000 left to earn interest at 8% compounded quarterly will amount to $3281 at the end of fifteen years. However, two important questions arise. Is it realistic to assume a yield of 8% for an extended period? Look at how the rates have fluctuated over just the last dozen years. Furthermore, even if, by some miracle, interest rates stabilized for a fifteen-year period, a second major consideration is the impact of taxes on investment yields. The table in Figure 6 summarizes the approximate Canadian personal tax brackets in force for 1993-94. Of course, the figures will vary from province to province but, in general, the difference isn't more than a few percentage points.

Figure 6
Canadian personal tax brackets (approximate)

Taxable Income	*Tax Bracket*
From $0-30,000	25%
$30,000-60,000	40%–45%
$60,000 and up	45%–60%

This book will tread very lightly on the subject of taxation. For the most part, I'll assume taxes at a 45% rate on investment income, partly because of the ease this gives me in presenting examples. Similarly, if you borrow to make investments, and the interest is tax-deductible, I'll make the same assumption that your cost of borrowing is reduced to 55% of the rate specified. Of course, you should make the required calculations using the rates applicable to your own situation. For example, if you're in a 44% tax bracket and you're earning interest at 9%, your after-tax yield is just about 5%. On the other hand, if your tax bracket is 40%, your actual yield is almost 5.5%.

In some circumstances, such as if you invest in a registered retirement savings plan (see Chapter Fifteen), your before-tax and your after-tax return are the same. In other cases, the return on an investment may be subject to capital gains taxes only and these are somewhat lower than taxes on ordinary income.

My point is, however, that to be of *any real use, interest tables must deal with a very broad range of potential rates*. Today it may be realistic to assume only a 5% *before-tax* rate of return (for which the compound interest figures are provided on page 128). This is also the actual after-tax yield for someone in a 45% bracket who earns interest at a rate of 9%. This is because almost one-half of the before-tax earnings will have to be removed from investment capital each year and paid over to the government. Only the remaining portion can be left to compound as savings.

Additional Applications for Table 1

So far, we've only used Table 1 in a very narrow context. Table 1 has many other applications as well. For example, you can answer the following question: If you lend your brother-in-law $1000 for five years and you charge him 13% annual interest compounded monthly, how much will he have to pay you as a lump sum at the end of that five-year period? In this case, you are the banker. The amount you lend your brother-in-law today is the present value and the amount you'll be repaid is the future value. If you look at the table on page 132 under the figures for 13% compounded monthly, the answer is $1000 x 1.909 or $1909. Of that amount, $909 will represent interest and the balance is your principal.

Here's another interesting application. You've inherited $10,000 and you're thinking of investing in the shares of Goldfinger Mining Limited which trade on the Vancouver Stock Exchange. The company owns several producing gold mines but doesn't pay a dividend. The stock is trading at $1 a share. Suppose this investment would only be attractive to you if you could earn an 18% return (before considering possible taxes on capital gains) compounded annually over the next four years. At what price would you have to sell your stock in order to realize your objective? From the table on page 134, you can see $1 left to compound at 18% annually for four years will amount to $1.939 at the end of this time. Therefore, for you to earn 18% on this stock market investment, your Goldfinger shares would have to be worth $19,390. This works out to just under $2 a share. In other words, before you make your investment, you must ask yourself what the chances are of this stock doubling within the next four years. This is essentially what must happen if you wish to realize your required rate of return. (In Chapter Thirteen, we will make more sophisticated calculations taking capital gains taxes as well as dividend yields into account.)

Compound Interest and Inflation

Inflation is always at work, eroding your investment yields. So, in setting goals and objectives for returns on investment, you must always take it into account. We can start our analysis of how inflation works right here in this chapter by simply using Table 1.

Let's assume, for example, that in 1963, the price of a cup of coffee was 10¢. If at that time, someone had guessed that inflation would average 8% a year, what would the price of a cup of coffee be thirty years later in 1993?

By looking at Table 1, on page 129, in the column for 8% compounded annually, we can see that $1 invested for thirty years would amount to $10.063 at the end of that time. Similarly, if something cost $1 thirty years ago, and the price went up by 8% compounded annually, that same purchase would cost $10.06 today.

If we consider a 10¢ cup of coffee in 1963, today's price would be $0.10 x 10.063, or about $1.00. And it is! In many restaurants across the country that's just about what you would have to pay (although many establishments don't charge for refills). In other words, we can conclude, on average, over the last thirty years the price of a cup of coffee has increased by 8% a year.

Now let's look to the future. If the price of a cup of coffee today is, say, $1.00, what will the price be in thirty years? Well, if we continue to assume an 8% average annual increase, the price in thirty years will be $1.00 x

10.063, roughly $10.06! Hard to believe, but what would your reaction have been in 1963 if someone had told you then the price of coffee would be about ten times as much thirty years later?

Inflation and Wages

Here's another example of a practical application to the theory behind compound interest. Assume you are forty-five years of age and are earning $30,000 a year from your employment. Also assume your employer has promised to give you a series of promotions coupled with an 8% raise compounded semi-annually (that is, 4% twice a year). You expect to retire at age fifty-seven with a pension equal to 60% of your final year's earnings. How much can you assume your pension will be in the first year after retirement?

If you are now earning $30,000 and expect to average an 8% increase each year (calculated semi-annually) your pay after eleven years (before age fifty-seven) can be calculated from Table 1, page 129. Your final pay will be $30,000 x 2.370, or $71,100. This is the future value of $30,000 today compounded semi-annually at 8% for eleven years. If your pension starting in year twelve is 60% of your final earnings figure, you can count on receiving 60% of $71,100, or $42,660 in that first year.

Can you then consider yourself wealthy? Well, the key question here is what has happened to your cost of living over that same period? Clearly, if your cost of living has compounded by the equivalent of 8% calculated semi-annually, it would take an income of $71,100 to purchase what $30,000 does today. This, of course, assumes that the impact of taxes on an income of $71,100 twelve years from now is no heavier a burden than the taxes on $30,000 today.

If the inflation rate exceeds your annual rate of salary increases, then you'll lose. Take another look at page 129. If money is invested at 8% compounded annually, $1 invested today will amount to $2 ($1.999) at the end of only nine years. By that same token, if an expenditure costs $1 today and the price increases by 8% a year, that same item will cost $2 in nine years.

The Rule of Seventy-Two

There is a very interesting rule of thumb which will allow you to determine approximately how long it'll take your money to double at various interest rates. This is called the rule of seventy-two. You simply divide the number 72 by the interest rate as shown in Figure 7.

Figure 7
The rule of seventy-two

Interest Rate Compounded Annually	*Length of Time for Money to Double*	*Future Value of $1 Compounded From Table 1*
6%	72÷ 6 = 12 years	12 years 2.012
8%	72÷ 8 = 9 years	9 years 1.999
12%	72÷12 = 6 years	6 years 1.974
18%	72÷18 = 4 years	4 years 1.939

As you can see from the last column in the illustration, this rule of thumb really works!

Summary

Take the time to go through Table 1 carefully. Get a feel for the numbers at various interest rates. You can see the longer the period, the more important it is to try to earn a higher rate. Similarly, it starts to make larger differences whether your interest is calculated monthly, quarterly, semi-annually or annually.

In your own life, there will be other considerations, such as income taxes, to be taken into account in determining actual yields. As you continue through this book, you'll see, however, nothing is really all that complicated. Money simply has a value that changes during the time over which it is used to make more money. To be realistic in your investments and business transactions, you have to know what these values are and how they're computed. In the next chapter, you'll be introduced to the concept of an annuity—what happens to you if you save money *all along* and invest it over a period of time.

THREE

The Future Value of a Series of Deposits

How Much Will $1 Invested at the End of Each Period Amount to at Some Point in the Future?

Many business and investment situations require the computation of the future value of not just a single amount, but a series of amounts. This is often referred to as an "ordinary annuity". Most people have only seen the term "annuity" used in the context of life insurance. Actually, the concept is much broader. To show you an annuity problem in its simplest form, you may want to answer the following question: If I put aside $100 a month for ten years and earn 9% interest calculated monthly, what will I have at the end?

In order to make such a calculation, you must make sure that:

- All the amounts are equal;
- The deposits occur at regular intervals whether they are monthly, quarterly, semi-annually or annually, and
- The deposits are made at the *end* of each period.

The amount you'll have once you have made your last deposit is called the "future value of your annuity".

Table 2 is all you need to make these kinds of calculations. But, remember GIGO—our warning from the computer experts—"garbage in, garbage out". If you don't use the numbers from the proper columns, your answer will be totally worthless and confusing. To illustrate how Table 2 works, let's just take an extract from the figures on page 139 which reflects an interest yield of 9%. If deposits of $1 are made to earn interest at 9%, Figure 1 shows the result at the end of ten years.

In this case, the final amount varies drastically under all four alternatives. This isn't simply because in the first column, the interest is calculated monthly, while in the column on the right, the interest is calculated once a year only. Rather, the difference is primarily because, in the first case, *the deposits are made monthly* (and the interest is calculated monthly) while in the fourth case *only one deposit a year is made* (with interest calculated annually, as well). In other words, Column 1 represents twelve monthly deposits of $1 each, Column 2, four quarterly deposits of $1 each, Column 3, two deposits a year, and Column 4 only one deposit. *Column 1 therefore reflects twelve times the number of deposits as Column 4.* Again, review the annuity rules outlined above. Note that Table 2 is very different from Table 1. When we looked at Table 1, the key point was how often interest would be calculated on a single amount. In using Table 2, the major consideration is the frequency of your deposits.

Figure 1
The future value of $1 invested at the end of each period after ten years

	Deposits are made and interest at 9% compounded			
End of Year	*Monthly*	*Quarterly*	*Semi–Annually*	*Annually*
10	193.514	63.786	31.371	15.193

Now it's time for a practical example. Suppose you deposit $100 a month into a savings account at the end of each month for the next ten years. The account pays 9% interest calculated monthly (9/12 of 1% per month). How much will you have at the end of the ten years? A time diagram would look like Figure 2.

Figure 2
Time diagram illustrating twelve monthly deposits of $100 at the end of each month over a ten-year period

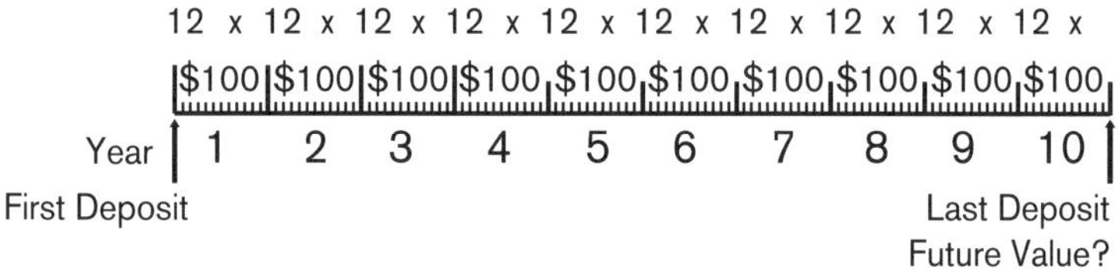

12 x 12 x 12 x 12 x 12 x 12 x 12 x 12 x 12 x 12 x
$100 $100 $100 $100 $100 $100 $100 $100 $100 $100
Year 1 2 3 4 5 6 7 8 9 10
First Deposit
Last Deposit
Future Value?

Note that the deposits are made at the end of each month. Also, in this instance, interest is calculated monthly as well. To find the future value, simply refer to the extract from Table 2 given in Figure 1. The answer is:

$100 x 193.514 = $19,351.40

Over this ten-year period, you will have deposited $12,000 in principal payments. The fact that you'll have just over $19,000 at the end means the total interest is in excess of $7000.

What would happen if, instead of depositing $ 100 a month at the end of each month for ten years, you deposited $1200 once a year for ten years at 9% interest compounded annually? What would you have at the end? Again, refer to Figure 1. The answer is:

$1200 x 15.193 = $18,231.60

Note that your total is $1119.80 less ($19,351.40 minus $18,231.60) than the results of $100 monthly deposits. There are two reasons for this.

First, the more frequent the deposits, the more you benefit from the compounding of interest. This was illustrated in Chapter Two. Secondly, in the first illustration not only are the deposits made monthly, but interest is presumed to be calculated monthly as well. In example two, the total reflects not only annual deposits but an annual compound interest calculation, as well.

You may want to check the accuracy of Table 2 for yourself. If you want, you can develop a calculation table, period by period. It should look like the calculations in Figure 3. A new deposit is added to the amount on deposit at the *end* of each period to obtain the amount on deposit at the start of the *following* period. As you can see, after ten years of making $1200 annual deposits, the amount in the account, *including* the final $1200 deposit is $18,231.52, which is almost the same as the answer obtained from Table 2. The difference of 8¢ is, of course, due to rounding.

Figure 3
Verifying the future value of a series of annual deposits

	Amount on Deposit Beginning of Year	*Interest for Year at 9%*	*Amount on Deposit End of Year*	*New Deposit*
1	$ 0.00	$ 0.00	$ 0.00	$1,200.00
2	1,200.00	108.00	1,308.00	1,200.00
3	2,508.00	225.72	2,733.72	1,200.00
4	3,933.72	354.03	4,287.75	1,200.00
5	5,487.75	493.90	5,981.65	1,200.00
6	7,181.65	646.35	7,828.00	1,200.00
7	9,028.00	812.52	9,840.52	1,200.00
8	11,040.52	993.65	12,034.17	1,200.00
9	13,234.17	1,191.08	14,425.25	1,200.00
10	15,625.25	1,406.27	17,031.52	1,200.00
	$18,231.52			

Income Tax Considerations

Take some time to familiarize yourself with Table 2 by scanning pages 135- to 143. You'll see that this table contains calculations at interest rates ranging from 3% to 18%. As described in Chapter Two, if you find it necessary to make calculations at an interest rate of say, 8½%, from a practical standpoint, you can get a good estimate by making calculations at 8% and 9% and then simply averaging.

For example, monthly deposits of $1 at 8% for ten years will amount to $182.95. At 9%, the amount is $193.51. Thus, presumably, if the interest rate is 8½%, you might expect the total to be *around* $188. Obviously, the longer the period, the greater your error, but the approximation is still worthwhile.

In case you've forgotten why this book deals with such a wide range of interest rates, I'll remind you that you can't project any true interest rates unless you're aware of the income tax consequences.

In Canada, interest received is generally taxable although there's one significant exception—investments in a registered retirement savings plan, which are discussed in detail in Chapter Fifteen.

A person in a 45% income tax bracket (taxable income around $60,000 in 1994) can't really earn, say, 9% interest even if a lending institution is offering this rate. Anyone in that bracket will have to withdraw almost half of the investment yield on an annual basis just to cover taxes. If you're earning enough to be in this bracket, you would be better off making your calculations using an after-tax yield of 5% only. Otherwise, your results will be tremendously misleading.

Take a moment to examine the Table 2 figures on page 137 for an interest rate of 5%, and assume your deposits will be made annually for ten years. Each dollar of annual deposits would amount to $12.58 at the end. This is a far cry from an accumulation of $15.19 if the interest rate were 9%. Figure 4 compares the results for annual deposits of $1200 given the two rates.

The difference of $3138.00 is partially the result of the required income tax outlays themselves and partially because your tax payments reduce your ability to earn compound income on an ongoing basis.

Figure 4
$1200 deposited at the end of each year for ten years

At 9% interest:	$1,200 x 15.193 = $18,231.60
At 5% interest:	$1,200 x 12.578 = $15,093.60
Difference	$ 3,138.00

Again, study the tables carefully. Most investment counselors will advise you to save for a rainy day. But it's hard to do so—especially if you don't have the proper motivation. Table 2 can help you find the motivation necessary to become a "saver".

Assume you can earn a long-term average return of 5% on your money after taxes. If you deposit $1 a month for thirty years you will have $832.26 at the end. Thus, putting aside $100 a month at the same interest rate for thirty years would give you over $83,000! Of course, what that $83,000 will be worth in thirty years in terms of buying power is another story. But whatever the inflation rate, I'd rather have $83,000 than not have it!

Another question you could ask yourself is whether it pays to shop seriously for the "best" rate available—even if it means moving money frequently from one financial institution to another. Assume that over a thirty-year period, you're able to squeeze out an extra *half a percentage point* after tax on your savings. Let's see how important this is.

We'll assume that, without much effort, you can earn a long-term average rate of return of 5% interest calculated semi-annually. If you invest $1 *twice a year* at 5%, this means that you will have $135.99 at the end. This sum consists of $60 of your own money ($2 a year for thirty years) and $75.99 of after-tax interest. At 6%, you would have $163.05. Therefore, at 5½%, you could expect to have somewhere between $135.99 and $163.05.

Summary

From the calculations shown in Figure 5, you can see how a rate difference of only one-half a per cent means a difference of approximately $13.53 for each $1 invested. What if your semi-annual savings were $500 instead of only $1? At the end of a thirty-year period, your difference would be 500 x $13.53, or $6765. Yes, it does pay to shop! Your own total capital of $500 deposited semi-annually for thirty years is $30,000. A $6765 net return on a total capital investment of $30,000 is quite a significant amount. A one-half per cent difference, more or less, doesn't seem very much when you look at it in isolation, but if you take the time to understand your tables, you'll begin to understand the importance of getting the best rates available. Remember, it's your money.

Figure 5
One dollar deposited semi-annually for thirty years

At 5% interest	$135.99		
At 6% interest	$163.05		
At 5½% interest approximately	($163.05 + $135.99) / 2	=	$149.52
Accumulated difference for each $1 invested	($149.52–$135.99)		$ 13.53

FOUR

What is a Dollar Due Sometime in the Future Worth Today?

In this chapter, I'll explain how to determine the value today (that is, the present value) of a single amount due sometime in the future. A typical example of the problem which you'll be able to solve after reading this chapter is: How much must I deposit in a savings account today in order to have $1000 after five years if the account pays, say, 9% interest, compounded quarterly? The answers can all be calculated by using Table 3 on pages 144-152.

But before you make the calculations of the amount needed today to attain your $1000 goal at the end of five years, it's again useful to prepare a time diagram similar to Figure 1 so that you can understand what you're trying to do.

Notice the direction of the time arrow. In Chapters Two and Three, we were moving from the present to the future. Here, we're moving from the future to the present. Now let's take a look at Table 3. With interest compounded quarterly at 9%, you would have to invest $0.6408 today in order to have $1 at the end of five years. Thus, to accumulate $1000 at the end of this same period, you would need a present investment of $640.80. In other words, a single deposit of $640.80 invested today and left alone for five years to earn 9% compounded quarterly, will amount to $1000 at the end of five years.

Figure 1
The present value of $1,000 due sometime in the future

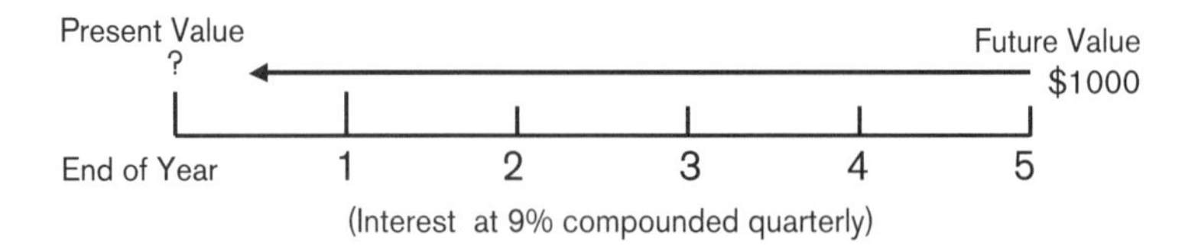

Of course, this answer can be verified. If we wanted to, we could make the calculations longhand and produce a schedule similar to the one on page 7 in Chapter Two. However, if we're compounding quarterly, this would entail twenty calculations, and really, all this work isn't necessary. To check our answer, all we need to do is refer to Table 1. This table tells us what $1 today is worth at some point in the future. Turn to page 130. Assuming interest at 9% compounded quarterly, $1 invested today would amount to $1.561 at the end of five years. Therefore, $640.80 invested today would amount to: $640.80 x 1.561 or $1000.28. Of course, the 28¢ is a rounding difference only.

From these calculations, you can see Table 1 and Table 3 are "reciprocals" or mirror images. Table 1 gives us the future value of a single present amount while Table 3 gives us the present value of a single future amount.

Now take a few minutes and flip through pages 144 to 152. You'll see Table 3 deals with interest rates ranging from 3% to 18%. Remember our old enemy, income taxes. In the previous example, we looked at earning interest at 9% compounded quarterly. However, what if you're in a 45% tax bracket? If you have to draw out almost half your earnings each year to pay taxes to the government, your interest isn't really going to compound at 9%, even if you could get this rate in the first place. Let's see what would happen if we make the assumption you can earn 5% on your money after tax. What would you then need to deposit in a savings account today if you want to have $1000 after five years, assuming interest is compounded quarterly? From page 146, we can determine you would need about $0.78 today to have $1 at the end of five years. Therefore, you would need about $780.00 if you wanted to attain your $1000 goal, considerably more than the $640.80 that would be required if taxes were not a factor.

Take a few minutes to carefully examine the structure of Table 3. The extract in Figure 2 gives us the present value of $1 due at the end of ten years with interest calculated at 8%.

Figure 2
The present value of $1 due at the end of ten years at 8% interest compounded

End of Year	*Monthly*	*Quarterly*	*Semi–Annually*	*Annually*
10	0.4505	0.4529	0.4564	0.4632

You'll notice the numbers are quite close to each other. Of course, if you can earn interest compounded monthly, you can deposit a smaller amount today to get $1 by the end of any given number of years. If your money is earning interest less frequently, an additional initial deposit is required. For example, if you can earn 8% after tax (highly unlikely in today's market) and you wish to have $1000 at the end of ten years, you need only deposit $450.50 today if interest is calculated monthly, while you must deposit $463.20 if the interest calculation will only be made once a year.

Let's take a look at a few more practical examples to show you where you may have occasion to refer to Table 3.

Assume you'll be retiring in ten years and you'd like to take a nice long vacation, which you figure will cost $7000. Suppose, as well, you have some savings and can earn 5% on your money compounded semi-annually after taxes. How much would you need in savings today so that you could draw out the necessary funds in time to pay for your trip?

Turn to page 146. If interest is calculated semi-annually, an investment of $0.6103 today will total $1 at the end of ten years. Therefore, if you want $7000 in ten years, you would need to have savings of 0.6103 x $7000 or $4272.10. If you have these savings, your vacation goal objective is readily attainable.

What if you're short? In the next chapter, you'll find out how to calculate the amount of *periodic deposits* you would have to make from time to time to accumulate your desired level of savings. (This is called a "sinking fund".)

Here's another example of a present value calculation. You're a shareholder in your family's business, which has just been sold. You're told you will receive a lump-sum of $50,000 at the end of three years on which you'll then have to pay $10,000 in capital gains taxes. (This example ignores the lifetime capital gains exemption.) How much can you borrow *today* at an annual rate of 12% compounded monthly so you can pay off your debt, principal plus interest, at the end of the three years out of the sales proceeds? Again, Table 3 will provide the answer.

What you really want to know is what single amount invested today will accumulate to $40,000 ($50,000 minus your taxes) at the end of three years, with interest at 12% compounded monthly. Your answer can be calculated from page 149. It is $40,000 x .6989 or $27,956. In other words, if you borrow $27,956 today, and allow interest to accumulate for three years, you would owe $40,000 at the end, which you could then pay off with your share of the money received from the sale of the business.

Understanding Inflation

Perhaps one of the most practical uses of Table 3 is as another aid to understanding inflation. Simply put, it was no doubt clear to you before you even began reading this book that $1 which you will either receive or pay out at some time in the future is worth considerably less than $1 today. From the last example, you can see if the annual inflation rate were 12% (with increases compounded monthly), $40,000 three years from now would be worth only as much as $27,956 is worth today. This is why you might be willing to borrow $27,956 today even if it means paying back $40,000 three years later.

Let's assume inflation compounds at 5% annually. Figure 3 is an extract from Table 3 which shows you what $1 due sometime in the future is worth today at an assumed interest rate of 5% compounded annually.

Basically, what this illustration shows us is, given a 5% inflation rate, $1 due at the end of next year is worth only approximately 95¢ today. Similarly, $1 due in nine years is worth 65¢ today while $1 due at the end of thirty years is worth only about 23¢ today.

Figure 3
The present value of $1 due at the end of various time periods at 5% interest compounded annually

End of Year		*End of Year*	
1	0.9524	16	0.4581
2	0.9070	17	0.4363
3	0.8638	18	0.4155
4	0.8227	19	0.3957
5	0.7835	20	0.3769
6	0.7462	21	0.3589
7	0.7107	22	0.3418
8	0.6768	23	0.3256
9	0.6446	24	0.3101
10	0.6139	25	0.2953
11	0.5847	26	0.2812
12	0.5568	27	0.2678
13	0.5303	28	0.2551
14	0.5051	29	0.2429
15	0.4810	30	0.2314

Some simple examples will further reinforce your understanding of present value. Assume you're age forty-three and you buy a life insurance policy which will pay your estate $100,000 at the time of your death. You're presently earning $30,000 a year. According to statistics, you probably won't die for another thirty years and your family will have to wait until then to collect on this $100,000 policy. If inflation averages 5% a year over that period, the equivalent present value of $100,000 due then is $100,000 x .2314, or $23,140. Compare that to your present income level. Instead of providing a benefit of more than three times your annual income, the "real" benefit is less than one year's salary.

However, before you conclude that life insurance is a rip-off, please wait until you read Chapter Sixteen. Remember, the assumption you will live for thirty more years is a statistical one. What happens if you get run over by a truck tomorrow? Then, the $100,000 death benefit is really worth $100,000!

Here's another example. You and your family are looking to buy a new house. Your agent shows you a property he or she is confident you can get for $100,000. "At the rate property values are going," says the agent, "this house should double in value over the next fifteen years." You immediately start to see the dollar signs. A $100,000 property worth $200,000 after "only" a fifteen-year period. And yet, what if inflation averages 5% a year? The present value of $200,000 due at the end of fifteen years, assuming a 5% compound interest factor, is $200,000 x .4810, or $96,200. In other words, if inflation averages 5% and your property *only* doubles over that fifteen-year period, you'll have actually lost $3800 in purchasing power!

One last example. Try this one on your own. Assume you have $10,000 to invest in the stock market. You feel a reasonable rate of return before tax is 15% a year, taking into account the risk of making almost any stock market investment. Your broker tells you about a mining stock presently trading at $5 a share which he thinks will be a $10 stock within the next four years. If you invest your $10,000 and the stock does double in that four-year period, will you attain your objective of a 15% return?

If you look at Table 3 on page 151, you'll see that at a 15% rate of return, $1 due at the end of four years has a present value of 57.18¢. Therefore $20,000 due at the end of four years has a present value of $11,436. In this case, if you only have to invest $10,000 and the broker's prediction holds true, you'll attain more than your 15% required rate of return. This kind of problem is discussed in more detail in Chapter Ten, which deals with discounted cash-flow techniques—the key behind the more sophisticated investment analyses contained in the later chapters of this book.

Summary

Of all the tables, Table 3 is certainly one of the most interesting. It'll help you to understand not only rates of return on investment, but also the workings of inflation. Take one last look at page 152. At 18% compounded annually, the present value of $1 due at the end of 25 years is .0160. In other words, if inflation ever reaches 18% a year, our dollar will lose 98% of its value over a twenty-five-year period. Comforting if you are trying to plan for retirement, isn't it?

FIVE

Saving Money to Meet Your Goals and Objectives

The last chapter addressed the question of how much you must invest today in order to accumulate a desired amount of money by the end of some future period.

What happens, however, if instead you want to save towards a definite goal by means of regular deposits? How much should you deposit at a time? For example, suppose you want to have $10,000 in your savings account after four years and you plan to make deposits at the end of each month. If the account pays 9% interest that is also compounded monthly, how large must each of your deposits be?

To solve this problem, we turn to Table 4, pages 153 to 161. Table 4 provides the necessary information to calculate how much must be invested at the end of various time periods to accumulate $1 by some future date. Like most of the tables in this book, Table 4 deals with investment yields ranging from 3% to 18%. The wide range is again because yields are in themselves meaningless unless you take income tax implications into account. The 9% yield referred to in the first example in this chapter is for illustration only. It may not be a particularly realistic after-tax rate of return.

Table 4 is structured to solve investment savings problems whether your deposits are made monthly, quarterly, semi-annually or annually. The extract from the table shown in Figure 1 gives the figures for an interest rate of 9% over four years.

Figure 1
How much must be invested at the end of each period to accumulate $1 after four years

	At 9% interest compounded and deposits made			
End of Year	*Monthly*	*Quarterly*	*Semi–Annually*	*Annually*
4	0.0174	0.0526	0.1066	0.2187

What this tells you is that deposits of $0.0174 or roughly 1¾¢ *per month* would amount to $1 by the end of four years if interest is compounded *monthly* at an annualized rate of 9%. Similarly, quarterly deposits of just over 5¼¢ will also amount to $1 after four years, with interest at 9% calculated *quarterly*. If your deposits are made *semi-annually*, just over 10⅔¢ would have to be deposited every half-year for four years to amount to $1 if interest at 9% is compounded *semi-annually*. Finally, it would take almost 22¢ deposited at the end of each *year* with interest at 9% compounded *annually* to reach a $1 objective by the end of the required four-year period.

Returning then to the example at the beginning of this chapter, anyone who wants to have $10,000 in savings after four years must make monthly deposits of $174 if interest at 9% will be calculated monthly. The time diagram in Figure 2 illustrates this point.

Figure 2
Time diagram illustrating twelve monthly deposits of $174 at the end of each month over a four-year period

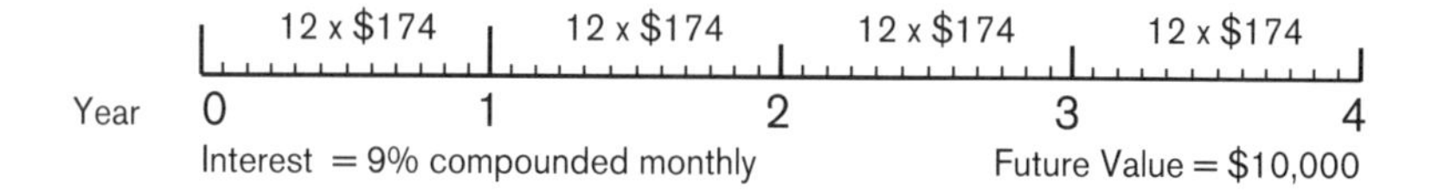

Can we verify our results? Certainly. All we have to do is turn back to Table 2. Table 2 gave us the future value of $1 invested at the end of each period. If you look at page 139, under the column for monthly deposits at 9%, you can calculate that $174 deposited monthly for four years will amount to $174 X 57.521 or $10,008.65. Again, because this book only contains tables to three or four decimal places, there is a rounding difference. In this case the rounding difference is $8.65. Tables 2 and 4 are "reciprocals" or reverse images. You can use either of these tables to check the other.

Here's another example. If you invest $1000 a year and earn 6% after-tax compounded annually, Table 2 (page 137) tells you that, at the end of ten years, you'll have $13,181 ($1000 x 13.181). Conversely, if you want to have $13,181 at the end of ten years, and you wish to make annual deposits with interest at 6%, Table 4 tells you that you must make deposits of $13,181 x .0759, which equals $1000.44. Again, Table 2 will enable you to verify Table 4 and vice versa.

Let's look at a few more practical examples of how Table 4 can assist you in your business or investment planning. Assume you're the proud parent of a newborn child. Eighteen years from now, you'd like to have $15,000 saved up for your child's college education. You'd like to make quarterly savings deposits beginning three months from now. You figure, on average, you can earn 6% after-tax compounded quarterly. How large will each deposit need to be to achieve your $15,000 goal at the end of eighteen years? Turn to page 155. The answer is simply $15,000 x .0078 or $117. (Note: in using the tables presented in this book, you don't have to concern yourself with the fact that there are seventy-two quarters in eighteen years.)

Shall we verify? Turn to Table 2, page 137. If deposits of $1 are made quarterly with interest at 6% over eighteen years, you'll have $128.08 at the end. Therefore, if your quarterly deposits are $117.00, your total will be $117.00 x 128.08 or $14,985.36. Again, the small difference of just under $15 is simply due to rounding.

How much better off would you be if you make your deposits monthly instead of quarterly? On an annual basis, four quarterly payments of $117.00 amount to $468 a year. To attain your $15,000 objective after eighteen years (assuming a 6% interest factor) would require monthly payments of $15,000 x .0026 or $39.00. This produces the same $468 in a year as if you made quarterly deposits. Actually, if you used sophisticated tables calculated to eight or ten decimal places, you'd find the year's total of your monthly payments would be slightly less than the annualized amount of your quarterly payments. The difference is not, however, too significant.

Here's another example just to show you how Table 4 can be used to help set investment goals and objectives. Many people dream of retiring by age sixty-five as millionaires. Assume you are age forty and would like to retire in twenty-five years with $1,000,000 in savings. Assume you can earn an after-tax yield at 7% calculated monthly. What monthly deposits would you need to accomplish your objective?

If you turn to page 156, you'll see that monthly deposits of .0012 for twenty-five years will amount to $1 at 7%. Therefore, if your objective is $1,000,000, simply multiply $1,000,000 by .0012 and you'll see that the answer is $1200 a month. Anyone who can save $1200 a month and earn an after-tax yield of 7% can become a millionaire in twenty-five years! See how simple it is?

Finally, it's time for our first "complicated" exercise in which we'll use two tables together in order to solve one investment problem. To do this, we can modify the facts of the last example, where we made calculations for someone who wants to be a millionaire at age 65 but who starts with *no savings* at age forty.

What if, however, our ambitious investor started out at age 40 with $50,000 in accumulated investments. What would he or she then need to set aside monthly to attain the $1,000,000 objective twenty-five years hence, again assuming the same 7% rate of return compounded monthly?

To solve this problem, we must use both Tables 1 and 4. From Table 1 on page 129, we can see that $1 left alone to earn a yield of 7% compounded monthly will amount to $5.725 at the end of twenty-five years. Therefore, $50,000 will become $50,000 x 5.725 or $286,250 by the time our hypothetical investor reaches age 65. Thus, our ambitious friend need only make monthly investments which would accumulate to $1,000,000 *minus* $286,250 over the next twenty-five years. In other words, he or she needs only accumulate *an additional* $713,750 over that twenty-five-year period to attain the goal. The other $286,250 will be provided out of the initial investment of $50,000 at age 40. Again, we return to Table 4, page 156. To accumulate $713,750 over the next twenty-five years assuming a yield of 7% compounded monthly would require monthly investments of $713,750 x .0012 or $856.50. This is only about 70% of the $1200 monthly amount which would otherwise be required if our investor had no funds to start with.

Summary

You'll find Table 4 useful in helping you set realistic goals and objectives for yourself. If you want to save towards a vacation, for a child's education, or to secure a comfortable retirement, you should be able to calculate what is necessary for you to attain your objectives. Once you've defined your goals, it's so much easier to go after them than to leave the build-up of your savings to haphazard and chancy investment methods.

SIX

To Borrow or Not to Borrow?

Before we examine Tables 5, 6, 7 and 8, which all deal with borrowing money, it would be worthwhile to take a fast look at some of the Canadian income tax rules with which you must be familiar before you can figure out the true cost of a loan and decide whether it's worth the risk. You must always compare the after-tax cost of investing to the capital growth needed to at least break even. Bear in mind that if a profit on the sale of property is treated as a capital gain, only three-quarters is taxable. Thus, if you're in a 45% personal tax bracket, the maximum tax on a capital gain is about 33%. Then again, there may be no tax at all if your capital gain is sheltered by the lifetime capital gains exemption which was explained in Chapter One. However, at this point, let's concentrate on the deductibility of your interest expense. If your interest is non-deductible, you'd require a much greater pre-tax return on investment in order to break even. This is illustrated in Figure 1.

The results are somewhat shocking. If interest expense is non-deductible, while capital growth is taxable, you require almost twice the return before taxes just to break even. In other words, *non-deductible interest is expensive.*

Figure 1
An individual in a 45% tax bracket borrows money at 12% to invest in a "growth" investment

	If Interest Expense is Deductible	*If Interest Expense is Non–Deductible*
Cost of borrowing (gross)	12.00%	12.00%
Less: Tax savings (45%)	5.40%	-
Cost of borrowing (net)	6.60%	12.00%
Annual capital growth required to break even (gross) if no capital gains exemption	9.90%	18.00%
Less: 33% tax on growth	3.30%	6.00%
Annual capital growth required to break even (net)	6.60%	12.00%

Interest Deductibility

When, then, is interest tax-deductible? In general, interest on money borrowed to acquire an interest in or finance the operations of a business is tax-deductible. There are, however, some important restrictions on the deductibility of interest on money borrowed for other purposes. First, interest on money borrowed to buy property for personal use is just not deductible. So, if you borrow to buy your own home or a vacation property, you'll be paying off the loan with whatever money you take home after-tax. Similarly, interest on money borrowed to put into registered retirement savings plans is not deductible. This will be dealt with more fully in Chapter Fifteen which deals with RRSPs.

On the other hand, if you borrow to buy a house or property that you'll rent out or take a loan so you can play the stock market, your interest will be tax-deductible. As you'll see in later chapters in this book, you can carry significantly more debt if you're receiving a government subsidy in the form of tax deductions.

There are, however, two special investments for which different rules apply. First, Canadian tax law states that interest on money borrowed to acquire raw land is not tax-deductible. You're permitted to use your interest expense to offset any miscellaneous income which you derive from your land holdings, but you can't create a loss.

Another area where caution is indicated involves transactions in investments such as gold and silver. Generally, profits from the disposition of gold and silver are subject to capital gains treatment. In the case of investments in bullion or coins, this is a result of administrative discretion on the part of Revenue Canada. Since bullion cannot pay interest or dividends and is held strictly as a speculation, whether short or long-term, any gains should theoretically be treated as 100% taxable income. However, it has historically been the policy of Revenue Canada to accept capital gains treatment on these transactions. Nevertheless, you must realize if you want capital gains treatment on your transactions in gold and silver, interest on money borrowed to make these investments is not deductible. If you decide, on the other hand, to deduct interest expense, you must be prepared to pay taxes on your full profits.

As you're no doubt well aware, the tax rules keep changing. Before borrowing money, always seek professional advice as to the tax consequences. This is the only way you can determine the real cost of carrying your investments. When you read Chapters Ten through Seventeen, you'll get a better feel for calculating after-tax costs and returns.

Introduction to Table 5

A very common financial situation involves finding the payment required to repay a loan over a period of time. Suppose you want to borrow $25,000 for five years. The lender wants to earn 11% interest compounded monthly. You're prepared to repay the loan in monthly installments beginning one month after you receive the $25,000. What is the amount of each of your monthly payments? Again, it might be useful to start with a time diagram.

Table 5 will tell you how to calculate the periodic payments needed to pay off or "amortize" a loan of $1 over a certain length of time. Turn to page 166. If the loan payments are to be made monthly, with interest at 11% also calculated monthly, twelve payments of .0217 will be required each year to repay a $1 loan over five years. Therefore, to repay $25,000, payments of $25,000 x .0217, or $542.50, are needed. After five years, you'll have made payments totaling $32,550 (sixty months x $542.50). Of this amount, $25,000 would be the full principal you would have paid back and $7550 would represent interest.

Figure 2
Time diagram illustrating the monthly payments required to amortize a loan of $25,000 over five years

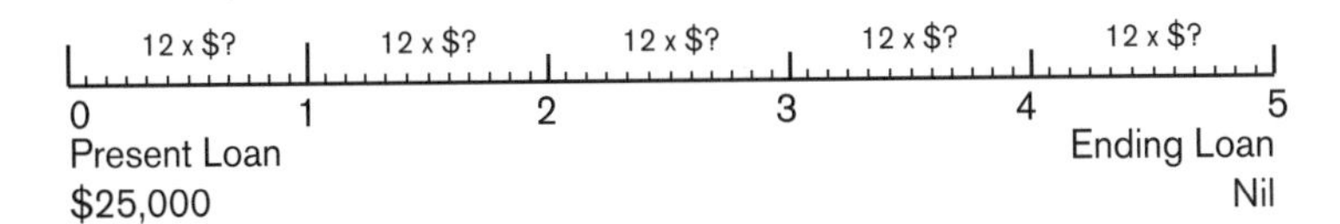

Is there any way to verify that a $25,000 loan at 11% with interest calculated monthly can be amortized by sixty payments of $542.50? Of course there is. Any lender who's willing to accept sixty payments of $542.50 in exchange for $25,000 must, in his or her own mind, *consider both alternatives as having equal value* over a five-year period. In other words, the future value of $25,000 earning interest at 11% calculated monthly for five years must have the same value as sixty payments of $542.50 also at an 11% interest rate. Let's examine Figure 3 to see if the two are, in fact, identical.

Figure 3
Sixty monthly payments of $542.50 are equivalent to $25,000 if money can be invested at 11% compounded monthly

Present Value	*5 Years With Interest at 11% Compounded Monthly*	*Future Value*
$25,000	$25,000 x 1.729 (Table 1, page 131)	$43,225
or		
Sixty monthly payments of $542.50	$542.50 x 79.518 (Table 2, page 140)	43,138
	Rounding difference	$ 87

The future value of $25,000 left to earn interest at 11% compounded monthly for five years is $43,225. Similarly, the future value of sixty monthly payments of $542.50 is $43,138, also assuming interest at 11% compounded monthly. Ignoring a small rounding difference, the values of both are identical.

You'll find Table 5 useful any time you face the prospect of borrowing money and would like to know the required monthly, quarterly, semi-annual or annual payments to discharge your debt.

Again, take the trouble to review pages 162 to 170. In using Table 5, *always be careful to make sure you're looking under the right column.* Otherwise, you'll become a victim of the "garbage in, garbage out" principle.

Note that in the first column of Table 5, monthly payments are assumed. It's also assumed that interest is compounded monthly as well. Similarly, in the third column, which details the required semi-annual payments, it's also assumed that interest is calculated semi-annually. Technically, it's conceivable that you could borrow money under an arrangement whereby your payments are made monthly although interest is calculated only semi-annually. In these circumstances, the figures in the first column will give you a close approximation of the required monthly payments although they won't be exact.

Actually, most Canadian mortgage loans call for monthly payments, even though interest is compounded semi-annually. This is why I have included Table 6, which is discussed in the next chapter.

Here's another application of Table 5. Let's assume you can borrow money at 10%. You are looking for a $10,000 loan and want to have a nine-year repayment program. How much would you need to pay? Figure 4 contains an extract from that table.

Figure 4
Periodic payments required to amortize a loan of $10,000 at 10% over nine years

Payments are made	*Monthly*	*Quarterly*	*Semi–Annually*	*Annually*
9 Years/$1	0.0141	0.0425	0.0855	0.1736
Periodic payments to amortize a loan of $10,000	$ 141	$ 425	$ 855	$1,736
	x 12	x 4	x 2	x 1
Annual Payments	$1,692	$1,700	$1,710	$1,736

You can see it really doesn't make a tremendous amount of difference whether your payments are made monthly or annually. Of course, the more frequently your payments are made, the cheaper it is for you to discharge your debt. Over a nine-year period, though, the difference between paying monthly and annually is only $44 x 9, or $396 on a $10,000 loan.

However, let's assume your payments will be made on a monthly basis since this is usually what most lenders require. Figure 5 is another extract from Table 5 showing the monthly payments required to discharge a loan of $1 with interest at 10% over one to thirty years.

If you look at these numbers carefully, I think you'll learn something very interesting. Obviously, if you want to get rid of a debt over one, two or even three years, the payments are quite high relative to the original debt. However, look what happens if the debt is extended over a long time period. *Your payments are virtually the same whether you choose to repay over fifteen years or thirty years. In other words, there is little point in extending any debt any longer than you absolutely require.* For example, let's assume the principal amount you borrow is $10,000. If you're willing to pay for the privilege of borrowing $10,000 at 10% over a thirty-year period, your monthly payments will be $10,000 x .0088, or $88 per month. However, if you want to, you can shorten the payout period to, say, fifteen years. Your payments then become $10,000 x .0107, or $107 per month. Thus, if you're willing to pay out an extra $19 a month, you can save a total cash outflow of $12,420. This is illustrated in Figure 6. Astounding, isn't it?

Figure 5
Monthly payments required to amortize a loan of $1 at 10% interest calculated monthly over one to thirty years

1	0.0879	16	0.0105
2	0.0461	17	0.0102
3	0.0323	18	0.0100
4	0.0254	19	0.0098
5	0.0212	20	0 0097
6	0.0185	21	0.0095
7	0.0166	22	0.0094
8	0.0152	23	0.0093
9	0.0141	24	0.0092
10	0.0132	25	0.0091
11	0.0125	26	0.0090
12	0.0120	27	0.0089
13	0.0115	28	0.0089
14	0.0111	29	0.0088
15	0.0107	30	0.0088

Figure 6
Paying off a debt of $10,000 over fifteen years vs. thirty years

$10,000 x 0.0088 = $ 88 /Month pays off $10,000 over thirty years
$10,000 x 0.0107 = $107 /Month pays off $10,000 over fifteen years
Monthly difference $ 19

Thirty years x 12 monthly payments x $ 88/month =	$31,680
Fifteen years x 12 monthly payments x $107/month =	19,260
Total difference	$12,420

Summary

In real life, any time you're negotiating for a loan which you'll repay with blended payments of principal and interest, you should always take a close look at Table 5. First, you can see how much you can afford to borrow depending on your ability to repay. Then, you'll find if you force yourself to make just slightly higher payments than the bare minimum you could afford to get away with under the lender's conditions, you'll be far ahead of the game.

SEVEN

Canadian Mortgage Loans

In the last chapter, we dealt with Table 5, which gives the periodic payments required to amortize a loan over various time periods. For each interest factor, the first column of Table 5 shows the loan payments which must be made monthly, assuming interest is also calculated on a monthly basis. Although Table 5 is useful in dealing with most conventional loans from lending institutions, it is not suitable for handling problems involving Canadian mortgage loans. This is because, under Canadian law, interest is compounded semi-annually, although most mortgage loan payments are made monthly. So, the payments required to discharge a Canadian mortgage loan are slightly smaller than they would be if interest were calculated monthly.

Figure 1 compares the monthly payment required to discharge a "conventional" loan of $1000 at 10% compounded monthly to the monthly payment required to amortize a Canadian mortgage loan at the same interest rate but with interest calculated semi-annually. Granted, the difference is only a few pennies for each $1000 of debt, but it doesn't hurt to be reasonably accurate—especially since most mortgages are only repaid over fifteen to twenty-five years.

Figure 1

Years	*Monthly payment required to amortize a loan of $1000 at 10% interest compounded monthly over various periods of time (from Table 5)*	*Monthly payment required to amortize a mortgage loan of $1000 at 10% interest compounded semi–annually over various periods of time (from Table 6)*
5	$21.20	$21.15
10	13.20	13.10
15	10.70	10.62
20	9.70	9.52
25	9.10	8.95

Table 6 provides you with all the information you'll need to construct Canadian mortgage amortization schedules. The interest rates for this table range from 5% to 16.875%, increasing by one-eighth of 1% each time. In this case, since fractional percentages are built into the table, it's not necessary for you to make any approximations. You may use this table to deal with amortizations from one to forty years. One word of caution, however. It almost goes without saying that in dealing with all mathematics tables, you must be sure not to make errors in your decimal places. Most of the tables in this book deal with present value and future value calculations for $1 amounts. The only exceptions are Tables 6 and 7 which refer to mortgage loans of $1000. For example, if you're trying to calculate the payments required to amortize a $50,000 mortgage loan at 12.375% over twenty years, your required payments would be 50 (not 50,000) x 11.058. (see page 179). The payments in this case are $552.90.

Most mortgage loans are made on the basis of a twenty-five-year amortization. Of course, they have to be renewed at the prevailing interest rate periodically. Table 7 provides you with the balance outstanding at the end of each year on a twenty-five-year mortgage loan of $1000 at various rates of interest, with interest compounded semi-annually. Figure 2 is an extract from this table showing the progression of a $100,000 mortgage loan at 12%. As time goes on, the principal balance outstanding on the mortgage continues to decrease.

Figure 2
Balance outstanding on a twenty-five year mortgage loan of $100,000 at 12% interest (Monthly Payment $1031.90; Rounded to Nearest $100)

End of Year		*End of Year*		*End of Year*	
1	$99,300	9	$89,400	17	$64,100
2	98,500	10	87,300	18	59,000
3	97,600	11	85,100	19	53,200
4	96,600	12	82,500	20	46,700
5	95,500	13	79,600	21	39,400
6	94,200	14	76,400	22	31,200
7	92,800	15	72,800	23	22,000
8	91,200	16	68,700	24	11,600
				25	0

By using Tables 6 and 7 together, you should be able to calculate with a reasonable degree of accuracy which portion of any given year's mortgage payments will be applied against principal or interest.

For example, at 12% interest compounded semi-annually, a mortgage loan of $100,000 can be discharged over twenty-five years with monthly payments of $1031.90. Yearly, the payments are $1031.90 x 12, or $12,382.80. Over the course of the first year, the mortgage principal declines from $100,000 to $99,300. This means that $700 out of payments totaling $12,383 apply towards principal in the first year. The balance of $11,683 therefore represents interest. Similarly, in year fifteen, the balance outstanding on principal declines from $76,400 to $72,800, a difference of $3600. Again, if the total payments are $12,383, the interest portion would have to be $8783. This is illustrated in Figure 3.

Figure 3
Amortizing a $100,000 mortgage at 12% over twenty-five years

Monthly payments: $100,000 x 10.319 = $ 1,031.90
$ 1,000

Annual payments: $1,031.90 x 12 = $12,382.80

Year	Payments Made	Principal	Interest
1	$12,383	$100,000–$99,300 = $ 700	$11,683
5	12,383	96,600 – 95,500 = 1,100	11,283
10	12,383	89,400 – 87,300 = 2,100	10,283
15	12,383	76,400 – 72,800 = 3,600	8,783
20	12,383	53,200 – 46,700 = 6,500	5,883
25	12,383	11,600 – 0 = 11,600	783

Income Tax Considerations

Since Canadians cannot deduct interest on money borrowed to buy a house for their own use, home ownership is an extremely expensive proposition. If your mortgage bears interest at 12% and you're in a 45% tax bracket, you must earn almost double the amount you have to pay off. For this reason, you must try to discharge a home mortgage as quickly as possible.

Many mortgages will allow the borrower to prepay up to ten percent on the anniversary date each year. If you make ordinary payments on a monthly basis coupled with seven or eight installments of 10% of the original balance, your mortgage can then be eliminated within seven or eight years. Take another look at Figure 2, which shows the balance outstanding on a twenty-five-year mortgage loan of $100,000 at 12%. At the end of the first year, the principal balance outstanding is $99,300 while at the end of year nine it is $89,400. Therefore, if you were to repay $9900 on the first anniversary of your mortgage, you would then be eliminating the next eight annual payments. In other words, if your monthly payments stay the same (which they would) and you make no further special payments against principal, your debt would be completely extinguished only sixteen years later. Given a special payment of $9900 at the end of the first year, you would then owe only $89,400 at the end of year two, $87,300 after year three, and so forth. Of course, if additional principal payments were made at the end of the second year (and subsequently) your debt would be extinguished that much more quickly. Certainly, most people are not in a position to pay down as much as 10% of their mortgage each year on the anniversary date—especially since they must use after-tax dollars to do this. However, whatever *you* can pay down will be quite helpful.

The Mortgage Term

Be careful never to confuse the *amortization* of a loan with its *term*. If you're told a mortgage is to be amortized over twenty-five years, you must never assume it has a twenty-five-year term. The term of a mortgage is the period of time given to the borrower before the lender can demand the principal balance owing on the loan. Until perhaps thirty years ago, lenders did in fact make loans for long periods, such as twenty-five years, at fixed rates of interest. Today, however, mortgage terms rarely exceed five years and often must be renewed each year. Thus, although an amortization schedule may reflect the payments necessary to discharge a debt over twenty-five years, the borrower, in most cases, must still repay the principal balance at the end of only one, two, or at most, four or five years. Of course, the lender will usually renew the mortgage at current prevailing rates.

Again, examine the schedule on page 35. If payments of $1031.90 are made monthly over twenty-five years, a loan of $100,000 at 12% would be extinguished. However, here is the problem posed by the fact that your mortgage might have, say, a three-year term. At the end of three years, the lender will want his money and, on a twenty-five-year loan, you'd still owe him $97,600. To repay that loan, you'd probably have to commit yourself to another mortgage and borrow the $97,600. Assume the new mortgage is for a further three years at the same rate and also with payments calculated over a twenty-five-year period. Figure 4 shows what your outstanding balance will be over the next three years in round figures.

Figure 4
Balance outstanding on a loan of $97,600 at 12%
(twenty-five year amortization)

End of Year		*Balance*
1	$97,600 x .993 =	$96,917
2	97,600 x .985 =	96,136
3	97,600 x .976 =	95,258

At the end of the second three-year period when you have to repay the loan, you may repeat the process. Each new three-year term will result in smaller monthly payments because the principal amount at the start of each succeeding term will be less. However, instead of amortizing the loan down to zero after twenty-five years, it may take over one hundred years to discharge the loan completely. *There is only one way a twenty-five-year mortgage can be paid off in full over twenty-five years. Each time a mortgage is renewed, you must arrange to have the remaining principal amortized for a period which is not longer than the remaining number of years in the original amortization.*

In other words, continuing with the preceding example, the $97,600 balance outstanding at the end of the first three-year period should be renewed with payments based on a *twenty-two-year* amortization. Then, the balance outstanding at the end of six years should be renewed for a further term based on an amortization period of only nineteen years and so on.

Especially in times of high interest rates, the tendency is to try to reduce monthly payments by lengthening the term over which a loan is amortized. As you'll shortly see, however, this can be an extremely costly mistake. The table in Figure 5 shows the payments necessary to amortize a $100,000 mortgage loan at 12% over various time periods.

Clearly, the longer the period, the smaller the monthly payments.

However, the longer the term, the greater the total cost. The analysis in Figure 5 compares the difference between a fifteen-year amortization and a twenty-five-year repayment. For each $100,000, the monthly difference is less than $150. However, extending the payment period an extra ten years costs $96,882 in the long run.

Figure 5
Amortization of $100,000 at 12% over various time periods

$100,000 at 12%	*15 Years*	*20 Years*	*25 Years*	*35 Years*
Monthly payment	$ 1,181.60	$ 1,081.00	$ 1,031.90	$ 992.70
Annual cost	14,179.20	12,972.00	12,382.80	11,912.40
Total cost	212,688.00	259,440.00	309,570.00	416,934.00
Total interest paid	112,688.00	159,440.00	209,570.00	316,934.00

Monthly payment over 15 years	$ 1,181.60
Monthly payment over 25 years	1,031.90
Difference	$ 149.70
Total interest over 25 years	$ 209,570.00
Total interest over 15 years	112,688.00
Difference	$ 96,882.00

Points

Many real estate loans involve special charges called "points". One point is one per cent of the loan principal. Lenders charge points in order to increase the real yield on the loan, without increasing the stated rate.

For example, if you're negotiating with a lender for a $50,000 twenty-five-year fixed rate, second mortgage loan at 14% annual interest, the monthly payment on such a loan would be $586.95 ($11.739 x 50).

If the lender also charges three points as a service fee, 3% of $50,000 is $1500. This amount is deducted from the $50,000, to give a net loan principal of $48,500. Now, what is the true interest rate? The monthly payment on the loan will be the same as calculated above, but the loan principal is only $48,500.

Using Table 6, you can calculate that $50,000 at 14% for twenty-five years requires monthly payments of:

$50,000 ÷ $1000 = 50
11.739 x 50 = $586.95

If the loan amount is reduced to $48,500 but the payments of $586.95 remain the same, then the interest rate must increase. Tracing the twenty-five-year amortization line further to the right, you can try various factors from Table 6 for the best fit:

$48,500 ÷ $1000 = 48.5
11.829 x 48.5 = 573.71 (14 1/8%)
11.919 x 48.5 = 578.07 (14 1/4%)
12.009 x 48.5 = 582.44 (14 3/8%)
12.099 x 48.5 = 586.80 (14 1/2%)

From this trial and error process, you can see the factor of 12.099 gives the closest approximation to a payment of $586.95 per month. This factor is for a 14.5% interest rate. In other words, the three points charged against the mortgage will cost you an extra 1/2% interest over the twenty-five-year life of the loan.

Summary

This chapter has explained the fundamentals of mortgages. In Chapter Eleven, we'll return to the topic of home ownership and deal with the question of how to evaluate a home as an investment. Then, Chapter Twelve covers investing in real estate other than a home. After reading these two chapters, you should be in a better position to decide whether it's worthwhile to discharge a debt quickly or if it makes sense to extend the term over which your financing obligations will be repaid. As you'll see, one of the key factors is the deductibility or non-deductibility of your interest expense.

EIGHT

How Much Can I Afford to Borrow?

Suppose you're looking for a loan and your income level will allow you to make up to $600 in monthly payments beginning one month from now. There's a lender who is willing to give you a five-year loan with annual interest of, say, 11% compounded monthly. How much will you be able to borrow?

Before we examine Table 8, which will give us the answer, it might again be appropriate to sketch a simple time diagram, as in Figure 1.

If you're faced with this type of problem, you'll notice that each payment occurs at the end of each period. In fact, most loans generally *do* require payments at the end of each period.

Now we can turn to Table 8, which gives us the present value of $1 per period payable at the end of each period. In simple terms, this table will tell you how much you can borrow today at various interest rates for each $1 you're able to pay back at the end of each period for a given number of periods. The figures for an interest rate of 11% appear on page 196.

If payments of $600 will be made monthly for five years, the amount you can borrow today is $600 x 45.993 or $27,595.80. In other words, if you're prepared to pay back $600 each month, you could borrow $27,595.80 and extinguish your debt over a sixty-month period. Your payments would provide both principal and interest to the lender. Once you know this amount, it's then easy to determine your principal-interest breakdown. In total, your payments will be sixty months x $600, or $36,000. Therefore, the total interest you would pay during the life of the loan is $36,000 minus $27,595.80, or $8,404.20.

Figure 1
How much can you borrow if you can afford to make monthly payments of $600 over five years with interest at 11%?

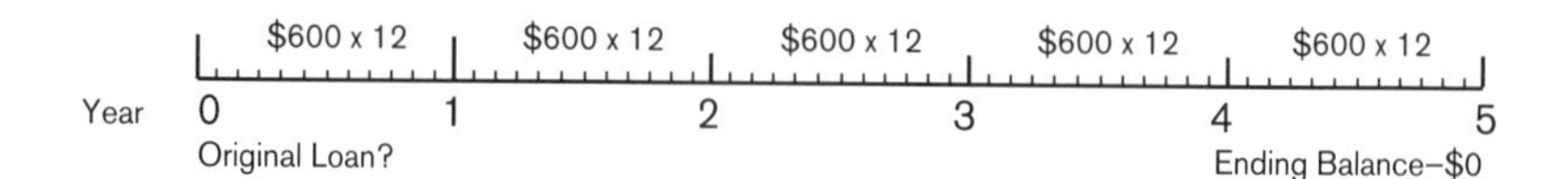

Can Your Results Be Verified?

In previous chapters, I explained you can generally prove whether your answers are correct. In this case, the solution can also be verified although it takes two steps to do so. The process is, however, important because it illustrates the meaning of "the present value of an annuity".

Let's take a look at the situation from the lender's standpoint. If our answer is correct, a lender who's willing to earn 11% on his money would be just as well off trading $27,595.80 for the right to receive $600 a month for the next five years. In other words, at 11% interest, his or her total accumulation would be the same. We can use Tables 1 and 2 to see whether this is, in fact, the case.

Figure 2
Future value of $27,595.80 after five years with interest compounded at 11%, calculated monthly

$27,595.80 x 1.729 (Table 1, page 131) = $47,713.14

Figure 3
Future value of sixty monthly payments of $600 with interest compounded at 11%, calculated monthly

$600 x 79.518 (Table 2, page 140) = $47,710.80

Except for a $2.34 rounding difference, the calculations shown in Figures 2 and 3 prove that the future value is equivalent; thus our initial answer was correct.

Perhaps there is one area of confusion. In the problem with which we've been dealing, the lender would be receiving sixty monthly payments of $600, or a total of $36,000. How does this amount reconcile with the calculations just made which show that the future value of these payments is $47,710? The answer is that the verification using future value equivalents assumes the lender *could reinvest each payment of $600* as it is received at 11%, so that, over a period of five years, he or she could earn *an additional $11,710* in interest.

The concept of equivalents of future values is one of the most important and fundamental ideas behind all financing arrangements. It shows why a lender would be willing to give up cash in exchange for future monthly payments.

Take the time to examine Table 8 in some detail. Notice for each percentage factor, the numbers are completely different in all four columns. This is because the first column deals with a monthly payback, while the second column deals with four quarterly payments, and column three reflects two semi-annual payments, while column four assumes one annual payment only. As is the case in Table 5, if monthly payments are to be made, it's assumed interest is also compounded monthly. Similarly, if annual payments are required, interest is assumed to compound annually.

The practical application of Table 8 is, as I already explained, its usefulness in helping you determine how much you can afford to borrow for investment based on your anticipated cash flow (that is, your ability to pay back). In the example described in the first few pages of this chapter, the assumption was made that a borrower could afford to repay $600 a month over a five-year period. This gave him or her the opportunity to borrow $27,596 today.

Often, when it comes to investing, you don't need a substantial amount of start-up capital. *All you need is the power to carry debt.* As you'll learn in later chapters, an initial borrowing which can be covered by cash flow from your job, business or profession can then be leveraged into *further* borrowings, provided the *additional* debt can be serviced out of cash flows generated from the investments themselves. In other words, if excess earnings of $600 a month from your job allows you to borrow, say, $27,500, and you invest in a stock that pays a 6% dividend, you'll find you can actually borrow substantially *more* than $27,500. This is because the dividend yield from the investment itself will help you pay down the additional debt commitment. The deductibility of investment interest for tax purposes can also enhance greatly your ability to carry a debt load.

Common sense should tell you two very important things about borrowing money: (1) The lower the interest rate, the more you can afford to borrow. (2) However, extending the term of a loan beyond, say, six or seven years, does not significantly increase the amount you can borrow. This is because your interest costs are so high in proportion to your total payments that it becomes more and more difficult to amortize the principal balance.

Figure 4 illustrates how Table 8 proves these common-sense points. It shows the amount of money you can borrow at various interest rates if you're prepared to pay $600 a month for five years. As you can see, the difference between borrowing at 10% and 18% is significant ($28,239 - $23,628 = $4611).

Figure 4
Principal amount of debt that can be amortized by monthly payments of $600 over five years at various rates of interest

Interest Rate	*Factor From Table 8*	*Initial Debt To Be Repaid Over 5 Years*
10%	$600 x 47.065	$28,239
12%	600 x 44.955	26,973
14%	600 x 42.977	25,786
16%	600 x 41.122	24,673
18%	600 x 39.380	23,628

On the other hand, Figure 5 shows you that, at any given interest rate, the amount you can borrow does not vary dramatically whether you commit yourself to make payments over fifteen years or over as long as twenty years. For purposes of illustration, I'll assume an interest rate of 14%.

The difference between a twenty-year and a fifteen-year repayment period represents the opportunity to borrow only an extra $3196 ($48,250 – $45,054). In exchange for that small amount, you'd have to make sixty additional payments of $600 each or $36,000.

Figure 5
Principal amount of debt that can be amortized by monthly payments of $600 at 14% interest over various time periods

Time Period Years	*Factor From Table 8*	*Initial Debt To Be Repaid*
15	$600 x 75.090	$45,054
16	600 x 76.470	45,882
17	600 x 77.671	46,603
18	600 x 78.716	47,230
19	600 x 79.626	47,776
20	600 x 80.417	48,250

Summary

Before you even think about borrowing money, your first question should be: If I borrow, how much can I afford to repay on a periodic basis (monthly, quarterly, etc.)? Of course, your answer depends on whether the property you buy with borrowed money will provide you with a cash inflow to subsidize your debt. Whenever you do borrow, you should generally try to extinguish your debts as soon as possible, even if it requires slightly higher cash outlays to do so. Over the long run, the savings in cash flow can be quite significant.

NINE

The Future and Present Value of Payments Made at the *Beginning* of Each Period

In our previous discussions of annuities, we always assumed that the periodic payments would be made at the *end* of each time period. In Chapter Three, for example, we calculated how much you could accumulate if you were to put aside a certain amount of money monthly, quarterly, semi-annually or annually at the *end* of each period. Similarly, in the last chapter, we calculated how much money you could afford to *borrow* if you were prepared to make *payments* at the *end* of various time periods. Savings are typically deposited at the end of various time intervals and loans are typically repaid on an ordinary annuity basis. Thus, the financial tables we've already examined in this book are directly applicable to most saving and loan situations.

Leasing, however, is also an extremely important financial activity. The problem with leases is that they usually call for periodic payments at the *beginning* of each time period. We're all familiar with the concept of paying rent in advance on the first of each month. *An annuity calling for payments at the beginning of each time period is called "an annuity due".*

Table 2 can't be used directly to calculate the future value of an annuity due. It can be modified using high-school algebra, but instead I've chosen to include a separate table in this book to determine the future value of $1 invested at the *beginning* of each period (Table 9).

How Do You Calculate the Future Value of an Annuity Due?

Suppose you deposit $100 each month in a savings account that pays 9% interest compounded monthly—just like in the first example in Chapter Three when we dealt with ordinary annuities. This time, however, you make your deposits at the *start* of each period rather than at the end. Deposits are made for ten years. Before doing the calculations, it would be, again, useful to construct a time diagram and then compare it to the one on page 16.

Like the diagram in Chapter Three, this one also calls for one hundred and twenty monthly payments. However, they are all moved *one period closer to the present.* Instead of waiting one month before making the first deposit, you do so immediately. The last deposit is made at the *start* of the

120th month. The future value of the sixty payments at 9% compounded monthly is 194.966 X $100 or $19,496.60. In the ordinary annuity problem (deposits made at the *end* of each month), the future value turned out to be $19,351.40. You'll notice the future value of the "annuity due" is higher because deposits into the account are made *sooner* and therefore *earn more interest.* The difference over a ten-year period is $145.

Figure 1
Time diagram illustrating twelve monthly deposits of $100 at the beginning of each month over a ten-year period

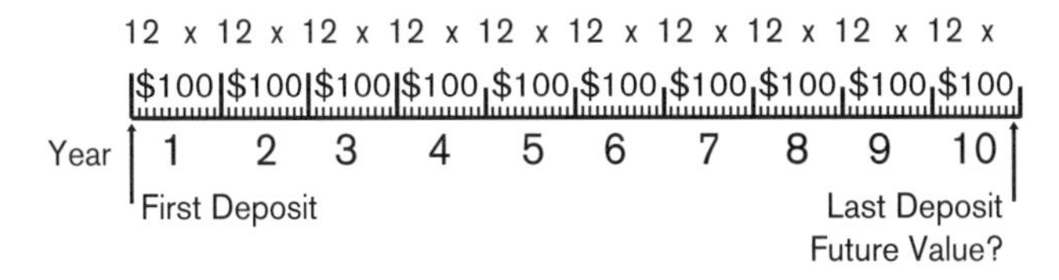

How Much Do I Have to Save to Meet My Goals and Objectives—If I Start NOW?

In Chapter Five, we saw that, in order to accumulate $10,000 in a savings account after four years with interest at 9% compounded monthly, you had to make monthly deposits of $174 on an ordinary annuity basis. But, what would have happened if, instead of making your deposits at the end of each month, you had made your first deposit right away? How much would each deposit have to be?

To solve this problem, you may use Table 10. The only difference between Table 10 and Table 4 is that Table 10 deals with payments made at the *beginning* of each period. From page 213, the monthly payment factor at 9% is 0.0173. In other words, you need only make monthly payments of $173 at the beginning of each month, if you wish to accumulate $10,000 after four years. The difference is $1 a month.

How Do You Determine the Present Value of an Annuity Due?

The present value of an annuity due is an important quantity to consider when you analyze a lease or an insurance policy. Both of these will be discussed later in this book, but here's a simple example just to illustrate the concept.

Suppose you purchase a computer with the intention of leasing it out for five years. You figure the property will have no value at the end of this time because it'll have been rendered obsolete by changes in technology. You want lease payments large enough to allow you to recover the cost of the computer as well as an 18% annual rate of return on your investment (compounded monthly). If you pay $30,000 for the computer, how much do you have to charge as a monthly lease payment in order to realize your objectives? Again, we should refer to a time diagram.

As you can see in Figure 2, this is an annuity due situation with the lease payments occurring at the start of each of the sixty consecutive monthly periods. If you look at Table 11, and the figures on page 45, you'll see that the answer is $30,000 x .0250, or $750 a month. If you can find a lessee who agrees to those terms, you'd receive 60 x $750 or $45,000 over the five-year period. This would cover your $30,000 cost and give you an 18% return on your investment with interest calculated monthly.

Figure 2
Time diagram illustrating the required monthly lease payments to recover $30,000 over five years with interest at 18%

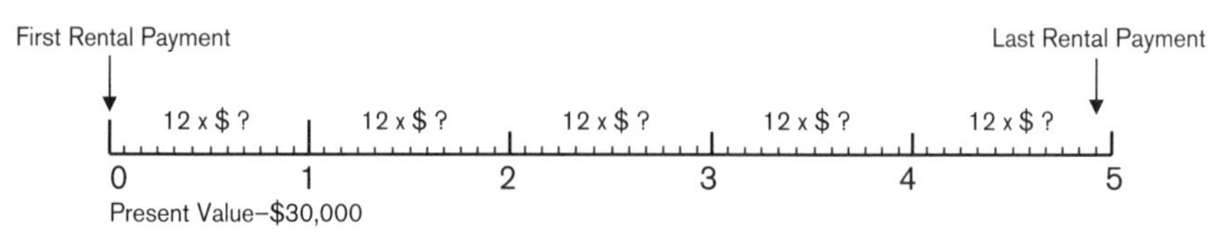

In this lease example, your only return on the computer is the annuity of sixty monthly payments. Again, please note the assumption made earlier that the computer itself would have no value after the five-year period. In Chapter Seventeen, we'll deal with more realistic examples, which make the assumption the property does have some value at the end of the lease. You'll see that the present value of the final sale price must be taken into account in determining a fair market value leasing rate.

As the final example in this chapter, suppose you understand from your cousin, who is a real estate broker, that duplexes in your city are renting for $600 a month ($300 for each side). You've just inherited a sizable amount of money and would like to buy a duplex property as long as you can earn a 16% return on your investment compounded monthly over the next twenty-five years. What is the most you should spend for the property?

In this case, you'd expect a return on investment of $600 a month for the next twenty-five years, starting immediately. The present value of an annuity due is given in Table 12. Table 12 is very similar to Table 6 except that Table 6 deals with the present value of payments made at the *end* of each period while Table 12 deals with payments made at the *beginning*.

At 16% interest, the present value of twenty-five years of $600 monthly payments can be determined from the figures on page 234. The answer is 74.571 multiplied by the $600 monthly rent, or $44,742.60. This amount represents the purchase price that would give you your 16% return over the next twenty-five years. If you can buy the house for less and still rent it out at $600 a month, your return will be greater than 16%. Of course, this example is not realistic since you'd expect rents to increase annually instead of being held constant over twenty-five years. Also, the example assumes the property would be worthless at the end of twenty-five years. Actually, you'd be able to sell the house at the end of that time.

Suppose the sales price is $150,000. The present value of $150,000 to be received thirty years from now can be found by using Table 3. Assuming a 16% return on investment factor, compounded monthly, the present value is $150,000 x .0188, or $2820. You can add this $2820 to the $44,742 present value of the lease payments to arrive at a total of approximately $47,500 you could pay for the house and attain your objectives (ignoring potential rent increases). Note the final sales proceeds do not make much of a difference in the calculations because the sale is projected to take place so far in the future. As you'll see in subsequent chapters, given shorter holding periods, the final sales price has a much more important effect on your investment decisions.

Also, please take note that these last few examples have not taken taxes into account. In a true situation, you'd have to compute your net income from rental payments and the net sales proceeds after taxes, including those which may be levied on capital gains, and *then* use the tables. But, for the time being, the more simplified computations will serve just to introduce the workings of the various tables.

Summary

To this stage, we've covered the applications of Tables 1 through 12 inclusive. The only table not yet discussed is Table 13, which deals with mortality rates. This will be discussed in Chapter Sixteen when we examine the subject of life insurance and annuities.

With what we've learned so far as background, we're almost ready to examine how the various tables can be used to assist you to make specific investment decisions beyond just earning or paying interest. But, before we do this, we must examine the concept of "discounted cash flow", which is the subject of the next chapter.

TEN

Discounted Cash-Flow Analysis

Most investments require an initial outlay of cash. Then, some investments will provide a cash return during the period of ownership, while others will require you to subsidize their costs through additional outflows of money. Finally, when an investment is sold, there's usually one final net cash inflow.

In making any financial analysis, the key point to remember is a dollar you'll either receive or pay out sometime in the future is worth less than a dollar today. How much less depends on the interest rate you choose for your calculations. This interest rate can be the presumed rate of inflation or it can be your own desired rate of return for an investment.

Often, in dealing with the concept of future dollars being worth less than dollars today, financial analysts refer to the process of "discounting". Future dollars are discounted at the selected interest rate to translate them into a more meaningful framework—today's dollars.

In this chapter and in the remainder of this book, we'll refer often to Table 3, which gives you the present value of $1 due at the end of various time periods. You'll need this to perform present value analysis, or discounting.

The excerpt from Table 3 in this section provides figures for an assumed annual investment rate of 10%. These figures can be read in one of two ways. First, if you invest 62 cents today at 10% and leave your money alone for five years, you'll have $1 at the end. Or we can take the opposite approach. If you're to receive $1 at the end of five years, this right is only worth an equivalent of 62 cents today, if a 10% annual interest/investment (or inflation) rate is assumed.

Figure 1
The present value of $1 due at the end of various time periods at 10% interest compounded annually

End of Year	
1	0.9091
2	0.8264
3	0.7513
4	0.6830
5	0.6209

Discounted Cash-Flow Techniques

Professional investment analysts use discounted cash-flow techniques to evaluate all kinds of property—including real estate, stock market transactions and other investments such as gold and silver. The actual technique used may vary from analyst to analyst but most have several common factors:

1. Income taxes are considered and calculations are made using after-tax values only.
2. The techniques consider the time value of money.
3. The emphasis is on cash flow and not net income since cash flow is regarded as the best test of investment performance.
4. A percentage rate of return is used to measure the value of the investment. This is something that is easily understood and interpreted. For example, if an investment yields a return of 14.73%, this result can be compared to other alternatives.
5. Discounted cash-flow techniques all take into account the actual amount you, as an investor, commit to an investment.

As long as you're willing to devote a bit of time and effort, these techniques are quite easy to apply. The most widely used discounted cash-flow techniques are called the *net present value method* and the *internal rate of return method.* Wherever possible, these should be used together when analyzing a potential investment.

The Net Present Value Method

To determine the net present value of an investment, you must go through several steps.

1. First, you must choose a minimum satisfactory after-tax rate of return for your investment. This is often referred to as the discount rate. How you select a satisfactory discount rate is discussed in the next section of this chapter.
2. Then, you must detail all of the after-tax cash flows from an investment on a year-by-year basis.
3. Next, you calculate the present value of each year's net after-tax cash flow using the discount rate established in Step 1. Add them together and the total is your net present value.
4. Finally, you analyze and interpret the result.

If the net present value is a positive number, then your investment is earning more than your required rate of return. A net present value less than zero means your investment is earning less than you wanted and should perhaps be discarded. The closer the net present value is to exactly zero, the closer the investment will perform according to your exact specifications.

How to Select the Required Rate of Return

To set your own required rate of return, you'll need two reference points: the rate of return offered at a particular time on other investments, and the degree of risk associated with the particular investment compared to the risk of alternatives.

For example, assume your simplest investment is a bank term deposit which might yield 8% before tax and would carry very little risk. However, if you're in a 45% marginal tax bracket, a yield of 8% translates to only 4.4% (8% x 55%) after taxes. Now, if you feel that a particular investment is just as safe as a term deposit, you could set the after-tax required rate of return at only 4.4%. On the other hand, if you feel that a prospective investment is riskier, you should increase that percentage. How much you add is purely a matter of your own judgment. If you feel that a potential investment is quite risky, you might add a 10% "risk premium" to the 4.4% to arrive at your required after-tax rate of return.

Clearly, the greater you set your required after-tax rate of return, the higher the investment performance has to be before the net present value will be positive. In other words, an investment that may have a positive net present value at a 10% required rate of return could have a negative net present value if your required return is 20%. In the following chapters, we'll often use a 12% to 18% factor for the required after-tax rate of return. Remember that an 18% return would be calculated *after taxes*, and is equivalent to as much as a 36% or 38% rate of return before tax, depending on your marginal tax bracket. However, in your own calculations, you're certainly free to choose whatever rates you desire.

Determining After-Tax Cash Flows

Of course, tax laws and tax rates are always changing. So I'll try to keep my examples relatively simple. I'll generally assume an investor is in a 45% income tax bracket. Most of the ground rules for tax assumptions have already been covered in Chapter Two.

Simplifying Your Investment Analysis

Wherever possible, you should keep your analysis as simple as you can. In the next chapter, we'll analyze a possible investment in a house. This will be followed with another example involving a vacation home. Both analyses are made with yearly projections, rather than monthly. By making a few such simplifications, the time required to prepare a financial analysis can be reduced to only a few minutes with no major loss of accuracy for purposes of decision making. Always remember most financial analysis relies on estimates. Future incomes are not certain nor are projections of future expenses, nor for that matter, tax rates.

Take a moment to examine the blank investment analysis form on pages 52-53. The first column represents the purchase of the investment. In this column, you would show your personal cash outlay to acquire whatever you are buying. Notice the first column includes not only your downpayment but any other initial costs associated with an investment. If you're buying a home, these could include legal fees or appraisal costs. In the case of a stock market investment, brokerage commissions would be a "front end" cost as well. Clearly, no matter what discount rate you're using, *the present value factor here is always 1.000*. This is because the initial outlay is made in *today's dollars*. Then, Columns 1 through 5 represent future years, starting with the first year after the date the initial investment is made.

The form in Figure 2 on the next two pages is geared to an investment in real estate. It can be adopted quite nicely, as you'll see in Chapters Thirteen and Fourteen, to deal with other investments as well, such as the stock market or gold. The various descriptions on the form are, for the most part, self-explanatory. In any example dealing with the purchase of a home, depreciation and income tax considerations are not applicable. In other cases, you may have to calculate these amounts on an annual basis and also compute potential taxes on capital gains at the time of sale.

An investment analysis form provides for the calculation of taxable income arising from the particular investment so you can determine any income taxes payable (over and above your other taxes). Then, items not affecting cash flow or income tax matters are accounted for separately. *Remember it is cash flow that really determines whether an investment is desirable and cash flow is quite different from net income.* In a given year, you could have a high net income but no cash flow. A good example would be if you use whatever revenue an investment provides to pay off debt owing against that investment. Remember you cannot reinvest your net income—you can only reinvest your cash. Again, this is why the net present value method is called a *discounted cash flow* technique.

One small formality. I suggest you use a simple accounting trick to help in your calculations. When a number represents a cash *outflow,* record it in parentheses. This is the same as a minus sign but is harder to miss.

The rate of return you require will determine the present value factor you must insert at the bottom of each column. For these purposes, you'll use Table 3. For example, if you require a 10% after-tax rate of return, a cash inflow or outflow at the end of one year has a present value of 0.9091 (see page 148), while an amount due at the end of two years has a present value of 0.8264. To translate after-tax cash flows into present dollars, simply multiply these cash flows by the present value factor.

Interpreting the Net Present Value

Once you've calculated your after-tax cash flows and have translated them into present dollars, you're ready to interpret your results. If your net present value is positive, this means you could have made an even larger initial investment and you still would have realized your desired rate of return. If the net present value is negative, then you're earning less than your target.

Reinvestment Assumption in the Net Present Value Method

You should be careful, however, when you use the concept of net present value analysis in real life. *The net present value you derive will only be true if you can reinvest all positive cash flows* during *the life of the investment at the required after-tax rate of return.* This is a reasonable assumption in many cases, unless you've established a required rate so high that the reinvestment of the "intermediate proceeds" at that rate is not possible or likely.

In the next chapter, we won't run into this potential problem because, if you buy a house, there are usually no positive cash flows until the house is eventually sold. The issue only arises when there are positive after-tax cash flows *before* the final year of the investment.

Figure 2
Investment analysis form to determine the net present value of an investment in a home

	Time of Acquisition	*Year 1*	*Year 2*	*Year 3*	*Year 4*	*Year 5*
Gross revenue before expense						
Operating expenses before interest and depreciation						
Property taxes						
Heating						
Utilities						
Maintenance						
Insurance						
Painting						
Other						
Total operating expenses						
Net profit (loss) before interest and depreciation						
Interest on debt						
Depreciation						
Total interest and depreciation						
Taxable income (loss)						

Estimated income taxes						
Net after-tax income (loss)						
Add: Depreciation						
Rent savings due to ownership						
Less: Capital outlays						
Cost of investment						
Expenses of acquisition						
Add: Sales proceeds net of expenses of sale						
Less: Debt repayment –principal						
Tax on gain						
After-tax cash flow						
Required rate of return						
Present value factor (Table 3)						
Net present value						

In Chapter Twelve, we'll look at investments in land and rental property. While no depreciation may be claimed with respect to land, depreciation may be taken on most rental property, although there are restrictions against creating losses for tax purposes. However, because depreciation is tax-deductible and can shelter cash flow, it's a major factor in the financial success of many real estate investments.

Also, don't over-estimate the validity of your conclusions just because you've used a rather sophisticated procedure to evaluate a potential investment. Similarly, don't assume you can compute your answers using tables to seven, eight, or even ten decimal places and achieve a great degree of precision and accuracy. The final result of any analytical technique is only as good as the data you put in. Remember that most of your input is estimates. In every real estate example, operating expenses and final sales proceeds are only estimates. *If a property actually appreciates by half of what you project, the entire analysis could show quite different results*

On the other hand, I don't mean to imply it's a waste of time to make such an analysis. This is because this process forces you to look at certain details of an investment you might otherwise pass over. A more cautious approach would be to prepare *three* analyses using the same data, estimating the appreciation of an investment at low, medium and high ranges with resulting differences in the ultimate sales price. Your results would then provide a reasonable mid-range estimate along with a forecast of the investment's maximum up-side and down-side potential.

The Internal Rate of Return

What if an investment yields either a positive or negative net present value at your selected rate of return? Can the actual return be calculated with any degree of precision? Of course, such a computation is possible and, again, you will find Table 3 useful.

By definition, the internal rate of return on an investment is the required rate of return or discount rate that results in a net present value of exactly zero. You can find the internal rate of return by using the present value factors from Table 3 and through trial and error.

For example, assume at a 10% desired rate of return, the net present value of an investment is +$5000. If you use a higher rate of return, the net present value will be reduced and it will eventually become zero. Try applying a 14% discount rate to your cash flows and recalculate your net present value. Perhaps it's now –$1750. From this, you can conclude your internal rate of return is between 10% and 14%. Repeat the procedure using a 13% discount rate and your final result might now be +$123. For most purposes, this is close enough and you can conclude your internal rate of return is "just over 13%." Once you become familiar with this approach, you'll be able to zero in on accurate numbers without too much difficulty.

Where Do I Go From Here?

Discounted cash-flow techniques can provide an essential tool for investment analysis. I hope this chapter has convinced you of their usefulness by introducing the basic mechanics involved in filling out a sample form. (Feel free to use it as your own worksheet.)

The following chapters will illustrate the application of these techniques. Chapter Eleven deals with home ownership. Even if you don't want to buy a home or aren't interested in analyzing the home you presently own, I recommend you read this chapter carefully. This is for two reasons. First, the examples are easy to relate to and don't require any in-depth knowledge of tax concepts. Second, once you understand these examples, you can go on to apply discounted cash-flow to other investments which may be more suitable to your preferences, such as real estate (other than a home), the stock market, gold or certain life insurance policies.

ELEVEN

How to Evaluate an Investment in a Home or Vacation Property

Possibly the most important investment any of us can make is to buy our own home. Historically, inflation has created a tremendous increase in residential values in many parts of the country. Of course, events of the last decade have shown us the real estate market is cyclical and if you can acquire property in a downturn phase, you can certainly get a better deal than during a boom period.

The reason home ownership is so important is because all of us need a place to live. From a Canadian perspective, mortgage interest on your own home is not deductible—but, then again, neither are rental costs. When faced with a choice between non-deductible mortgage payments and non-deductible rent, you're still better off in the long run, at least in theory, as an owner so *you* can gain from the appreciation.

In this chapter, we'll examine how to use the tables and techniques introduced in previous chapters to assess home ownership as an investment. Of course, there are many subjective factors such as the size of your family and your lifestyle. However, it is only after you've made a comprehensive analysis that you can really answer the question intelligently: Should I own or rent?

Then, after going through a typical example of a home purchase, we'll examine the subject of a second home or vacation cottage since there can be one major difference between a principal residence and a second home. The capital gain on the eventual sale of a primary residence is tax-free; capital growth (after 1981) on a second home may be subject to capital gains tax at the time of sale. This tax can reduce your investment potential significantly.

Buying a Home

Let's assume you've always lived in a rented apartment. You're now considering buying your first home and, based on your current income level, you feel you can afford to buy a house for $90,000. You have $22,000 in savings and you can get a $68,000 mortgage at a variable interest rate you think might average as much as 13% over the next five years. At the end of five years, your goal is to sell the house and perhaps move into something a bit more luxurious. You figure property values will probably appreciate 10% a year, although your selling costs will be about 3% of the final sales price.

You've estimated the operating expenses on this property in the first year as described in Figure 1, and you've projected reasonable annual increases as well.

Figure 1
Projected operating expenses of a proposed investment in a home

	Year of Acquisition	*Estimated Annual Increase*
Property taxes	$1,600	10%
Heating	1,200	12%
Utilities	1,200	12%
Maintenance	600	5%
Insurance	400	7%
Painting		$1,500 in Year 4

Rent Savings Due to Ownership

If you buy and occupy this house, you'll no longer be paying rent. Your annual rent is $7800 and you figure it would rise, on average, 8% a year. The concept of rent savings due to ownership is one of the most important and yet most often overlooked factors when deciding about a home as an investment. *Many home buyers fail to consider that the rent savings is a real, positive cash flow.* This is why a separate line for this item has been provided for in the analysis sheets.

Making Your Analysis

Your first step is to prepare a mortgage amortization schedule to determine the total principal and interest year-by-year. You can do this quite easily using Tables 6 and 7. As mentioned in Chapter Seven, most mortgage payments are calculated over a twenty-five-year period. Assuming a 13% rate, the monthly payment required for a $68,000 mortgage at 13% is $749.63 (68 x 11.024). Of course, if you can arrange to obtain financing with a twenty-year amortization you could pay back your debt that much more quickly. However, the monthly payments then become 68 x 11.475 or $780.30. Unfortunately, since your previous rent was $650 a month, a twenty-five-year amortization already means an outlay of an additional $100 each month. You therefore decide to stick with a twenty-five-year period. Using Table 7, we can prepare the amortization schedule shown in Figure 2.

Now we are almost ready to prepare a complete investment analysis form. At the time of acquisition the outlays are $22,000, representing the initial cash downpayment, plus the expenses of acquisition (including moving), which we will estimate to be $1000 in total. Since this is an immediate outlay, no matter what we assume for a required rate of return on investment, the present value is always 1.000. This is because the initial outlay is made in today's dollars.

Figure 2
Mortgage amortization schedule: $68,000 at 13% (first five years)

25 year amortization 68 x 11.024 = $ 749.63 /Month
= $8,995.56/Year

End of Year	*Outstanding Principal Balance*	*Annual Payment*	*Principal*	*Interest*
0	$68,000	$8,996		
1	.994 x $68,000 =$67,592	$8,996	$408	$8,588
2	.987 x 68,000 = 67,116	8,996	476	8,520
3	.979 x 68,000 = 66,572	8,996	544	8,452
4	.971 x 68,000 = 66,028	8,996	544	8,452
5	.961 x 68,000 = 65,348	8,996	680	8,316

What About the Required Rate of Return?

Normally, as I explained in the last chapter, you might require a 15% to 16% after-tax return on any investment that involves even a modest risk factor. On the other hand, when we consider a house and take into account the fact that you need shelter for yourself and your family in any event, it might be appropriate to use a 10% required rate of return. Again, what you do is up to you, although the investment analysis form has been completed on the basis of an annual return of 10%. The present value factors are taken from Table 3.

The only other table computation you need to make refers back to the anticipated appreciation. You'll recall that this hypothetical investment is assumed to appreciate by 10% over each of the next five years. So, the 10% will be compounded annually. Selling costs are then projected to be 3% of the final sales price. The selling price at the end of year five is calculated from Table 1. The future value of $90,000 at 10% interest compounded annually after five years is $90,000 x 1.611, or $144,990. If expenses to sell are 3%, the net anticipated selling price is therefore 97% of $144,990, or $140,640. Out of those funds, the debt owing at the end of five years ($65,348) must be repaid.

Since this investment involves a principal residence, we don't have to concern ourselves with tax calculations. Take a few moments and review the investment analysis form in Figure 3 on pages 60 and 61. You'll notice that the operating cost figures in Year 1 come from the assumptions which were made in Figure 1. The operating expenses are then estimated to increase annually as illustrated, while the rent savings is computed at $7800 in the first year, increasing by 8% a year. Interest on debt is calculated using the schedule in Figure 2. No depreciation is permitted since this is a principal residence and because the investment is not a rental property, there is no gross revenue.

The conclusion we can draw is that the owner of this property investment *would* get an after-tax rate of return slightly in excess of 10%, as well as providing shelter for the entire family.

Interpretation of the Net Present Value

What does the $27 net present value figure on the investment analysis form signify? Since the figure is positive, it means the present value of the after-tax cash inflows (of which there is only one in the example) exceeds the present value of the after-tax outflows (of which there are five) by $27. This means the initial outlay of $23,000 could have been $27 higher and the investment would still have yielded the required 10% after-tax rate of return. Remember the financial decision rule described in Chapter Ten—any investment with a positive net present value is acceptable while investments with (large) negative net present values should be rejected. Another way to look at this situation is that your $23,000 investment would be earning the required 10% rate of return plus an extra $27. If it earned exactly the required rate of return, the net present value would be zero. If the rate of return were less than you desired, the net present value would be negative.

The Internal Rate of Return

But what is the actual rate of return? All you know to this point is that it is more than 10%. To find the approximate rate of return on your $23,000 investment, you should calculate the internal rate of return. We'll continue the example with which we've been working.

As I explained in Chapter Ten, *the internal rate of return is the required rate of return or discount rate that results in a net present value of exactly zero.* You can find the internal rate of return by using the present value factors in Table 3 and through trial and error. You know when 10% is used, the net present value comes out to +$27. If you use a higher rate of return, the net present value will be reduced and, eventually, the net present value will become zero. Again, the required rate that produces a net present value of exactly zero is the internal rate of return. Let's assume instead of a 10% discount rate, we use a rate of, say, 11%. Figure 4 shows the computation of net present value using 11% as the discount rate.

Figure 4
Calculating the internal rate of return on an investment in a home

Year	*Present Value Factor at 11%*	*Present Value of Cash Flow*	*Cash Flow*
0	1.000	($23,000)	($23,000)
1	.901	(6,196)	(5,582)
2	.812	(6,078)	(4,935)
3	.731	(5,964)	(4,360)
4	.659	(7,356)	(4,848)
5	.594	69,536	41,304
			($1,421)

In this case, at 11%, the net present value is already negative. Therefore the internal rate of return really is almost exactly 10%! Again, you shouldn't be concerned about being more than one or two percentage points away from the true internal rate of return, because your initial assumptions are

Figure 3
Investment analysis form to determine the net present value of an investment in a home

	Time of Acquisition	*Year 1*	*Year 2*	*Year 3*	*Year 4*	*Year 5*
Gross revenue before expenses		-	-	-	-	-
Operating expenses before interest and depreciation						
Property taxes		(1,600)	(1,760)	(1,936)	(2,130)	(2,343)
Heating		(1,200)	(1,344)	(1.505)	(1,685)	(1,887)
Utilities		(1,200)	(1,344)	(1.505)	(1,685)	(1,887)
Maintenance		(600)	(630)	(662)	(695)	(730)
Insurance		(400)	(428)	(458)	(490)	(524)
Painting		-	-	-	(1,500)	-
Other		-	-	-	-	-
Total operating expenses		(5,000)	(5,506)	(6,066)	(8,185)	(7,371)
Net profit (loss) before interest and depreciation		(5,000)	(5,506)	(6,066)	(8,185)	(7,371)
Interest on debt		(8,588)	(8,520)	(8,452)	(8,452)	(8,316)
Depreciation		-	-	-	-	-
Total interest and depreciation		(8,588)	(8,520)	(8,452)	(8,452)	(8,316)
Taxable income (loss)		(13,588)	(14,026)	(14,518)	(16,637)	(15,687)

Estimated income taxes		-	-	-	-	-
Net after-tax income (loss)		(13,588)	(14,026)	(14,518)	(16,637)	(15,687)
Add: Depreciation		-	-	-	-	-
Rent savings due to ownership		7,800	8,424	9,098	9,825	10,611
Less: Capital outlays						
Cost of investment	(22,000)	-	-	-	-	-
Expenses of acquisition	(1,000)					
Add: Sales proceeds net of expenses of sale						140,640
Less: Debt repayment –principal		(408)	(476)	(544)	(544)	(680)
						(65,348)
Tax on gain		-	-	-	-	-
After-tax cash flow	(23,000)	(6,196)	(6,078)	(5,964)	(7,356)	69,536
Required rate of return	10%					
Present value factor (Table 3)	1.000	.909	.826	.751	.683	.621
Net present value	(23,000)	(5,632)	(5,020)	(4,479)	(5,024)	43,182

Net present value $27

likely to contain several errors. In other words, if your required rate of return on a particular investment is 15% and the internal rate of return comes out at 14%, this doesn't necessarily mean the investment should be rejected.

The 10% internal rate of return computed in the example which we've just looked at is an after-tax rate. Remember, to keep 10% after paying taxes on ordinary income, you would need to earn approximately 18%-21% *before* taxes. To earn 10% on an investment where capital gains tax applies, your investment would have to pay you at least a 15% return before tax. So, to get an idea of relative performance, compare the after-tax return on an investment in your home to other alternatives such as savings accounts, stock market investments, other real estate projects, or investments in gold and silver.

Summary of Home Evaluation

Any potential investment in a home can be analyzed by using the approach shown in this chapter. *Remember, if you buy a home, you will save the rent you are otherwise going to pay.*

In the example, I assumed the buyer has $23,000 to invest and I calculated an after-tax rate of return of 10%. What if the rate of return were, say, only 2%? Under those circumstances, our conclusions might be that the family is better off renting and investing its savings elsewhere.

Even if you already own your home, you can still make similar calculations to see whether you're getting a reasonable return on investment. Just substitute your present net equity in your home for the $23,000 original investment in the example. To determine your net equity take today's selling price and deduct your costs to sell plus all amounts owing against the property.

Go on, try it ...

A Summer Cottage

In the second part of this chapter, we'll examine a possible investment in a summer cottage. You'll see we can prepare the same kind of analysis as we did for a principal residence, subject to two changes. First, there will be no rent savings due to ownership as there was with a principal residence. On the other hand, *you may use the line on the investment analysis form for rent savings to record the vacation savings that your family would realize as a result of vacation property ownership.* In this respect, therefore, there is a similarity between your home and a vacation property.

The major difference, however, is with respect to capital gains. In the example of a home purchase, we assumed the property could be sold for $140,640 tax-free. By way of contrast, a profit on the sale of a second residence may be taxed as a capital gain. In the illustration which follows, we'll assume no capital gains tax exemption would apply and the effective tax cost will be 33% of the gain. This is the most conservative approach. If there is no tax, your net return will obviously be higher.

Financial Analysis of a Second Residence

Assume you'd like to buy a country house. You've found a nice property which will cost $60,000. Because it's somewhat harder to borrow against country property than it is to borrow against a city house, you'd need a $25,000 downpayment and there would be about $1000 in closing costs. The $35,000 balance could be bank-financed over a five-year term at 14%. Since this is a regular bank loan instead of a mortgage loan, the interest will be compounded monthly. You estimate expenses on the property will be as shown in Figure 5.

Figure 5
Projected operating expenses of a proposed investment in a vacation property

	Year of Acquisition	*Estimated Annual Increase*
Property taxes	$600	10%
Heating	800	12%
Utilities	500	12%
Maintenance	300	7%
Insurance	200	10%

By using the country house, you estimate you'll save approximately $4000 a year in vacation costs in today's dollars. You think these costs would go up by 10% a year. However, you realize you must immediately lay out approximately $5000 for furnishings which, for all practical purposes, will be worthless after a five-year period.

You don't really expect to sell the house in the near future, although you do expect the value of the property to increase about 10% a year. If you were to sell, you are confident you could do so privately and avoid incurring any substantial selling costs.

What you are really interested in doing is assessing the merits of this country house as an investment over the next five years, because you recognize that your initial downpayment plus furnishings and closing costs represent an investment of $31,000. You'd be satisfied with a 10% after-tax rate of return on your investment capital since a vacation home does not appear to be a very risky investment.

Before you can prepare an investment analysis form similar to the one in Figure 8, you must first prepare a loan amortization schedule. In this case, we turn to Table 5, which gives us the monthly payments required to pay off a five-year loan at 14% with interest calculated monthly. As illustrated in Figure 6, the payments are $35,000 x .0233, or $815.50 a month. Over the five-year period, your total payments will be 60 x $815.50, or $48,930. Note for this problem, we would not use the regular mortgage amortization schedules, which call for monthly payments with interest compounded semi-annually.

Allocation Between Principal and Interest

Clearly, if your total payments over five years are $48,930 and your principal amortization is $35,000, the difference of $13,930 represents interest. If we were working with a problem involving a revenue property, it would be important to have separate figures for principal and interest in order to determine taxable income and taxes payable. In this case, however, we needn't bother. This is because *none* of the expenses are tax-deductible — in spite of the fact that the capital gain at the time of sale may be subject to income tax! Remember, we are concerned with cash flow and, in this case, the cash outflow against the loan is $9786 a year for five years. As you'll see, the investment analysis form for a vacation property treats interest and principal together.

In order to assess the value of the property five years down the road, we turn to Table 1, which gives us the future value of an investment made today. Page 130 contains the factors for a compound interest rate of 10%. If our projections are correct, a vacation property worth $60,000 today would be worth $60,000 x 1.611, or $96,660 in five years. The capital gains tax (assuming no exemption) is computed in Figure 7.

Figure 6
Loan amortization schedule: $35,000 at 14% compounded monthly over five years

Payments: From Table 5
$35,000 x .0233 = $815.50
Total Payments: 60 x $815.50 = $48,930
Payment Each Year: 1/5 x $48,930 = $ 9,786

$48,930	Total Payments
35,000	Principal
$13,930	Interest

Figure 7
Computation of capital gain and taxes payable on the sale of a vacation property ignoring possible exemption.

Value of second home after five years
Assuming a 10% annual growth in value
$60,000 x 1.611 = $96,660

Anticipated selling price		$96,660
Cost of property: Original cost	$60,000	
Expenses of acquisition	1,000	
Furnishings	5,000	66,000
Capital gain		$30,660
Taxable capital gain (3/4) ignoring any exemption		$22,995
Income tax at an assumed tax rate of 45%		$10,348

Now, examine the completed investment analysis form in Figure 8 on pages 66 and 67. In this case, the investment fails to provide a 10% rate of return. *The rate would be almost 10% if there were no tax on the capital gain.*

Let's try to determine what the rate of return really is. The calculations in Figure 9 use present value factors at 5% from Table 3. In this case, assuming a 5% net after-tax return on investment were acceptable, this investment would be more than adequate. Therefore, the real rate of return is somewhere *between* 5% and 10%.

Figure 9
Calculating the internal rate of return on an investment in vacation property

Year	Present Value Factor at 5%	Cash Flow	Present Value of Cash Flow
0	1.000	($31,000)	($31,000)
1	.952	(8,186)	(7,793)
2	.907	(8,043)	(7,295)
3	.864	(7,887)	(6,814)
4	.823	(7,719)	(6,352)
5	.784	79,003	61,938
			$ 2,684

Finally, let's make calculations assuming a 7% return is acceptable. As we can see from Figure 10, in this case, the internal rate of return is less than 7%. Try using 6% on your own!

Figure 10
Calculating the internal rate of return on an investment in vacation property

Year	Present Value Factor at 7%	Cash Flow	Present Value of Cash Flow
0	1.000	($31,000)	($31,000)
1	.935	(8,186)	(7,654)
2	.873	(8,043)	(7,021)
3	.816	(7,887)	(6,436)
4	.763	(7,719)	(5,889)
5	.713	79,003	56,329
			($ 1,671)

Summary—Is a Country House Really a Good Investment?

Can we come to any general conclusions from this example? Again, note that your final results are strictly a function of the input provided in the first place. If your annual vacation cost is well in excess of $4000 (the assumption made in this investment), clearly the opportunity to save more dollars would increase your rate of return.

On the other hand, what if the property does not appreciate by 10% a year? In this instance, it appears that carrying the property over the first four years is really quite expensive, since the net outflows are about $8000 a year. Remember, however, that over the first four-year period, approximately $28,000 out of $35,000 of debt principal is being discharged. *In other words, even before considering capital growth, the investor's equity in the property is increasing.*

Figure 8
Investment analysis form to determine the net present value of an investment in a vacation property

	Time of Acquisition	*Year 1*	*Year 2*	*Year 3*	*Year 4*	*Year 5*
Gross revenue before expenses		-	-	-	-	-
Operating expenses before interest and depreciation						
Property taxes		(600)	(660)	(726)	(799)	(878)
Heating		(800)	(896)	(1,003)	(1,123)	(1,258)
Utilities		(500)	(560)	(627)	(702)	(787)
Maintenance		(300)	(321)	(343)	(367)	(393)
Insurance		(200)	(220)	(242)	(266)	(293)
Other						
Total operating expenses		(2,400)	(2,657)	(2,941)	(3,257)	(3,609)
Net profit (loss) before interest and depreciation		(2,400)	(2,657)	(2,941)	(3,257)	(3,609)
Interest and principal on debt		(9,786)	(9,786)	(9,786)	(9,786)	(9,786)
Depreciation		-	-	-	-	-
Total interest and depreciation		(9,786)	(9,786)	(9,786)	(9,786)	(9,786)
Income (loss)		(12,186)	(12,443)	(12,727)	(13,043)	(13,395)

Estimated income taxes		-	-	-	-	-
Net income (loss)		(12,186)	(12,443)	(12,727)	(13,043)	(13,395)
Add: Depreciation		-	-	-	-	-
Vacation cost savings due to ownership		4,000	4,400	4,840	5,324	6,086
Less: Capital outlays						
Cost of investment	(25,000)					
Expenses of acquisition	(1,000)					
Furnishings	(5,000)					
Add: Sales proceeds net of expenses of sale						96,660
Less: Debt repayment				Included above		Already repaid
Tax on gain						(10,348)
After-tax cash flow	(31,000)	(8,186)	(8,043)	(7,887)	(7,719)	79,003
Required rate of return	10%					
Present value factor (Table 3)	1.000	.909	.826	.751	.683	.621
Net present value $(7,218)	(31,000)	(7,441)	(6,643)	(5,923)	(5,272)	49,061

My major point is this example is only hypothetical. However, try to apply the concepts to your own circumstances. If you own a house or a vacation property or are planning to buy either one, you won't be sorry you took the time to make this kind of analysis.

TWELVE

Real Estate Investment for Fun and Profit

Just as basic mathematical techniques can help evaluate the purchase of real estate for personal use, so can they be used in the assessment of investment properties acquired primarily for future growth. There are really only a few differences, primarily with respect to tax-related matters. If you concentrate on a few basic rules which will be highlighted in this chapter, you shouldn't get confused. If, from time to time, you have some tax questions, a few minutes spent with your own advisers can give you the answers you need to complete your analysis. So let's get started.

Investing in Raw Land

Suppose you've found a nice parcel of farm land priced at $100,000. The vendor will take back a $60,000 mortgage against the property with interest at 14% compounded annually for five years. He does, however, require that you make annual principal payments of $2000 at the end of each year. The only expenses you'd have to consider besides interest are property and school taxes, which are presently $500 a year but are anticipated to increase by 10% annually. There is a farmer who lives three miles away who is prepared to pay you $300 a year for the right to cut hay on the property. Because this amount is so small, you don't think it's worthwhile to negotiate an annual escalation clause.

The big attraction is you expect to be able to sell the land for $200,000 after a five-year holding period because the neighbouring municipality is expanding rapidly. Of course, you would have a sizable commitment of funds—$40,000 down and the obligation to pay $2000 a year in principal payments, plus rather expensive interest on your financing. Also, an investment in raw land is a little tricky. What if the municipality starts to expand in the other direction? Because of the risk factor, you decide if the investment doesn't have the potential to yield a net 18% return, you're going to pass. After all, if this opportunity isn't good enough, there are always others. You remember to budget for a 33% tax on capital gains since you are in a 45% tax bracket.

So, How Do You Proceed?

The first step is to phone your tax adviser and confirm the current tax implications of such an investment. You learn that, in Canada, rental losses on raw or vacant land are generally not tax-deductible. However, to the extent they arise as a result of mortgage interest and property taxes, they are added to the cost of the land and therefore decrease the capital gain for tax purposes in the year of sale. In other words, for the first four years in which you hold this investment, there will be neither any tax benefits nor any costs.

Your next step is to prepare a mortgage amortization schedule so you can calculate cash flows. In this case, none of the tables in this book will help you because the financial arrangement calls for interest at 14% compounded annually, subject to annual principal payments of $2000 a year. There really is no shortcut to a longhand computation unless you have access to a computer. Fortunately, however, the calculations are not difficult, as illustrated by Figure 1.

Figure 1
Amortization of a $60,000 loan at 14% compounded annually with $2000 principal payments at the end of each year

Year	*Principal Owing Beginning of Year*	*Interest at 14%*	*Principal Payment*	*Principal Owing End of Year*
1	$60,000	$8,400	$2,000	$58,000
2	58,000	8,120	2,000	56,000
5	56,000	7,840	2,000	54,000
4	54,000	7,560	2,000	52,000
5	52,000	7,280	52,000	0

In this case, we'll assume that the entire balance owing is paid off at the end of five years, at the same time that the property is sold.

Now we're ready to start preparing the investment analysis form, Figure 2 on pages 72-73. Because losses arising from undeveloped land are added to the tax cost of the land itself, we can't calculate the anticipated capital gain and related income taxes until we are part way through the analysis. We can, however, prepare the figures for the first four years and then complete the capital gains schedule just below (Figure 3) after.

Figure 3
Calculation of capital gains tax on sale of land (ignoring the lifetime capital gains exemption)

Anticipated sales price			$200,000
Original cost		$100,000	
Property taxes and interest in excess of rental revenue	$8,600		
	8,370		
	8,145		
	7,925		
	7,712	40,752	140,752
Capital gain			$ 59,248
Taxable capital gain (3/4)			$ 44,436
Tax payable by investor in a 45% tax bracket			$ 19,996

If you examine the investment analysis form in Figure 2, you'll see that this particular investment won't come close to providing an 18% annual return based on the assumptions made. As illustrated in Figure 4, the actual internal rate of return is even less than 12%. This example illustrates one of the fundamental concepts in this book—*a dollar due sometime in the future isn't worth anything close to a dollar today.* On the surface, a property which doubles in value over five years appears to be an attractive investment, and yet when you take into account carrying costs, the return can be considerably below your expectations.

(Of course, this deal involved raw land only, on which the gross revenue was projected to be negligible. In the next example, we'll take a look at a rental property where most of the carrying costs are defrayed by rental income. You'll see how this changes the picture.)

Figure 4
Calculating the internal rate of return on an investment in raw land

Year	*Present Value Factor at 12% (From Table 3)*	*Cash Flow*	*Present Value of Cash Flow*
0	1.000	($40,000)	($40,000)
1	.893	(10,600)	(9,466)
2	.797	(10,370)	(8,265)
3	.712	(10,145)	(7,223)
4	.636	(9,925)	(6,312)
5	.567	120,292	68,206
			($ 3,060)

Before leaving this particular land investment, we might ask ourselves what the selling price would have to be at the end of five years to achieve our desired 18% rate of return. If we use a little common sense, we can figure this out. As it stands, the investment is short by $15,156 in providing the required rate of return. Since all the positive cash flow is deferred until year five, what is needed is a selling price sufficient to provide enough cash so that the present value is an additional $15,156.

The additional cash flow required would be $15,156 ÷ .437, or $34,682. In other words, if the after-tax cash flow in year five were $34,682 higher than the anticipated after-tax cash flow of $120,292, the present value of this extra $34,682 would be .437 x $34,682, or $15,156. This would make the net present value zero and would therefore result in an internal rate of return of 18%.

However, given an income tax rate of 33% on the gross capital gain, the $34,682 additional after-tax cash flow would have to represent *two-thirds* of the *additional selling price*. If the total selling price were $252,023 instead of $200,000, the capital gain would be $52,023 higher. Of that amount, the investor would retain 67%, or $34,682 and, again, the present value of this would be $15,156.

In round numbers, therefore, the property would have to command a selling price of $250,000 to provide the required 18% rate of return on investment over the five-year holding period.

Figure 2
Investment analysis form to determine the net present value of an investment in raw land

	Time of Acquisition	*Year 1*	*Year 2*	*Year 3*	*Year 4*	*Year 5*
Gross revenue before expenses		300	300	300	300	300
Operating expenses before interest and depreciation						
Property taxes		(500)	(550)	(605)	(665)	(732)
Heating						
Utilities						
Maintenance						
Insurance						
Other						
Total operating expenses		(500)	(550)	(605)	(665)	(732)
Net profit (loss) before interest and depreciation		(200)	(250)	(305)	(365)	(432)
Interest on debt		(8,400)	(8,120)	(7,840)	(7,560)	(7,280)
Depreciation		-	-	-	-	-
Total interest and depreciation		(8,400)	(8,120)	(7,840)	(7,560)	(7,280)

Taxable income (loss)		(8,600)	(8,370)	(8,145)	(7,925)	(7,712)
Estimated income taxes		-	-	-	-	-
Net after-tax income (loss)		(8,600)	(8,370)	(8,145)	(7,925)	(7,712)
Add: Depreciation		-	-	-	-	-
Less: Capital outlays						
Cost of investment	(40,000)	-	-	-	-	-
Expenses of acquisition						
Add: Sales proceeds net of expenses of sale						200,000
Less: Debt repayment		(2,000)	(2,000)	(2,000)	(2,000)	(52,000)
Tax on gain		-	-	-	-	(19,996)
After-tax cash flow	(40,000)	(10,600)	(10,370)	(10,145)	(9,925)	120,292
Required rate of return	18%					
Present value factor (Table 3)	1.000	.847	.718	.609	.516	.437
Net present value $(15,156)	(40,000)	(8,978)	(7,446)	(6,178)	(5,121)	52,567

A Condominium Investment

Our next real estate example shows an analysis of a condominium investment acquired for rental income and capital growth potential. Here, you'll see how income tax considerations—beyond just capital gains—interact with the other financial aspects that we looked at before.

Specifically, rental losses may be deducted from income which is otherwise taxable and the tax refund then provides a positive cash flow. Of course, if a property yields a positive rental income after all expenses, taxes payable during the ownership period reduce your cash flow.

In all cases, taxable income may be affected by depreciation (a percentage write-off which is also known as capital cost allowance). Depreciation may be used to reduce taxable income from a rental property down to zero as long as you don't exceed the maximum allowable percentage for that type of property. However, in general, *capital cost allowance can't be used to create or increase a rental loss.*

In working out an example such as this one, tax depreciation must be calculated year-by-year. Since depreciation reduces the net income for tax purposes, but not the actual cash flow, the tax write-off is added back in the lower part of the investment analysis form. Now, let's look at a specific example.

Assume your neighbour is a real estate broker and he tells you about a "super" condominium investment that has come on the market. The present owner has just died and the estate is very eager to sell in order to gain some liquidity.

The condominium has a purchase price of $95,000. Of this amount, $5000 can reasonably be allocated to land, $85,000 to the building itself, and $5000 for furniture and fixtures (stove, dishwasher, refrigerator, etc.). The agent tells you the estate will provide a $70,000 mortgage at 14% with a twenty-five-year amortization. "At the rate real estate values are going," he says, "you should be able to sell the condominium for $135,000 after five years. It doesn't matter that the interest rate is a couple of points higher than it should be." He presents you with the analysis of projected incomes and expenses shown here as Figure 5.

Figure 5
Condominium investment—projected income and expenses

	First Year	*Annual % Increase*
Rental income	$12,600	8%
Property taxes	1,200	12%
Maintenance	900	10%
Insurance	400	10%
Utilities	Paid by Tenant	–

Your accountant tells you that tax depreciation (capital cost allowance) may be claimed at 2% of the cost of a building in the year of acquisition and at 4% of the undepreciated cost (cost minus accumulated depreciation, or the declining balance) every year thereafter. You're also told that the depreciation on the furniture and fixtures is 10% in the year of acquisition and 20% (declining balance) in subsequent years. However, he cautions you to be aware that capital cost allowance may not be used to create or increase a rental loss. Assume you are in a 45% tax bracket because of your other income.

As you can see, this property would require a commitment of $25,000 of your own funds if you don't wish to obtain a second mortgage. You find the idea of owning real estate intriguing, but only if you can earn a 15% rate of return on your investment capital over the five-year projected term of this investment.

Before you can complete an analysis form similar to the one in Figure 9 on pages 76 and 77, you will first have to prepare a mortgage amortization schedule using Tables 6 and 7 and a schedule of projected capital cost allowances. The capital cost allowances should be calculated *year-by-year*, keeping in mind the prohibition against creating rental losses. See Figures 6 and 7 for these schedules.

You won't be able to finalize your figures for year five until you calculate the tax on your projected capital gain (see Figure 8). In this case, there is not only a capital gain on sale but "recaptured depreciation" as well. Recaptured depreciation comes about in the year of sale if capital cost allowance has been claimed but the property has *not* really depreciated. In this case, since the selling price is well in excess of the original cost, we can assume that all the depreciation will be recaptured. But keep in mind that the difference between the selling price of $135,000 and the original cost of $95,000 will be taxed as a capital gain, at only three-quarters of your normal rate.

Figure 6
Condominium investment mortgage amortization schedule
$70,000 mortgage @ 14% — twenty-five-year amortization

Monthly Payments: From Table 7

$$\frac{\$70{,}000}{1{,}000} \times 11.739 = \$821.73$$

Annual Payments: 12 x $821.73 = $9,860.76

Year	Opening Balance	Principal Payments	Interest Payments	Balance End of Year From Table
1	$70,000	$350	$9,511	.995 x $70,000 = $69,650
2	69,650	420	9,441	.989 x 70,000 = 69,230
3	69,230	490	9,371	.982 x 70,000 = 68,740
4	68,740	490	9,371	.975 x 70,000 = 68,250
5	68,250	630	9,231	.966 x 70,000 = 67,620

Why Claim Depreciation?

Why bother claiming depreciation on a property if there will be a recapture in the year of sale? The answer, of course, ties into the fact that a dollar today is worth more than a dollar in the future. *In other words, the tax savings from depreciation in years one through four are worth more than the offsetting*

Figure 9
Investment analysis form to determine the net present value of an investment in a condominium

	Time of Acquisition	*Year 1*	*Year 2*	*Year 3*	*Year 4*	*Year 5*
Gross revenue before expenses		12,600	13,608	14,697	15,872	17,142
Operating expenses before interest and depreciation						
Property taxes		(1,200)	(1,344)	(1,505)	(1,686)	(1,888)
Heating		-	-	-	-	-
Utilities		-	-	-	-	-
Maintenance		(900)	(990)	(1,089)	(1,198)	(1,318)
Insurance		(400)	(440)	(484)	(532)	(586)
Other		-	-	-	-	-
Total operating expenses		(2,500)	(2,774)	(3,078)	(3,416)	(3,792)
Net profit (loss) before interest and depreciation		10,100	10,834	11,619	12,456	13,350
Interest on debt		(9,511)	(9,441)	(9,371)	(9,371)	(9,231)
Depreciation		(589)	(1,393)	(2,248)	(3,085)	-
Total interest and depreciation		(10,100)	(10,834)	(11,619)	(12,456)	(9,231)
Taxable income (loss)		-	-	-	-	4,119

Estimated income taxes		-	-	-	-	(1,854)
Net after-tax income (loss)		-	-	-	-	2,265
Add: Depreciation		589	1,393	2,248	3,085	-
Less: Capital outlays						
Cost of investment	(25,000)	-	-	-	-	-
Expenses of acquisition						
Add: Sales proceeds net of expenses of sale						135,000
Less: Debt repayment						(67,620)
		(350)	(420)	(490)	(490)	(630)
Tax on gain and recapture						(16,792)
After-tax cash flow	(25,000)	239	973	1,758	2,595	52,223
Required rate of return	15%					
Present value factor (Table 3)	1.000	.870	.756	.658	.572	.497
Net present value	(25,000)	208	735	1,156	1,484	25,955
$4,538						

tax on recapture in year five. This is, of course, provided your tax bracket doesn't start out low and then increase substantially in the year of sale. In this case, we have assumed you would be in a 45% bracket throughout the period.

If you examine the depreciation schedule in this case study (Figure 7) carefully, you'll see that the net rental income after operating expenses (including interest) is never large enough to permit a full capital cost allowance claim. Again, this is because of the general rule that depreciation can't be used to create a rental loss.

The results of the investment analysis form in Figure 9 indicate clearly that the projected return on investment is well in excess of the required rate of 15%. In fact, the internal rate of return is really well over 18%. Of course, bear in mind that all the calculations are based on projections only.

Figure 7
Condominium investment capital cost allowance schedule

	Building	*Furniture & Fixtures*
Capital Cost Allowance (CCA)		
–first year	2%	10%
–thereafter	4%	20%
Cost	$85,000	$5,000
Year 1 (maximum)	589	–
	84,411	5,000
Year 2 (maximum)	1,393	–
	83,018	5,000
Year 3 (maximum)	2,248	–
	80,770	5,000
Year 4 (maximum)	3,085	–
	$77,685	$5,000

Notes:

1. No capital cost allowance is claimed on the furniture and fixtures because the capital cost allowance on the building is enough to reduce the net rental income to zero in years one through four.
2. No capital cost allowance is claimed in year five because it's anticipated that a sale will take place at the end of that year. Any depreciation taken would automatically be recaptured in any event.

Figure 8
Condominium investment calculation of taxes on projected gain

		Tax Payable
Anticipated selling price	$135,000	
Cost	95,000	
Capital gain	$ 40,000	
Taxable capital gain (3/4)	$ 30,000	
Tax at 45% assumed tax rate		$13,500
Recaptured depreciation: $85,000–$77,685	$ 7,315	
Tax at 45% assumed tax rate		3,292
Total Tax		$16,792

Summary

Financial analysis procedures are essential if you want to make a proper evaluation of the desirability of any particular investment opportunity. Most mistakes are made by investors who make commitments without sufficient careful thought and planning.

An investment analysis also represents a *plan* for the future—a sort of road map to get you to your destination of making profits. It can tell you whether the destination is worth reaching (if the net present value is greater than zero at your selected required after-tax rate of return). If you decide an investment looks good and you proceed with the project, the year-by-year figures in the analysis will serve as a guide to let you know whether your plan is being realized as scheduled. If you find you're falling behind because cash outflows are greater than planned, or inflows are smaller, you can try to improve your situation. On the other hand, if you have no plan or no guideline analysis, you have no standard against which to measure your investment performance. You won't know when corrective action becomes necessary and you won't know how well you could or should have done with your investment.

THIRTEEN

Investing in the Stock Market

As much as I want to help you make money in the stock market, you'll probably understand why I can't recommend any particular stock to you. By the time you read this, the investment climate can be considerably different from the way it was at the time this was written.

What I can do, however, is provide you with some practical guidelines to help you decide whether the purchase of a particular stock is consistent with your investment objectives. Everybody wants to double their money as quickly as possible. But, as you have already seen, the longer it takes for a profit to be made, the less valuable this profit is in today's dollars. Again, turn to Table 3 (see page 152). If you require an 18% rate of return on invested capital to make an investment palatable, a profit of $1 payable four years from now is only worth about 51¢ in today's money.

In this chapter, we'll use an investment analysis form that is somewhat different from the one designed for use in real estate. The stock market form takes into account dividends and carrying charges instead of rental income and operating expenses. You'll note, if you flip through this chapter quickly, I have prepared all my sample investment analysis over three-year periods. Technically, you can buy a stock and hold it forever but, from a practical standpoint, I don't think it's too likely you would contemplate holding any particular stock for a much longer term than three years.

If you have any interest in investment (and you must if you are reading this book) you don't need me to tell you the stock market goes up and down. It doesn't seem possible we will ever find a way to eliminate the business cycle and there is no point in buying a stock, watching it increase in value and then holding on to it long enough for your gain to be completely wiped out in the next downturn.

So, again, all I can do here is help you analyze a potential investment mathematically. If reasonable assumptions are made, can a particular investment help you attain your goals and objectives?

Receipt of Dividends

Before we can make any kind of analysis, we must understand the Canadian tax rules pertaining to dividends, carrying charges and capital gains. The rules here are somewhat different than the tax provisions in other countries.

Many stocks pay dividends to their shareholders and these dividends can provide a flow of income to be used on an after-tax basis either for personal living expenses or for additional investment capital.

The receipt of cash dividends from Canadian securities is treated quite differently for tax purposes than the receipt of interest. A dividend received by an individual is included in taxable income, subject to a calculation which "grosses up" the amount received, but also provides an offsetting dividend tax credit to reduce the tax payable. The "gross-up" is one-quarter of the cash dividend received.

Thus, for example, if you buy a stock that pays you a $100 dividend, you'll include $125 in your income. Then, in arriving at your taxes payable, you'll reduce your total tax by the amount of the gross-up. In other words, although your income is inflated by $25 for each $100 of dividends received, your total tax is reduced by the same $25. (Actually, the federal dividend tax credit is approximately three-quarters of the gross-up while a reduction in provincial income taxes payable provides the remaining credit for the balance.)

The dividend tax credit is provided for two reasons, one being that dividends are a distribution out of after-tax corporate earnings. If the system taxed the same dollar as income to both the corporation which earned it and the individual who ultimately received it, this would create double taxation. Second, the dividend tax credit provides a major incentive for Canadians to invest in their own corporations.

Figure 1 illustrates that taxpayers in all marginal brackets will retain more after tax from receipts of dividends than they would from equivalent receipts of interest.

Essentially, you must earn one-and-a-quarter times as much interest as dividends to wind up with the same after-tax dollars in your hands. This example shows you something that is, as already mentioned, uniquely Canadian. By comparison, in the United States, both interest and dividends are simply taxed in your top marginal bracket.

Figure 1
Comparative after-tax retention on Canadian dividends vs. interest

Individual's marginal tax bracket	*25%*	*40%*	*45%*
Alternative 1–$100 Canadian dividends			
Cash dividend	$100	$100	$100
1/4 gross–up	25	25	25
Taxable income	$125	$125	$125
Tax in marginal bracket	$ 31	$ 50	$ 56
Dividend tax credit (combined federal and provincial)	25	25	25
Net tax	$ 6	$25	$ 31
Net retention (cash dividend minus tax)	$ 94	$75	$ 69
Alternative 2–$100 Canadian interest			
Interest	$100	$100	$100
Tax in marginal bracket	25	40	45
Net retention	$ 75	$ 60	$ 55
Ratio of after–tax retention Dividends:Interest	1.25:1	1.25:1	1.25:1

From this example, you should now understand a very important point: for anyone with taxable income, a 6% dividend is equivalent to a 7.5% (before tax) interest yield, while an 8% dividend is equivalent to interest at 10%. In other words, a dividend yield on a Canadian security is certainly much more attractive than first meets the eye. I must stress, however, this mathematical relationship is only valid where an individual is taxable in the first place. A dividend yield may not be that attractive to a senior citizen who has a few thousand dollars of savings and needs some income over and above government pensions.

Borrowing for Stock Market Investments

If you borrow to invest in the shares of Canadian public companies, you are always permitted to deduct your interest expense and other carrying charges, such as safekeeping fees, against other income. First you must apply as much of these expenses as you can to offset your grossed-up dividends. Even if the stocks you buy don't presently bear dividends, your interest and other expenses are nevertheless tax-deductible. This is an extremely important factor in evaluating cash flows.

Perhaps the most important consideration of all, however, is that *carrying charges do not affect the availability of a dividend tax credit.* It is therefore possible in Canada to obtain a tremendous advantage from the fact that *a dividend tax credit can offset carrying charges which are significantly higher than the actual dividends received.* Figure 2 shows the receipt of a cash dividend of $10,000 where an investor has incurred investment carrying charges of $12,500.

Because a dividend must be grossed-up by one-quarter, it can fully offset the amount of the carrying charges incurred in arriving at the individual's income. However, although none of the dividend is in fact taxable, the investor is still entitled to claim the dividend tax credit against the taxes on his or her other income. In terms of cash flow, the individual in this example will find that his or her tax savings make up for the fact that he or she has paid $2,500 more in carrying charges than he or she has received in dividends.

Figure 2
Effect of dividend tax credit on carrying charges

Assumptions:	
■ Cash dividend	$10,000
■ Carrying charges	12,500
Cash dividend	$10,000
Gross–up	2,500
Grossed–up dividend	12,500
Less: Carrying charges	(12,500)
Effect on taxable income	Nil
Carrying charges – cash dividend	$ 2,500
Less: Tax savings from dividend tax credit	(2,500)
Negative cash flow	Nil

Even if a stock doesn't pay a dividend, you should note the carrying costs are always reduced substantially by tax savings. For example, an individual in a 45% bracket who borrows money at 12% is only incurring a cost of under 7% after tax.

Capital Gains

Capital gains are not generally taxed until property is sold. At that time, three-quarters of any gain is included in income, although any available lifetime exemption must be taken into account.

Ignoring the exemption, simple arithmetic can show you how an individual who borrows money at almost 12% for a stock market investment can come out ahead of the game even if the investment appreciates in value by only 10% per annum. This is illustrated in Figure 3.

Figure 3
It pays to borrow at 12% interest to buy Canadian securities—as long as the investment appreciates by at least 10% a year

Assumed capital growth before taxes	10.00%
Less: Assumed tax on capital gain	
Three–quarters of gain taxed in 45% tax bracket	
(7.50% x 45%)	3.38
Net capital growth after taxes	6.62%
Carrying cost of investment	12.00%
Less: Tax saving in 45% tax bracket from interest write–off	5.40
Net cost to borrow	6.60%

Investment Carrying Charges and the Capital Gains Exemption

The June 1987 tax reform introduced legislation under which net taxable capital gains eligible for the lifetime exemption are reduced in cases where an individual claims investment losses after 1987 in computing income for tax purposes.

For purposes of these rules, where an individual's investment expenses exceed his or her investment income, an equivalent amount of capital gains are not eligible for the exemption. Only capital gains realized *after* investment losses have been "recaptured" now qualify.

For example, what if an individual's only investment involves borrowing $10,000 on January 1, 1994 to purchase 100 shares of a public company. Assume the annual interest expense on the loan is $1,200 and the shares pay no dividends. Assume further that the shares are then sold at the end of 1995 for $22,000. This produces a $12,000 capital gain of which $9,000 (or three-quarters of $12,000) is a taxable capital gain. Ignoring any other facts that may be relevant to this person's position, the maximum capital gains exemption that could be claimed in 1995 would be $6,600—that is, $9,000 of taxable capital gain less the cumulative net investment loss at the end of 1995 of $2,400 (two years of interest expense).

Again, however, for purposes of this book, the lifetime capital gains exemption is not generally considered. This provides the most conservative approach in making investment analyses.

A "Real Life" Example

Let's now take a realistic example which calculates the *actual* return on invested capital if a stock is purchased for a medium-term holding period, such as three years. To do this, we may use an investment analysis form such as the one in Figure 4.

Figure 4
Investment analysis form to evaluate the net present value of a stock market investment

	Time of Acquisition	*Year 1*	*Year 2*	*Year 3*
Cash dividend		6,000	6,000	6,000
Gross–up		1,500	1,500	1,500
Taxable dividend		7,500	7,500	7,500
Less: Investment carrying charges				
–interest expense				
–other				
Taxable income (loss)		7,500	7,500	7,500
Estimated income taxes				
–(payable)		(3,300)	3,300)	(3,300)
–recovered				
Net after–tax income (loss)		4,200	4,200	4,200
Less: Dividend gross–up		(1,500)	1,500)	(1,500)
Add: Tax savings from dividend tax credit (equal to gross–up)		1,500	1,500	1,500
Less: Capital outlays				
–cash invested	(100,000)			
–expenses of acquisition	(2,000)			
Add: Proceeds from sale				150,000
Less: Expenses to sell				(2,000)
Debt repayment				–
Tax on gain				(15,525)
After–tax cash flow	(102,000)	4,200	4,200	136,675
Required rate of return	18%			
Present value factor (Table 3)	1.000	.848	.718	.609
Net present value ($12,187)	(102,000)	3,562	3,016	83,235

Assume you have a little over $100,000 to invest and you buy 10,000 shares of a public company at $10 each, incurring, at the same time, $2000 in brokerage costs. The stock you buy is expected to bear a 6% annual dividend. You further believe that the stock can be sold at the end of three years at $15 a share. This would represent a 50% increase in value over that three year period. You're examining this potential investment and would be inclined to pursue it if you can earn an 18% net after-tax return on invested capital each year. Is this, in fact, feasible? To be conservative, you decide to ignore any potential benefits from the lifetime capital gains tax exemption.

Now take a few moments and examine the completed investment analysis form in Figure 4.

At the time of acquisition, the cash outlay is $102,000 including expenses of acquisition. Then each year for a three-year period, a $6000 cash dividend is anticipated. For tax purposes, this dividend is grossed-up to $7500, resulting in taxes payable of about $3300 before the dividend tax credit. The dividend tax credit is approximately equal to the gross-up and it results in a cash-flow saving. On the other hand, the dividend gross-up itself doesn't represent an inflow of funds. Thus, when the smoke clears, this investment produces a net after-tax cash flow of $4200 in the first two years for an investor in a 45% tax bracket. In the third year, we assume net proceeds of sale of $148,000 ($150,000 minus $2000 in selling expenses). The capital gain and tax are computed in Figure 5.

Returning to the investment analysis form, we see that in year three the net after-tax cash flow is $136,675. Assuming a rate of return of 18% is, however, required, the after-tax cash flow in year three is only worth roughly 61¢ on the dollar in today's money. You can see that the investment falls well short of the 18% target. In fact, the internal rate of return is actually a little less than 13%, as illustrated in Figure 6.

Figure 5
Calculation of capital gain and taxes on the disposition of a stock market investment (ignoring possible benefits from the lifetime capital gains exemption)

Net selling price	$148,000
Cost of investment including expenses of acquisition	102,000
Capital gain	$ 46,000
Taxable capital gain (3/4)	$ 34,500
Tax payable by investor in 45% bracket	$ 15,525

Figure 6
Calculating the internal rate of return on a stock market investment

Year	*After–Tax Cash Flow*	*Present Value Factor at 13%*	*Present Value of Cash Flow*
0	$(102,000)	1.000	$(102,000)
1	4,200	.885	3,717
2	4,200	.783	3,289
3	136,675	.693	94,716
			$ (278)

Now let's make one fundamental change. Instead of investing $102,000, let's assume you choose to invest $52,000 in cash and borrow $50,000 at 12% over a three-year period with no principal payments required (as long as the stock doesn't decline substantially in value). The investment analysis form in Figure 7 shows that realizing (just over) your required 18% rate of return is now possible. There are two reasons why this is true. First, the investment carrying charges of $6000 a year are tax-deductible, and second, you have a smaller initial cash outflow to recoup. In other words, if the investment performs in accordance with your objectives, you will benefit substantially from the use of *leverage*. The $50,000 pre-tax capital gain, instead of representing a 50% return on invested capital, now becomes a 100% return! Of course, it is deferred three years and, as such, the value of the profit is again only 61¢ on the dollar in today's money.

Figure 7
Investment analysis form to evaluate the net present value of a stock market investment

	Time of Acquisition	*Year 1*	*Year 2*	*Year 3*
Cash dividend		6,000	6,000	6,000
Gross–up		1,500	1,500	1,500
Taxable dividend		7,500	7,500	7,500
Less: Investment carrying charges				
–interest expense		(6,000)	(6,000)	(6,000)
–other				
Taxable income (loss)		1,500	1,500	1,500
Estimated income taxes				
–(payable)		(660)	(660)	(660)
–recovered				
Net after–tax income (loss)		840	840	840
Less: Dividend gross–up		(1,500)	(1,500)	(1,500)
Add: Tax savings from dividend tax credit (equal to gross–up)		1,500	1,500	1,500
Less: Capital outlays				
–cash invested	(50,000)			
–expenses of acquisition	(2,000)			
Add: Proceeds from sale				150,000
Less: Expenses to sell				(2,000)
Debt repayment				(50,000)
Tax on gain				(15,525)
After–tax cash flow	(52,000)	840	840	83,315
Required rate of return	18%			
Present value factor (Table 3)	1.000	.848	.718	.609
Net present value $54	(52,000)	712	603	50,739

Preparing an analysis such as the one in Figure 7 is extremely important because it will help you decide whether it's to your advantage to borrow for investment purposes. In this case, although you are laying out $6000 in interest charges while receiving the same $6000 in cash dividends, you are ahead by $840 a year. This is, of course, hard to believe but it's nevertheless true. The positive cash flow results from tax savings from the dividend tax credit. (Of course, if your investment has been heavily financed by debt and it declines in value you've got problems.)

Stock Dividends

Until a number of years ago, special tax rules applied in Canada for public companies which paid stock dividends. A stock dividend is simply a payment in the form of additional shares. In the past, stock dividends paid by public companies didn't trigger any immediate tax consequences, since they weren't treated as ordinary dividends. Instead, the shares received were assigned a zero cost for tax purposes and this created larger capital gains at the time the shares were ultimately sold.

Several years ago, however, the government repealed the special rules relating to stock dividends. Their value is now taxed on an ongoing basis in the same way as regular dividends, even if no cash is received. Of course, shares received under a stock dividend can always be sold to cover any taxes pertaining to the receipt of these shares. Since the tax benefits have been taken away, stock dividends have become less popular in recent years.

Retractable Preferred Shares

If you're going to invest in stocks in order to earn dividend yields, you should ask what type of security is worth holding. The answer is generally one of several retractable preferred share issues which blue chip companies in Canada have issued in recent years in order to raise capital. A preferred share is one that bears dividends before the common shareholders receive any return on their investment.

The fact that a share is retractable means the holder has the right to demand that his or her share be redeemed for cash at the end of a stipulated time. In other words, unless the company runs into severe financial difficulties, the investor would get his or her money back at the end of this period. Thus, retractable preferreds are quite attractive since they combine all of the best features of both bonds and stocks. Often, these shares have a limited life span, such as five years. Sometimes, these shares also offer the option of converting them into the issuing corporation's common stock. Thus, if the corporation performs well, there is the potential for a capital gain. Alternatively, if prevailing interest rates drop, the dividend yield on these shares becomes more attractive. In some circumstances, a sale even before redemption can result in a capital gain.

Many of these issues pay substantial dividends, and remember, a dividend is worth one and one-quarter times as much as interest to an investor who would be taxable upon receipt.

How to Find Stocks to Buy and Sell

Of course, the most difficult question concerning the stock market is which stock to buy, when to buy it, and when to sell. In an effort to deal with this question, two diametrically opposite schools of thought have evolved.

One of these is the school which advocates "fundamental analysis" and the other practices "technical analysis."

Fundamental analysis is a rational process which focuses on the value of the corporation whose stock is being examined. The proper stock to buy is the one which is undervalued—where the value of the company's assets, income, or expectations of income isn't fully reflected in the stock's market price. Those who practice fundamental analysis assume the market will eventually recognize that this particular corporation's shares are undervalued and therefore the stock price is eventually bound to rise. Alternatively, if the same approach indicates a stock is overvalued, this may mean that the particular security is undesirable and should be sold.

Fundamental analysis is an approach which is most suitable for long-term holdings because there is really no way to determine *when* the market will recognize its "error" in having undervalued a stock in the first place. Thus, fundamental analysis is of limited use for investors who wish to trade or speculate. In order to locate an undervalued stock, you must be prepared to analyze corporate financial statements through a series of steps. These include the use of many arithmetic ratios to determine liquidity, financial strength and profitability. You must also be willing to acquire knowledge of the industry itself, the products, the management philosophy of the company and many other factors which would have an impact upon the value of the stock price.

Fundamental analysis can be very time-consuming and for the average person the arithmetic approach in itself is very tedious. The biggest drawback of fundamental analysis is that it does not indicate *when* to buy or sell other than to tell you if you hold the stock long enough, then, supposedly, the intrinsic value will be recognized by the market.

As you can see from the analysis in this chapter, any time you are forced to hold a stock which does not move for several years, it is both frustrating and expensive. The fundamental approach also does not indicate *when* to sell for short-term profits.

If you practice fundamental analysis, you may in fact find a truly valuable stock in terms of long-term appreciation. However, if you have to hold it for three years and virtually all of the growth takes place in the last six months, you must consider the opportunity loss in the first two and a half years of the holding period.

One of the most significant factors mitigating *against* the use of fundamental analysis is the accounting information which forms the basis of much of the review. Accounting statements are generally based on historical cost concepts. In other words, asset values on a corporate balance sheet don't necessarily reflect the fair market values of these particular properties. Furthermore, different companies within the same industry may adopt different depreciation policies. They may also have different methods of reporting certain potential liabilities, such as pension commitments. There is sometimes a time lag between the end of a particular reporting period and the date on which financial statements are made generally available. In the interim, there can be severe changes in conditions affecting the market as a whole, the industry in which the corporation is active, or the company itself.

So, in the past few years, an entirely different method of stock market analysis has developed, which perhaps is better suited to the fast-moving and more speculative economy we witness today. This is technical analysis.

Technical analysis makes an effort to determine what the trend of stock prices is at any given point in time and where they presently stand within that trend. It tries to predict the tops and bottoms of current trends that evolve from time to time. The philosophy behind this approach is that the market has its own distinct personality, which is a composite of the tens of thousands of living personalities who are involved on a day-to-day basis. Therefore, the actions of the market are more a product of psychology than logic. Technical analysts feel investment success is dependent upon understanding and being able to interpret the indicators of what the market is presently doing. By its very nature, technical analysis tends to focus on the more or less short-term picture. It makes the assumption that it is inefficient for an investor to commit his or her money in expectation of a profit which may be several years down the road.

Technical analysis is not concerned with the intrinsic value of particular corporations. Analysts who use this approach interpret what the market is presently doing and what it is likely to do in the near future by studying the highs and lows, the Dow Jones Industrial Average, the advance-decline line and on-balance volume figures. If, for example, many stocks are reaching high points at which they have traded over the last few years, this generally is an indication that the market is moving upwards. Similarly, if more issues go up than those which decline over a particular period, this too is an indicator the market is advancing. Fortunately, none of the indicators is particularly complicated and virtually all information is available on a day-to-day basis in large newspapers. Stock brokers all have the benefit of studies done by analysts who use this approach.

Summary

Whether you use fundamental analysis or technical analysis to select stocks, you'll still find it worthwhile to make the calculations I've suggested in this chapter. It's only after you've analyzed your projections that you can determine a realistic projected rate of return. Then, the object of the exercise is to compare this to rates available from other investments taking into account relative risk factors. I wish you good luck in your stock market endeavours!

FOURTEEN

Investing in Gold

Over the centuries, gold has been the universal medium of international financial exchange. This alone necessitates examining it as an investment. History has witnessed the rise and fall of many powerful civilizations. When all else of value lay in rubble, gold alone remained. To the present day, many people have credited their survival to having held substantial investments in gold. Gold is portable and can be bartered for food or, in fact, for one's life. Even in North America, the uncertain economic climate prompts many investment counselors to suggest that every individual keep at least some investment capital in gold as a contingency.

At present it's very difficult to predict where the price of gold is headed. In fact, the price may not fluctuate to any great extent until there is some kind of panic internationally. For example, a large-scale war would almost certainly send the price of gold spiraling upwards. Also, if government deficits continue to increase and vast quantities of paper money are printed to pay outstanding bills, the potential hyperinflation could create a tremendous demand for this metal.

In this book, I'll consider a mathematical approach towards gold as an investment. In one major respect, this precious metal differs from most real estate investments or from investing in the stock market. Specifically, the ownership of gold doesn't provide any income yield *during* the period in which it is held. It's only upon sale that a profit or loss is realized. If you buy gold today at a certain price and hold it for several years, remember the most important lesson you've learned in this book—a profit due several years from now is worth only a fraction in today's money.

The Tax Consequences of Transactions in Gold

It's impossible to evaluate gold as an investment without understanding the tax implications, which are somewhat particular to Canada. Generally, profits from the disposition of gold, whether it's held in physical form (bullion or coins) or in certificates are subject to capital gains treatment. This is as a result of administrative discretion on the part of the Revenue authorities. Since gold has no capacity to pay interest or dividends and is held strictly as a speculation, whether short or long-term, any gain should theoretically be fully taxable. However, it has historically been the policy of Revenue Canada to accept capital gains treatment on these transactions.

You must nevertheless realize *if you wish to benefit from capital gains treatment on your gold transactions, interest on money borrowed to make your investments is not deductible.* If you decide, on the other hand, to deduct interest expense, you must be prepared to pay taxes on your *full* profits.

An Approach to Investing in Gold

Most of the remainder of this chapter will be devoted to three specific case studies involving a hypothetical investment in gold. To start with, there are two broad possibilities: either you buy gold using your own money only, or the acquisition is financed, at least in part, with borrowed funds. If borrowed funds are used, there's another choice to be made. Either you claim an interest expense deduction for tax purposes on an ongoing basis and pay tax on your entire profit at the time of sale or you treat your interest expense as non-deductible in favour of capital gains treatment at the time of sale. We'll see that the return on investment varies by at least several percentage points depending on whether:

- An investment in gold is made without borrowing money;
- Borrowed money is used and the interest is claimed as a tax deduction; or
- Borrowed money is used with the interest treated as non-deductible.

Background to a Hypothetical Case

Let's assume you'd like to invest $100,000 in the purchase of gold. If gold were trading at $500 an ounce, this means you could afford to buy 200 ounces. Assume you're looking at a medium-term holding period of, say, three years. Your criterion for successful investment performance is that you get an annual 15% net after-tax rate of return on invested capital.

Figure 1
Summary of a case study: Buy Gold for $100,000

Assumption: Required rate of return is 15% for next three years

Net selling price required after three years (from Table 1)

$100,000 x 1.521 = $152,100

However, profit on sale is subject to tax.

If capital gain, tax is 33%*

Therefore 67% of total profit = $52,100

Therefore, profit needed to return 15% net is

$52,100 ÷ 67 = $77,761

Therefore, total selling price needed for a 15% net return over three years is $177,761 (approximately $178,000)

*(This ignores the potential use of the lifetime capital gains tax exemption.)

Even before we proceed with the investment analysis forms, we can calculate the selling price needed in order to attain a 15% return on investment over a three-year period. If we turn to Table 1, which deals with the compound value of $1 invested at various interest rates, and we look at page 133, we can see that to realize a 15% return annually over three years, a $100,000 investment must then be worth $100,000 x 1.521 or $152,100. In other words, $100,000 invested today at 15% would total $152,100 at the end of three years. Thus, on the surface, it would appear that if the price of gold rises from $500 to $760.50 an ounce, your 200-ounce investment will have met your objective of a 15% annual net increase in value.

However, what about income taxes? In order to achieve a 15% net after-tax rate of return, the growth of $52,100 must be an *after-tax* figure. If we assume that you're in a 45% tax bracket, the effective tax on a capital gain is 33%, again ignoring the possibility of using the lifetime exemption in the interests of a conservative approach. Therefore, to realize a 15% net after-tax growth, 67% of your total profit must equal $52,100. This would allow a 33% factor to cover your income tax liability. Thus, the *real* profit needed to return 15% *net* over three years is: $52,100 divided by .67, or $77,761. In other words, unless you could sell your gold at the end of three years for $177,761, your rate of return on invested capital would not be 15%. To round the numbers, you really need a selling price (based on 200 ounces) of $890 an ounce.

In summary, to realize a 15% annual rate of return, the price of an ounce of gold (in this example) would have to increase by $390 over a three-year period.

Figure 2
Calculation of tax on capital gain on sale of gold (ignoring possible exemption)

Selling price of gold	$178,000
Cost	100,000
Capital gain	$ 78,000
Taxable capital gain (3/4)	$ 58,500
Tax at 45%	$ 26,325

In Figure 3, you see the first of three investment analysis forms. This one corresponds to the scenario with which we have just dealt. Specifically, it assumes a purchase of 200 ounces of gold at $500 per ounce, funded without borrowed money. Then, at the end of three years, a sale is projected for $178,000. Capital gains taxes on the $78,000 profit are $26,325 as shown in Figure 2.

The net return at the end of three years is $151,675 and, using Table 3, the present value factor at 15% is .658 x $151,675, or $99,802. Thus, the net present value is -$198, which means that the investment does provide a return just slightly less than 15%, *if gold is worth $890 an ounce after three years.*

Let's now look at a second alternative. Again, we'll assume you can buy 200 ounces of gold at $500, for a total investment of $100,000. This

Figure 3
Investment analysis form to evaluate the net present value of an investment in gold

		Time of Acquisition	*Year 1*	*Year 2*	*Year 3*
Purchase price					
200 oz. x $500	Total	$100,000			
Cash outlay		100,000			
Portion financed		-			
Total		$100,000			
Interest expense on financing					
Less: Income tax saving from deduction of interest (optional)					
Net after-tax loss					
Less: Capital outlay					
-cash invested		(100,000)			
-expenses of acquisition					
-interest (if not claimed for tax)					
Add: Proceeds from sale net of expenses to sell					178,000
Less: Debt repayment					-
Tax on profit					(26,325)
After–tax cash flow		(100,000)	-	-	151,675
Required rate of return		15%			
Present value factor (Table 3)		1.000	.870	.756	.658
Net present value ($198)		(100,000)	-	-	99,802

time, however, we'll see what happens if you put down $50,000 of your own money and borrow the rest at 11% interest. We'll assume you can arrange with your lending institution to pay interest only against the loan because the lending institution will hold your gold as collateral. In real life, this wouldn't be an uncommon arrangement. The annual interest on your $50,000 debt at 11% is $5,500.

Say, in this case, you'd like to claim the interest expense as a tax write-off. In exchange, you're prepared to pay full income taxes at regular tax rates on any gain from eventual sale. Now take a look at the investment analysis form shown as Figure 4.

In our second investment analysis there's an initial cash outlay of $50,000. In each of the next two years, the only outlay is the interest expense, which after considering tax savings, produces a negative cash flow of $3,025 a year. Of course, the present value of this outflow is only $4,919 over the two-year period. Then, at the end of year three, we again assume your investment can be sold for $178,000 and your debt of $50,000 would then be repaid. However, as Figure 5 illustrates, your *full profit* of $78,000 on sale would be taxable and the government's share is $35,100.

Figure 4
Investment analysis form to evaluate the net present value of an investment in gold

		Time of Acquisition	*Year 1*	*Year 2*	*Year 3*
Purchase price 200 oz. x $500	Total	$100,000			
Cash outlay		50,000			
Portion financed		50,000			
Total		$100,000			
Interest expense on financing			(5,500)	(5,500)	(5,500)
Less: Income tax saving from deduction of interest (optional)			2,475	2,475	2,475
Net after–tax loss			(3,025)	(3,025)	(3,025)
Less:					
Capital outlay – cash invested		(50,000)			
– expenses of acquisition					
– interest (if not claimed for tax)					
Add: Proceeds from sale net of expenses to sell					178,000
Less: Debt repayment					(50,000)
Tax on profit					(35,100)
After–tax cash flow		(50,000)	(3,025)	(3,025)	89,875
Required rate of return		15%			
Present value factor (Table 3)		1.000	.870	.756	.685
Net present value	$4,219	(50,000)	(2,632)	(2,287)	59,138

Figure 5
Calculation of tax on profit from sale of gold (no capital gains treatment)

Selling price of gold	$178,000
Cost	100,000
Profit from sale	$ 78,000
Tax at 45%	$ 35,100

The after-tax cash flow of year three ($89,875) has a present value of only $59,138, given a 15% discount factor. In the end, we see that the investment generates more than your required rate of return of 15%. In fact, the actual rate of return works out to be almost exactly 18% (as shown in Figure 6).

Figure 6
Calculating the internal rate of return on an investment in gold

Year	Cash Flow	Present Value Factor at 18%	Present Value of Cash Flow
0	$(50,000)	1.000	$(50,000)
1	(3,025)	.848	(2,565)
2	(3,025)	.718	(2,172)
3	89,875	.609	54,733
			($4)

Now let's look at a final alternative. You'll still buy $100,000 worth of gold using $50,000 of borrowed money with the remainder coming from your own capital. In this case, however, we'll assume you do *not* try to deduct your interest expense. This is because you want your profit on sale treated as a capital gain. Comparing the third investment analysis (Figure 7) to the

Figure 7
Investment analysis form to evaluate the net present value of an investment in gold

	Time of Acquisition	Year 1	Year 2	Year 3
Purchase price 200 oz. x $500 Total	$100,000			
Cash outlay	50,000			
Portion financed	50,000			
Total	$100,000			
Interest expense on financing				
Less: Income tax saving from deduction of interest (optional)				
Net after–tax loss				
Less:				
Capital outlay				
– cash invested	(50,000)			
– expenses of acquisition				
– interest (if not claimed for tax)	(5,500)	(5,500)	(5,500)	
Add: Proceeds from sale net of expenses to sell				178,000
Less: Debt repayment				(50,000)
Tax on profit				(26,325)
After–tax cash flow	(50,000)	(5,500)	(5,500)	96,175
Required rate of return	15%			
Present value factor (Table 3)	1.000	.870	.756	.685
Net present value $4,340	(50,000)	(4,785)	(4,158)	63,283

one on page 94, you can see that, in years one and two, the cost of not deducting interest is somewhat higher. However, this is more than offset in the third year by the fact that the tax on your eventual profit, as calculated in Figure 8, is that much smaller.

In this particular case, the investment again returns substantially *more* than your required 15% rate of return, and the results in Figure 7 are marginally better than the results in Figure 4.

Figure 8
Calculation of tax on capital gain on sale of gold (ignoring possible exemption)

Selling price of gold	$178,000
Original cost	100,000
Capital gain	$ 78,000
Taxable capital gain (3/4)	$ 58,500
Tax at 45%	$ 26,325

Summary

As with any other type of investment, it's possible to quantify your goals and objectives. Do you think it's conceivable that the price of gold could increase by $350 an ounce over three years? Is an after-tax rate of return of 15% adequate for your purposes? On the other hand, is it more than you would really require? Should you use borrowed money to make such an investment? If so, should you attempt to deduct the interest expense? None of these questions can be answered without some mathematical analysis. And yet, as you can see, the procedure is certainly not difficult.

Finally, don't let the numbers scare you. In this chapter, I've chosen an investment of $100,000 because of the ease in dealing with nice round numbers. Remember, an investment in gold can be made by people at all income levels. At the time this is being written, a 1/10 oz. gold coin costs less than $100. Of course, whether the price will eventually go up or down, and by how much, remains a matter for conjecture.

FIFTEEN

Investing in a Registered Retirement Savings Plan

In Chapter Two, I suggested that you think twice before making interest-bearing investments at modest rates solely for the sake of earning interest income—if you'll be taxed in a high bracket. However, earning interest income even at relatively low rates can be profitable as long as it's tax-sheltered.

One of the best ways Canadians can earn tax-sheltered income is through a personal registered retirement savings plan (RRSP) program. This is probably the only interest-bearing investment that's safe to hold over an extended period of time. As you'll see, an RRSP provides the opportunity to use untaxed dollars for your own investment portfolio, while also earning a tax-deferred investment yield.

Under the RRSP program, you are allowed to make tax-deductible contributions in a given calendar year or within sixty days following the end of that year. For 1994, RRSP contributions may not exceed 18% of your *1993* "earned income" to a maximum dollar amount of $13,500.

If you're a member of a pension plan or deferred profit sharing plan, your allowable limit is reduced by a "pension adjustment" that reflects your contributions and those of your employer to the plan. The maximum RRSP limit is slated to jump by $1,000 a year, reaching $15,500 by 1996. After that, limits will be indexed with reference to annual inflation.

Earned income is basically the sum of *net* receipts from employment, self-employment (business), rentals, and alimony. If you're not a member of an employer-sponsored pension or deferred profit-sharing program, the "magic" 1993 earned income required for full participation in an RRSP in 1994 is $75,000. This is because 18% of $75,000 is $13,500.

The RRSP program is a fairly straightforward investment. Each year contributions are made, they are tax-deductible. As long as the amounts are invested in qualified investments such as term deposits or guaranteed income certificates, Canadian public company stocks and bonds, Canada Savings Bonds, or mortgages, the income earned within an RRSP compounds on a tax-deferred basis. After several years of ongoing contributions, the available capital starts to snowball and the build-up of capital continues until retirement. At that time, you can liquidate the assets in your plan and purchase an annuity that'll provide you with a cash flow after your retirement. Although withdrawals from an RRSP are taxable, you'll often be in a lower tax bracket after retirement than previously.

The benefits of an RRSP are substantial, as we can confirm by simply taking a look at Table 2 (pages 135-143). Assuming a 10% yield, deposits of $1 a year made for ten years will amount to almost $16 at the end. After twenty years, you would have $57.28 and, after thirty years, $164.49.

For purposes of this chapter, I'll assume you can afford to contribute $2000 a year to your RRSP for various periods of time. Figure 1 illustrates how Table 2 can be used to calculate your total accumulation at various investment yields over these periods. For example, if you can earn an average of 10% on your money for thirty years, you'll have $2000 x 164.49, or $328,988 at the end. Clearly, the higher the investment yield, the more significant the accumulation.

Table 2 provides you with calculations assuming deposits are made monthly, quarterly, semi-annually as well as annually. What if, instead of investing $2000 a year *once* a year, you were to invest $166.67 each month? Let's assume you're, say, twenty-five years away from retirement. From Figure 2, you can see that putting aside money on a monthly basis produces a sizable advantage. The difference is $24,449.

Figure 1
Value of an investment of $2000 each year into a registered retirement savings plan

Yield	*10%*	*12%*	*14%*	*16%*
Investment of $2000 a year for:				
10 years	$ 31,875	$ 35,098	$ 88,674	$ 42,642
15 years	63,545	74,560	87,684	103,320
20 years	114,550	144,104	182,050	230,760
25 years	196,694	266,668	363,742	498,428
30 years	328,988	482,666	713,574	1,060,624
35 years	542,048	863,326	1,387,146	2,241,426

Figure 2
Comparison of monthly investments vs. one annual investment in an RRSP

Investment of $166.67 per month at 10% for 25 years	$221,143
Investment of $2000 per year at 10% for 25 years	196,694
Difference	$ 24,449

You can keep an RRSP open until you reach age seventy-one. After that time, you must start drawing funds out, generally in the form of an annuity. Annuities will be discussed later in this chapter.

I've provided detailed discussions of RRSP programs in several other books. Here, I'll just caution you that interest on money borrowed to acquire an RRSP investment is *not* tax-deductible. On the other hand, you *are* permitted to split your contribution between a personal plan and a plan in the name of your spouse. The purpose of doing this would be to eventually receive *two* flows of annuity income and make use of the low tax bracket twice. I recommend that you read up on the RRSP rules, or discuss them with your own tax adviser, so you can take maximum advantage of this program.

Should I Have an RRSP?

One of the most common questions serious investors ask is whether an RRSP is advisable, especially because of investment restrictions. Real estate is a non-qualified investment, as are precious metals such as gold and silver, and you can't invest to any great extent in foreign securities. Despite the limitations placed on an RRSP portfolio, I don't think you really have much choice—you *must* have an RRSP.

Let's examine the alternatives. Assume you're in a 40% income tax bracket and can save $2000 a year before income taxes. Assume the average yield you can earn on invested capital is 10%. You then have the choice between investing $2000 a year at 10% for, say, twenty-five years or having $1200 a year earning 6% for that same period of time. At the end of twenty-five years, assume you completely deregister your RRSP investment in one lump-sum. Even if the tax cost at that point is 50% of the amount withdrawn, Figure 3 shows you will still have made $32,509 more than you would without the RRSP. (The calculations to support this conclusion are also made using Table 2.)

Figure 3
Comparison of an investment in an RRSP to "outside" savings

RRSP investment of $2000 per year at 10% for 25 years	$196,694
Less Income taxes on withdrawal at 50%	98,347
	98,347
Non–RRSP investment of $1200 per year at 6% for 25 years	65,838
Advantage of RRSP	$ 32,509

So, in dealing with the question of whether or not an RRSP is attractive, simply ask yourself, what better choice is there?

What Kind of Plan Should I Have?

RRSPs are administered by trust companies, banks and insurance companies. In addition, you're allowed to have a self-directed plan where you appoint trustees (or a trust company) and the trustees make whatever investments you, as planholder, desire. Of course, your investments must fall within the acceptable tax guidelines discussed previously. Traditionally, people wait until the end of February to purchase their RRSP for the preceding year. Many millions of dollars are spent annually by companies trying to promote their own particular plans. To attempt to compare all the different alternative investments is a full-time job for a qualified investment counselor. When it comes to selecting an RRSP, you can't even rely on past performance. Remember that the performance of a particular program is only a function of those people employed as fund managers.

You should, however, try to get the best return available. While a difference of 1% or 2% in the long run is not going to make or break the average middle-income or upper-income investor, the difference can still be very substantial over twenty-five years. Figure 4 uses Table 2 to show you the difference between a return of 10% and 11% on annual investments of $2000 over a twenty-five year period. The difference is $32,132.

You are permitted to move your money from one RRSP to another even if you change your trustees. Of course, you must always consider handling fees. If the increased return on investment is more than offset by additional handling costs, then it clearly won't be worthwhile to move your funds.

Figure 4
Comparison of investments in an RRSP at different rates of return over twenty-five years

Investment of $2000 per year at 11% for 25 years	$228,826
Investment of $2000 per year at 10% for 25 years	196,694
Difference	$ 32,132

Cashing-In an RRSP

In Figure 3, we saw what happens when you invest in an RRSP for an extended period of time (twenty-five years) and then simply deregister the entire accumulation of $196,694 and pay taxes. This is not ordinarily what you would do. Instead, you would probably buy an annuity. This would provide you with a cash flow to subsidize your living costs after your retirement.

Until about fifteen years ago, there was only one way to cash-in an RRSP without paying immediate taxes. The Income Tax Act required that you use the RRSP funds to purchase a life annuity from an insurance company before you reached the age of seventy-one. The annuity benefits were then taxable as and when they were received. The only alternative was to make a lump-sum withdrawal from the RRSP and pay income tax on all amounts received at that time.

To safeguard against an early death, an individual was also permitted to modify the ordinary life annuity by adding a "guaranteed term" rider. A guaranteed term means that payments continue for at least that length of time, even if the buyer dies before then. However, any time an individual lives beyond the guaranteed term, the payments only continue until the time of death. The maximum guaranteed term permitted under current legislation is twenty years. In addition, you're allowed to arrange a joint-and-last-survivor annuity program where RRSP payments continue until both husband and wife die. Even the joint-and-last survivor option can be structured to have a guaranteed term of up to twenty years. You should also explore Registered Retirement Income Funds (RRIFs) with your tax adviser. A detailed discussion of RRIFs is beyond the scope of this book.

Most people don't understand annuities, especially annuities beginning at age seventy-one. If you're seventy-one years old and you go to an insurance company with $200,000 in your RRSP, you may find that you could get approximately $30,000 a year if you don't opt for any guaranteed term. Of course, you wouldn't ordinarily think this is any bargain. If you're a male, you're probably conscious of the fact that your average life expectancy is only seventy-two years. So, how would you feel about receiving only one or two years worth of annuity payments, or perhaps only $60,000 out of a $200,000 initial investment?

If you think this is a problem, you've fallen into the common trap. While it's true the average life expectancy of a male would be approximately seventy-two years, *this is only true if that male person is younger than age forty*. Once you pass age forty, your life expectancy begins to *increase*.

It's now time to introduce the last of our tables, on page 236. This is the standard Canadian Mortality Table. If you look at this table closely, you can see that a seventy-year-old male has a life expectancy of another eleven years and a female of the same age is projected to live another fourteen years. Thus, you would *not* be mistreated if you were offered $30,000 a year as an RRSP yield. In preparing calculations, the insurance company must budget for a payout of eleven to fourteen years, even without any guarantee.

Naturally, if you retire when you're sixty-five and begin to take an RRSP annuity at that age, you can expect to receive substantially less than if you wait until age seventy-one. Also, a woman may be offered a lower annual yield than a man, since she's expected to live longer.

Calculating Annuity Yields

In order to calculate annuity yields, we can use Table 5. This table provides us with periodic payments at the end of each period required to amortize a loan of $1 over a period of time. We've made use of Table 5 in Chapter Six in dealing with loans other than Canadian mortgages. In the previous application, we assumed you're a borrower and you're paying back a loan with interest over a period of time. In an annuity situation the tables turn. In other words, *you* become the *lender* who deposits a sum of money with an insurance or trust company and then the insurance or trust company (i.e., the borrower) pays you back over a period of time, with interest.

Figure 5
Calculating annuity yields

		Male	*Female*
Life expectancy at age 70 (from Table 13)		10.9	13.85
Assumed value of RRSP at age 70	(A)	$ 200,000	$ 200,000
Monthly annuity to yield 10% for		11 years	14 years
Factor (from Table 5)	(B)	.0125	.0111
(A) x (B)		$2500/mo.	$2220/mo.
Proof			
Present value of	(A)	$2500/mo.	$2220/mo.
for		11 years	14 years
at		10%	10%
Factor (from Table 8)	(B)	79.873	90.236
(A) x (B)		$ 199,683	$ 200,324

Let's assume you're dealing with an insurance company and you're seventy-one years old. As I mentioned before, even without any guarantee, the insurance company must budget for a payout of eleven to fourteen years. Say you have $200,000 in your RRSP at that time and the going rate of interest is 10%. The insurance company will be prepared to pay you a monthly annuity for eleven to fourteen years in exchange for your $200,000 deposit. From Table 5, we can see that to amortize a loan of $1 at 10% interest over eleven years requires a monthly payment of $0.0125 and, over fourteen years, the factor is .0111. Thus, a $200,000 deposit can be amortized with monthly payments of $2500 a month over eleven years and $2220 a month over fourteen years. Therefore, a yield of $30,000 a year from age seventy is not the least bit unrealistic or unreasonable—as long as the going rate of interest is 10% as in this example.

We can prove our numbers using Table 8. Table 8 gives us the present value of $1 per period payable at the end of each period. At 10% interest, the right to receive $2500 a month for eleven years is worth $199,683 ($2500 x 79.873). Of course, the difference between this amount and $200,000 is a result of rounding. Similarly, the present value of the right to receive $2220 a month for fourteen years at 10% is $200,324 ($2220 x 90.236). Again, the $324 difference is due to rounding. Figure 5 illustrates these points in table form.

Evaluating Annuity Yields

By now you can appreciate why it isn't possible to evaluate an annuity yield unless you have a clear understanding of the concept of life expectancy. In fact, in the next chapter you'll see that a consideration of life expectancy is crucial when evaluating the cost of any life insurance policy.

Let's return to the situation where you have $200,000 in an RRSP and you'd like to buy a life annuity. This time, suppose you don't want to take a chance on dying prematurely and, instead, decide to opt for a guaranteed term. Figure 6 is an extract from Table 5 which will enable you to determine the approximate monthly yield if you take a guaranteed term of ten to fifteen years. It also includes the factors for twenty years at different interest rates.

Figure 6
Monthly payments required to amortize a loan of $1 over various time periods (from Table 5)

Years	*10%*	*11%*	*12%*	*13%*	*14%*	*15%*
10	.0132	.0138	.0143	.0149	.0155	.0161
11	.0125	.0131	.0137	.0143	.0149	.0155
12	.0120	.0125	.0131	.0137	.0144	.0150
13	.0115	.0121	.0127	.0133	.0140	.0146
14	.0111	.0117	.0123	.0130	.0136	.0143
15	.0107	.0114	.0120	.0127	.0133	.0140
20	.0097	.0103	.0110	.0117	.0124	.0132

Now let's assume a seventy-year-old man opts to convert a $200,000 RRSP accumulation into an annuity with a guaranteed term of fifteen years.

Assume he can get 10% on his money. His monthly income will then be \$200,000 x .0107 or \$2140. In other words, he would be sacrificing \$360 a month in exchange for the guarantee.

Determining An Annuity Rate

Any time you wish to calculate the rate of return on an annuity, you need only know two things: the original amount invested and the anticipated length of time over which payments will be received. Then, by calculating your monthly return for each \$1 of investment, you can determine the percentage yield from your tables.

Table 5 can be used to determine annuity yields when you know the initial deposit and the payments to be received on a monthly basis. For example, assume at the age of seventy a man has \$200,000 in an RRSP and he's told by another insurance company that they will give him \$2970 per month for life with no guaranteed term. What is the rate of return? First, we have to examine the individual's life expectancy, which is eleven years. Then, if \$200,000 provides \$2970 a month, a \$1 investment would provide 1/200,000 x \$2970, or \$0.01485 per month.

Now, turning to the extract from Table 5 in Figure 6, we can scan along the columns opposite an eleven-year payout and try to find the number that most closely approximates the factor we have just calculated. In this case, it's found under the column for a 14% return. In other words, if an insurance company were willing to provide \$2970 per month for life with no guaranteed term in exchange for a lump-sum payment of \$200,000 at age seventy, the yield is calculated to be approximately 14%. Of course, the actual yield may be greater or smaller depending on the age at death.

What if this same individual decided he would rather have a life annuity with a twenty-year guaranteed term? Assume, in these circumstances, the insurance company was willing to provide \$2670 a month. In this case, the return for each dollar of original investment is 1/\$200,000 x \$2670, or \$0.01335 per month.

If we now examine the numbers on the last line of our extract from Table 5 in Figure 6, we can see that the rate of return is slightly more than 15% over a twenty-year period. In the unlikely event that the individual survives beyond age ninety, the yield would be larger.

Summary

For most Canadians, the RRSP is the cornerstone to building a comfortable retirement. While the opportunity to set aside perhaps only a few thousand dollars a year may not seem to be attractive at the outset, the tax-deductibility of contributions along with the opportunity to compound earnings without tax on an ongoing basis makes such a program extremely rewarding. This is especially true once you understand what is actually available at the end of the line.

SIXTEEN

Understanding Life Insurance Policies

How is this for a deal? Assume you are a thirty-five-year-old male and a life insurance company offers you a $100,000 policy under the following terms. You pay $100 a month for ten years. At the end of ten years, you'll have paid a total of $12,000 in premiums and this amount will then be refunded to you. In other words, you get your money back. Then, whenever you die (even if this happens before the ten years are up) the policy will pay $100,000 to your estate.

Sounds as if you're getting something for nothing. But is this really the case? As you'll learn in the next few pages, it's impossible to properly evaluate a life insurance policy without a basic understanding of the math tables in this book.

Let's take a closer look at the "free" insurance offer. We'll assume for illustration that an insurance company can earn 12% a year on its money. If you deposit $100 at the beginning of each month for ten years at 12% interest, Table 9 tells you that this will accumulate to $23,234. Then, when you're age forty-five, the insurance company could give you back your original capital investment of $12,000 and still retain $11,234.

Now it's time to look at Table 13—the standard Canadian Mortality Table. At age forty-five, a male can be expected to live an additional 28.77 years. So according to statistics, the insurance company will be allowed to keep $11,234 for twenty-eight years to earn 12% compounded annually—if this investment yield continues to hold. From Table 1, the future value of $11,234 invested at 12% is $11,234 x 23.884, or $268,313. Then, if *you* die at the end of twenty-eight years, the insurance company will be able to pay the death benefit of $100,000 and still retain $168,313 towards overhead and profit. In other words, as Figure 1 illustrates, you don't get anything for nothing.

This is not to say that insurance companies should be condemned. First of all, the example I just gave you is purely hypothetical. Second, there is no guarantee that the insurance company will be able to earn an average of 12% net after-tax each year for the next thirty-eight years. Finally, what if *you* happen to die prematurely? The insurance company is taking the risk. All insurance companies are in business to make a profit. What you get in return if you take out a policy are two things:

1. Protection in the event of an *early* death, and

2. The security of knowing that you'll have dollars available *when needed* to pay taxes or to provide income to your family.

Figure 1
Example of refundable premium insurance policy

Future value of $100 per month invested at the beginning of each month for 10 years at 12% (from Table 9) $100 x 232.339 =	$ 23,233.90
Less: Original capital refunded after ten years $100 x 120 months	12,000.00
Funds retained by life insurance company	$ 11,233.90
Future value of $11,234 invested to earn compound interest at 12% for a further 28 years (from Table 1) $11,234 x 23.884 =	$268,313.00
Less: Life insurance proceeds paid at age 73	100,000.00
Net contribution to overhead and profits of insurance company	$168,313.00

If any of us was assured of living for many, many years, life insurance would probably not be necessary. Take a look at Table 4, which tells us how much must be invested at the end of each month to accumulate $1. Assume you wish to have $100,000 at the end of thirty-eight years and you think you can earn an average of 6% a year after tax. You need only invest $100,000 x .0006, or $60 a month.

Anyone who can guarantee a long life would be better off investing his or her money instead of paying insurance premiums. *Traditional life insurance policies are not an investment even though they are sometimes sold as such.* You'll soon see life insurance represents a cost. Again, its purpose is to provide protection as well as a source of cash when it's most needed.

Before tackling a mathematical approach to insurance policy evaluation, a little background is warranted. As a bare minimum, I think you should insure your life so, at the time of death, there need be no forced sale of assets solely for the purpose of paying income taxes. For that reason, some kind of permanent insurance is necessary and term insurance will not usually be sufficient. Remember that a term policy will not help if it expires before your death. *Many term policies are not renewable beyond age seventy.* Keep in mind you will probably live several years beyond your seventieth birthday, whether you are male or female. Take a good look at Table 13. It will tell you how much time you have left.

The tables in this book can help you determine the amount of insurance you'll require to pay taxes, as long as you know how the law operates. Basically, the tax rules provide that, upon death, you are "deemed" or considered to have sold all your properties at fair market value. The exception is where you leave property to a spouse. In such a case, any increase in value will not ordinarily be taxed until your spouse dies.

From time to time, you should try to estimate the potential taxes resulting from death. You should project the future value of your investments and then compare these amounts with your costs. Then, you should apply combined federal and provincial marginal tax rates to your anticipated gains. To the extent you have capital gains, three-quarters is taxable. In order to be conservative, you should generally assume a tax rate of about 45% -50%, and you might be well advised to discount the potential benefits of the lifetime capital gains exemption. You might note, however, taxes produced by any deemed dispositions on death may be spread over ten years but each installment bears interest and the interest is not tax-deductible.

If you insure against your ultimate tax liability, one of the most important points to keep in mind is that no one will have to pay tax on your life insurance *benefits*. On the other hand, you generally *cannot* deduct the cost of your life insurance *premiums* from your income.

Insurance Programs Provide Income to Dependents

Many people rely totally on group life and pension programs instituted by their employers. This is a mistake, since the present level of such benefits will not generally provide adequately for either a middle-income or a highly paid key executive. In some cases, these shortcomings are created by government regulations, while others are caused by restrictions imposed by insurers themselves. For example, assume a male executive has annual earnings of $50,000. His company program limits his coverage to 2½ times earnings under its group life package. Let's assume this executive now dies and his widow inherits $125,000 of tax-free insurance proceeds. Assume the funds are then invested at 8% to yield $10,000 a year. Compare these (before-tax) earnings to the deceased's annual income of $50,000. If the widow wishes to retain her capital intact, she must make a drastic change in her lifestyle. The thought of an 80% reduction in the level of family income is certainly not particularly attractive.

What about an employer-sponsored pension program? Take the example of another male executive age fifty-five who anticipates retiring at age sixty-five after thirty-five years of service. (Actually, such a long period of service would be extremely rare in practice.) Again, assume a present income level of $50,000 a year and—assuming, for example, a 10% annual increase in pay—a final income of $118,000.

Traditionally, most pension plans are based on the average of the highest salaries earned over a five-year period. In this case, the average of the best five years would also be the last five years, or $98,000. Assume the pension benefit is 2% for each year of service multiplied by the average of the best five years. This would provide an annual cash flow of 2% multiplied by thirty-five years multiplied by $98,000, or $68,000.

As a percentage of *final* earnings, this works out to only 57% in our case. If the retired individual decides to take his pension as an annuity guaranteed for fifteen years, the annual pension might be only approximately $54,000, or 46% of the final year's earnings. If taken as a joint-and-last-survivor annuity guaranteed for ten years (assuming a spouse who is five years younger) the pension may only be $43,200, or 37% of final income. Then, if we assume the pensioner dies shortly after retirement, we can see that again his spouse is faced with the prospect of receiving an income which is only a fraction of what was previously received.

If you stop and think for a moment, a "standard" executive compensation program is often not sufficient to meet your needs. Thus, the first role of the insurance you hold personally is to provide income to your surviving spouse and other dependents in the event that earned income from employment, business or a professional practice ceases.

A second use of life insurance is, as I described previously, to pay income taxes arising from deemed dispositions on death and on other income generated at that time. Also, insurance proceeds can be used to pay debts owing at the time of death and debts created by death itself (such as funeral costs, executors' fees and professional fees).

Insurance Provides Liquidity

In addition, one of the most important reasons for carrying life insurance is to provide liquidity to an estate so assets yielding little or no current income can be retained. Your family home is one example. This is especially important if you've borrowed money to acquire these assets in the first place. Several times, this book has suggested you consider borrowing money for investment purposes if you can finance your costs from surplus earnings from your job, business or profession. The actual amount you decide to borrow depends largely on several facts, including the type of investment you choose to acquire, the deductibility of interest and your own "comfort level".

The concept of borrowing money makes sense for many people—*but only as long as they are alive.* If your earnings cease, so does the cash flow needed to maintain debt. You never want to be in a position where assets must be sold at fire-sale prices just because your estate can no longer afford to carry them. As you know, all investment markets tend to be somewhat cyclical, and if your heirs must sell at a time when your particular investments are depressed, there can be a substantial penalty.

A general rule of thumb is you should always carry sufficient insurance to cover *all debts owing at the time of death as well as debts created.* In other words, even if you don't adopt an aggressive investment philosophy, you should still insure your mortgage, car loans and any other personal debts. Then, additional insurance should be provided to maintain a flow of income so your dependents don't have to suffer a reduction in their lifestyles. The amount of insurance required is not necessarily mind-boggling. For example, if you have a $50,000 mortgage against your house at 11% and there's insurance to cover that debt at the time of your death, technically your family could then afford to live on your take-home pay prior to death *minus* $481 a month (ignoring any inflation factor). The $481 represents the amount previously required to meet your monthly mortgage payments.

Other Uses for Insurance

One of the most underrated advantages of carrying life insurance is that it can facilitate distributions of an estate among family members. If, for example, you own a family farm or small business, you may wish to pass that on to one child rather than divide it equally among all your children. This is especially true if the one child is active in the farming or business operation. Leaving such an enterprise to be shared by all your children can create some serious inequities. Why should the one child who is active be forced to support inactive brothers and sisters? In addition, if the business can comfortably support one or two families, what happens when that business is then drained by the requirements of four or five families? In other words, it doesn't always make sense to give all your intended beneficiaries equal shares of each and every asset.

Does this mean you must disinherit some of your children? Certainly not. The idea is to carry life insurance in sufficient amounts so that a family farm or business can pass to one child while the other children receive equivalent cash values from the insurance proceeds.

Life insurance can also be useful to meet obligations with respect to charitable bequests, or in special situations where you wish to provide for handicapped children or elderly parents. In addition, an insurance policy can help you achieve independence if you're contemplating a career change with an attendant loss of employer-benefit programs. If you own a part-interest in a private business, life insurance is almost mandatory to assist the surviving partners in buying out the estates of those who die first.

Borrowing Against Life Insurance Policies

As time goes on, some insurance policies develop "cash surrender values". A cash surrender value is the amount you'd receive from the insurance company if you were to cancel the policy. In most cases, I wouldn't recommend you surrender your insurance—if for no other reason than the fact that the older you get, the more expensive it becomes to replace your coverage. In some cases, however, insurance companies will allow you to borrow against the cash surrender value at rates lower than those of other institutions. If you borrow for investment purposes, the interest is tax-deductible.

Unfortunately, the income tax rules surrounding life insurance policies are somewhat complex. Accordingly, I recommend before you consider borrowing against any policy, you review the income tax implications with representatives of the insurance company that has issued the policy as well as with your own accountant.

Types of Life Insurance Products

Broadly speaking, there are two types of life insurance:

- term insurance, and
- permanent insurance

For individuals who maintain liquid estates and who require most of their protection in the early years, perhaps term insurance would be advisable. When it comes to a business situation, however, most advisers recommend a more permanent type of coverage. This is because most term insurance policies expire when the holder reaches age seventy, whereas the average individual will probably not die until one or two years later. Term insurance therefore provides protection for your early needs while your children are young, but it's not adequate for long-range business planning and the preservation of property that isn't liquid, such as real estate. When it comes to investment and estate planning, a good insurance agent is just as important a member of the team as your accountant or lawyer.

Generally, I recommend in the decade between age twenty-five and thirty-five, while you are advancing in a career and at the same time beginning to raise a family, you should acquire term insurance to protect your family in the event of a premature death. Then, once you are more established, you should begin to transfer your coverage into more permanent-type policies. This is because the longer you wait, the more expensive permanent insurance becomes.

Characteristics of a Term Insurance Policy

As you would expect, term insurance tends to give the most protection for the least initial outlay. However, many term insurance policies do, in fact, expire by the time the individual reaches age seventy. Thus, the one major deficiency is the lack of *permanent* coverage. Nevertheless, if you're considering a term insurance policy, there are several special considerations. First, there should be a guarantee that you can convert and renew it without providing evidence of your adequate health.

Generally, term insurance policies must be renewed annually or every few years and may be converted into whole-life insurance. You would want the right to obtain these benefits, especially if at some point your health should deteriorate and you would be unable to pass a medical examination. A guaranteed convertibility and renewability feature can easily be built into most term policies. You would also look for a provision which provides a waiver of premiums if you become disabled. This means the policy would continue in force without your making any additional premium payments. Finally, you might also look for "double indemnity". This feature means the policy would pay-off double if you die accidentally. This would be especially appealing if your lifestyle or job requires you to do a lot of travelling.

Permanent Insurance

There are many kinds of permanent insurance policies. Most common is the "whole-life" policy where payments continue until the time of death. As a variation, there is also the concept of "limited pay life" where your insurance premiums cease at a certain age (generally at the time of retirement). When I make recommendations for permanent insurance coverage, I generally suggest a person shouldn't take any policy requiring insurance premiums to be paid after retirement. This is because, in many cases, one's cash flow tends to decrease once the "earned income years" are over. In addition to whole-life policies, permanent insurance also includes "endowment" policies and "single premium" policies. Endowment policies have become somewhat unpopular in the last few years and single-premium policies have been rendered unattractive as a result of certain income tax changes.

An endowment policy provides a specific death benefit, or if one survives, the face amount is paid at age sixty five (or seventy). Proceeds from the surrender of the policy in excess of total premiums are fully taxable. This vehicle hasn't been popular since other savings plans can provide better yields.

Last-to-Die Policies

The "last-to-die" concept lends itself nicely to estate planning where the object is to pass assets intact to the next generation. Under Canadian law, a husband pays no tax on property he leaves to his wife and vice versa. It's therefore not necessary to pay taxes on death until both husband and wife die. (Fortunately, none of the Canadian provinces any longer levy provincial succession duties at the time of a person's death.) A last-to-die policy can provide inexpensive insurance if one spouse is considerably younger than the other. It can also be useful if one spouse is not medically fit and the premiums to carry insurance on that person's life alone would otherwise be very high. As a variation on this theme, a last-to-die policy can be structured so that premium payments cease when the first spouse (or income earner) dies. The policy would still pay off at the time of the second death.

Evaluating Life Insurance Products

If you become conversant with the tables in this book, you'll be able to evaluate any insurance product, no matter what type of policy it is and no matter which company is promoting it.

To illustrate what I mean, let's take the example of a forty-year-old man who is looking for insurance coverage of $100,000. Let's assume his agent brings him three alternative policies. The first is a five-year renewable term-life program to age seventy. Under this type of policy, the premiums increase every five years. The second type of policy is a whole-life arrangement where premiums will have to be paid until the date of death. The premiums are however fixed each year, as is the death benefit. The third type is also a whole-life policy, but it involves higher premium payments and a death benefit which increases each year.

The place to start is with life expectancy. In this case, for a male age forty, we must project payments for thirty-three years. Let's say yearly premiums are paid at the beginning of each year and a reasonable after-tax rate of return on investment capital is 8% a year. *Really, the rate of return you use doesn't make much difference as long as you're consistent and it's reasonable in relation to the prevailing interest rates.* The entire scenario is illustrated in Figure 2.

The first step in the analysis is to determine the present value of the premium costs. The present value of either whole-life policy is easily determined in a one-step calculation. From Table 12, the present value of thirty-three payments of $1 made at the beginning of each year assuming an 8% interest factor is $12.435. Thus, the present value of payments of $1160 and $2610 may be easily calculated.

On the other hand, calculating the present value of the term insurance policy is much more difficult. Essentially, you must first determine the present value of five payments of $430. Table 12 again tells us the factor at 8% interest for five years is 4.312 multiplied by the premium. Next you must determine the present value of five payments of $650 using the same factor (4.312) from Table 12. However, you must *then* take the present value of the five payments of $650 ($2803) *back five years* using Table 3. Similarly, the present value of five payments of $940 must be brought back ten years and the present value of five payments of $1360 must be brought back fifteen years, and so on.

Figure 2
A present value approach to life insurance products (numbers are for illustration only)

Male age 40 *Initial coverage – $100,000* *Years*	*5 Year Renewable Term to Age 70*	*Premium Cost Whole Life Policy – Fixed Death Benefit*	*Whole Life Policy – Increasing Death Benefit*
1– 5	430	1,160	2,610
6–10	650	1,160	2,610
11–15	940	1,160	2,610
16–20	1,360	1,160	2,610
21–25	2,090	1,160	2,610
26–30	3,380	1,160	2,610
Death benefit at age 70 – 1 day	$100,000	$100,000	$278,000
Death benefit at age 70 + 1 day	0	100,000	278,000
Death Benefit at age 73	0	100,000	341,000

Life expectancy from Table 13 is 33 years.
Assume a reasonable after–tax rate of return is 8% per annum and premiums are paid at the beginning of each year.

In the final analysis, the total present value is, as illustrated in Figure 3, $11,546. Also, take a look at Figure 4, which is a time diagram showing exactly what's being done. In each case, you must first determine the present value of five payments and then bring that total figure back to today.

Figure 3
Calculation of the present value cost of term insurance

Annual Premiums	$430	$650	$940	$1,360	$2,090	$3,380
Present value of 5 annual payments factor (Table 12)	4.312	4.312	4.312	4.312	4.312	4.312
Present value end of year	0	5	10	15	20	25
Present value today	$1,854	$2,803	$4,053	$5,864	$9,012	$14,575
(Table 3) factor	1.000	.6806	.4632	.3152	.2145	.1460
Present value $11,546	$1,854	$1,907	$1,877	$1,848	$1,933	$ 2,127

Figure 4
Calculation of the present value (PV) cost of term insurance

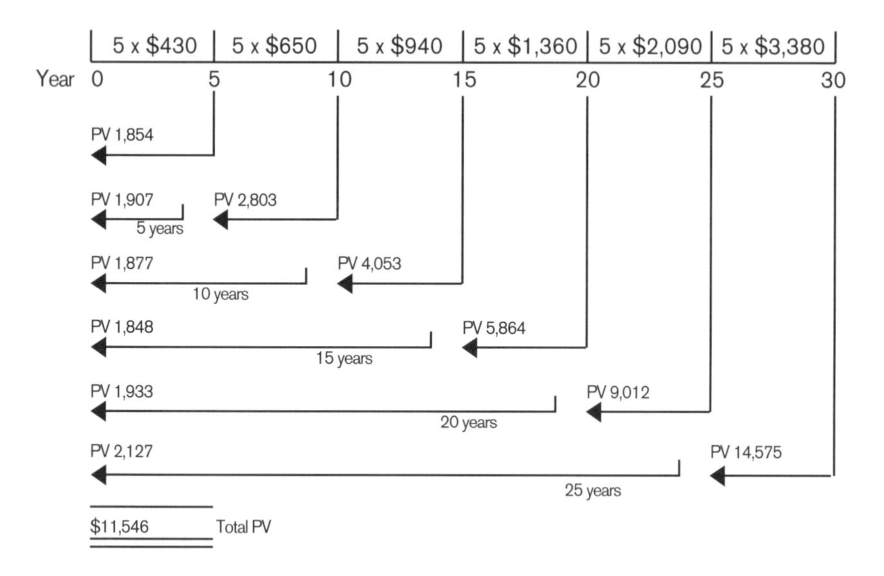

Once you've calculated the present value of the future premiums, the next step is to calculate the present value of the death benefit. This amount can be determined by using Table 3. Take a look at Figure 5.

The present value cost of the term insurance premiums is, as calculated, $11,546. Since the policy expires after thirty years, the present value of the death benefit, thirty-three years down the road, is clearly zero. In other words, if the insured person lives out his normal life expectancy, the net cost of his insurance becomes $11,546. Under the whole-life policy with the fixed benefit, the present value of thirty-three payments of $1160 is $14,424. On the other hand, the present value of the $100,000 death benefit at the end of thirty-three years is only $7890. The difference represents the net cost of insurance.

A comparison of this whole-life policy with the second one, which provides an increasing death benefit, is extremely interesting. On the one hand, the premiums paid are two-and-a-quarter times as high while the death benefit at age seventy-three is 3.41 times as high. Nevertheless, when you apply present value techniques, the difference in cost is less than $1000. In other words, although the estate will wind up with $341,000 instead of $100,000, the deceased will have paid for the extra benefits.

Before leaving this example, however, there's one further possibility that's worth looking into. Let's assume death occurs *one day* before the insured person's seventieth birthday. In other words, just less than thirty years after the policy is taken out.

Figure 5
Calculating the cost of different insurance policies if death occurs at age seventy-three

If Death Occurs After 33 Years (Age 73)	*5 Year Renewable Term Insurance to Age 70*	*Whole Life Policy Fixed Death Benefit*	*Whole Life Policy Increasing Death Benefit*
Present value of insurance premiums as calculated	$11,546		
Present value of 33 payments made at the beginning of each year at 8% interest (Table 12)			
$1,160 x 12.435		$14,424	
$2,610 x 12.435			$32,455
Present value of death benefit payable at the end of 33 years assuming 8% interest			
Policy expires after 30 years	0		
$100,000 x .0789 (Table 3)		7,890	
$341,000 x .0789 (Table 3)			26,905
Net cost of insurance	$11,546	$ 6,534	$ 5,550

If this is the case, the term insurance policy becomes the one that has the smallest cost. Although the present value cost of the premiums hasn't changed, there's suddenly a death benefit of $100,000. In today's money, assuming an 8% interest factor, the present value of this benefit is $9940 and the net cost of insurance becomes only $1606. Since the death benefit is brought three years closer under options two and three, the net cost of insurance is reduced as well. Again, the difference between the two whole-life alternatives is negligible.

In all cases, it becomes clear that life insurance is, as I mentioned previously, a *cost, not an investment.*

On the other hand, before you rush out to cancel your insurance, you must understand that, if the results didn't work out as shown, the insurance companies would all go bankrupt. Any business that pays out more than it takes in goes out of business very quickly.

Why then, would anybody pay out more than what he or she hoped to receive? The answer is, protection. What happens if our hypothetical male age forty dies well before age seventy-three? He would then be paying smaller premiums for each year of decreased life span. Also, his estate would receive the insurance proceeds that much sooner.

On the other hand, if our forty-year-old male *outlives* his normal life expectancy, the cost of insurance becomes even more expensive. This is because he would be paying his premiums for more than thirty-three years and his estate would only receive the death benefit at a later time. The point, however, is that *insurance provides policyholders with protection.*

What if *you* are the one who dies prematurely? What happens if *your* dependents require income at an earlier time than they would if you were to live out your normal life expectancy?

Figure 6
Calculating the cost of different insurance policies if death occurs just before age seventy

If Death Occurs at Age 70 Minus 1 Day (just under 30 years)	*5 Year Renewable Term Insurance to Age 70*	*Whole Life Policy Fixed Death Benefit*	*Whole Life Policy Increasing Death Benefit*
Present value of insurance premiums as calculated	$11,546		
Present value of 30 payments made at the beginning of each year at 8% interest (Table 12)			
$1,160 x 12.158		$14,103	
$2,610 x 12.158			$31,732
Present value of death benefit payable at the end of 30 years (Table 3) assuming 8% interest			
$100,000 x .0994	9,940		
$100,000 x .0994		9,940	
$278,000 x .0994			27,633
Net cost of insurance	$ 1,606	$ 4,163	$ 4,099

How Much Insurance is Enough?

Realizing insurance is a cost, you may decide to "buy term and invest the difference". Buying term insurance at a relatively cheap cost at an early age and investing the difference can be the best move you will ever make—if you *are sure you are going to die younger than most.* However, what happens if you outlive your policy? This too may not be a serious problem if, by that time, you have substantial liquid assets and if the needs of your dependents are more than adequately met from other sources. On the other hand, if you have invested heavily in liquid investments and your family enjoys an expensive lifestyle, term insurance is probably not the answer.

Of course, one of the biggest problems is inflation. If you died today and your spouse inherited perhaps $300,000 of insurance, he or she could take these funds and invest conservatively to earn $20,000 a year before taxes. While your family might be able to live on this income today, what about five years from now, ten years from now or twenty years from now? Again, study Table 3. The present value of $1 due thirty years from now at 8% is only about 10¢.

On the other hand, if you were to carry double the insurance, your premium costs today would also be double. You must ask yourself whether it's worth depriving yourself and your family of disposable income today for the sake of insuring a future. How far you should go to obtain insurance coverage is a matter of personal choice. So sharpen your pencil and weigh the alternatives mathematically.

Summary

By using the present value analysis techniques illustrated in this chapter, it's not only possible to compare different types of policies issued by the same company but also to compare policies issued by different companies. One word of caution is, however, in order. If a policy is structured to provide a specific death benefit and premiums that are not subject to change, the analysis techniques described in this chapter will allow you to determine your cost with no great effort.

However, in many cases, insurance policy premiums and benefits are structured to be flexible. If, for example, interest rates jump drastically, it's possible that an insurance company will pass on the savings. This can be done in the form of either decreased premiums or increased death benefits, or, in fact, a combination of the two. Usually, insurance companies, in making quotations, will specify the rate of return at which their calculations are made. In insurance jargon this is referred to as the "dividend" rate. Obviously, if one company projects a dividend rate of 12%, while another company projects a rate of 17%, the second company's figures will appear much more attractive.

Don't try to compare apples and oranges. What you should do is ask the agent who presented you with the figures to have one insurance company recalculate its numbers using assumptions that are consistent with those made on the other projection. Then, if over the life of the policy the actual results exceed the revised budget, you can only benefit. In other words, there won't be any unpleasant surprises.

Generally, insurance companies tend to be rather competitive. If, after applying present value analysis, you find there are significant differences with respect to net costs, take an hour or so and sit down with your own independent financial advisers. They can help you determine whether your calculations are correct or whether, in fact, an error has been made.

SEVENTEEN

To Lease or Buy—That Is the Question

Not only business owners but all of us in our personal financial planning often have a hard time deciding whether to buy things or lease them. Even with the aid of mathematical analysis, the decision is a tough one because it involves factors beyond dollars and cents.

For example, if you're considering a piece of equipment subject to quick obsolescence, you might be better off with a leasing rather than a purchase arrangement. This is because many leasing companies will allow you to "trade up". Within a business environment, leasing can also be beneficial since it doesn't tie up working capital or a line of credit. Assume, for instance, a small business has a bank line of $75,000 and the owner requires a car which will be used for both business and pleasure. If the car the owner wants costs $15,000, it would probably not be a good idea to tie up 20% of the line of credit in such a purchase. This is especially true since the car will depreciate over time.

On the other hand, consider the case of an individual who has just inherited $200,000. Suppose he or she is very conservative and has most of his or her money tied up in term deposits yielding 7% interest. If this person is considering the alternatives of buying or leasing a $15,000 car, I would generally recommend a purchase. This is because the lease on that vehicle will reflect an interest rate significantly higher than 7%, and one would have to question whether it pays to earn 7% on one investment and pay out perhaps double to carry another.

A further factor to consider is maintenance. Again, my comments here are somewhat subjective, but many people feel a company that leases equipment will tend to provide better service on these properties than if the customer owns. After all, the lessee does have the option of stopping his or her monthly payments (whether or not he or she is legally entitled to do so) if he or she is not satisfied with performance.

Then, of course, we must take income tax implications into account, especially in a business environment. Generally, lease payments are tax-deductible in the same way as office rent, provided any option to buy is reasonable in relation to the anticipated fair market value of the property at the end of the lease period. There is, however, a tax rule in Canada which states if a lease option is exercised and the property is then sold, any gain made is not treated as a capital gain but is fully taxable. This serves to reimburse the government in cases where the initial leasing write-offs were too generous. For example, say that I lease a $15,000 car for my business at $500 a month for three years. Then, I have an option to buy the vehicle for $2000. My business exercises the option and sells the car for $6000. The $4000 gain becomes ordinary income. This is because the business *previously* wrote off *all* of the $500 monthly payments as an expense for tax purposes.

Figure 1
Extract from Canadian capital cost allowance regulations

Description of Property	*First Year Depreciation*	*Subsequent Depreciation*
Furniture and fixtures	10% of cost	20% of undepreciated* capital cost every year thereafter on a declining balance basis
Automobiles**	15% of cost	30% of undepreciated* capital cost every year thereafter on a declining balance basis

* Undepreciated capital cost is cost minus the accumulated depreciation claimed previously
** For acquisitions after August 31, 1989, only the first $24,000 of cost is eligible for capital cost allowance

If depreciable assets are bought for use in a business, interest on money borrowed to fund such purchases is tax-deductible. Then, the cost of the properties can be depreciated in accordance with the capital cost allowance rules. There are, at the time this is being written, forty-three different "classes" of property for Canadian income tax purposes, each with its own unique write-off rules and rates. Since this isn't a book on taxes, Figure 1 only shows two of the more significant rates.

In a real life situation, before making any arithmetic analysis such as those which appear in the rest of this chapter, you would be well advised to contact your accountant, who can give you tax information which is up-to-date and accurate in your circumstances.

Whenever you face a question of buying or leasing, it's important to start with as many hard facts as you possibly can and also try to ensure that your data is comparable. For example, if you're looking to buy property using borrowed funds, ask yourself what rate of interest you will have to pay. Second, don't try to compare the cost of buying a Volkswagen to the cost of leasing a Cadillac. Make sure that you're always talking about identical property, whether it's a car, a piece of computer equipment, a boat or whatever.

The Mathematics Behind Leasing Arrangements

To make calculations involving leasing arrangements, you must always keep in mind the fact that payments will be made at the *beginning* of each period and not at the end. Thus, to evaluate leases, you'll have to rely on two of the tables which were introduced in Chapter Nine. The first is Table 11, which gives you the periodic payments at the beginning of each period required to amortize a loan of $1 over a period of time. This table will help you determine the effective interest rate of the lease.

The second is Table 12, which gives you the value today of a series of payments where the payments start immediately. This table will tell you the present value of your future lease payments.

Let's take a look at a simple example in which you try to determine whether to buy or lease a $15,000 car. We'll first examine this question on the assumption that the car will be used for *personal purposes only*. In other words, tax write-offs will *not* be considered since they would have no relevance. (Later in the chapter, we'll see what happens if the vehicle will be used by someone in a 44% tax bracket who'll be able to claim his or her entire costs for income tax purposes. A practical application would be the purchase or lease of a vehicle by a travelling salesman who has another car which is owned as a pleasure vehicle.)

Assume you are deciding between the purchase or lease of a $15,000 car. If you buy the car, you can obtain a bank loan of $15,000 for a three-year period at 14% interest. Then, after three years, you figure that the car will be worth $6000. This last factor, which is often referred to by accountants as the "residual value", is extremely important. This is because you would always want to determine the real cost of ownership or leasing over a certain specific length of time. Ignoring present value concepts for the moment, what you're really looking at is the purchase of a $15,000 car which can then be sold for $6000 three years from now, giving you a *net cost* of $9000.

Suppose, however, you're offered two alternatives to buying. You can lease an identical car for $400 a month for thirty-six months with an option to buy for $6000, or you can lease for $500 a month for that same thirty-six month period with an option to buy for only $2000.

Figure 2
Case study involving the purchase or lease of a car

Alternative A
Buy a $15,000 car with borrowed funds @ 14%
Pay for it over 3 years and then sell it for $6000
OR
Alternative B
Lease the same car at $400/month for 36 months
With an option to buy for $6000 at the end of this period
OR
Alternative C
Lease the same car at $500/month for 36 months
With an option to buy for $2000 at the end of this period

Before preparing any sophisticated evaluations, you can see that the option to buy for $6000 under the $400 a month lease really has no value. This is because, if you exercise your option and then sell the car for the same amount, the net cost or benefit at that point is zero. On the other hand, if you decide to pay the higher monthly lease payments of $500 a month and then exercise your option to buy for $2000, you'll have a $4000 *profit* at the end of that three-year period. This is because I've assumed the car could then be sold for $6000. The present value of that profit will *decrease* your cost under this second leasing option. The three alternatives are outlined in Figure 2 for your easy reference.

At this point, you should note the operating costs will generally be the same whether you buy or lease. In cases where you lease property and maintenance is included in your monthly payment, you should attempt to subtract the maintenance costs from your figures and deal with the "raw" lease alone. Otherwise, you won't be in a position to compare "apples to apples".

Now let's proceed with our analysis. The first step is to determine the actual cost of ownership in today's dollars.

The cost to buy the car is, of course, $15,000. But this is before considering the trade-in value in three years. If we assume a 14% interest rate, the present value of $6000 due at the end of three years can be determined from Table 3: $6000 x .6750, or $4050. Thus, the actual cost of buying the car in today's dollars is, as calculated in Figure 3, $10,950.

Figure 3
Calculating the present value cost of buying a car

Present value of original cost	$15,000
Less: Present value of selling price in three years @ 14% ($6000 x .6750)	4,050
Net present value cost	$10,950

Under the second alternative, the same car can be leased for $400 a month with payments starting immediately for a thirty-six month period. From Table 12, we learn that the present value of $400 per month for thirty-six months (at the 14% rate it would cost you to borrow it) is: $400 x 29.600, or $11,840. Here, we don't have to be concerned with the present value of the option to buy. This is because the option to buy is for the same price as the anticipated selling price at the end of three years. In other words, if the car were bought for $6000 at that time, it could then be sold immediately for the same price. There would be no profit then, and, of course, the present value of a zero profit three years from now is zero.

The third alternative, however, is more interesting. In this case, the choice is to pay $500 a month for thirty-six months. The present value of this cash outflow can also be calculated (using a 14% rate) from Table 12 as $500 x 29.600. The cost here is $14,800 in today's dollars. On the other hand, at the end of three years there is a benefit. If you take this last option, you could buy the car for $2000 and sell it for $6000. In other words, there is a profit of $4000 three years down the road. If we assume the prevailing interest rate is still 14% (so that's what money is worth) and use Table 3, the present value of $4000 in three years is $4000 x .675, or $2700. The net cost under Alternative C is therefore $14,800 minus $2700 or $12,100. Thus, Alternative A ($10,950) is the cheapest, Alternative B ($11,840) comes second and Alternative C ($12,100) is third.

However, before making any final decisions, please keep in mind that the numbers used in these examples are purely hypothetical. Also, it would pay to reread the beginning of this chapter, since there are so many variables that should be taken into account in any specific situation. For example, do you really want to tie up a line of credit at your bank for the sake of only a few hundred dollars?

What is the Interest Rate?

Very often, you'll find yourself in the position where you are given a quotation on a lease and you're curious as to what the interest rate is. Let's take the previous example and continue with it. You've just calculated that if you bought a particular car for $15,000 which would be worth $6000 at the end of three years, your present value cost is $10,950. What then is the interest cost built into a lease of $400 a month for thirty-six months with the same option to buy?

For all intents and purposes, what you would be doing is paying off a $10,950 cost over thirty-six months at $400 a month. The monthly factor is $400 divided by $10,950 = 0.0365. Now turn to Table 11. This table shows you the required payments beginning immediately which will amortize a loan of $1 over a period of time. Look through the table and try to find the monthly payment needed to discharge a loan of $1 over three years at various rates of interest. You'll see that the factor (on page 225) for 18% is 0.0356. Thus, for all intents and purposes, you can conclude that the interest rate built into the lease in my hypothetical example, is slightly in excess of 18%.

Be very careful when you apply Table 11. Remember that *your lease payments don't usually amortize the full cost of the property you are leasing.* There is usually a buy-out option at the end, and thus, what your lease payments are doing is amortizing *the price minus the present value of that future buy-out option.* In the previous case study, the $400 monthly payments amortized a cost of $10,950, not $15,000.

Taking Income Tax Implications Into Account

Now, let's see what happens if the person who will use the leased or purchased vehicle is in a position to treat the property as a business asset. If the car is leased, the monthly rent of $400 (using the figures in Alternative B) will be tax-deductible. If the car is purchased, capital cost allowance can be taken and the interest becomes deductible as well.

Before we can prepare an investment analysis form to cover this situation, we must first prepare a loan amortization schedule and a capital cost allowance schedule. These factors are important because, without them, we can't determine after-tax cash flows under the purchase option.

From Table 5, we see that the monthly payments required to amortize a loan of $15,000 over three years at 14% are $15,000 x .0342, or $513 a month. The annual payments are therefore $513 x 12, or $6156. The table in Figure 4 shows the breakdown over the three-year period between interest and principal payments. You'll note at the end of the first year, 71.1% of the principal is still outstanding. Then, at the end of the second year, 37.9% of the original loan is still owing, while, at the end of the third year, the balance is zero.

Figure 4
Periodic payments to amortize a loan of $15,000 over three years at 14%

Monthly Payments: $15,000 x .0342 (Table 5) = $513
Annual Payments: $513 x 12 = $6,156

Year	*Loan Beginning of Year*	*Loan End of Year*	*Principal*	*Interest*
1	$15,000	.711 x $15,000 = $10,665	$4,335	$1,821
2	10,665	.379 x 15,000 = 5,685	4,980	1,176
3	5,685	.000 x 15,000 = 0	5,685	471

Space doesn't permit me to include all conceivable math tables in this book. Table 8 shows the balance outstanding each year on twenty-five-year Canadian mortgage loans but this table cannot be used for our purposes here. This is because we're dealing with a three-year loan only. If necessary, you could get the principal and interest breakdowns from your lending institution at the time you make your application for financing. Alternatively, if the loan is of short duration, you could take the interest evenly throughout the period or make a reasonable attempt to apportion it. The differences should not be that significant.

Next, in Figure 5 we calculate the capital cost allowance for each year using the formula provided on page 117.

You can see that, after normal capital cost allowances, there's still an undepreciated balance of $6,248 at the end of the third year. If the car is then sold for $6,000 and no other vehicle is purchased, the remaining $248 balance becomes a tax write-off. This is because the actual depreciation is a bit larger than the depreciation previously allowed for income tax purposes.

Now we are ready to tackle the investment analysis form in Figure 6.

Under the purchase option, the interest on the loan over a three-year period is a tax-deductible expenditure along with capital cost allowance.

Figure 5
Calculation of capital cost allowance (tax depreciation) on an automobile

Original cost	$15,000	
CCA–Year 1	2,250	$15,000 x 15%
	12,750	
CCA–Year 2	3,825	$12,750 x 30%
	8,925	
CCA–Year 3	2,677	$8,925 x 30%
	6,248	
Selling price	(6,000)	
Additional tax write–off in Year 3	$ 248	

Figure 6
Investment analysis form to compare ownership vs. leasing

Option 1: Purchase	*Year 1*	*Year 2*	*Year 3*
Interest on loan to acquire property	(1,821)	(1,176)	(471)
Capital cost allowance	(2,250)	(3,825)	(2,925)
Deductible expenditures for tax purposes	(4,071)	(5,001)	(3,396)
Tax savings in 44% bracket	1,791	2,200	1,494
Net after–tax cost	(2,280)	(2,801)	(1,902)
Less: Capital cost allowance	2,250	3,825	2,925
	(30)	1,024	1,023
Principal payments on debt	(4,335)	(4,980)	(5,685)
Selling price			6,000
Less: tax on recaptured depreciation			-
	(4,365)	(3,956)	1,338
Required rate of return 14%			
Present value factor (Table 3)	.877	.770	.675
Present value cost $(5,971)	(3,828)	(3,046)	903

Option 2: Lease			
Lease payments	(4,800)	(4,800)	(4,800)
Less: Tax savings thereon (44%)	2,112	2,112	2,112
Net after–tax cost	(2,688)	(2,688)	(2,688)
Option price			(6,000)
Selling price			6,000
			(2,688)
Required rate of return 14%			
Present value factor (Table 3)	.877	.770	.675
Present value cost $(6,241)	(2,357)	(2,070)	(1,814)

From a cash-flow standpoint, the tax saving represents a cash in-flow. Notice the net after-tax cost of ownership is *decreased* by the capital cost allowance, which doesn't represent an outflow of funds. The cash outflows are, however, increased by the principal payments on the debt, in this case $15,000 over three years. At the end of the third year, there is one further in-flow, which is the proceeds from sale. In this example, there is no recaptured depreciation. If we assume the prevailing interest rate is 14%, the present value of the two outflows and the positive cash flow in year three represents a negative amount of $5971. *This is the cost of ownership in today's dollars.*

In the example on page 119, the cost of ownership was calculated at $10,950. Why the difference? *This is because the last series of calculations takes into account the tax benefits from deducting interest and capital cost allowance. This reduces the cost of ownership by almost half.*

Now, let's consider the lease. This involves a relatively straightforward set of calculations. The lease payments in all three years are tax-deductible, which means that the net cost becomes only 56% (100% – 44% tax savings). Applying the same present value factors, we can see that the present value cost of leasing in this example is virtually identical to the cost of ownership ($5971 versus $6241). In other words, the tax advantages of leasing pretty well offset the results of the first analysis on pages 118 and 119, which showed that the net present cost of leasing was more expensive where there are no tax write-offs. This is why you must always prepare a detailed analysis before you can decide which alternative to choose.

Summary

Deciding whether to lease or buy is a difficult task. However, no matter how complex the arrangement might initially seem to be, if you keep your wits about you and go slowly, you can make an intelligent comparison. But you won't know until you try. Keep this book with you and use it before making any business or investment financing decision. You'll find that the procedures I've illustrated can be adapted to help you manage your money and make it grow.

TABLES

TABLE 1

The compound amount of $1

What is $1 invested today worth at some time in the future at various interest rates if interest is calculated at the end of each month, quarterly, semi-annually, or annually?

Applications

Chapter Two

- Compound interest calculations
- What will $1 invested today be worth at some time in the future?
- If you lend $1 to someone else at various interest rates, how much will he or she have to pay you as a single lump sum sometime in the future?
- By how much must an investment appreciate over a period of time to give you a required rate of return?
- What will the price of an item be after various time periods assuming different rates of inflation?
- How much can you expect to be earning if you are given percentage salary increases over various time periods?

Chapter Eleven

- What will a real estate property be worth in the future if it appreciates by a certain percentage each year?

The compound amount of $1

End of Year	3% Interest compounded Monthly	Quarterly	Semi-Annually	Annually	4% Interest compounded Monthly	Quarterly	Semi-Annually	Annually
1	1.030	1.030	1.030	1.030	1.041	1.041	1.040	1.040
2	1.062	1.062	1.061	1.061	1.083	1.083	1.082	1.082
3	1.094	1.094	1.093	1.093	1.127	1.127	1.126	1.125
4	1.127	1.127	1.126	1.126	1.173	1.173	1.172	1.170
5	1.162	1.161	1.161	1.159	1.221	1.220	1.219	1.217
6	1.197	1.196	1.196	1.194	1.271	1.270	1.268	1.265
7	1.233	1.233	1.232	1.230	1.323	1.321	1.319	1.316
8	1.271	1.270	1.269	1.267	1.376	1.375	1.373	1.369
9	1.310	1.309	1.307	1.305	1.432	1.431	1.428	1.423
10	1.349	1.348	1.347	1.344	1.491	1.489	1.486	1.480
11	1.390	1.389	1.388	1.384	1.552	1.549	1.546	1.539
12	1.433	1.431	1.430	1.426	1.615	1.612	1.608	1.601
13	1.476	1.475	1.473	1.469	1.681	1.678	1.673	1.665
14	1.521	1.520	1.517	1.513	1.749	1.746	1.741	1.732
15	1.567	1.566	1.563	1.558	1.820	1.817	1.811	1.801
16	1.615	1.613	1.610	1.605	1.894	1.890	1.885	1.873
17	1.664	1.662	1.659	1.653	1.972	1.967	1.961	1.948
18	1.715	1.713	1.709	1.702	2.052	2.047	2.040	2.026
19	1.767	1.765	1.761	1.754	2.136	2.130	2.122	2.107
20	1.821	1.818	1.814	1.806	2.223	2.217	2.208	2.191
21	1.876	1.873	1.869	1.860	2.313	2.307	2.297	2.279
22	1.933	1.930	1.925	1.916	2.407	2.400	2.390	2.370
23	1.992	1.989	1.984	1.974	2.505	2.498	2.487	2.465
24	2.053	2.049	2.043	2.033	2.608	2.599	2.587	2.563
25	2.115	2.111	2.105	2.094	2.714	2.705	2.692	2.666
26	2.179	2.175	2.169	2.157	2.824	2.815	2.800	2.772
27	2.246	2.241	2.234	2.221	2.939	2.929	2.913	2.883
28	2.314	2.309	2.302	2.288	3.059	3.048	3.031	2.999
29	2.384	2.379	2.372	2.357	3.184	3.172	3.154	3.119
30	2.457	2.451	2.443	2.427	3.313	3.300	3.281	3.243
31	2.532	2.526	2.517	2.500	3.448	3.434	3.414	3.373
32	2.609	2.602	2.593	2.575	3.589	3.574	3.551	3.508
33	2.688	2.681	2.672	2.652	3.735	3.719	3.695	3.648
34	2.770	2.763	2.752	2.732	3.887	3.870	3.844	3.794
35	2.854	2.846	2.835	2.814	4.046	4.027	4.000	3.946
36	2.941	2.933	2.921	2.898	4.211	4.191	4.161	4.104
37	3.030	3.022	3.009	2.985	4.382	4.361	4.329	4.268
38	3.122	3.113	3.100	3.075	4.561	4.538	4.504	4.439
39	3.217	3.208	3.194	3.167	4.746	4.722	4.686	4.616
40	3.315	3.305	3.291	3.262	4.940	4.914	4.875	4.801
41	3.416	3.406	3.390	3.360	5.141	5.113	5.072	4.993
42	3.520	3.509	3.493	3.461	5.351	5.321	5.277	5.193
43	3.627	3.615	3.598	3.565	5.569	5.537	5.491	5.400
44	3.737	3.725	3.707	3.671	5.795	5.762	5.712	5.617
45	3.851	3.838	3.819	3.782	6.032	5.996	5.943	5.841
46	3.968	3.954	3.934	3.895	6.277	6.239	6.183	6.075
47	4.089	4.074	4.053	4.012	6.533	6.493	6.433	6.318
48	4.213	4.198	4.176	4.132	6.799	6.756	6.693	6.571
49	4.341	4.325	4.302	4.256	7.076	7.031	6.963	6.833
50	4.473	4.457	4.432	4.384	7.365	7.316	7.245	7.107

The compound amount of $1

End of Year	5% Interest compounded Monthly	Quarterly	Semi-Annually	Annually	6% Interest compounded Monthly	Quarterly	Semi-Annually	Annually
1	1.051	1.051	1.051	1.050	1.062	1.061	1.061	1.060
2	1.105	1.104	1.104	1.103	1.127	1.126	1.126	1.124
3	1.161	1.161	1.160	1.158	1.197	1.196	1.194	1.191
4	1.221	1.220	1.218	1.216	1.270	1.269	1.267	1.262
5	1.283	1.282	1.280	1.276	1.349	1.347	1.344	1.338
6	1.349	1.347	1.345	1.340	1.432	1.430	1.426	1.419
7	1.418	1.416	1.413	1.407	1.520	1.517	1.513	1.504
8	1.491	1.488	1.485	1.477	1.614	1.610	1.605	1.594
9	1.567	1.564	1.560	1.551	1.714	1.709	1.702	1.689
10	1.647	1.644	1.639	1.629	1.819	1.814	1.806	1.791
11	1.731	1.727	1.722	1.710	1.932	1.925	1.916	1.898
12	1.820	1.815	1.809	1.796	2.051	2.043	2.033	2.012
13	1.913	1.908	1.900	1.886	2.177	2.169	2.157	2.133
14	2.011	2.005	1.996	1.980	2.312	2.302	2.288	2.261
15	2.114	2.107	2.098	2.079	2.454	2.443	2.427	2.397
16	2.222	2.215	2.204	2.183	2.605	2.593	2.575	2.540
17	2.336	2.327	2.315	2.292	2.766	2.752	2.732	2.693
18	2.455	2.446	2.433	2.407	2.937	2.921	2.898	2.854
19	2.581	2.571	2.556	2.527	3.118	3.100	3.075	3.026
20	2.713	2.701	2.685	2.653	3.310	3.291	3.262	3.207
21	2.851	2.839	2.821	2.786	3.514	3.493	3.461	3.400
22	2.997	2.984	2.964	2.925	3.731	3.707	3.671	3.604
23	3.151	3.136	3.114	3.072	3.961	3.934	3.895	3.820
24	3.312	3.296	3.271	3.225	4.206	4.176	4.132	4.049
25	3.481	3.463	3.437	3.386	4.465	4.432	4.384	4.292
26	3.659	3.640	3.611	3.556	4.740	4.704	4.651	4.549
27	3.847	3.825	3.794	3.733	5.033	4.993	4.934	4.822
28	4.043	4.020	3.986	3.920	5.343	5.299	5.235	5.112
29	4.250	4.225	4.188	4.116	5.673	5.624	5.553	5.418
30	4.468	4.440	4.400	4.322	6.023	5.969	5.892	5.743
31	4.696	4.666	4.623	4.538	6.394	6.336	6.250	6.088
32	4.937	4.904	4.857	4.765	6.788	6.724	6.631	6.453
33	5.189	5.154	5.102	5.003	7.207	7.137	7.035	6.841
34	5.455	5.417	5.361	5.253	7.652	7.575	7.463	7.251
35	5.734	5.693	5.632	5.516	8.124	8.040	7.918	7.686
36	6.027	5.983	5.917	5.792	8.625	8.533	8.400	8.147
37	6.335	6.287	6.217	6.081	9.157	9.057	8.912	8.636
38	6.660	6.608	6.532	6.385	9.721	9.613	9.454	9.154
39	7.000	6.944	6.862	6.705	10.321	10.202	10.030	9.704
40	7.358	7.298	7.210	7.040	10.957	10.828	10.641	10.286
41	7.735	7.670	7.575	7.392	11.633	11.493	11.289	10.903
42	8.131	8.061	7.958	7.762	12.351	12.198	11.976	11.557
43	8.547	8.471	8.361	8.150	13.113	12.947	12.706	12.250
44	8.984	8.903	8.784	8.557	13.921	13.741	13.480	12.985
45	9.443	9.356	9.229	8.985	14.780	14.584	14.300	13.765
46	9.927	9.833	9.696	9.434	15.692	15.479	15.171	14.590
47	10.435	10.334	10.187	9.906	16.659	16.429	16.095	15.466
48	10.968	10.860	10.703	10.401	17.687	17.437	17.076	16.394
49	11.530	11.414	11.244	10.921	18.778	18.507	18.115	17.378
50	12.119	11.995	11.814	11.467	19.936	19.643	19.219	18.420

The compound amount of $1

End of Year	7% Interest compounded Monthly	Quarterly	Semi-Annually	Annually	8% Interest compounded Monthly	Quarterly	Semi-Annually	Annually
1	1.072	1.072	1.071	1.070	1.083	1.082	1.082	1.080
2	1.150	1.149	1.148	1.145	1.173	1.172	1.170	1.166
3	1.233	1.231	1.229	1.225	1.270	1.268	1.265	1.260
4	1.322	1.320	1.317	1.311	1.376	1.373	1.369	1.360
5	1.418	1.415	1.411	1.403	1.490	1.486	1.480	1.469
6	1.520	1.516	1.511	1.501	1.614	1.608	1.601	1.587
7	1.630	1.625	1.619	1.606	1.747	1.741	1.732	1.714
8	1.748	1.742	1.734	1.718	1.892	1.885	1.873	1.851
9	1.874	1.867	1.857	1.838	2.050	2.040	2.026	1.999
10	2.010	2.002	1.990	1.967	2.220	2.208	2.191	2.159
11	2.155	2.145	2.132	2.105	2.404	2.390	2.370	2.332
12	2.311	2.300	2.283	2.252	2.603	2.587	2.563	2.518
13	2.478	2.465	2.446	2.410	2.819	2.800	2.772	2.720
14	2.657	2.642	2.620	2.579	3.053	3.031	2.999	2.937
15	2.849	2.832	2.807	2.759	3.307	3.281	3.243	3.172
16	3.055	3.035	3.007	2.952	3.581	3.551	3.508	3.426
17	3.276	3.253	3.221	3.159	3.879	3.844	3.794	3.700
18	3.513	3.487	3.450	3.380	4.201	4.161	4.104	3.996
19	3.766	3.738	3.696	3.617	4.549	4.504	4.439	4.316
20	4.039	4.006	3.959	3.870	4.927	4.875	4.801	4.661
21	4.331	4.294	4.241	4.141	5.336	5.277	5.193	5.034
22	4.644	4.603	4.543	4.430	5.779	5.712	5.617	5.437
23	4.979	4.934	4.867	4.741	6.258	6.183	6.075	5.871
24	5.339	5.288	5.214	5.072	6.778	6.693	6.571	6.341
25	5.725	5.668	5.585	5.427	7.340	7.245	7.107	6.848
26	6.139	6.075	5.983	5.807	7.949	7.842	7.687	7.396
27	6.583	6.512	6.409	6.214	8.609	8.488	8.314	7.988
28	7.059	6.980	6.865	6.649	9.324	9.188	8.992	8.627
29	7.569	7.482	7.354	7.114	10.098	9.945	9.726	9.317
30	8.116	8.019	7.878	7.612	10.936	10.765	10.520	10.063
31	8.703	8.595	8.439	8.145	11.843	11.653	11.378	10.868
32	9.332	9.213	9.040	8.715	12.826	12.613	12.306	11.737
33	10.007	9.875	9.684	9.325	13.891	13.653	13.311	12.676
34	10.730	10.585	10.374	9.978	15.044	14.778	14.397	13.690
35	11.506	11.345	11.113	10.677	16.293	15.996	15.572	14.785
36	12.338	12.161	11.904	11.424	17.645	17.315	16.842	15.968
37	13.230	13.034	12.752	12.224	19.109	18.742	18.217	17.246
38	14.186	13.971	13.660	13.079	20.695	20.287	19.703	18.625
39	15.212	14.975	14.633	13.995	22.413	21.960	21.311	20.115
40	16.311	16.051	15.676	14.974	24.273	23.770	23.050	21.725
41	17.491	17.205	16.792	16.023	26.288	25.729	24.931	23.462
42	18.755	18.441	17.988	17.144	28.470	27.850	26.965	25.339
43	20.111	19.766	19.269	18.344	30.833	30.146	29.165	27.367
44	21.565	21.186	20.642	19.628	33.392	32.631	31.545	29.556
45	23.123	22.709	22.112	21.002	36.164	35.321	34.119	31.920
46	24.795	24.341	23.687	22.473	39.165	38.232	36.903	34.474
47	26.588	26.090	25.374	24.046	42.416	41.384	39.915	37.232
48	28.510	27.965	27.182	25.729	45.936	44.795	43.172	40.211
49	30.570	29.974	29.118	27.530	49.749	48.488	46.695	43.427
50	32.780	32.128	31.191	29.457	53.878	52.485	50.505	46.902

The compound amount of $1

End of Year	9% Interest compounded Monthly	Quarterly	Semi-Annually	Annually	10% Interest compounded Monthly	Quarterly	Semi-Annually	Annually
1	1.094	1.093	1.092	1.090	1.105	1.104	1.103	1.100
2	1.196	1.195	1.193	1.188	1.220	1.218	1.216	1.210
3	1.309	1.306	1.302	1.295	1.348	1.345	1.340	1.331
4	1.431	1.428	1.422	1.412	1.489	1.485	1.477	1.464
5	1.566	1.561	1.553	1.539	1.645	1.639	1.629	1.611
6	1.713	1.706	1.696	1.677	1.818	1.809	1.796	1.772
7	1.873	1.865	1.852	1.828	2.008	1.996	1.980	1.949
8	2.049	2.038	2.022	1.993	2.218	2.204	2.183	2.144
9	2.241	2.228	2.208	2.172	2.450	2.433	2.407	2.358
10	2.451	2.435	2.412	2.367	2.707	2.685	2.653	2.594
11	2.681	2.662	2.634	2.580	2.991	2.964	2.925	2.853
12	2.933	2.910	2.876	2.813	3.304	3.271	3.225	3.138
13	3.208	3.180	3.141	3.066	3.650	3.611	3.556	3.452
14	3.509	3.477	3.430	3.342	4.032	3.986	3.920	3.797
15	3.838	3.800	3.745	3.642	4.454	4.400	4.322	4.177
16	4.198	4.154	4.090	3.970	4.920	4.857	4.765	4.595
17	4.592	4.541	4.466	4.328	5.436	5.361	5.253	5.054
18	5.023	4.963	4.877	4.717	6.005	5.917	5.792	5.560
19	5.494	5.425	5.326	5.142	6.633	6.532	6.385	6.116
20	6.009	5.930	5.816	5.604	7.328	7.210	7.040	6.727
21	6.573	6.482	6.352	6.109	8.095	7.958	7.762	7.400
22	7.189	7.086	6.936	6.659	8.943	8.784	8.557	8.140
23	7.864	7.745	7.574	7.258	9.880	9.696	9.434	8.954
24	8.602	8.466	8.271	7.911	10.914	10.703	10.401	9.850
25	9.408	9.254	9.033	8.623	12.057	11.814	11.467	10.835
26	10.291	10.115	9.864	9.399	13.319	13.040	12.643	11.918
27	11.256	11.057	10.772	10.245	14.714	14.394	13.939	13.110
28	12.312	12.086	11.763	11.167	16.255	15.888	15.367	14.421
29	13.467	13.211	12.845	12.172	17.957	17.538	16.943	15.863
30	14.731	14.441	14.027	13.268	19.837	19.358	18.679	17.449
31	16.112	15.785	15.318	14.462	21.915	21.368	20.594	19.194
32	17.624	17.255	16.728	15.763	24.209	23.586	22.705	21.114
33	19.277	18.861	18.267	17.182	26.744	26.035	25.032	23.225
34	21.085	20.616	19.948	18.728	29.545	28.737	27.598	25.548
35	23.063	22.535	21.784	20.414	32.639	31.721	30.426	28.102
36	25.227	24.633	23.789	22.251	36.056	35.014	33.545	30.913
37	27.593	26.926	25.978	24.254	39.832	38.648	36.984	34.004
38	30.182	29.432	28.369	26.437	44.003	42.661	40.774	37.404
39	33.013	32.172	30.979	28.816	48.611	47.089	44.954	41.145
40	36.110	35.167	33.830	31.409	53.701	51.978	49.561	45.259
41	39.497	38.440	36.943	34.236	59.324	57.374	54.641	49.785
42	43.202	42.018	40.343	37.318	65.536	63.330	60.242	54.764
43	47.255	45.929	44.056	40.676	72.398	69.904	66.417	60.240
44	51.688	50.205	48.110	44.337	79.979	77.161	73.225	66.264
45	56.537	54.878	52.537	48.327	88.354	85.172	80.730	72.890
46	61.840	59.986	57.372	52.677	97.606	94.014	89.005	80.180
47	67.641	65.570	62.651	57.418	107.827	103.774	98.128	88.197
48	73.986	71.673	68.417	62.585	119.118	114.547	108.186	97.017
49	80.927	78.345	74.713	68.218	131.591	126.438	119.276	106.719
50	88.518	85.637	81.589	74.358	145.370	139.564	131.501	117.391

The compound amount of $1

End of Year	11% Interest compounded Monthly	Quarterly	Semi-Annually	Annually	12% Interest compounded Monthly	Quarterly	Semi-Annually	Annually
1	1.116	1.115	1.113	1.110	1.127	1.126	1.124	1.120
2	1.245	1.242	1.239	1.232	1.270	1.267	1.262	1.254
3	1.389	1.385	1.379	1.368	1.431	1.426	1.419	1.405
4	1.550	1.544	1.535	1.518	1.612	1.605	1.594	1.574
5	1.729	1.720	1.708	1.685	1.817	1.806	1.791	1.762
6	1.929	1.918	1.901	1.870	2.047	2.033	2.012	1.974
7	2.152	2.137	2.116	2.076	2.307	2.288	2.261	2.211
8	2.401	2.382	2.355	2.305	2.599	2.575	2.540	2.476
9	2.679	2.655	2.621	2.558	2.929	2.898	2.854	2.773
10	2.989	2.960	2.918	2.839	3.300	3.262	3.207	3.106
11	3.335	3.299	3.248	3.152	3.719	3.671	3.604	3.479
12	3.721	3.677	3.615	3.498	4.191	4.132	4.049	3.896
13	4.152	4.099	4.023	3.883	4.722	4.651	4.549	4.363
14	4.632	4.569	4.478	4.310	5.321	5.235	5.112	4.887
15	5.168	5.092	4.984	4.785	5.996	5.892	5.743	5.474
16	5.766	5.676	5.547	5.311	6.756	6.631	6.453	6.130
17	6.433	6.327	6.174	5.895	7.613	7.463	7.251	6.866
18	7.178	7.052	6.872	6.544	8.579	8.400	8.147	7.690
19	8.008	7.860	7.649	7.263	9.667	9.454	9.154	8.613
20	8.935	8.761	8.513	8.062	10.893	10.641	10.286	9.646
21	9.969	9.765	9.476	8.949	12.274	11.976	11.557	10.804
22	11.123	10.884	10.546	9.934	13.831	13.480	12.985	12.100
23	12.410	12.132	11.739	11.026	15.585	15.171	14.590	13.552
24	13.846	13.522	13.065	12.239	17.561	17.076	16.394	15.179
25	15.448	15.072	14.542	13.585	19.788	19.219	18.420	17.000
26	17.236	16.800	16.186	15.080	22.298	21.631	20.697	19.040
27	19.230	18.726	18.015	16.739	25.126	24.346	23.255	21.325
28	21.455	20.872	20.051	18.580	28.313	27.401	26.129	23.884
29	23.938	23.264	22.317	20.624	31.903	30.840	29.359	26.750
30	26.708	25.931	24.840	22.892	35.950	34.711	32.988	29.960
31	29.799	28.903	27.647	25.410	40.509	39.068	37.065	33.555
32	33.247	32.216	30.772	28.206	45.647	43.971	41.646	37.582
33	37.094	35.909	34.250	31.308	51.436	49.490	46.794	42.092
34	41.387	40.025	38.121	34.752	57.959	55.701	52.577	47.143
35	46.176	44.612	42.430	38.575	65.310	62.692	59.076	52.800
36	51.519	49.726	47.226	42.818	73.592	70.560	66.378	59.136
37	57.481	55.426	52.563	47.528	82.926	79.416	74.582	66.232
38	64.133	61.779	58.504	52.756	93.443	89.384	83.800	74.180
39	71.554	68.860	65.117	58.559	105.294	100.602	94.158	83.081
40	79.834	76.753	72.476	65.001	118.648	113.229	105.796	93.051
41	89.073	85.550	80.668	72.151	133.695	127.440	118.872	104.217
42	99.380	95.356	89.786	80.088	150.651	143.435	133.565	116.723
43	110.880	106.286	99.934	88.897	169.757	161.437	150.074	130.730
44	123.711	118.468	111.229	98.676	191.287	181.699	168.623	146.418
45	138.027	132.047	123.800	109.530	215.547	204.503	189.465	163.988
46	153.999	147.183	137.793	121.579	242.884	230.170	212.882	183.666
47	171.820	164.053	153.367	134.952	273.687	259.059	239.195	205.706
48	191.703	182.857	170.701	149.797	308.398	291.573	268.759	230.391
49	213.887	203.816	189.995	166.275	347.510	328.168	301.978	258.038
50	238.637	227.178	211.469	184.565	391.583	369.356	339.302	289.002

The compound amount of $1

End of Year	13% Interest compounded Monthly	Quarterly	Semi-Annually	Annually	14% Interest compounded Monthly	Quarterly	Semi-Annually	Annually
1	1.138	1.136	1.134	1.130	1.149	1.148	1.145	1.140
2	1.295	1.292	1.286	1.277	1.321	1.317	1.311	1.300
3	1.474	1.468	1.459	1.443	1.518	1.511	1.501	1.482
4	1.677	1.668	1.655	1.630	1.745	1.734	1.718	1.689
5	1.909	1.896	1.877	1.842	2.006	1.990	1.967	1.925
6	2.172	2.155	2.129	2.082	2.305	2.283	2.252	2.195
7	2.472	2.449	2.415	2.353	2.649	2.620	2.579	2.502
8	2.813	2.783	2.739	2.658	3.045	3.007	2.952	2.853
9	3.202	3.163	3.107	3.004	3.500	3.450	3.380	3.252
10	3.644	3.594	3.524	3.395	4.022	3.959	3.870	3.707
11	4.147	4.085	3.997	3.836	4.623	4.543	4.430	4.226
12	4.719	4.642	4.533	4.335	5.314	5.214	5.072	4.818
13	5.370	5.276	5.141	4.898	6.107	5.983	5.807	5.492
14	6.112	5.996	5.832	5.535	7.019	6.865	6.649	6.261
15	6.955	6.814	6.614	6.254	8.068	7.878	7.612	7.138
16	7.915	7.744	7.502	7.067	9.272	9.040	8.715	8.137
17	9.008	8.801	8.509	7.986	10.657	10.374	9.978	9.276
18	10.251	10.002	9.651	9.024	12.249	11.904	11.424	10.575
19	11.666	11.367	10.947	10.197	14.078	13.660	13.079	12.056
20	13.277	12.918	12.416	11.523	16.180	15.676	14.974	13.743
21	15.109	14.681	14.083	13.021	18.597	17.988	17.144	15.668
22	17.195	16.685	15.973	14.714	21.374	20.642	19.628	17.861
23	19.568	18.962	18.117	16.627	24.566	23.687	22.473	20.362
24	22.270	21.550	20.549	18.788	28.235	27.182	25.729	23.212
25	25.343	24.491	23.307	21.231	32.451	31.191	29.457	26.462
26	28.842	27.833	26.435	23.991	37.298	35.793	33.725	30.167
27	32.823	31.632	29.983	27.109	42.868	41.073	38.612	34.390
28	37.353	35.949	34.008	30.633	49.270	47.132	44.207	39.204
29	42.509	40.855	38.572	34.616	56.628	54.085	50.613	44.693
30	48.377	46.431	43.750	39.116	65.085	62.064	57.946	50.950
31	55.055	52.768	49.622	44.201	74.805	71.220	66.343	58.083
32	62.654	59.969	56.283	49.947	85.976	81.727	75.956	66.215
33	71.302	68.153	63.837	56.440	98.816	93.783	86.962	75.485
34	81.144	77.455	72.406	63.777	113.573	107.619	99.563	86.053
35	92.345	88.025	82.124	72.069	130.534	123.495	113.989	98.100
36	105.092	100.039	93.148	81.437	150.029	141.713	130.506	111.834
37	119.598	113.692	105.650	92.024	172.434	162.619	149.417	127.491
38	136.106	129.208	119.831	103.987	198.186	186.609	171.067	145.340
39	154.893	146.842	135.916	117.506	227.783	214.138	195.855	165.687
40	176.273	166.882	154.159	132.782	261.801	245.729	224.234	188.884
41	200.605	189.657	174.851	150.043	300.899	281.979	256.726	215.327
42	228.295	215.541	198.320	169.549	345.836	323.578	293.926	245.473
43	259.807	244.957	224.940	191.590	397.484	371.313	336.515	279.839
44	295.668	278.388	255.132	216.497	456.845	426.090	385.276	319.017
45	336.480	316.381	289.377	244.641	525.071	488.948	441.103	363.679
46	382.925	359.560	328.219	276.445	603.486	561.079	505.019	414.594
47	435.782	408.631	372.274	312.383	693.612	643.852	578.196	472.637
48	495.934	464.399	422.243	352.992	797.197	738.834	661.977	538.807
49	564.389	527.779	478.918	398.881	916.252	847.830	757.897	614.239
50	642.293	599.808	543.201	450.736	1053.087	972.904	867.716	700.233

The compound amount of $1

End of Year	15% Interest compounded Monthly	Quarterly	Semi-Annually	Annually	16% Interest compounded Monthly	Quarterly	Semi-Annually	Annually
1	1.161	1.159	1.156	1.150	1.172	1.170	1.166	1.160
2	1.347	1.342	1.335	1.323	1.374	1.369	1.360	1.346
3	1.564	1.555	1.543	1.521	1.611	1.601	1.587	1.561
4	1.815	1.802	1.783	1.749	1.888	1.873	1.851	1.811
5	2.107	2.088	2.061	2.011	2.214	2.191	2.159	2.100
6	2.446	2.419	2.382	2.313	2.595	2.563	2.518	2.436
7	2.839	2.803	2.752	2.660	3.042	2.999	2.937	2.826
8	3.296	3.248	3.181	3.059	3.566	3.508	3.426	3.278
9	3.825	3.763	3.676	3.518	4.181	4.104	3.996	3.803
10	4.440	4.360	4.248	4.046	4.901	4.801	4.661	4.411
11	5.154	5.052	4.909	4.652	5.745	5.617	5.437	5.117
12	5.983	5.854	5.673	5.350	6.735	6.571	6.341	5.936
13	6.944	6.782	6.556	6.153	7.895	7.687	7.396	6.886
14	8.061	7.858	7.576	7.076	9.255	8.992	8.627	7.988
15	9.356	9.105	8.755	8.137	10.850	10.520	10.063	9.266
16	10.860	10.550	10.117	9.358	12.719	12.306	11.737	10.748
17	12.606	12.223	11.692	10.761	14.910	14.397	13.690	12.468
18	14.633	14.163	13.512	12.375	17.478	16.842	15.968	14.463
19	16.985	16.410	15.614	14.232	20.489	19.703	18.625	16.777
20	19.715	19.013	18.044	16.367	24.019	23.050	21.725	19.461
21	22.885	22.029	20.852	18.822	28.157	26.965	25.339	22.574
22	26.564	25.524	24.098	21.645	33.008	31.545	29.556	26.186
23	30.834	29.574	27.848	24.891	38.694	36.903	34.474	30.376
24	35.791	34.266	32.182	28.625	45.360	43.172	40.211	35.236
25	41.544	39.702	37.190	32.919	53.174	50.505	46.902	40.874
26	48.223	46.001	42.977	37.857	62.334	59.084	54.706	47.414
27	55.975	53.299	49.666	43.535	73.073	69.120	63.809	55.000
28	64.973	61.754	57.395	50.066	85.661	80.860	74.427	63.800
29	75.417	71.552	66.327	57.575	100.418	94.595	86.812	74.009
30	87.541	82.903	76.649	66.212	117.717	110.663	101.257	85.850
31	101.614	96.056	88.578	76.144	137.996	129.460	118.106	99.586
32	117.948	111.295	102.363	87.565	161.769	151.449	137.759	115.520
33	136.909	128.953	118.293	100.700	189.637	177.174	160.682	134.003
34	158.918	149.411	136.702	115.805	222.305	207.269	187.420	155.443
35	184.465	173.115	157.977	133.176	260.602	242.475	218.606	180.314
36	214.118	200.580	182.562	153.152	305.496	283.662	254.983	209.164
37	248.539	232.402	210.973	176.125	358.124	331.844	297.412	242.631
38	288.493	269.273	243.805	202.543	419.819	388.211	346.901	281.452
39	334.869	311.993	281.748	232.925	492.141	454.152	404.625	326.484
40	388.701	361.490	325.595	267.864	576.923	531.293	471.955	378.721
41	451.186	418.841	376.265	308.043	676.310	621.538	550.488	439.317
42	523.716	485.290	434.821	354.250	792.818	727.111	642.089	509.607
43	607.906	562.282	502.491	407.387	929.398	850.618	748.933	591.144
44	705.630	651.488	580.691	468.495	1089.506	995.102	873.555	685.727
45	819.063	754.847	671.061	538.769	1277.196	1164.129	1018.915	795.444
46	950.731	874.604	775.494	619.585	1497.220	1361.866	1188.463	922.715
47	1103.565	1013.360	896.181	712.522	1755.147	1593.191	1386.223	1070.349
48	1280.968	1174.130	1035.649	819.401	2057.508	1863.808	1616.890	1241.605
49	1486.890	1360.406	1196.822	942.311	2411.956	2180.392	1885.941	1440.262
50	1725.914	1576.235	1383.077	1083.657	2827.466	2550.750	2199.761	1670.704

The compound amount of $1

End of Year	17% Interest compounded Monthly	Quarterly	Semi-Annually	Annually	18% Interest compounded Monthly	Quarterly	Semi-Annually	Annually
1	1.184	1.181	1.177	1.170	1.196	1.193	1.188	1.180
2	1.402	1.395	1.386	1.369	1.430	1.422	1.412	1.392
3	1.659	1.648	1.631	1.602	1.709	1.696	1.677	1.643
4	1.964	1.946	1.921	1.874	2.043	2.022	1.993	1.939
5	2.326	2.299	2.261	2.192	2.443	2.412	2.367	2.288
6	2.753	2.715	2.662	2.565	2.921	2.876	2.813	2.700
7	3.260	3.207	3.133	3.001	3.493	3.430	3.342	3.185
8	3.859	3.788	3.689	3.511	4.176	4.090	3.970	3.759
9	4.569	4.474	4.342	4.108	4.993	4.877	4.717	4.435
10	5.409	5.285	5.112	4.807	5.969	5.816	5.604	5.234
11	6.404	6.242	6.018	5.624	7.137	6.936	6.659	6.176
12	7.581	7.373	7.085	6.580	8.533	8.271	7.911	7.288
13	8.975	8.709	8.340	7.699	10.202	9.864	9.399	8.599
14	10.626	10.286	9.818	9.007	12.198	11.763	11.167	10.147
15	12.580	12.150	11.558	10.539	14.584	14.027	13.268	11.974
16	14.893	14.351	13.607	12.330	17.437	16.728	15.763	14.129
17	17.632	16.950	16.018	14.426	20.848	19.948	18.728	16.672
18	20.874	20.021	18.857	16.879	24.927	23.789	22.251	19.673
19	24.713	23.647	22.199	19.748	29.803	28.369	26.437	23.214
20	29.258	27.931	26.133	23.106	35.633	33.830	31.409	27.393
21	34.638	32.991	30.764	27.034	42.603	40.343	37.318	32.324
22	41.008	38.967	36.217	31.629	50.937	48.110	44.337	38.142
23	48.548	46.025	42.635	37.006	60.901	57.372	52.677	45.008
24	57.476	54.363	50.191	43.297	72.815	68.417	62.585	53.109
25	68.046	64.211	59.086	50.658	87.059	81.589	74.358	62.669
26	80.559	75.842	69.558	59.270	104.089	97.296	88.344	73.949
27	95.373	89.581	81.885	69.345	124.451	116.027	104.962	87.260
28	112.911	105.808	96.397	81.134	148.796	138.364	124.705	102.967
29	133.674	124.975	113.481	94.927	177.903	165.002	148.162	121.501
30	158.256	147.614	133.593	111.065	212.704	196.768	176.031	143.371
31	187.358	174.354	157.269	129.946	254.313	234.650	209.143	169.177
32	221.811	205.938	185.141	152.036	304.061	279.824	248.483	199.629
33	262.600	243.243	217.953	177.883	363.540	333.695	295.222	235.563
34	310.891	287.306	256.580	208.123	434.656	397.938	350.753	277.964
35	368.061	339.351	302.052	243.503	519.682	474.549	416.730	327.997
36	435.744	400.823	355.583	284.899	621.341	565.908	495.117	387.037
37	515.874	473.432	418.601	333.332	742.887	674.856	588.249	456.703
38	610.739	559.193	492.788	389.998	888.209	804.778	698.898	538.910
39	723.049	660.490	580.122	456.298	1061.959	959.713	830.361	635.914
40	856.011	780.136	682.935	533.869	1269.698	1144.475	986.552	750.378
41	1013.425	921.456	803.968	624.626	1518.073	1364.808	1172.122	885.446
42	1199.785	1088.375	946.451	730.813	1815.036	1627.559	1392.598	1044.827
43	1420.416	1285.532	1114.185	855.051	2170.090	1940.895	1654.546	1232.896
44	1681.618	1518.404	1311.647	1000.410	2594.599	2314.553	1965.766	1454.817
45	1990.854	1793.459	1544.104	1170.479	3102.150	2760.147	2335.527	1716.684
46	2356.955	2118.340	1817.757	1369.461	3708.987	3291.527	2774.839	2025.687
47	2790.380	2502.073	2139.909	1602.269	4434.532	3925.207	3296.786	2390.311
48	3303.508	2955.318	2519.155	1874.655	5302.007	4680.883	3916.912	2820.567
49	3910.996	3490.667	2965.612	2193.346	6339.176	5582.040	4653.683	3328.269
50	4630.195	4122.994	3491.193	2566.215	7579.235	6656.686	5529.041	3927.357

TABLE 2

The future value of $1 invested at the *end* of each period

The future value of an "ordinary annuity" assuming deposits are made monthly, quarterly, semi-annually or annually at various interest rates

Applications

Chapter Three

- How much will $1 invested at the end of each period amount to at some time in the future?

Chapter Fifteen

- Evaluating registered retirement savings plan yields.

The future value of $1 invested at the *end* of each period

End of Year	3% Interest compounded and Deposits made				4% Interest compounded and Deposits made			
	Monthly	*Quarterly*	*Semi-Annually*	*Annually*	*Monthly*	*Quarterly*	*Semi-Annually*	*Annually*
1	12.166	4.045	2.015	1.000	12.222	4.060	2.020	1.000
2	24.703	8.213	4.091	2.030	24.943	8.286	4.122	2.040
3	37.621	12.508	6.230	3.091	38.182	12.683	6.308	3.122
4	50.931	16.932	8.433	4.184	51.960	17.258	8.583	4.246
5	64.647	21.491	10.703	5.309	66.299	22.019	10.950	5.416
6	78.779	26.188	13.041	6.468	81.223	26.973	13.412	6.633
7	93.342	31.028	15.450	7.662	96.754	32.129	15.974	7.898
8	108.347	36.015	17.932	8.892	112.919	37.494	18.639	9.214
9	123.809	41.153	20.489	10.159	129.741	43.077	21.412	10.583
10	139.741	46.446	23.124	11.464	147.250	48.886	24.297	12.006
11	156.158	51.901	25.838	12.808	165.471	54.932	27.299	13.486
12	173.074	57.521	28.634	14.192	184.435	61.223	30.422	15.026
13	190.505	63.311	31.514	15.618	204.172	67.769	33.671	16.627
14	208.466	69.277	34.481	17.086	224.713	74.581	37.051	18.292
15	226.973	75.424	37.539	18.599	246.090	81.670	40.568	20.024
16	246.043	81.758	40.688	20.157	268.339	89.046	44.227	21.825
17	265.693	88.283	43.933	21.762	291.494	96.722	48.034	23.698
18	285.940	95.007	47.276	23.414	315.592	104.710	51.994	25.645
19	306.804	101.935	50.720	25.117	340.673	113.022	56.115	27.671
20	328.302	109.073	54.268	26.870	366.775	121.672	60.402	29.778
21	350.454	116.427	57.923	28.676	393.940	130.672	64.862	31.969
22	373.280	124.004	61.689	30.537	422.212	140.038	69.503	34.248
23	396.800	131.812	65.568	32.453	451.636	149.785	74.331	36.618
24	421.035	139.856	69.565	34.426	482.259	159.927	79.354	39.083
25	446.008	148.145	73.683	36.459	514.130	170.481	84.579	41.646
26	471.740	156.684	77.925	38.553	547.298	181.464	90.016	44.312
27	498.255	165.483	82.295	40.710	581.819	192.893	95.673	47.084
28	525.576	174.549	86.798	42.931	617.745	204.785	101.558	49.968
29	553.728	183.890	91.436	45.219	655.136	217.161	107.681	52.966
30	582.737	193.514	96.215	47.575	694.049	230.039	114.052	56.085
31	612.628	203.431	101.138	50.003	734.549	243.440	120.679	59.328
32	643.428	213.648	106.210	52.503	776.698	257.385	127.575	62.701
33	675.165	224.175	111.435	55.078	820.564	271.896	134.749	66.210
34	707.867	235.021	116.818	57.730	866.217	286.996	142.213	69.858
35	741.564	246.197	122.364	60.462	913.731	302.710	149.978	73.652
36	776.285	257.712	128.077	63.276	963.180	319.062	158.057	77.598
37	812.063	269.576	133.963	66.174	1014.644	336.077	166.463	81.702
38	848.929	281.799	140.027	69.159	1068.205	353.784	175.208	85.970
39	886.917	294.394	146.275	72.234	1123.948	372.209	184.306	90.409
40	926.060	307.371	152.711	75.401	1181.961	391.383	193.772	95.026
41	966.393	320.742	159.342	78.663	1242.339	411.335	203.620	99.827
42	1007.953	334.518	166.173	82.023	1305.176	432.097	213.867	104.820
43	1050.777	348.712	173.210	85.484	1370.573	453.702	224.527	110.012
44	1094.904	363.337	180.460	89.048	1438.635	476.185	235.618	115.413
45	1140.373	378.406	187.930	92.720	1509.470	499.580	247.157	121.029
46	1187.225	393.932	195.625	96.501	1583.190	523.926	259.162	126.871
47	1235.502	409.928	203.553	100.397	1659.914	549.259	271.652	132.945
48	1285.247	426.410	211.720	104.408	1739.764	575.622	284.647	139.263
49	1336.506	443.393	220.134	108.541	1822.868	603.055	298.166	145.834
50	1389.323	460.890	228.803	112.797	1909.356	631.602	312.232	152.667

The future value of $1 invested at the *end* of each period

End of Year	5% Interest compounded and Deposits made				6% Interest compounded and Deposits made			
	Monthly	*Quarterly*	*Semi-Annually*	*Annually*	*Monthly*	*Quarterly*	*Semi-Annually*	*Annually*
1	12.279	4.076	2.025	1.000	12.336	4.091	2.030	1.000
2	25.186	8.359	4.153	2.050	25.432	8.433	4.184	2.060
3	38.753	12.860	6.388	3.153	39.336	13.041	6.468	3.184
4	53.015	17.591	8.736	4.310	54.098	17.932	8.892	4.375
5	68.006	22.563	11.203	5.526	69.770	23.124	11.464	5.637
6	83.764	27.788	13.796	6.802	86.409	28.634	14.192	6.975
7	100.329	33.279	16.519	8.142	104.074	34.481	17.086	8.394
8	117.741	39.050	19.380	9.549	122.829	40.688	20.157	9.897
9	136.043	45.116	22.386	11.027	142.740	47.276	23.414	11.491
10	155.282	51.490	25.545	12.578	163.879	54.268	26.870	13.181
11	175.506	58.188	28.863	14.207	186.323	61.689	30.537	14.972
12	196.764	65.228	32.349	15.917	210.150	69.565	34.426	16.870
13	219.109	72.627	36.012	17.713	235.447	77.925	38.553	18.882
14	242.598	80.403	39.860	19.599	262.305	86.798	42.931	21.015
15	267.289	88.575	43.903	21.579	290.819	96.215	47.575	23.276
16	293.243	97.163	48.150	23.657	321.091	106.210	52.503	25.673
17	320.525	106.188	52.613	25.840	353.231	116.818	57.730	28.213
18	349.202	115.674	57.301	28.132	387.353	128.077	63.276	30.906
19	379.347	125.642	62.227	30.539	423.580	140.027	69.159	33.760
20	411.034	136.119	67.403	33.066	462.041	152.711	75.401	36.786
21	444.342	147.129	72.840	35.719	502.874	166.173	82.023	39.993
22	479.354	158.700	78.552	38.505	546.226	180.460	89.048	43.392
23	516.158	170.861	84.554	41.430	592.251	195.625	96.501	46.996
24	554.844	183.641	90.860	44.502	641.116	211.720	104.408	50.816
25	595.510	197.072	97.484	47.727	692.994	228.803	112.797	54.865
26	638.256	211.188	104.444	51.113	748.072	246.934	121.696	59.156
27	683.189	226.023	111.757	54.669	806.547	266.178	131.137	63.706
28	730.421	241.613	119.440	58.403	868.628	286.602	141.154	68.528
29	780.070	257.998	127.511	62.323	934.539	308.280	151.780	73.640
30	832.259	275.217	135.992	66.439	1004.515	331.288	163.053	79.058
31	887.117	293.314	144.901	70.761	1078.807	355.708	175.013	84.802
32	944.783	312.332	154.262	75.299	1157.681	381.627	187.702	90.890
33	1005.399	332.320	164.096	80.064	1241.420	409.135	201.163	97.343
34	1069.116	353.326	174.429	85.067	1330.323	438.332	215.444	104.184
35	1136.092	375.401	185.284	90.320	1424.710	469.321	230.594	111.435
36	1206.496	398.602	196.689	95.836	1524.919	502.211	246.667	119.121
37	1280.501	422.985	208.672	101.628	1631.308	537.119	263.719	127.268
38	1358.293	448.609	221.261	107.710	1744.259	574.170	281.810	135.904
39	1440.065	475.540	234.487	114.095	1864.177	613.494	301.002	145.058
40	1526.020	503.842	248.383	120.800	1991.491	655.231	321.363	154.762
41	1616.373	533.586	262.982	127.840	2126.657	699.529	342.964	165.048
42	1711.349	564.845	278.321	135.232	2270.160	746.545	365.881	175.951
43	1811.183	597.697	294.436	142.993	2422.514	796.447	390.193	187.508
44	1916.126	632.222	311.366	151.143	2584.265	849.411	415.985	199.758
45	2026.437	668.507	329.154	159.700	2755.993	905.625	443.349	212.744
46	2142.393	706.640	347.843	168.685	2938.312	965.288	472.379	226.508
47	2264.280	746.715	367.477	178.119	3131.876	1028.612	503.177	241.099
48	2392.404	788.833	388.106	188.025	3337.379	1095.822	535.850	256.565
49	2527.083	833.096	409.779	198.427	3555.557	1167.157	570.513	272.958
50	2668.652	879.614	432.549	209.348	3787.191	1242.869	607.288	290.336

The future value of $1 invested at the *end* of each period

End of Year	7% Interest compounded and Deposits made				8% Interest compounded and Deposits made			
	Monthly	Quarterly	Semi-Annually	Annually	Monthly	Quarterly	Semi-Annually	Annually
1	12.393	4.106	2.035	1.000	12.450	4.122	2.040	1.000
2	25.681	8.508	4.215	2.070	25.933	8.583	4.246	2.080
3	39.930	13.225	6.550	3.215	40.536	13.412	6.633	3.246
4	55.209	18.282	9.052	4.440	56.350	18.639	9.214	4.506
5	71.593	23.702	11.731	5.751	73.477	24.297	12.006	5.867
6	89.161	29.511	14.602	7.153	92.025	30.422	15.026	7.336
7	107.999	35.738	17.677	8.654	112.113	37.051	18.292	8.923
8	128.199	42.412	20.971	10.260	133.869	44.227	21.825	10.637
9	149.859	49.566	24.500	11.978	157.430	51.994	25.645	12.488
10	173.085	57.234	28.280	13.816	182.946	60.402	29.778	14.487
11	197.990	65.453	32.329	15.784	210.580	69.503	34.248	16.645
12	224.695	74.263	36.667	17.888	240.508	79.354	39.083	18.977
13	253.331	83.705	41.313	20.141	272.920	90.016	44.312	21.495
14	284.037	93.827	46.291	22.550	308.023	101.558	49.968	24.215
15	316.962	104.675	51.623	25.129	346.038	114.052	56.085	27.152
16	352.268	116.303	57.335	27.888	387.209	127.575	62.701	30.324
17	390.126	128.767	63.453	30.840	431.797	142.213	69.858	33.750
18	430.721	142.126	70.008	33.999	480.086	158.057	77.598	37.450
19	474.250	156.446	77.029	37.379	532.383	175.208	85.970	41.446
20	520.927	171.794	84.550	40.995	589.020	193.772	95.026	45.762
21	570.977	188.245	92.607	44.865	650.359	213.867	104.820	50.423
22	624.646	205.878	101.238	49.006	716.788	235.618	115.413	55.457
23	682.194	224.779	110.484	53.436	788.731	259.162	126.871	60.893
24	743.902	245.037	120.388	58.177	866.645	284.647	139.263	66.765
25	810.072	266.752	130.998	63.249	951.026	312.232	152.667	73.106
26	881.024	290.027	142.363	68.676	1042.411	342.092	167.165	79.954
27	957.106	314.974	154.538	74.484	1141.381	374.413	182.845	87.351
28	1038.688	341.714	167.580	80.698	1248.565	409.398	199.806	95.339
29	1126.168	370.375	181.551	87.347	1364.645	447.267	218.150	103.966
30	1219.971	401.096	196.517	94.461	1490.359	488.258	237.991	113.283
31	1320.555	434.025	212.549	102.073	1626.508	532.628	259.451	123.346
32	1428.411	469.320	229.723	110.218	1773.958	580.655	282.662	134.214
33	1544.064	507.151	248.120	118.933	1933.645	632.641	307.767	145.951
34	1668.077	547.700	267.827	128.259	2106.587	688.913	334.921	158.627
35	1801.055	591.164	288.938	138.237	2293.882	749.823	364.290	172.317
36	1943.646	637.750	311.552	148.913	2496.724	815.754	396.057	187.102
37	2096.544	687.685	335.778	160.337	2716.400	887.120	430.415	203.070
38	2260.496	741.207	361.729	172.561	2954.310	964.369	467.577	220.316
39	2436.300	798.576	389.528	185.640	3211.966	1047.986	507.771	238.941
40	2624.813	860.067	419.307	199.635	3491.008	1138.495	551.245	259.057
41	2826.954	925.977	451.207	214.610	3793.210	1236.466	598.267	280.781
42	3043.707	996.623	485.379	230.632	4120.494	1342.512	649.125	304.244
43	3276.130	1072.346	521.985	247.776	4474.943	1457.299	704.134	329.583
44	3525.354	1153.510	561.199	266.121	4858.811	1581.549	763.631	356.950
45	3792.595	1240.506	603.205	285.749	5274.540	1716.042	827.983	386.506
46	4079.154	1333.754	648.203	306.752	5724.774	1861.620	897.587	418.426
47	4386.429	1433.702	696.407	329.224	6212.377	2019.199	972.870	452.900
48	4715.917	1540.833	748.043	353.270	6740.452	2189.768	1054.296	490.132
49	5069.224	1655.662	803.358	378.999	7312.356	2374.397	1142.367	530.343
50	5448.071	1778.742	862.612	406.529	7931.727	2574.245	1237.624	573.770

The future value of $1 invested at the *end* of each period

End of Year	9% Interest compounded and Deposits made				10% Interest compounded and Deposits made			
	Monthly	Quarterly	Semi-Annually	Annually	Monthly	Quarterly	Semi-Annually	Annually
1	12.508	4.137	2.045	1.000	12.566	4.153	2.050	1.000
2	26.188	8.659	4.278	2.090	26.447	8.736	4.310	2.100
3	41.153	13.602	6.717	3.278	41.782	13.796	6.802	3.310
4	57.521	19.005	9.380	4.573	58.722	19.380	9.549	4.641
5	75.424	24.912	12.288	5.985	77.437	25.545	12.578	6.105
6	95.007	31.367	15.464	7.523	98.111	32.349	15.917	7.716
7	116.427	38.424	18.932	9.200	120.950	39.860	19.599	9.487
8	139.856	46.138	22.719	11.028	146.181	48.150	23.657	11.436
9	165.483	54.570	26.855	13.021	174.054	57.301	28.132	13.579
10	193.514	63.786	31.371	15.193	204.845	67.403	33.066	15.937
11	224.175	73.861	36.303	17.560	238.860	78.552	38.505	18.531
12	257.712	84.873	41.689	20.141	276.438	90.860	44.502	21.384
13	294.394	96.910	47.571	22.953	317.950	104.444	51.113	24.523
14	334.518	110.068	53.993	26.019	363.809	119.440	58.403	27.975
15	378.406	124.450	61.007	29.361	414.470	135.992	66.439	31.772
16	426.410	140.172	68.666	33.003	470.436	154.262	75.299	35.950
17	478.918	157.356	77.030	36.974	532.263	174.429	85.067	40.545
18	536.352	176.141	86.164	41.301	600.563	196.689	95.836	45.599
19	599.173	196.674	96.138	46.018	676.016	221.261	107.710	51.159
20	667.887	219.118	107.030	51.160	759.369	248.383	120.800	57.275
21	743.047	243.651	118.925	56.765	851.450	278.321	135.232	64.002
22	825.257	270.468	131.914	62.873	953.174	311.366	151.143	71.403
23	915.180	299.781	146.098	69.532	1065.549	347.843	168.685	79.543
24	1013.538	331.822	161.588	76.790	1189.692	388.106	188.025	88.497
25	1121.122	366.847	178.503	84.701	1326.833	432.549	209.348	98.347
26	1238.798	405.131	196.975	93.324	1478.336	481.605	232.856	109.182
27	1367.514	446.979	217.146	102.723	1645.702	535.755	258.774	121.100
28	1508.304	492.722	239.174	112.968	1830.595	595.525	287.348	134.210
29	1662.301	542.723	263.229	124.135	2034.847	661.501	318.851	148.631
30	1830.743	597.379	289.498	136.308	2260.488	734.326	353.584	164.494
31	2014.987	657.122	318.184	149.575	2509.756	814.711	391.876	181.943
32	2216.515	722.426	349.510	164.037	2785.126	903.441	434.093	201.138
33	2436.947	793.809	383.719	179.800	3089.331	1001.382	480.638	222.252
34	2678.057	871.836	421.075	196.982	3425.389	1109.491	531.953	245.477
35	2941.784	957.127	461.870	215.711	3796.638	1228.823	588.529	271.024
36	3230.252	1050.356	506.418	236.125	4206.761	1360.544	650.903	299.127
37	3545.779	1152.264	555.066	258.376	4659.830	1505.938	719.670	330.039
38	3890.905	1263.658	608.191	282.630	5160.340	1666.426	795.486	364.043
39	4268.407	1385.420	666.205	309.066	5713.261	1843.575	879.074	401.448
40	4681.320	1518.517	729.558	337.882	6324.080	2039.115	971.229	442.593
41	5132.968	1664.002	798.740	369.292	6998.859	2254.954	1072.830	487.852
42	5626.983	1823.030	874.289	403.528	7744.296	2493.199	1184.845	537.637
43	6167.341	1996.861	956.791	440.846	8567.791	2756.178	1308.341	592.401
44	6758.388	2186.872	1046.884	481.522	9477.516	3046.457	1444.496	652.641
45	7404.878	2394.571	1145.269	525.859	10482.502	3366.872	1594.607	718.905
46	8112.015	2621.602	1252.707	574.186	11592.722	3720.549	1760.105	791.795
47	8885.485	2869.767	1370.033	626.863	12819.197	4110.942	1942.565	871.975
48	9731.513	3141.031	1498.155	684.280	14174.100	4541.863	2143.728	960.172
49	10656.903	3437.546	1638.068	746.866	15670.879	5017.520	2365.510	1057.190
50	11669.102	3761.661	1790.856	815.084	17324.391	5542.556	2610.025	1163.909

The future value of $1 invested at the *end* of each period

End of Year	11% Interest compounded and Deposits made				12% Interest compounded and Deposits made			
	Monthly	Quarterly	Semi-Annually	Annually	Monthly	Quarterly	Semi-Annually	Annually
1	12.624	4.168	2.055	1.000	12.683	4.184	2.060	1.000
2	26.709	8.814	4.342	2.110	26.973	8.892	4.375	2.120
3	42.423	13.992	6.888	3.342	43.077	14.192	6.975	3.374
4	59.956	19.764	9.722	4.710	61.223	20.157	9.897	4.779
5	79.518	26.197	12.875	6.228	81.670	26.870	13.181	6.353
6	101.344	33.368	16.386	7.913	104.710	34.426	16.870	8.115
7	125.695	41.361	20.293	9.783	130.672	42.931	21.015	10.089
8	152.864	50.270	24.641	11.859	159.927	52.503	25.673	12.300
9	183.177	60.200	29.481	14.164	192.893	63.276	30.906	14.776
10	216.998	71.268	34.868	16.722	230.039	75.401	36.786	17.549
11	254.733	83.605	40.864	19.561	271.896	89.048	43.392	20.655
12	296.834	97.356	47.538	22.713	319.062	104.408	50.816	24.133
13	343.807	112.683	54.966	26.212	372.209	121.696	59.156	28.029
14	396.216	129.767	63.234	30.095	432.097	141.154	68.528	32.393
15	454.690	148.809	72.435	34.405	499.580	163.053	79.058	37.280
16	519.930	170.034	82.677	39.190	575.622	187.702	90.890	42.753
17	592.719	193.691	94.077	44.501	661.308	215.444	104.184	48.884
18	673.932	220.061	106.765	50.396	757.861	246.667	119.121	55.750
19	764.542	249.452	120.887	56.939	866.659	281.810	135.904	63.440
20	865.638	282.213	136.606	64.203	989.255	321.363	154.762	72.052
21	978.433	318.729	154.100	72.265	1127.400	365.881	175.951	81.699
22	1104.279	359.430	173.573	81.214	1283.065	415.985	199.758	92.503
23	1244.689	404.796	195.246	91.148	1458.473	472.379	226.508	104.603
24	1401.347	455.362	219.368	102.174	1656.126	535.850	256.565	118.155
25	1576.133	511.724	246.217	114.413	1878.847	607.288	290.336	133.334
26	1771.145	574.547	276.101	127.999	2129.814	687.691	328.281	150.334
27	1988.724	644.570	309.363	143.079	2412.610	778.186	370.917	169.374
28	2231.481	722.620	346.383	159.817	2731.272	880.039	418.822	190.699
29	2502.329	809.615	387.588	178.397	3090.348	994.675	472.649	214.583
30	2804.520	906.583	433.450	199.021	3494.964	1123.700	533.128	241.333
31	3141.679	1014.664	484.496	221.913	3950.896	1268.917	601.083	271.293
32	3517.855	1135.135	541.311	247.324	4464.651	1432.361	677.437	304.848
33	3937.561	1269.413	604.548	275.529	5043.562	1616.319	763.228	342.429
34	4405.834	1419.083	674.932	306.837	5695.895	1823.365	859.623	384.521
35	4928.296	1585.908	753.271	341.590	6430.959	2056.397	967.932	431.663
36	5511.217	1771.855	840.465	380.164	7259.249	2318.676	1089.629	484.463
37	6161.592	1979.115	937.513	422.982	8192.586	2613.874	1226.367	543.599
38	6887.229	2210.132	1045.531	470.511	9244.293	2946.122	1380.006	609.831
39	7696.835	2467.628	1165.757	523.267	10429.383	3320.070	1552.634	684.010
40	8600.127	2754.639	1299.571	581.826	11764.773	3740.952	1746.600	767.091
41	9607.948	3074.547	1448.510	646.827	13269.523	4214.658	1964.540	860.142
42	10732.392	3431.123	1614.283	718.978	14965.113	4747.818	2209.417	964.359
43	11986.956	3828.571	1798.793	799.065	16875.746	5347.895	2484.561	1081.083
44	13386.696	4271.575	2004.156	887.963	19028.696	6023.286	2793.712	1211.813
45	14948.413	4765.356	2232.731	986.639	21454.693	6783.445	3141.075	1358.230
46	16690.850	5315.735	2487.140	1096.169	24188.368	7639.011	3531.372	1522.218
47	18634.920	5929.200	2770.304	1217.747	27268.741	8601.958	3969.910	1705.884
48	20803.955	6612.980	3085.473	1352.700	30739.782	9685.763	4462.651	1911.590
49	23223.988	7375.136	3436.264	1502.497	34651.038	10905.595	5016.294	2141.981
50	25924.065	8224.651	3826.702	1668.771	39058.340	12278.527	5638.368	2400.018

The future value of $1 invested at the *end* of each period

End of Year	13% Interest compounded and Deposits made: Monthly	Quarterly	Semi-Annually	Annually	14% Interest compounded and Deposits made: Monthly	Quarterly	Semi-Annually	Annually
1	12.741	4.199	2.065	1.000	12.801	4.215	2.070	1.000
2	27.242	8.972	4.407	2.130	27.513	9.052	4.440	2.140
3	43.743	14.395	7.064	3.407	44.423	14.602	7.153	3.440
4	62.523	20.559	10.077	4.850	63.858	20.971	10.260	4.921
5	83.894	27.564	13.494	6.480	86.195	28.280	13.816	6.610
6	108.216	35.525	17.371	8.323	111.868	36.667	17.888	8.536
7	135.895	44.573	21.767	10.405	141.376	46.291	22.550	10.730
8	167.394	54.855	26.754	12.757	175.290	57.335	27.888	13.233
9	203.242	66.541	32.410	15.416	214.269	70.008	33.999	16.085
10	244.037	79.822	38.825	18.420	259.069	84.550	40.995	19.337
11	290.463	94.915	46.102	21.814	310.560	101.238	49.006	23.045
12	343.298	112.067	54.355	25.650	369.740	120.388	58.177	27.271
13	403.426	131.561	63.715	29.985	437.758	142.363	68.676	32.089
14	471.853	153.715	74.333	34.883	515.935	167.580	80.698	37.581
15	549.726	178.893	86.375	40.417	605.786	196.517	94.461	43.842
16	638.347	207.507	100.034	46.672	709.056	229.723	110.218	50.980
17	739.202	240.026	115.526	53.739	827.749	267.827	128.259	59.118
18	853.977	276.983	133.097	61.725	964.167	311.552	148.913	68.394
19	984.595	318.984	153.027	70.749	1120.959	361.729	172.561	78.969
20	1133.242	366.716	175.632	80.947	1301.166	419.307	199.635	91.025
21	1302.408	420.964	201.271	92.470	1508.286	485.379	230.632	104.768
22	1494.924	482.614	230.352	105.491	1746.337	561.199	266.121	120.436
23	1714.014	552.679	263.336	120.205	2019.939	648.203	306.752	138.297
24	1963.345	632.305	300.747	136.831	2334.401	748.043	353.270	158.659
25	2247.092	722.799	343.180	155.620	2695.826	862.612	406.529	181.871
26	2570.005	825.643	391.308	176.850	3111.227	994.082	467.505	208.333
27	2937.490	942.523	445.896	200.841	3588.665	1144.947	537.316	238.499
28	3355.701	1075.354	507.812	227.950	4137.404	1318.067	617.244	272.889
29	3831.638	1226.313	578.038	258.583	4768.093	1516.728	708.752	312.094
30	4373.270	1397.874	657.690	293.199	5492.971	1744.695	813.520	356.787
31	4989.665	1592.850	748.033	332.315	6326.103	2006.292	933.469	407.737
32	5691.142	1814.435	850.503	376.516	7283.657	2306.481	1070.799	465.820
33	6489.446	2066.261	966.727	426.463	8384.214	2650.956	1228.028	532.035
34	7397.941	2352.455	1098.551	482.903	9649.130	3046.247	1408.039	607.520
35	8431.839	2677.707	1248.069	546.681	11102.951	3499.854	1614.134	693.573
36	9608.448	3047.349	1417.656	618.749	12773.890	4020.378	1850.092	791.673
37	10947.468	3467.438	1610.006	700.187	14694.369	4617.691	2120.241	903.507
38	12471.315	3944.859	1828.174	792.211	16901.656	5303.121	2429.533	1030.998
39	14205.503	4487.437	2075.625	896.198	19438.585	6089.669	2783.643	1176.338
40	16179.066	5104.063	2356.291	1013.704	22354.383	6992.250	3189.063	1342.025
41	18425.044	5804.844	2674.629	1146.486	25705.633	8027.983	3653.228	1530.909
42	20981.040	6601.265	3035.696	1296.529	29557.365	9216.510	4184.651	1746.236
43	23889.846	7506.378	3445.227	1466.078	33984.323	10580.372	4793.076	1991.709
44	27200.162	8535.017	3909.728	1657.668	39072.411	12145.435	5489.663	2271.548
45	30967.409	9704.041	4436.576	1874.165	44920.365	13941.381	6287.185	2590.565
46	35254.659	11032.608	5034.141	2118.806	51641.665	16002.270	7200.269	2954.244
47	40133.689	12542.493	5711.913	2395.251	59366.736	18367.188	8245.658	3368.838
48	45686.183	14258.441	6480.660	2707.633	68245.486	21080.985	9442.523	3841.475
49	52005.102	16208.574	7352.591	3060.626	78450.206	24195.131	10812.815	4380.282
50	59196.236	18424.854	8341.558	3459.507	90178.920	27768.684	12381.662	4994.521

The future value of $1 invested at the *end* of each period

End of Year	15% Monthly	15% Quarterly	15% Semi-Annually	15% Annually	16% Monthly	16% Quarterly	16% Semi-Annually	16% Annually
	15% Interest compounded and Deposits made				*16% Interest compounded and Deposits made*			
1	12.860	4.231	2.075	1.000	12.920	4.246	2.080	1.000
2	27.788	9.133	4.473	2.150	28.066	9.214	4.506	2.160
3	45.116	14.812	7.244	3.473	45.822	15.026	7.336	3.506
4	65.228	21.393	10.446	4.993	66.636	21.825	10.637	5.066
5	88.575	29.017	14.147	6.742	91.036	29.778	14.487	6.877
6	115.674	37.852	18.424	8.754	119.639	39.083	18.977	8.977
7	147.129	48.088	23.366	11.067	153.169	49.968	24.215	11.414
8	183.641	59.947	29.077	13.727	192.476	62.701	30.324	14.240
9	226.023	73.689	35.677	16.786	238.554	77.598	37.450	17.519
10	275.217	89.610	43.305	20.304	292.571	95.026	45.762	21.321
11	332.320	108.057	52.119	24.349	355.892	115.413	55.457	25.733
12	398.602	129.431	62.305	29.002	430.122	139.263	66.765	30.850
13	475.540	154.197	74.076	34.352	517.140	167.165	79.954	36.786
14	564.845	182.891	87.679	40.505	619.149	199.806	95.339	43.672
15	668.507	216.137	103.399	47.580	738.730	237.991	113.283	51.660
16	788.833	254.658	121.566	55.717	878.912	282.662	134.214	60.925
17	928.501	299.290	142.560	65.075	1043.243	334.921	158.627	71.673
18	1090.623	351.003	166.820	75.836	1235.884	396.057	187.102	84.141
19	1278.805	410.921	194.857	88.212	1461.711	467.577	220.316	98.603
20	1497.239	480.344	227.257	102.444	1726.442	551.245	259.057	115.380
21	1750.788	560.782	264.698	118.810	2036.777	649.125	304.244	134.841
22	2045.095	653.980	307.967	137.632	2400.575	763.631	356.950	157.415
23	2386.714	761.965	357.969	159.276	2827.044	897.587	418.426	183.601
24	2783.249	887.082	415.753	184.168	3326.982	1054.296	490.132	213.978
25	3243.530	1032.049	482.530	212.793	3913.044	1237.624	573.770	249.214
26	3777.802	1200.014	559.699	245.712	4600.067	1452.091	671.326	290.088
27	4397.961	1394.628	648.877	283.569	5405.445	1702.988	785.114	337.502
28	5117.814	1620.117	751.933	327.104	6349.566	1996.501	917.837	392.503
29	5953.386	1881.380	871.028	377.170	7456.331	2339.871	1072.645	456.303
30	6923.280	2184.092	1008.657	434.745	8753.759	2741.564	1253.213	530.312
31	8049.088	2534.830	1167.704	500.957	10274.696	3211.489	1463.828	616.162
32	9355.876	2941.213	1351.503	577.100	12057.647	3761.234	1709.489	715.747
33	10872.736	3412.068	1563.905	664.666	14147.748	4404.358	1996.028	831.267
34	12633.438	3957.624	1809.363	765.365	16597.912	5156.723	2330.247	965.270
35	14677.180	4589.734	2093.020	881.170	19470.168	6036.882	2720.080	1120.713
36	17049.464	5322.128	2420.821	1014.346	22837.229	7066.545	3174.781	1301.027
37	19803.102	6170.716	2799.637	1167.498	26784.337	8271.105	3705.145	1510.191
38	22999.401	7153.934	3237.405	1343.622	31411.417	9680.269	4323.761	1752.822
39	26709.519	8293.139	3743.301	1546.165	36835.607	11328.792	5045.315	2034.273
40	31016.055	9613.079	4327.927	1779.090	43194.226	13257.331	5886.935	2360.757
41	36014.886	11142.429	5003.536	2046.954	50648.251	15513.449	6868.601	2739.478
42	41817.302	12914.411	5784.286	2354.997	59386.385	18152.787	8013.617	3178.795
43	48552.483	14967.518	6686.541	2709.246	69629.846	21240.440	9349.163	3688.402
44	56370.374	17346.352	7729.209	3116.633	81637.955	24852.557	10906.943	4279.546
45	65445.027	20102.588	8934.142	3585.128	95714.711	29078.223	12723.939	4965.274
46	75978.471	23296.103	10326.593	4123.898	112216.481	34021.654	14843.282	5760.718
47	88205.213	26996.270	11935.744	4743.482	131561.024	39804.770	17315.284	6683.433
48	102397.460	31283.470	13795.319	5456.005	154238.067	46570.197	20198.627	7753.782
49	118871.175	36250.836	15944.291	6275.405	180821.702	54484.790	23561.759	8995.387
50	137993.114	42006.277	18427.696	7217.716	211984.922	63743.745	27484.516	10435.649

The future value of $1 invested at the *end* of each period

End of Year	17% Interest compounded and Deposits made				18% Interest compounded and Deposits made			
	Monthly	*Quarterly*	*Semi-Annually*	*Annually*	*Monthly*	*Quarterly*	*Semi-Annually*	*Annually*
1	12.981	4.262	2.085	1.000	13.041	4.278	2.090	1.000
2	28.348	9.297	4.540	2.170	28.634	9.380	4.573	2.180
3	46.542	15.243	7.429	3.539	47.276	15.464	7.523	3.572
4	68.081	22.267	10.831	5.141	69.565	22.719	11.028	5.215
5	93.581	30.563	14.835	7.014	96.215	31.371	15.193	7.154
6	123.771	40.361	19.549	9.207	128.077	41.689	20.141	9.442
7	159.512	51.935	25.099	11.772	166.173	53.993	26.019	12.142
8	201.825	65.605	31.632	14.773	211.720	68.666	33.003	15.327
9	251.920	81.751	39.323	18.285	266.178	86.164	41.301	19.086
10	311.226	100.823	48.377	22.393	331.288	107.030	51.160	23.521
11	381.439	123.349	59.036	27.200	409.135	131.914	62.873	28.755
12	464.563	149.956	71.583	32.824	502.211	161.588	76.790	34.931
13	562.972	181.382	86.355	39.404	613.494	196.975	93.324	42.219
14	679.479	218.501	103.744	47.103	746.545	239.174	112.968	50.818
15	817.410	262.345	124.215	56.110	905.625	289.498	136.308	60.965
16	980.706	314.130	148.314	66.649	1095.822	349.510	164.037	72.939
17	1174.030	375.297	176.684	78.979	1323.226	421.075	196.982	87.068
18	1402.905	447.543	210.081	93.406	1595.115	506.418	236.125	103.740
19	1673.868	532.877	249.398	110.285	1920.189	608.191	282.630	123.414
20	1994.659	633.668	295.683	130.033	2308.854	729.558	337.882	146.628
21	2374.441	752.718	350.170	153.139	2773.549	874.289	403.528	174.021
22	2824.062	893.334	414.314	180.172	3329.147	1046.884	481.522	206.345
23	3356.364	1059.422	489.825	211.801	3993.430	1252.707	574.186	244.487
24	3986.552	1255.596	578.720	248.808	4787.659	1498.155	684.280	289.494
25	4732.626	1487.307	683.368	292.105	5737.253	1790.856	815.084	342.603
26	5615.898	1760.992	806.563	342.763	6872.606	2139.907	970.491	405.272
27	6661.595	2084.254	951.592	402.032	8230.053	2556.157	1155.130	479.221
28	7899.588	2466.074	1122.322	471.378	9853.042	3052.543	1374.500	566.481
29	9365.238	2917.060	1323.311	552.512	11793.518	3644.493	1635.134	669.447
30	11100.408	3449.742	1559.920	647.439	14113.585	4350.404	1944.792	790.948
31	13154.662	4078.917	1838.462	758.504	16887.500	5192.216	2312.698	934.319
32	15586.676	4822.067	2166.368	888.449	20204.044	6196.092	2749.806	1103.496
33	18465.917	5699.836	2552.387	1040.486	24169.363	7393.233	3269.134	1303.125
34	21874.628	6736.611	3006.819	1218.368	28910.371	8820.846	3886.149	1538.688
35	25910.171	7961.196	3541.788	1426.491	34578.806	10523.301	4619.223	1816.652
36	30687.818	9407.612	4171.566	1669.994	41356.090	12553.511	5490.189	2144.649
37	36344.034	11116.042	4912.957	1954.894	49459.133	14974.573	6524.984	2531.686
38	43040.382	13133.951	5785.741	2288.225	59147.280	17861.735	7754.423	2988.389
39	50968.133	15517.400	6813.204	2678.224	70730.604	21304.730	9215.120	3527.299
40	60353.732	18332.606	8022.759	3134.522	84579.836	25410.565	10950.574	4163.213
41	71465.264	21657.780	9446.677	3668.391	101138.230	30306.850	13012.467	4913.591
42	84620.116	25585.302	11122.950	4293.017	120935.747	36145.760	15462.202	5799.038
43	100194.036	30224.286	13096.299	5023.830	144606.018	43108.769	18372.732	6843.865
44	118631.871	35703.612	15419.376	5878.881	172906.624	51412.288	21830.733	8076.760
45	140460.272	42175.506	18154.160	6879.291	206743.343	61314.387	25939.184	9531.577
46	166302.734	49819.770	21373.616	8049.770	247199.139	73122.826	30820.435	11248.261
47	196897.412	58848.775	25163.640	9419.231	295568.824	87204.608	36619.849	13273.948
48	233118.198	69513.365	29625.351	11021.500	353400.498	103997.395	43510.132	15664.259
49	275999.687	82109.822	34877.789	12896.155	422545.099	124023.106	51696.478	18484.825
50	326766.727	96988.100	41061.090	15089.502	505215.639	147904.139	61422.675	21813.094

TABLE 3

The present value of $1 due at the *end* of various time periods

"Compound Discount Table for $1 Principal"

How much must be invested today to have $1 accumulated at some point in the future at various interest rates compounded monthly, quarterly, semi-annually or annually?

Applications

Chapter Four

- What is $1 due sometime in the future worth today?
- How much do I have to invest today to have $1 at the end of various time periods?
- How much can I borrow today so that I can repay my debt, principal plus interest, out of money which I have coming in at the end of a certain time period?
- What is the value of an insurance policy today where the benefits are payable sometime in the future, given a presumed rate for inflation?
- What is the present value of a future profit from the sale of a house or a stock market investment?

Chapters Eleven and Twelve

- Evaluating an investment in a home, vacation property or real estate using discounted cash flow.

Chapters Thirteen and Fourteen

- Evaluating an investment in the stock market or gold using discounted cash flow.

Chapter Sixteen

- Calculating the present value of an insurance policy death benefit.

The present value of $1 due at the *end* of various time periods

End of Year	3% Interest compounded Monthly	Quarterly	Semi-Annually	Annually	4% Interest compounded Monthly	Quarterly	Semi-Annually	Annually
1	0.9705	0.9706	0.9707	0.9709	0.9609	0.9610	0.9612	0.9615
2	0.9418	0.9420	0.9422	0.9426	0.9232	0.9235	0.9238	0.9246
3	0.9140	0.9142	0.9145	0.9151	0.8871	0.8874	0.8880	0.8890
4	0.8871	0.8873	0.8877	0.8885	0.8524	0.8528	0.8535	0.8548
5	0.8609	0.8612	0.8617	0.8626	0.8190	0.8195	0.8203	0.8219
6	0.8355	0.8358	0.8364	0.8375	0.7869	0.7876	0.7885	0.7903
7	0.8108	0.8112	0.8118	0.8131	0.7561	0.7568	0.7579	0.7599
8	0.7869	0.7873	0.7880	0.7894	0.7265	0.7273	0.7284	0.7307
9	0.7636	0.7641	0.7649	0.7664	0.6981	0.6989	0.7002	0.7026
10	0.7411	0.7416	0.7425	0.7441	0.6708	0.6717	0.6730	0.6756
11	0.7192	0.7198	0.7207	0.7224	0.6445	0.6454	0.6468	0.6496
12	0.6980	0.6986	0.6995	0.7014	0.6193	0.6203	0.6217	0.6246
13	0.6774	0.6780	0.6790	0.6810	0.5950	0.5961	0.5976	0.6006
14	0.6574	0.6581	0.6591	0.6611	0.5717	0.5728	0.5744	0.5775
15	0.6380	0.6387	0.6398	0.6419	0.5494	0.5504	0.5521	0.5553
16	0.6192	0.6199	0.6210	0.6232	0.5279	0.5290	0.5306	0.5339
17	0.6009	0.6016	0.6028	0.6050	0.5072	0.5083	0.5100	0.5134
18	0.5831	0.5839	0.5851	0.5874	0.4873	0.4885	0.4902	0.4936
19	0.5659	0.5667	0.5679	0.5703	0.4683	0.4694	0.4712	0.4746
20	0.5492	0.5500	0.5513	0.5537	0.4499	0.4511	0.4529	0.4564
21	0.5330	0.5338	0.5351	0.5375	0.4323	0.4335	0.4353	0.4388
22	0.5173	0.5181	0.5194	0.5219	0.4154	0.4166	0.4184	0.4220
23	0.5020	0.5029	0.5042	0.5067	0.3991	0.4003	0.4022	0.4057
24	0.4872	0.4881	0.4894	0.4919	0.3835	0.3847	0.3865	0.3901
25	0.4728	0.4737	0.4750	0.4776	0.3685	0.3697	0.3715	0.3751
26	0.4589	0.4597	0.4611	0.4637	0.3541	0.3553	0.3571	0.3607
27	0.4453	0.4462	0.4475	0.4502	0.3402	0.3414	0.3432	0.3468
28	0.4322	0.4331	0.4344	0.4371	0.3269	0.3281	0.3299	0.3335
29	0.4194	0.4203	0.4217	0.4243	0.3141	0.3153	0.3171	0.3207
30	0.4070	0.4079	0.4093	0.4120	0.3018	0.3030	0.3048	0.3083
31	0.3950	0.3959	0.3973	0.4000	0.2900	0.2912	0.2929	0.2965
32	0.3834	0.3843	0.3856	0.3883	0.2786	0.2798	0.2816	0.2851
33	0.3720	0.3730	0.3743	0.3770	0.2677	0.2689	0.2706	0.2741
34	0.3611	0.3620	0.3633	0.3660	0.2572	0.2584	0.2601	0.2636
35	0.3504	0.3513	0.3527	0.3554	0.2472	0.2483	0.2500	0.2534
36	0.3401	0.3410	0.3423	0.3450	0.2375	0.2386	0.2403	0.2437
37	0.3300	0.3309	0.3323	0.3350	0.2282	0.2293	0.2310	0.2343
38	0.3203	0.3212	0.3225	0.3252	0.2193	0.2204	0.2220	0.2253
39	0.3108	0.3117	0.3131	0.3158	0.2107	0.2118	0.2134	0.2166
40	0.3016	0.3025	0.3039	0.3066	0.2024	0.2035	0.2051	0.2083
41	0.2927	0.2936	0.2950	0.2976	0.1945	0.1956	0.1971	0.2003
42	0.2841	0.2850	0.2863	0.2890	0.1869	0.1879	0.1895	0.1926
43	0.2757	0.2766	0.2779	0.2805	0.1796	0.1806	0.1821	0.1852
44	0.2676	0.2685	0.2698	0.2724	0.1725	0.1736	0.1751	0.1780
45	0.2597	0.2605	0.2619	0.2644	0.1658	0.1668	0.1683	0.1712
46	0.2520	0.2529	0.2542	0.2567	0.1593	0.1603	0.1617	0.1646
47	0.2446	0.2454	0.2467	0.2493	0.1531	0.1540	0.1554	0.1583
48	0.2374	0.2382	0.2395	0.2420	0.1471	0.1480	0.1494	0.1522
49	0.2303	0.2312	0.2324	0.2350	0.1413	0.1422	0.1436	0.1463
50	0.2235	0.2244	0.2256	0.2281	0.1358	0.1367	0.1380	0.1407

The present value of $1 due at the *end* of various time periods

End of Year	5% Interest compounded Monthly	Quarterly	Semi-Annually	Annually	6% Interest compounded Monthly	Quarterly	Semi-Annually	Annually
1	0.9513	0.9515	0.9518	0.9524	0.9419	0.9422	0.9426	0.9434
2	0.9050	0.9054	0.9060	0.9070	0.8872	0.8877	0.8885	0.8900
3	0.8610	0.8615	0.8623	0.8638	0.8356	0.8364	0.8375	0.8396
4	0.8191	0.8197	0.8207	0.8227	0.7871	0.7880	0.7894	0.7921
5	0.7792	0.7800	0.7812	0.7835	0.7414	0.7425	0.7441	0.7473
6	0.7413	0.7422	0.7436	0.7462	0.6983	0.6995	0.7014	0.7050
7	0.7052	0.7062	0.7077	0.7107	0.6577	0.6591	0.6611	0.6651
8	0.6709	0.6720	0.6736	0.6768	0.6195	0.6210	0.6232	0.6274
9	0.6382	0.6394	0.6412	0.6446	0.5835	0.5851	0.5874	0.5919
10	0.6072	0.6084	0.6103	0.6139	0.5496	0.5513	0.5537	0.5584
11	0.5776	0.5789	0.5809	0.5847	0.5177	0.5194	0.5219	0.5268
12	0.5495	0.5509	0.5529	0.5568	0.4876	0.4894	0.4919	0.4970
13	0.5228	0.5242	0.5262	0.5303	0.4593	0.4611	0.4637	0.4688
14	0.4973	0.4987	0.5009	0.5051	0.4326	0.4344	0.4371	0.4423
15	0.4731	0.4746	0.4767	0.4810	0.4075	0.4093	0.4120	0.4173
16	0.4501	0.4516	0.4538	0.4581	0.3838	0.3856	0.3883	0.3936
17	0.4282	0.4297	0.4319	0.4363	0.3615	0.3633	0.3660	0.3714
18	0.4073	0.4088	0.4111	0.4155	0.3405	0.3423	0.3450	0.3503
19	0.3875	0.3890	0.3913	0.3957	0.3207	0.3225	0.3252	0.3305
20	0.3686	0.3702	0.3724	0.3769	0.3021	0.3039	0.3066	0.3118
21	0.3507	0.3522	0.3545	0.3589	0.2845	0.2863	0.2890	0.2942
22	0.3336	0.3351	0.3374	0.3418	0.2680	0.2698	0.2724	0.2775
23	0.3174	0.3189	0.3211	0.3256	0.2524	0.2542	0.2567	0.2618
24	0.3019	0.3034	0.3057	0.3101	0.2378	0.2395	0.2420	0.2470
25	0.2872	0.2887	0.2909	0.2953	0.2240	0.2256	0.2281	0.2330
26	0.2733	0.2747	0.2769	0.2812	0.2110	0.2126	0.2150	0.2198
27	0.2600	0.2614	0.2636	0.2678	0.1987	0.2003	0.2027	0.2074
28	0.2473	0.2487	0.2509	0.2551	0.1872	0.1887	0.1910	0.1956
29	0.2353	0.2367	0.2388	0.2429	0.1763	0.1778	0.1801	0.1846
30	0.2238	0.2252	0.2273	0.2314	0.1660	0.1675	0.1697	0.1741
31	0.2129	0.2143	0.2163	0.2204	0.1564	0.1578	0.1600	0.1643
32	0.2026	0.2039	0.2059	0.2099	0.1473	0.1487	0.1508	0.1550
33	0.1927	0.1940	0.1960	0.1999	0.1388	0.1401	0.1421	0.1462
34	0.1833	0.1846	0.1865	0.1904	0.1307	0.1320	0.1340	0.1379
35	0.1744	0.1757	0.1776	0.1813	0.1231	0.1244	0.1263	0.1301
36	0.1659	0.1672	0.1690	0.1727	0.1159	0.1172	0.1190	0.1227
37	0.1578	0.1591	0.1609	0.1644	0.1092	0.1104	0.1122	0.1158
38	0.1502	0.1513	0.1531	0.1566	0.1029	0.1040	0.1058	0.1092
39	0.1429	0.1440	0.1457	0.1491	0.0969	0.0980	0.0997	0.1031
40	0.1359	0.1370	0.1387	0.1420	0.0913	0.0923	0.0940	0.0972
41	0.1293	0.1304	0.1320	0.1353	0.0860	0.0870	0.0886	0.0917
42	0.1230	0.1241	0.1257	0.1288	0.0810	0.0820	0.0835	0.0865
43	0.1170	0.1180	0.1196	0.1227	0.0763	0.0772	0.0787	0.0816
44	0.1113	0.1123	0.1138	0.1169	0.0718	0.0728	0.0742	0.0770
45	0.1059	0.1069	0.1084	0.1113	0.0677	0.0686	0.0699	0.0727
46	0.1007	0.1017	0.1031	0.1060	0.0637	0.0646	0.0659	0.0685
47	0.0958	0.0968	0.0982	0.1009	0.0600	0.0609	0.0621	0.0647
48	0.0912	0.0921	0.0934	0.0961	0.0565	0.0573	0.0586	0.0610
49	0.0867	0.0876	0.0889	0.0916	0.0533	0.0540	0.0552	0.0575
50	0.0825	0.0834	0.0846	0.0872	0.0502	0.0509	0.0520	0.0543

The present value of $1 due at the *end* of various time periods

End of Year	*7% Interest compounded*				*8% Interest compounded*			
	Monthly	*Quarterly*	*Semi-Annually*	*Annually*	*Monthly*	*Quarterly*	*Semi-Annually*	*Annually*
1	0.9326	0.9330	0.9335	0.9346	0.9234	0.9238	0.9246	0.9259
2	0.8697	0.8704	0.8714	0.8734	0.8526	0.8535	0.8548	0.8573
3	0.8111	0.8121	0.8135	0.8163	0.7873	0.7885	0.7903	0.7938
4	0.7564	0.7576	0.7594	0.7629	0.7269	0.7284	0.7307	0.7350
5	0.7054	0.7068	0.7089	0.7130	0.6712	0.6730	0.6756	0.6806
6	0.6578	0.6594	0.6618	0.6663	0.6198	0.6217	0.6246	0.6302
7	0.6135	0.6152	0.6178	0.6227	0.5723	0.5744	0.5775	0.5835
8	0.5721	0.5740	0.5767	0.5820	0.5284	0.5306	0.5339	0.5403
9	0.5336	0.5355	0.5384	0.5439	0.4879	0.4902	0.4936	0.5002
10	0.4976	0.4996	0.5026	0.5083	0.4505	0.4529	0.4564	0.4632
11	0.4641	0.4661	0.4692	0.4751	0.4160	0.4184	0.4220	0.4289
12	0.4328	0.4349	0.4380	0.4440	0.3841	0.3865	0.3901	0.3971
13	0.4036	0.4057	0.4088	0.4150	0.3547	0.3571	0.3607	0.3677
14	0.3764	0.3785	0.3817	0.3878	0.3275	0.3299	0.3335	0.3405
15	0.3510	0.3531	0.3563	0.3624	0.3024	0.3048	0.3083	0.3152
16	0.3273	0.3295	0.3326	0.3387	0.2792	0.2816	0.2851	0.2919
17	0.3053	0.3074	0.3105	0.3166	0.2578	0.2601	0.2636	0.2703
18	0.2847	0.2868	0.2898	0.2959	0.2381	0.2403	0.2437	0.2502
19	0.2655	0.2675	0.2706	0.2765	0.2198	0.2220	0.2253	0.2317
20	0.2476	0.2496	0.2526	0.2584	0.2030	0.2051	0.2083	0.2145
21	0.2309	0.2329	0.2358	0.2415	0.1874	0.1895	0.1926	0.1987
22	0.2153	0.2173	0.2201	0.2257	0.1731	0.1751	0.1780	0.1839
23	0.2008	0.2027	0.2055	0.2109	0.1598	0.1617	0.1646	0.1703
24	0.1873	0.1891	0.1918	0.1971	0.1475	0.1494	0.1522	0.1577
25	0.1747	0.1764	0.1791	0.1842	0.1362	0.1380	0.1407	0.1460
26	0.1629	0.1646	0.1671	0.1722	0.1258	0.1275	0.1301	0.1352
27	0.1519	0.1536	0.1560	0.1609	0.1162	0.1178	0.1203	0.1252
28	0.1417	0.1433	0.1457	0.1504	0.1073	0.1088	0.1112	0.1159
29	0.1321	0.1337	0.1360	0.1406	0.0990	0.1005	0.1028	0.1073
30	0.1232	0.1247	0.1269	0.1314	0.0914	0.0929	0.0951	0.0994
31	0.1149	0.1163	0.1185	0.1228	0.0844	0.0858	0.0879	0.0920
32	0.1072	0.1085	0.1106	0.1147	0.0780	0.0793	0.0813	0.0852
33	0.0999	0.1013	0.1033	0.1072	0.0720	0.0732	0.0751	0.0789
34	0.0932	0.0945	0.0964	0.1002	0.0665	0.0677	0.0695	0.0730
35	0.0869	0.0881	0.0900	0.0937	0.0614	0.0625	0.0642	0.0676
36	0.0811	0.0822	0.0840	0.0875	0.0567	0.0578	0.0594	0.0626
37	0.0756	0.0767	0.0784	0.0818	0.0523	0.0534	0.0549	0.0580
38	0.0705	0.0716	0.0732	0.0765	0.0483	0.0493	0.0508	0.0537
39	0.0657	0.0668	0.0683	0.0715	0.0446	0.0455	0.0469	0.0497
40	0.0613	0.0623	0.0638	0.0668	0.0412	0.0421	0.0434	0.0460
41	0.0572	0.0581	0.0596	0.0624	0.0380	0.0389	0.0401	0.0426
42	0.0533	0.0542	0.0556	0.0583	0.0351	0.0359	0.0371	0.0395
43	0.0497	0.0506	0.0519	0.0545	0.0324	0.0332	0.0343	0.0365
44	0.0464	0.0472	0.0484	0.0509	0.0299	0.0306	0.0317	0.0338
45	0.0432	0.0440	0.0452	0.0476	0.0277	0.0283	0.0293	0.0313
46	0.0403	0.0411	0.0422	0.0445	0.0255	0.0262	0.0271	0.0290
47	0.0376	0.0383	0.0394	0.0416	0.0236	0.0242	0.0251	0.0269
48	0.0351	0.0358	0.0368	0.0389	0.0218	0.0223	0.0232	0.0249
49	0.0327	0.0334	0.0343	0.0363	0.0201	0.0206	0.0214	0.0230
50	0.0305	0.0311	0.0321	0.0339	0.0186	0.0191	0.0198	0.0213

The present value of $1 due at the *end* of various time periods

End of Year	9% Interest compounded Monthly	Quarterly	Semi-Annually	Annually	10% Interest compounded Monthly	Quarterly	Semi-Annually	Annually
1	0.9142	0.9148	0.9157	0.9174	0.9052	0.9060	0.9070	0.9091
2	0.8358	0.8369	0.8386	0.8417	0.8194	0.8207	0.8227	0.8264
3	0.7641	0.7657	0.7679	0.7722	0.7417	0.7436	0.7462	0.7513
4	0.6986	0.7005	0.7032	0.7084	0.6714	0.6736	0.6768	0.6830
5	0.6387	0.6408	0.6439	0.6499	0.6078	0.6103	0.6139	0.6209
6	0.5839	0.5862	0.5897	0.5963	0.5502	0.5529	0.5568	0.5645
7	0.5338	0.5363	0.5400	0.5470	0.4980	0.5009	0.5051	0.5132
8	0.4881	0.4907	0.4945	0.5019	0.4508	0.4538	0.4581	0.4665
9	0.4462	0.4489	0.4528	0.4604	0.4081	0.4111	0.4155	0.4241
10	0.4079	0.4106	0.4146	0.4224	0.3694	0.3724	0.3769	0.3855
11	0.3730	0.3757	0.3797	0.3875	0.3344	0.3374	0.3418	0.3505
12	0.3410	0.3437	0.3477	0.3555	0.3027	0.3057	0.3101	0.3186
13	0.3117	0.3144	0.3184	0.3262	0.2740	0.2769	0.2812	0.2897
14	0.2850	0.2876	0.2916	0.2992	0.2480	0.2509	0.2551	0.2633
15	0.2605	0.2631	0.2670	0.2745	0.2245	0.2273	0.2314	0.2394
16	0.2382	0.2407	0.2445	0.2519	0.2032	0.2059	0.2099	0.2176
17	0.2178	0.2202	0.2239	0.2311	0.1840	0.1865	0.1904	0.1978
18	0.1991	0.2015	0.2050	0.2120	0.1665	0.1690	0.1727	0.1799
19	0.1820	0.1843	0.1878	0.1945	0.1508	0.1531	0.1566	0.1635
20	0.1664	0.1686	0.1719	0.1784	0.1365	0.1387	0.1420	0.1486
21	0.1521	0.1543	0.1574	0.1637	0.1235	0.1257	0.1288	0.1351
22	0.1391	0.1411	0.1442	0.1502	0.1118	0.1138	0.1169	0.1228
23	0.1272	0.1291	0.1320	0.1378	0.1012	0.1031	0.1060	0.1117
24	0.1163	0.1181	0.1209	0.1264	0.0916	0.0934	0.0961	0.1015
25	0.1063	0.1081	0.1107	0.1160	0.0829	0.0846	0.0872	0.0923
26	0.0972	0.0989	0.1014	0.1064	0.0751	0.0767	0.0791	0.0839
27	0.0888	0.0904	0.0928	0.0976	0.0680	0.0695	0.0717	0.0763
28	0.0812	0.0827	0.0850	0.0895	0.0615	0.0629	0.0651	0.0693
29	0.0743	0.0757	0.0778	0.0822	0.0557	0.0570	0.0590	0.0630
30	0.0679	0.0692	0.0713	0.0754	0.0504	0.0517	0.0535	0.0573
31	0.0621	0.0634	0.0653	0.0691	0.0456	0.0468	0.0486	0.0521
32	0.0567	0.0580	0.0598	0.0634	0.0413	0.0424	0.0440	0.0474
33	0.0519	0.0530	0.0547	0.0582	0.0374	0.0384	0.0399	0.0431
34	0.0474	0.0485	0.0501	0.0534	0.0338	0.0348	0.0362	0.0391
35	0.0434	0.0444	0.0459	0.0490	0.0306	0.0315	0.0329	0.0356
36	0.0396	0.0406	0.0420	0.0449	0.0277	0.0286	0.0298	0.0323
37	0.0362	0.0371	0.0385	0.0412	0.0251	0.0259	0.0270	0.0294
38	0.0331	0.0340	0.0353	0.0378	0.0227	0.0234	0.0245	0.0267
39	0.0303	0.0311	0.0323	0.0347	0.0206	0.0212	0.0222	0.0243
40	0.0277	0.0284	0.0296	0.0318	0.0186	0.0192	0.0202	0.0221
41	0.0253	0.0260	0.0271	0.0292	0.0169	0.0174	0.0183	0.0201
42	0.0231	0.0238	0.0248	0.0268	0.0153	0.0158	0.0166	0.0183
43	0.0212	0.0218	0.0227	0.0246	0.0138	0.0143	0.0151	0.0166
44	0.0193	0.0199	0.0208	0.0226	0.0125	0.0130	0.0137	0.0151
45	0.0177	0.0182	0.0190	0.0207	0.0113	0.0117	0.0124	0.0137
46	0.0162	0.0167	0.0174	0.0190	0.0102	0.0106	0.0112	0.0125
47	0.0148	0.0153	0.0160	0.0174	0.0093	0.0096	0.0102	0.0113
48	0.0135	0.0140	0.0146	0.0160	0.0084	0.0087	0.0092	0.0103
49	0.0124	0.0128	0.0134	0.0147	0.0076	0.0079	0.0084	0.0094
50	0.0113	0.0117	0.0123	0.0134	0.0069	0.0072	0.0076	0.0085

The present value of $1 due at the *end* of various time periods

End of Year	*11% Interest compounded* Monthly	Quarterly	Semi-Annually	Annually	*12% Interest compounded* Monthly	Quarterly	Semi-Annually	Annually
1	0.8963	0.8972	0.8985	0.9009	0.8874	0.8885	0.8900	0.8929
2	0.8033	0.8049	0.8072	0.8116	0.7876	0.7894	0.7921	0.7972
3	0.7200	0.7221	0.7252	0.7312	0.6989	0.7014	0.7050	0.7118
4	0.6453	0.6479	0.6516	0.6587	0.6203	0.6232	0.6274	0.6355
5	0.5784	0.5813	0.5854	0.5935	0.5504	0.5537	0.5584	0.5674
6	0.5184	0.5215	0.5260	0.5346	0.4885	0.4919	0.4970	0.5066
7	0.4646	0.4679	0.4726	0.4817	0.4335	0.4371	0.4423	0.4523
8	0.4164	0.4197	0.4246	0.4339	0.3847	0.3883	0.3936	0.4039
9	0.3733	0.3766	0.3815	0.3909	0.3414	0.3450	0.3503	0.3606
10	0.3345	0.3379	0.3427	0.3522	0.3030	0.3066	0.3118	0.3220
11	0.2998	0.3031	0.3079	0.3173	0.2689	0.2724	0.2775	0.2875
12	0.2687	0.2719	0.2767	0.2858	0.2386	0.2420	0.2470	0.2567
13	0.2409	0.2440	0.2486	0.2575	0.2118	0.2150	0.2198	0.2292
14	0.2159	0.2189	0.2233	0.2320	0.1879	0.1910	0.1956	0.2046
15	0.1935	0.1964	0.2006	0.2090	0.1668	0.1697	0.1741	0.1827
16	0.1734	0.1762	0.1803	0.1883	0.1480	0.1508	0.1550	0.1631
17	0.1554	0.1581	0.1620	0.1696	0.1314	0.1340	0.1379	0.1456
18	0.1393	0.1418	0.1455	0.1528	0.1166	0.1190	0.1227	0.1300
19	0.1249	0.1272	0.1307	0.1377	0.1034	0.1058	0.1092	0.1161
20	0.1119	0.1141	0.1175	0.1240	0.0918	0.0940	0.0972	0.1037
21	0.1003	0.1024	0.1055	0.1117	0.0815	0.0835	0.0865	0.0926
22	0.0899	0.0919	0.0948	0.1007	0.0723	0.0742	0.0770	0.0826
23	0.0806	0.0824	0.0852	0.0907	0.0642	0.0659	0.0685	0.0738
24	0.0722	0.0740	0.0765	0.0817	0.0569	0.0586	0.0610	0.0659
25	0.0647	0.0663	0.0688	0.0736	0.0505	0.0520	0.0543	0.0588
26	0.0580	0.0595	0.0618	0.0663	0.0448	0.0462	0.0483	0.0525
27	0.0520	0.0534	0.0555	0.0597	0.0398	0.0411	0.0430	0.0469
28	0.0466	0.0479	0.0499	0.0538	0.0353	0.0365	0.0383	0.0419
29	0.0418	0.0430	0.0448	0.0485	0.0313	0.0324	0.0341	0.0374
30	0.0374	0.0386	0.0403	0.0437	0.0278	0.0288	0.0303	0.0334
31	0.0336	0.0346	0.0362	0.0394	0.0247	0.0256	0.0270	0.0298
32	0.0301	0.0310	0.0325	0.0355	0.0219	0.0227	0.0240	0.0266
33	0.0270	0.0278	0.0292	0.0319	0.0194	0.0202	0.0214	0.0238
34	0.0242	0.0250	0.0262	0.0288	0.0173	0.0180	0.0190	0.0212
35	0.0217	0.0224	0.0236	0.0259	0.0153	0.0160	0.0169	0.0189
36	0.0194	0.0201	0.0212	0.0234	0.0136	0.0142	0.0151	0.0169
37	0.0174	0.0180	0.0190	0.0210	0.0121	0.0126	0.0134	0.0151
38	0.0156	0.0162	0.0171	0.0190	0.0107	0.0112	0.0119	0.0135
39	0.0140	0.0145	0.0154	0.0171	0.0095	0.0099	0.0106	0.0120
40	0.0125	0.0130	0.0138	0.0154	0.0084	0.0088	0.0095	0.0107
41	0.0112	0.0117	0.0124	0.0139	0.0075	0.0078	0.0084	0.0096
42	0.0101	0.0105	0.0111	0.0125	0.0066	0.0070	0.0075	0.0086
43	0.0090	0.0094	0.0100	0.0112	0.0059	0.0062	0.0067	0.0076
44	0.0081	0.0084	0.0090	0.0101	0.0052	0.0055	0.0059	0.0068
45	0.0072	0.0076	0.0081	0.0091	0.0046	0.0049	0.0053	0.0061
46	0.0065	0.0068	0.0073	0.0082	0.0041	0.0043	0.0047	0.0054
47	0.0058	0.0061	0.0065	0.0074	0.0037	0.0039	0.0042	0.0049
48	0.0052	0.0055	0.0059	0.0067	0.0032	0.0034	0.0037	0.0043
49	0.0047	0.0049	0.0053	0.0060	0.0029	0.0030	0.0033	0.0039
50	0.0042	0.0044	0.0047	0.0054	0.0026	0.0027	0.0029	0.0035

The present value of $1 due at the *end* of various time periods

End of Year	13% Interest compounded Monthly	Quarterly	Semi-Annually	Annually	14% Interest compounded Monthly	Quarterly	Semi-Annually	Annually
1	0.8787	0.8799	0.8817	0.8850	0.8701	0.8714	0.8734	0.8772
2	0.7721	0.7742	0.7773	0.7831	0.7570	0.7594	0.7629	0.7695
3	0.6785	0.6813	0.6853	0.6931	0.6586	0.6618	0.6663	0.6750
4	0.5962	0.5995	0.6042	0.6133	0.5731	0.5767	0.5820	0.5921
5	0.5239	0.5275	0.5327	0.5428	0.4986	0.5026	0.5083	0.5194
6	0.4603	0.4641	0.4697	0.4803	0.4338	0.4380	0.4440	0.4556
7	0.4045	0.4084	0.4141	0.4251	0.3774	0.3817	0.3878	0.3996
8	0.3554	0.3594	0.3651	0.3762	0.3284	0.3326	0.3387	0.3506
9	0.3123	0.3162	0.3219	0.3329	0.2857	0.2898	0.2959	0.3075
10	0.2744	0.2782	0.2838	0.2946	0.2486	0.2526	0.2584	0.2697
11	0.2412	0.2448	0.2502	0.2607	0.2163	0.2201	0.2257	0.2366
12	0.2119	0.2154	0.2206	0.2307	0.1882	0.1918	0.1971	0.2076
13	0.1862	0.1895	0.1945	0.2042	0.1637	0.1671	0.1722	0.1821
14	0.1636	0.1668	0.1715	0.1807	0.1425	0.1457	0.1504	0.1597
15	0.1438	0.1468	0.1512	0.1599	0.1240	0.1269	0.1314	0.1401
16	0.1263	0.1291	0.1333	0.1415	0.1078	0.1106	0.1147	0.1229
17	0.1110	0.1136	0.1175	0.1252	0.0938	0.0964	0.1002	0.1078
18	0.0975	0.1000	0.1036	0.1108	0.0816	0.0840	0.0875	0.0946
19	0.0857	0.0880	0.0914	0.0981	0.0710	0.0732	0.0765	0.0829
20	0.0753	0.0774	0.0805	0.0868	0.0618	0.0638	0.0668	0.0728
21	0.0662	0.0681	0.0710	0.0768	0.0538	0.0556	0.0583	0.0638
22	0.0582	0.0599	0.0626	0.0680	0.0468	0.0484	0.0509	0.0560
23	0.0511	0.0527	0.0552	0.0601	0.0407	0.0422	0.0445	0.0491
24	0.0449	0.0464	0.0487	0.0532	0.0354	0.0368	0.0389	0.0431
25	0.0395	0.0408	0.0429	0.0471	0.0308	0.0321	0.0339	0.0378
26	0.0347	0.0359	0.0378	0.0417	0.0268	0.0279	0.0297	0.0331
27	0.0305	0.0316	0.0334	0.0369	0.0233	0.0243	0.0259	0.0291
28	0.0268	0.0278	0.0294	0.0326	0.0203	0.0212	0.0226	0.0255
29	0.0235	0.0245	0.0259	0.0289	0.0177	0.0185	0.0198	0.0224
30	0.0207	0.0215	0.0229	0.0256	0.0154	0.0161	0.0173	0.0196
31	0.0182	0.0190	0.0202	0.0226	0.0134	0.0140	0.0151	0.0172
32	0.0160	0.0167	0.0178	0.0200	0.0116	0.0122	0.0132	0.0151
33	0.0140	0.0147	0.0157	0.0177	0.0101	0.0107	0.0115	0.0132
34	0.0123	0.0129	0.0138	0.0157	0.0088	0.0093	0.0100	0.0116
35	0.0108	0.0114	0.0122	0.0139	0.0077	0.0081	0.0088	0.0102
36	0.0095	0.0100	0.0107	0.0123	0.0067	0.0071	0.0077	0.0089
37	0.0084	0.0088	0.0095	0.0109	0.0058	0.0061	0.0067	0.0078
38	0.0073	0.0077	0.0083	0.0096	0.0050	0.0054	0.0058	0.0069
39	0.0065	0.0068	0.0074	0.0085	0.0044	0.0047	0.0051	0.0060
40	0.0057	0.0060	0.0065	0.0075	0.0038	0.0041	0.0045	0.0053
41	0.0050	0.0053	0.0057	0.0067	0.0033	0.0035	0.0039	0.0046
42	0.0044	0.0046	0.0050	0.0059	0.0029	0.0031	0.0034	0.0041
43	0.0038	0.0041	0.0044	0.0052	0.0025	0.0027	0.0030	0.0036
44	0.0034	0.0036	0.0039	0.0046	0.0022	0.0023	0.0026	0.0031
45	0.0030	0.0032	0.0035	0.0041	0.0019	0.0020	0.0023	0.0027
46	0.0026	0.0028	0.0030	0.0036	0.0017	0.0018	0.0020	0.0024
47	0.0023	0.0024	0.0027	0.0032	0.0014	0.0016	0.0017	0.0021
48	0.0020	0.0022	0.0024	0.0028	0.0013	0.0014	0.0015	0.0019
49	0.0018	0.0019	0.0021	0.0025	0.0011	0.0012	0.0013	0.0016
50	0.0016	0.0017	0.0018	0.0022	0.0009	0.0010	0.0012	0.0014

The present value of $1 due at the *end* of various time periods

End of Year	15% Interest compounded Monthly	Quarterly	Semi-Annually	Annually	16% Interest compounded Monthly	Quarterly	Semi-Annually	Annually
1	0.8615	0.8631	0.8653	0.8696	0.8530	0.8548	0.8573	0.8621
2	0.7422	0.7449	0.7488	0.7561	0.7277	0.7307	0.7350	0.7432
3	0.6394	0.6429	0.6480	0.6575	0.6207	0.6246	0.6302	0.6407
4	0.5509	0.5549	0.5607	0.5718	0.5295	0.5339	0.5403	0.5523
5	0.4746	0.4789	0.4852	0.4972	0.4517	0.4564	0.4632	0.4761
6	0.4088	0.4133	0.4199	0.4323	0.3853	0.3901	0.3971	0.4104
7	0.3522	0.3567	0.3633	0.3759	0.3287	0.3335	0.3405	0.3538
8	0.3034	0.3079	0.3144	0.3269	0.2804	0.2851	0.2919	0.3050
9	0.2614	0.2657	0.2720	0.2843	0.2392	0.2437	0.2502	0.2630
10	0.2252	0.2293	0.2354	0.2472	0.2040	0.2083	0.2145	0.2267
11	0.1940	0.1979	0.2037	0.2149	0.1741	0.1780	0.1839	0.1954
12	0.1672	0.1708	0.1763	0.1869	0.1485	0.1522	0.1577	0.1685
13	0.1440	0.1474	0.1525	0.1625	0.1267	0.1301	0.1352	0.1452
14	0.1241	0.1273	0.1320	0.1413	0.1080	0.1112	0.1159	0.1252
15	0.1069	0.1098	0.1142	0.1229	0.0922	0.0951	0.0994	0.1079
16	0.0921	0.0948	0.0988	0.1069	0.0786	0.0813	0.0852	0.0930
17	0.0793	0.0818	0.0855	0.0929	0.0671	0.0695	0.0730	0.0802
18	0.0683	0.0706	0.0740	0.0808	0.0572	0.0594	0.0626	0.0691
19	0.0589	0.0609	0.0640	0.0703	0.0488	0.0508	0.0537	0.0596
20	0.0507	0.0526	0.0554	0.0611	0.0416	0.0434	0.0460	0.0514
21	0.0437	0.0454	0.0480	0.0531	0.0355	0.0371	0.0395	0.0443
22	0.0376	0.0392	0.0415	0.0462	0.0303	0.0317	0.0338	0.0382
23	0.0324	0.0338	0.0359	0.0402	0.0258	0.0271	0.0290	0.0329
24	0.0279	0.0292	0.0311	0.0349	0.0220	0.0232	0.0249	0.0284
25	0.0241	0.0252	0.0269	0.0304	0.0188	0.0198	0.0213	0.0245
26	0.0207	0.0217	0.0233	0.0264	0.0160	0.0169	0.0183	0.0211
27	0.0179	0.0188	0.0201	0.0230	0.0137	0.0145	0.0157	0.0182
28	0.0154	0.0162	0.0174	0.0200	0.0117	0.0124	0.0134	0.0157
29	0.0133	0.0140	0.0151	0.0174	0.0100	0.0106	0.0115	0.0135
30	0.0114	0.0121	0.0130	0.0151	0.0085	0.0090	0.0099	0.0116
31	0.0098	0.0104	0.0113	0.0131	0.0072	0.0077	0.0085	0.0100
32	0.0085	0.0090	0.0098	0.0114	0.0062	0.0066	0.0073	0.0087
33	0.0073	0.0078	0.0085	0.0099	0.0053	0.0056	0.0062	0.0075
34	0.0063	0.0067	0.0073	0.0086	0.0045	0.0048	0.0053	0.0064
35	0.0054	0.0058	0.0063	0.0075	0.0038	0.0041	0.0046	0.0055
36	0.0047	0.0050	0.0055	0.0065	0.0033	0.0035	0.0039	0.0048
37	0.0040	0.0043	0.0047	0.0057	0.0028	0.0030	0.0034	0.0041
38	0.0035	0.0037	0.0041	0.0049	0.0024	0.0026	0.0029	0.0036
39	0.0030	0.0032	0.0035	0.0043	0.0020	0.0022	0.0025	0.0031
40	0.0026	0.0028	0.0031	0.0037	0.0017	0.0019	0.0021	0.0026
41	0.0022	0.0024	0.0027	0.0032	0.0015	0.0016	0.0018	0.0023
42	0.0019	0.0021	0.0023	0.0028	0.0013	0.0014	0.0016	0.0020
43	0.0016	0.0018	0.0020	0.0025	0.0011	0.0012	0.0013	0.0017
44	0.0014	0.0015	0.0017	0.0021	0.0009	0.0010	0.0011	0.0015
45	0.0012	0.0013	0.0015	0.0019	0.0008	0.0009	0.0010	0.0013
46	0.0011	0.0011	0.0013	0.0016	0.0007	0.0007	0.0008	0.0011
47	0.0009	0.0010	0.0011	0.0014	0.0006	0.0006	0.0007	0.0009
48	0.0008	0.0009	0.0010	0.0012	0.0005	0.0005	0.0006	0.0008
49	0.0007	0.0007	0.0008	0.0011	0.0004	0.0005	0.0005	0.0007
50	0.0006	0.0006	0.0007	0.0009	0.0004	0.0004	0.0005	0.0006

The present value of $1 due at the *end* of various time periods

End of Year	17% Interest compounded Monthly	Quarterly	Semi-Annually	Annually	18% Interest compounded Monthly	Quarterly	Semi-Annually	Annually
1	0.8447	0.8466	0.8495	0.8547	0.8364	0.8386	0.8417	0.8475
2	0.7135	0.7168	0.7216	0.7305	0.6995	0.7032	0.7084	0.7182
3	0.6026	0.6069	0.6129	0.6244	0.5851	0.5897	0.5963	0.6086
4	0.5090	0.5138	0.5207	0.5337	0.4894	0.4945	0.5019	0.5158
5	0.4300	0.4350	0.4423	0.4561	0.4093	0.4146	0.4224	0.4371
6	0.3632	0.3683	0.3757	0.3898	0.3423	0.3477	0.3555	0.3704
7	0.3068	0.3118	0.3191	0.3332	0.2863	0.2916	0.2992	0.3139
8	0.2591	0.2640	0.2711	0.2848	0.2395	0.2445	0.2519	0.2660
9	0.2189	0.2235	0.2303	0.2434	0.2003	0.2050	0.2120	0.2255
10	0.1849	0.1892	0.1956	0.2080	0.1675	0.1719	0.1784	0.1911
11	0.1562	0.1602	0.1662	0.1778	0.1401	0.1442	0.1502	0.1619
12	0.1319	0.1356	0.1412	0.1520	0.1172	0.1209	0.1264	0.1372
13	0.1114	0.1148	0.1199	0.1299	0.0980	0.1014	0.1064	0.1163
14	0.0941	0.0972	0.1019	0.1110	0.0820	0.0850	0.0895	0.0985
15	0.0795	0.0823	0.0865	0.0949	0.0686	0.0713	0.0754	0.0835
16	0.0671	0.0697	0.0735	0.0811	0.0573	0.0598	0.0634	0.0708
17	0.0567	0.0590	0.0624	0.0693	0.0480	0.0501	0.0534	0.0600
18	0.0479	0.0499	0.0530	0.0592	0.0401	0.0420	0.0449	0.0508
19	0.0405	0.0423	0.0450	0.0506	0.0336	0.0353	0.0378	0.0431
20	0.0342	0.0358	0.0383	0.0433	0.0281	0.0296	0.0318	0.0365
21	0.0289	0.0303	0.0325	0.0370	0.0235	0.0248	0.0268	0.0309
22	0.0244	0.0257	0.0276	0.0316	0.0196	0.0208	0.0226	0.0262
23	0.0206	0.0217	0.0235	0.0270	0.0164	0.0174	0.0190	0.0222
24	0.0174	0.0184	0.0199	0.0231	0.0137	0.0146	0.0160	0.0188
25	0.0147	0.0156	0.0169	0.0197	0.0115	0.0123	0.0134	0.0160
26	0.0124	0.0132	0.0144	0.0169	0.0096	0.0103	0.0113	0.0135
27	0.0105	0.0112	0.0122	0.0144	0.0080	0.0086	0.0095	0.0115
28	0.0089	0.0095	0.0104	0.0123	0.0067	0.0072	0.0080	0.0097
29	0.0075	0.0080	0.0088	0.0105	0.0056	0.0061	0.0067	0.0082
30	0.0063	0.0068	0.0075	0.0090	0.0047	0.0051	0.0057	0.0070
31	0.0053	0.0057	0.0064	0.0077	0.0039	0.0043	0.0048	0.0059
32	0.0045	0.0049	0.0054	0.0066	0.0033	0.0036	0.0040	0.0050
33	0.0038	0.0041	0.0046	0.0056	0.0028	0.0030	0.0034	0.0042
34	0.0032	0.0035	0.0039	0.0048	0.0023	0.0025	0.0029	0.0036
35	0.0027	0.0029	0.0033	0.0041	0.0019	0.0021	0.0024	0.0030
36	0.0023	0.0025	0.0028	0.0035	0.0016	0.0018	0.0020	0.0026
37	0.0019	0.0021	0.0024	0.0030	0.0013	0.0015	0.0017	0.0022
38	0.0016	0.0018	0.0020	0.0026	0.0011	0.0012	0.0014	0.0019
39	0.0014	0.0015	0.0017	0.0022	0.0009	0.0010	0.0012	0.0016
40	0.0012	0.0013	0.0015	0.0019	0.0008	0.0009	0.0010	0.0013
41	0.0010	0.0011	0.0012	0.0016	0.0007	0.0007	0.0009	0.0011
42	0.0008	0.0009	0.0011	0.0014	0.0006	0.0006	0.0007	0.0010
43	0.0007	0.0008	0.0009	0.0012	0.0005	0.0005	0.0006	0.0008
44	0.0006	0.0007	0.0008	0.0010	0.0004	0.0004	0.0005	0.0007
45	0.0005	0.0006	0.0006	0.0009	0.0003	0.0004	0.0004	0.0006
46	0.0004	0.0005	0.0006	0.0007	0.0003	0.0003	0.0004	0.0005
47	0.0004	0.0004	0.0005	0.0006	0.0002	0.0003	0.0003	0.0004
48	0.0003	0.0003	0.0004	0.0005	0.0002	0.0002	0.0003	0.0004
49	0.0003	0.0003	0.0003	0.0005	0.0002	0.0002	0.0002	0.0003
50	0.0002	0.0002	0.0003	0.0004	0.0001	0.0002	0.0002	0.0003

TABLE 4

How much must be invested at the *end* of each period to accumulate $1 by some future date, assuming deposits are made monthly, quarterly, semi-annually or annually at various interest rates?

Applications

Chapter Five

- Periodic deposits at the end of each period required to attain a certain savings level by the end of a given time period.
- How much must be deposited periodically in order to save a desired amount towards a child's college education?
- How much must you set aside on a periodic basis to become a millionaire by the time you retire?

How much must be invested at the *end* of each period to accumulate $1

End of Year	At 3% Interest compounded and Deposits made				At 4% Interest compounded and Deposits made			
	Monthly	Quarterly	Semi-Annually	Annually	Monthly	Quarterly	Semi-Annually	Annually
1	0.0822	0.2472	0.4963	1.0000	0.0818	0.2463	0.4950	1.0000
2	0.0405	0.1218	0.2444	0.4926	0.0401	0.1207	0.2426	0.4902
3	0.0266	0.0800	0.1605	0.3235	0.0262	0.0788	0.1585	0.3203
4	0.0196	0.0591	0.1186	0.2390	0.0192	0.0579	0.1165	0.2355
5	0.0155	0.0465	0.0934	0.1884	0.0151	0.0454	0.0913	0.1846
6	0.0127	0.0382	0.0767	0.1546	0.0123	0.0371	0.0746	0.1508
7	0.0107	0.0322	0.0647	0.1305	0.0103	0.0311	0.0626	0.1266
8	0.0092	0.0278	0.0558	0.1125	0.0089	0.0267	0.0537	0.1085
9	0.0081	0.0243	0.0488	0.0984	0.0077	0.0232	0.0467	0.0945
10	0.0072	0.0215	0.0432	0.0872	0.0068	0.0205	0.0412	0.0833
11	0.0064	0.0193	0.0387	0.0781	0.0060	0.0182	0.0366	0.0741
12	0.0058	0.0174	0.0349	0.0705	0.0054	0.0163	0.0329	0.0666
13	0.0052	0.0158	0.0317	0.0640	0.0049	0.0148	0.0297	0.0601
14	0.0048	0.0144	0.0290	0.0585	0.0045	0.0134	0.0270	0.0547
15	0.0044	0.0133	0.0266	0.0538	0.0041	0.0122	0.0246	0.0499
16	0.0041	0.0122	0.0246	0.0496	0.0037	0.0112	0.0226	0.0458
17	0.0038	0.0113	0.0228	0.0460	0.0034	0.0103	0.0208	0.0422
18	0.0035	0.0105	0.0212	0.0427	0.0032	0.0096	0.0192	0.0390
19	0.0033	0.0098	0.0197	0.0398	0.0029	0.0088	0.0178	0.0361
20	0.0030	0.0092	0.0184	0.0372	0.0027	0.0082	0.0166	0.0336
21	0.0029	0.0086	0.0173	0.0349	0.0025	0.0077	0.0154	0.0313
22	0.0027	0.0081	0.0162	0.0327	0.0024	0.0071	0.0144	0.0292
23	0.0025	0.0076	0.0153	0.0308	0.0022	0.0067	0.0135	0.0273
24	0.0024	0.0072	0.0144	0.0290	0.0021	0.0063	0.0126	0.0256
25	0.0022	0.0068	0.0136	0.0274	0.0019	0.0059	0.0118	0.0240
26	0.0021	0.0064	0.0128	0.0259	0.0018	0.0055	0.0111	0.0226
27	0.0020	0.0060	0.0122	0.0246	0.0017	0.0052	0.0105	0.0212
28	0.0019	0.0057	0.0115	0.0233	0.0016	0.0049	0.0098	0.0200
29	0.0018	0.0054	0.0109	0.0221	0.0015	0.0046	0.0093	0.0189
30	0.0017	0.0052	0.0104	0.0210	0.0014	0.0043	0.0088	0.0178
31	0.0016	0.0049	0.0099	0.0200	0.0014	0.0041	0.0083	0.0169
32	0.0016	0.0047	0.0094	0.0190	0.0013	0.0039	0.0078	0.0159
33	0.0015	0.0045	0.0090	0.0182	0.0012	0.0037	0.0074	0.0151
34	0.0014	0.0043	0.0086	0.0173	0.0012	0.0035	0.0070	0.0143
35	0.0013	0.0041	0.0082	0.0165	0.0011	0.0033	0.0067	0.0136
36	0.0013	0.0039	0.0078	0.0158	0.0010	0.0031	0.0063	0.0129
37	0.0012	0.0037	0.0075	0.0151	0.0010	0.0030	0.0060	0.0122
38	0.0012	0.0035	0.0071	0.0145	0.0009	0.0028	0.0057	0.0116
39	0.0011	0.0034	0.0068	0.0138	0.0009	0.0027	0.0054	0.0111
40	0.0011	0.0033	0.0065	0.0133	0.0008	0.0026	0.0052	0.0105
41	0.0010	0.0031	0.0063	0.0127	0.0008	0.0024	0.0049	0.0100
42	0.0010	0.0030	0.0060	0.0122	0.0008	0.0023	0.0047	0.0095
43	0.0010	0.0029	0.0058	0.0117	0.0007	0.0022	0.0045	0.0091
44	0.0009	0.0028	0.0055	0.0112	0.0007	0.0021	0.0042	0.0087
45	0.0009	0.0026	0.0053	0.0108	0.0007	0.0020	0.0040	0.0083
46	0.0008	0.0025	0.0051	0.0104	0.0006	0.0019	0.0039	0.0079
47	0.0008	0.0024	0.0049	0.0100	0.0006	0.0018	0.0037	0.0075
48	0.0008	0.0023	0.0047	0.0096	0.0006	0.0017	0.0035	0.0072
49	0.0007	0.0023	0.0045	0.0092	0.0005	0.0017	0.0034	0.0069
50	0.0007	0.0022	0.0044	0.0089	0.0005	0.0016	0.0032	0.0066

How much must be invested at the *end* of each period to accumulate $1

End of Year	At 5% Interest compounded and Deposits made				At 6% Interest compounded and Deposits made			
	Monthly	*Quarterly*	*Semi-Annually*	*Annually*	*Monthly*	*Quarterly*	*Semi-Annually*	*Annually*
1	0.0814	0.2454	0.4938	1.0000	0.0811	0.2444	0.4926	1.0000
2	0.0397	0.1196	0.2408	0.4878	0.0393	0.1186	0.2390	0.4854
3	0.0258	0.0778	0.1565	0.3172	0.0254	0.0767	0.1546	0.3141
4	0.0189	0.0568	0.1145	0.2320	0.0185	0.0558	0.1125	0.2286
5	0.0147	0.0443	0.0893	0.1810	0.0143	0.0432	0.0872	0.1774
6	0.0119	0.0360	0.0725	0.1470	0.0116	0.0349	0.0705	0.1434
7	0.0100	0.0300	0.0605	0.1228	0.0096	0.0290	0.0585	0.1191
8	0.0085	0.0256	0.0516	0.1047	0.0081	0.0246	0.0496	0.1010
9	0.0074	0.0222	0.0447	0.0907	0.0070	0.0212	0.0427	0.0870
10	0.0064	0.0194	0.0391	0.0795	0.0061	0.0184	0.0372	0.0759
11	0.0057	0.0172	0.0346	0.0704	0.0054	0.0162	0.0327	0.0668
12	0.0051	0.0153	0.0309	0.0628	0.0048	0.0144	0.0290	0.0593
13	0.0046	0.0138	0.0278	0.0565	0.0042	0.0128	0.0259	0.0530
14	0.0041	0.0124	0.0251	0.0510	0.0038	0.0115	0.0233	0.0476
15	0.0037	0.0113	0.0228	0.0463	0.0034	0.0104	0.0210	0.0430
16	0.0034	0.0103	0.0208	0.0423	0.0031	0.0094	0.0190	0.0390
17	0.0031	0.0094	0.0190	0.0387	0.0028	0.0086	0.0173	0.0354
18	0.0029	0.0086	0.0175	0.0355	0.0026	0.0078	0.0158	0.0324
19	0.0026	0.0080	0.0161	0.0327	0.0024	0.0071	0.0145	0.0296
20	0.0024	0.0073	0.0148	0.0302	0.0022	0.0065	0.0133	0.0272
21	0.0023	0.0068	0.0137	0.0280	0.0020	0.0060	0.0122	0.0250
22	0.0021	0.0063	0.0127	0.0260	0.0018	0.0055	0.0112	0.0230
23	0.0019	0.0059	0.0118	0.0241	0.0017	0.0051	0.0104	0.0213
24	0.0018	0.0054	0.0110	0.0225	0.0016	0.0047	0.0096	0.0197
25	0.0017	0.0051	0.0103	0.0210	0.0014	0.0044	0.0089	0.0182
26	0.0016	0.0047	0.0096	0.0196	0.0013	0.0040	0.0082	0.0169
27	0.0015	0.0044	0.0089	0.0183	0.0012	0.0038	0.0076	0.0157
28	0.0014	0.0041	0.0084	0.0171	0.0012	0.0035	0.0071	0.0146
29	0.0013	0.0039	0.0078	0.0160	0.0011	0.0032	0.0066	0.0136
30	0.0012	0.0036	0.0074	0.0151	0.0010	0.0030	0.0061	0.0126
31	0.0011	0.0034	0.0069	0.0141	0.0009	0.0028	0.0057	0.0118
32	0.0011	0.0032	0.0065	0.0133	0.0009	0.0026	0.0053	0.0110
33	0.0010	0.0030	0.0061	0.0125	0.0008	0.0024	0.0050	0.0103
34	0.0009	0.0028	0.0057	0.0118	0.0008	0.0023	0.0046	0.0096
35	0.0009	0.0027	0.0054	0.0111	0.0007	0.0021	0.0043	0.0090
36	0.0008	0.0025	0.0051	0.0104	0.0007	0.0020	0.0041	0.0084
37	0.0008	0.0024	0.0048	0.0098	0.0006	0.0019	0.0038	0.0079
38	0.0007	0.0022	0.0045	0.0093	0.0006	0.0017	0.0035	0.0074
39	0.0007	0.0021	0.0043	0.0088	0.0005	0.0016	0.0033	0.0069
40	0.0007	0.0020	0.0040	0.0083	0.0005	0.0015	0.0031	0.0065
41	0.0006	0.0019	0.0038	0.0078	0.0005	0.0014	0.0029	0.0061
42	0.0006	0.0018	0.0036	0.0074	0.0004	0.0013	0.0027	0.0057
43	0.0006	0.0017	0.0034	0.0070	0.0004	0.0013	0.0026	0.0053
44	0.0005	0.0016	0.0032	0.0066	0.0004	0.0012	0.0024	0.0050
45	0.0005	0.0015	0.0030	0.0063	0.0004	0.0011	0.0023	0.0047
46	0.0005	0.0014	0.0029	0.0059	0.0003	0.0010	0.0021	0.0044
47	0.0004	0.0013	0.0027	0.0056	0.0003	0.0010	0.0020	0.0041
48	0.0004	0.0013	0.0026	0.0053	0.0003	0.0009	0.0019	0.0039
49	0.0004	0.0012	0.0024	0.0050	0.0003	0.0009	0.0018	0.0037
50	0.0004	0.0011	0.0023	0.0048	0.0003	0.0008	0.0016	0.0034

How much must be invested at the *end* of each period to accumulate $1

End of Year	At 7% Interest compounded and Deposits made				At 8% Interest compounded and Deposits made			
	Monthly	*Quarterly*	*Semi-Annually*	*Annually*	*Monthly*	*Quarterly*	*Semi-Annually*	*Annually*
1	0.0807	0.2435	0.4914	1.0000	0.0803	0.2426	0.4902	1.0000
2	0.0389	0.1175	0.2373	0.4831	0.0386	0.1165	0.2355	0.4808
3	0.0250	0.0756	0.1527	0.3111	0.0247	0.0746	0.1508	0.3080
4	0.0181	0.0547	0.1105	0.2252	0.0177	0.0537	0.1085	0.2219
5	0.0140	0.0422	0.0852	0.1739	0.0136	0.0412	0.0833	0.1705
6	0.0112	0.0339	0.0685	0.1398	0.0109	0.0329	0.0666	0.1363
7	0.0093	0.0280	0.0566	0.1156	0.0089	0.0270	0.0547	0.1121
8	0.0078	0.0236	0.0477	0.0975	0.0075	0.0226	0.0458	0.0940
9	0.0067	0.0202	0.0408	0.0835	0.0064	0.0192	0.0390	0.0801
10	0.0058	0.0175	0.0354	0.0724	0.0055	0.0166	0.0336	0.0690
11	0.0051	0.0153	0.0309	0.0634	0.0047	0.0144	0.0292	0.0601
12	0.0045	0.0135	0.0273	0.0559	0.0042	0.0126	0.0256	0.0527
13	0.0039	0.0119	0.0242	0.0497	0.0037	0.0111	0.0226	0.0465
14	0.0035	0.0107	0.0216	0.0443	0.0032	0.0098	0.0200	0.0413
15	0.0032	0.0096	0.0194	0.0398	0.0029	0.0088	0.0178	0.0368
16	0.0028	0.0086	0.0174	0.0359	0.0026	0.0078	0.0159	0.0330
17	0.0026	0.0078	0.0158	0.0324	0.0023	0.0070	0.0143	0.0296
18	0.0023	0.0070	0.0143	0.0294	0.0021	0.0063	0.0129	0.0267
19	0.0021	0.0064	0.0130	0.0268	0.0019	0.0057	0.0116	0.0241
20	0.0019	0.0058	0.0118	0.0244	0.0017	0.0052	0.0105	0.0219
21	0.0018	0.0053	0.0108	0.0223	0.0015	0.0047	0.0095	0.0198
22	0.0016	0.0049	0.0099	0.0204	0.0014	0.0042	0.0087	0.0180
23	0.0015	0.0044	0.0091	0.0187	0.0013	0.0039	0.0079	0.0164
24	0.0013	0.0041	0.0083	0.0172	0.0012	0.0035	0.0072	0.0150
25	0.0012	0.0037	0.0076	0.0158	0.0011	0.0032	0.0066	0.0137
26	0.0011	0.0034	0.0070	0.0146	0.0010	0.0029	0.0060	0.0125
27	0.0010	0.0032	0.0065	0.0134	0.0009	0.0027	0.0055	0.0114
28	0.0010	0.0029	0.0060	0.0124	0.0008	0.0024	0.0050	0.0105
29	0.0009	0.0027	0.0055	0.0114	0.0007	0.0022	0.0046	0.0096
30	0.0008	0.0025	0.0051	0.0106	0.0007	0.0020	0.0042	0.0088
31	0.0008	0.0023	0.0047	0.0098	0.0006	0.0019	0.0039	0.0081
32	0.0007	0.0021	0.0044	0.0091	0.0006	0.0017	0.0035	0.0075
33	0.0006	0.0020	0.0040	0.0084	0.0005	0.0016	0.0032	0.0069
34	0.0006	0.0018	0.0037	0.0078	0.0005	0.0015	0.0030	0.0063
35	0.0006	0.0017	0.0035	0.0072	0.0004	0.0013	0.0027	0.0058
36	0.0005	0.0016	0.0032	0.0067	0.0004	0.0012	0.0025	0.0053
37	0.0005	0.0015	0.0030	0.0062	0.0004	0.0011	0.0023	0.0049
38	0.0004	0.0013	0.0028	0.0058	0.0003	0.0010	0.0021	0.0045
39	0.0004	0.0013	0.0026	0.0054	0.0003	0.0010	0.0020	0.0042
40	0.0004	0.0012	0.0024	0.0050	0.0003	0.0009	0.0018	0.0039
41	0.0004	0.0011	0.0022	0.0047	0.0003	0.0008	0.0017	0.0036
42	0.0003	0.0010	0.0021	0.0043	0.0002	0.0007	0.0015	0.0033
43	0.0003	0.0009	0.0019	0.0040	0.0002	0.0007	0.0014	0.0030
44	0.0003	0.0009	0.0018	0.0038	0.0002	0.0006	0.0013	0.0028
45	0.0003	0.0008	0.0017	0.0035	0.0002	0.0006	0.0012	0.0026
46	0.0002	0.0007	0.0015	0.0033	0.0002	0.0005	0.0011	0.0024
47	0.0002	0.0007	0.0014	0.0030	0.0002	0.0005	0.0010	0.0022
48	0.0002	0.0006	0.0013	0.0028	0.0001	0.0005	0.0009	0.0020
49	0.0002	0.0006	0.0012	0.0026	0.0001	0.0004	0.0009	0.0019
50	0.0002	0.0006	0.0012	0.0025	0.0001	0.0004	0.0008	0.0017

How much must be invested at the *end* of each period to accumulate $1

End of Year	At 9% Interest compounded and Deposits made				At 10% Interest compounded and Deposits made			
	Monthly	*Quarterly*	*Semi-Annually*	*Annually*	*Monthly*	*Quarterly*	*Semi-Annually*	*Annually*
1	0.0800	0.2417	0.4890	1.0000	0.0796	0.2408	0.4878	1.0000
2	0.0382	0.1155	0.2337	0.4785	0.0378	0.1145	0.2320	0.4762
3	0.0243	0.0735	0.1489	0.3051	0.0239	0.0725	0.1470	0.3021
4	0.0174	0.0526	0.1066	0.2187	0.0170	0.0516	0.1047	0.2155
5	0.0133	0.0401	0.0814	0.1671	0.0129	0.0391	0.0795	0.1638
6	0.0105	0.0319	0.0647	0.1329	0.0102	0.0309	0.0628	0.1296
7	0.0086	0.0260	0.0528	0.1087	0.0083	0.0251	0.0510	0.1054
8	0.0072	0.0217	0.0440	0.0907	0.0068	0.0208	0.0423	0.0874
9	0.0060	0.0183	0.0372	0.0768	0.0057	0.0175	0.0355	0.0736
10	0.0052	0.0157	0.0319	0.0658	0.0049	0.0148	0.0302	0.0627
11	0.0045	0.0135	0.0275	0.0569	0.0042	0.0127	0.0260	0.0540
12	0.0039	0.0118	0.0240	0.0497	0.0036	0.0110	0.0225	0.0468
13	0.0034	0.0103	0.0210	0.0436	0.0031	0.0096	0.0196	0.0408
14	0.0030	0.0091	0.0185	0.0384	0.0027	0.0084	0.0171	0.0357
15	0.0026	0.0080	0.0164	0.0341	0.0024	0.0074	0.0151	0.0315
16	0.0023	0.0071	0.0146	0.0303	0.0021	0.0065	0.0133	0.0278
17	0.0021	0.0064	0.0130	0.0270	0.0019	0.0057	0.0118	0.0247
18	0.0019	0.0057	0.0116	0.0242	0.0017	0.0051	0.0104	0.0219
19	0.0017	0.0051	0.0104	0.0217	0.0015	0.0045	0.0093	0.0195
20	0.0015	0.0046	0.0093	0.0195	0.0013	0.0040	0.0083	0.0175
21	0.0013	0.0041	0.0084	0.0176	0.0012	0.0036	0.0074	0.0156
22	0.0012	0.0037	0.0076	0.0159	0.0010	0.0032	0.0066	0.0140
23	0.0011	0.0033	0.0068	0.0144	0.0009	0.0029	0.0059	0.0126
24	0.0010	0.0030	0.0062	0.0130	0.0008	0.0026	0.0053	0.0113
25	0.0009	0.0027	0.0056	0.0118	0.0008	0.0023	0.0048	0.0102
26	0.0008	0.0025	0.0051	0.0107	0.0007	0.0021	0.0043	0.0092
27	0.0007	0.0022	0.0046	0.0097	0.0006	0.0019	0.0039	0.0083
28	0.0007	0.0020	0.0042	0.0089	0.0005	0.0017	0.0035	0.0075
29	0.0006	0.0018	0.0038	0.0081	0.0005	0.0015	0.0031	0.0067
30	0.0005	0.0017	0.0035	0.0073	0.0004	0.0014	0.0028	0.0061
31	0.0005	0.0015	0.0031	0.0067	0.0004	0.0012	0.0026	0.0055
32	0.0005	0.0014	0.0029	0.0061	0.0004	0.0011	0.0023	0.0050
33	0.0004	0.0013	0.0026	0.0056	0.0003	0.0010	0.0021	0.0045
34	0.0004	0.0011	0.0024	0.0051	0.0003	0.0009	0.0019	0.0041
35	0.0003	0.0010	0.0022	0.0046	0.0003	0.0008	0.0017	0.0037
36	0.0003	0.0010	0.0020	0.0042	0.0002	0.0007	0.0015	0.0033
37	0.0003	0.0009	0.0018	0.0039	0.0002	0.0007	0.0014	0.0030
38	0.0003	0.0008	0.0016	0.0035	0.0002	0.0006	0.0013	0.0027
39	0.0002	0.0007	0.0015	0.0032	0.0002	0.0005	0.0011	0.0025
40	0.0002	0.0007	0.0014	0.0030	0.0002	0.0005	0.0010	0.0023
41	0.0002	0.0006	0.0013	0.0027	0.0001	0.0004	0.0009	0.0020
42	0.0002	0.0005	0.0011	0.0025	0.0001	0.0004	0.0008	0.0019
43	0.0002	0.0005	0.0010	0.0023	0.0001	0.0004	0.0008	0.0017
44	0.0001	0.0005	0.0010	0.0021	0.0001	0.0003	0.0007	0.0015
45	0.0001	0.0004	0.0009	0.0019	0.0001	0.0003	0.0006	0.0014
46	0.0001	0.0004	0.0008	0.0017	0.0001	0.0003	0.0006	0.0013
47	0.0001	0.0003	0.0007	0.0016	0.0001	0.0002	0.0005	0.0011
48	0.0001	0.0003	0.0007	0.0015	0.0001	0.0002	0.0005	0.0010
49	0.0001	0.0003	0.0006	0.0013	0.0001	0.0002	0.0004	0.0009
50	0.0001	0.0003	0.0006	0.0012	0.0001	0.0002	0.0004	0.0009

How much must be invested at the *end* of each period to accumulate $1

End of Year	*At 11% Interest compounded and Deposits made*				*At 12% Interest compounded and Deposits made*			
	Monthly	*Quarterly*	*Semi-Annually*	*Annually*	*Monthly*	*Quarterly*	*Semi-Annually*	*Annually*
1	0.0792	0.2399	0.4866	1.0000	0.0788	0.2390	0.4854	1.0000
2	0.0374	0.1135	0.2303	0.4739	0.0371	0.1125	0.2286	0.4717
3	0.0236	0.0715	0.1452	0.2992	0.0232	0.0705	0.1434	0.2963
4	0.0167	0.0506	0.1029	0.2123	0.0163	0.0496	0.1010	0.2092
5	0.0126	0.0382	0.0777	0.1606	0.0122	0.0372	0.0759	0.1574
6	0.0099	0.0300	0.0610	0.1264	0.0096	0.0290	0.0593	0.1232
7	0.0080	0.0242	0.0493	0.1022	0.0077	0.0233	0.0476	0.0991
8	0.0065	0.0199	0.0406	0.0843	0.0063	0.0190	0.0390	0.0813
9	0.0055	0.0166	0.0339	0.0706	0.0052	0.0158	0.0324	0.0677
10	0.0046	0.0140	0.0287	0.0598	0.0043	0.0133	0.0272	0.0570
11	0.0039	0.0120	0.0245	0.0511	0.0037	0.0112	0.0230	0.0484
12	0.0034	0.0103	0.0210	0.0440	0.0031	0.0096	0.0197	0.0414
13	0.0029	0.0089	0.0182	0.0382	0.0027	0.0082	0.0169	0.0357
14	0.0025	0.0077	0.0158	0.0332	0.0023	0.0071	0.0146	0.0309
15	0.0022	0.0067	0.0138	0.0291	0.0020	0.0061	0.0126	0.0268
16	0.0019	0.0059	0.0121	0.0255	0.0017	0.0053	0.0110	0.0234
17	0.0017	0.0052	0.0106	0.0225	0.0015	0.0046	0.0096	0.0205
18	0.0015	0.0045	0.0094	0.0198	0.0013	0.0041	0.0084	0.0179
19	0.0013	0.0040	0.0083	0.0176	0.0012	0.0035	0.0074	0.0158
20	0.0012	0.0035	0.0073	0.0156	0.0010	0.0031	0.0065	0.0139
21	0.0010	0.0031	0.0065	0.0138	0.0009	0.0027	0.0057	0.0122
22	0.0009	0.0028	0.0058	0.0123	0.0008	0.0024	0.0050	0.0108
23	0.0008	0.0025	0.0051	0.0110	0.0007	0.0021	0.0044	0.0096
24	0.0007	0.0022	0.0046	0.0098	0.0006	0.0019	0.0039	0.0085
25	0.0006	0.0020	0.0041	0.0087	0.0005	0.0016	0.0034	0.0075
26	0.0006	0.0017	0.0036	0.0078	0.0005	0.0015	0.0030	0.0067
27	0.0005	0.0016	0.0032	0.0070	0.0004	0.0013	0.0027	0.0059
28	0.0004	0.0014	0.0029	0.0063	0.0004	0.0011	0.0024	0.0052
29	0.0004	0.0012	0.0026	0.0056	0.0003	0.0010	0.0021	0.0047
30	0.0004	0.0011	0.0023	0.0050	0.0003	0.0009	0.0019	0.0041
31	0.0003	0.0010	0.0021	0.0045	0.0003	0.0008	0.0017	0.0037
32	0.0003	0.0009	0.0018	0.0040	0.0002	0.0007	0.0015	0.0033
33	0.0003	0.0008	0.0017	0.0036	0.0002	0.0006	0.0013	0.0029
34	0.0002	0.0007	0.0015	0.0033	0.0002	0.0005	0.0012	0.0026
35	0.0002	0.0006	0.0013	0.0029	0.0002	0.0005	0.0010	0.0023
36	0.0002	0.0006	0.0012	0.0026	0.0001	0.0004	0.0009	0.0021
37	0.0002	0.0005	0.0011	0.0024	0.0001	0.0004	0.0008	0.0018
38	0.0001	0.0005	0.0010	0.0021	0.0001	0.0003	0.0007	0.0016
39	0.0001	0.0004	0.0009	0.0019	0.0001	0.0003	0.0006	0.0015
40	0.0001	0.0004	0.0008	0.0017	0.0001	0.0003	0.0006	0.0013
41	0.0001	0.0003	0.0007	0.0015	0.0001	0.0002	0.0005	0.0012
42	0.0001	0.0003	0.0006	0.0014	0.0001	0.0002	0.0005	0.0010
43	0.0001	0.0003	0.0006	0.0013	0.0001	0.0002	0.0004	0.0009
44	0.0001	0.0002	0.0005	0.0011	0.0001	0.0002	0.0004	0.0008
45	0.0001	0.0002	0.0004	0.0010	0.0000	0.0001	0.0003	0.0007
46	0.0001	0.0002	0.0004	0.0009	0.0000	0.0001	0.0003	0.0007
47	0.0001	0.0002	0.0004	0.0008	0.0000	0.0001	0.0003	0.0006
48	0.0000	0.0002	0.0003	0.0007	0.0000	0.0001	0.0002	0.0005
49	0.0000	0.0001	0.0003	0.0007	0.0000	0.0001	0.0002	0.0005
50	0.0000	0.0001	0.0003	0.0006	0.0000	0.0001	0.0002	0.0004

How much must be invested at the *end* of each period to accumulate $1

	At 13% Interest compounded and Deposits made				*At 14% Interest compounded and Deposits made*			
End of Year	*Monthly*	*Quarterly*	*Semi-Annually*	*Annually*	*Monthly*	*Quarterly*	*Semi-Annually*	*Annually*
1	0.0785	0.2381	0.4843	1.0000	0.0781	0.2373	0.4831	1.0000
2	0.0367	0.1115	0.2269	0.4695	0.0363	0.1105	0.2252	0.4673
3	0.0229	0.0695	0.1416	0.2935	0.0225	0.0685	0.1398	0.2907
4	0.0160	0.0486	0.0992	0.2062	0.0157	0.0477	0.0975	0.2032
5	0.0119	0.0363	0.0741	0.1543	0.0116	0.0354	0.0724	0.1513
6	0.0092	0.0281	0.0576	0.1202	0.0089	0.0273	0.0559	0.1172
7	0.0074	0.0224	0.0459	0.0961	0.0071	0.0216	0.0443	0.0932
8	0.0060	0.0182	0.0374	0.0784	0.0057	0.0174	0.0359	0.0756
9	0.0049	0.0150	0.0309	0.0649	0.0047	0.0143	0.0294	0.0622
10	0.0041	0.0125	0.0258	0.0543	0.0039	0.0118	0.0244	0.0517
11	0.0034	0.0105	0.0217	0.0458	0.0032	0.0099	0.0204	0.0434
12	0.0029	0.0089	0.0184	0.0390	0.0027	0.0083	0.0172	0.0367
13	0.0025	0.0076	0.0157	0.0334	0.0023	0.0070	0.0146	0.0312
14	0.0021	0.0065	0.0135	0.0287	0.0019	0.0060	0.0124	0.0266
15	0.0018	0.0056	0.0116	0.0247	0.0017	0.0051	0.0106	0.0228
16	0.0016	0.0048	0.0100	0.0214	0.0014	0.0044	0.0091	0.0196
17	0.0014	0.0042	0.0087	0.0186	0.0012	0.0037	0.0078	0.0169
18	0.0012	0.0036	0.0075	0.0162	0.0010	0.0032	0.0067	0.0146
19	0.0010	0.0031	0.0065	0.0141	0.0009	0.0028	0.0058	0.0127
20	0.0009	0.0027	0.0057	0.0124	0.0008	0.0024	0.0050	0.0110
21	0.0008	0.0024	0.0050	0.0108	0.0007	0.0021	0.0043	0.0095
22	0.0007	0.0021	0.0043	0.0095	0.0006	0.0018	0.0038	0.0083
23	0.0006	0.0018	0.0038	0.0083	0.0005	0.0015	0.0033	0.0072
24	0.0005	0.0016	0.0033	0.0073	0.0004	0.0013	0.0028	0.0063
25	0.0004	0.0014	0.0029	0.0064	0.0004	0.0012	0.0025	0.0055
26	0.0004	0.0012	0.0026	0.0057	0.0003	0.0010	0.0021	0.0048
27	0.0003	0.0011	0.0022	0.0050	0.0003	0.0009	0.0019	0.0042
28	0.0003	0.0009	0.0020	0.0044	0.0002	0.0008	0.0016	0.0037
29	0.0003	0.0008	0.0017	0.0039	0.0002	0.0007	0.0014	0.0032
30	0.0002	0.0007	0.0015	0.0034	0.0002	0.0006	0.0012	0.0028
31	0.0002	0.0006	0.0013	0.0030	0.0002	0.0005	0.0011	0.0025
32	0.0002	0.0006	0.0012	0.0027	0.0001	0.0004	0.0009	0.0021
33	0.0002	0.0005	0.0010	0.0023	0.0001	0.0004	0.0008	0.0019
34	0.0001	0.0004	0.0009	0.0021	0.0001	0.0003	0.0007	0.0016
35	0.0001	0.0004	0.0008	0.0018	0.0001	0.0003	0.0006	0.0014
36	0.0001	0.0003	0.0007	0.0016	0.0001	0.0002	0.0005	0.0013
37	0.0001	0.0003	0.0006	0.0014	0.0001	0.0002	0.0005	0.0011
38	0.0001	0.0003	0.0005	0.0013	0.0001	0.0002	0.0004	0.0010
39	0.0001	0.0002	0.0005	0.0011	0.0001	0.0002	0.0004	0.0009
40	0.0001	0.0002	0.0004	0.0010	0.0000	0.0001	0.0003	0.0007
41	0.0001	0.0002	0.0004	0.0009	0.0000	0.0001	0.0003	0.0007
42	0.0000	0.0002	0.0003	0.0008	0.0000	0.0001	0.0002	0.0006
43	0.0000	0.0001	0.0003	0.0007	0.0000	0.0001	0.0002	0.0005
44	0.0000	0.0001	0.0003	0.0006	0.0000	0.0001	0.0002	0.0004
45	0.0000	0.0001	0.0002	0.0005	0.0000	0.0001	0.0002	0.0004
46	0.0000	0.0001	0.0002	0.0005	0.0000	0.0001	0.0001	0.0003
47	0.0000	0.0001	0.0002	0.0004	0.0000	0.0001	0.0001	0.0003
48	0.0000	0.0001	0.0002	0.0004	0.0000	0.0000	0.0001	0.0003
49	0.0000	0.0001	0.0001	0.0003	0.0000	0.0000	0.0001	0.0002
50	0.0000	0.0001	0.0001	0.0003	0.0000	0.0000	0.0001	0.0002

How much must be invested at the *end* of each period to accumulate $1

End of Year	At 15% Interest compounded and Deposits made				At 16% Interest compounded and Deposits made			
	Monthly	Quarterly	Semi-Annually	Annually	Monthly	Quarterly	Semi-Annually	Annually
1	0.0778	0.2364	0.4819	1.0000	0.0774	0.2355	0.4808	1.0000
2	0.0360	0.1095	0.2236	0.4651	0.0356	0.1085	0.2219	0.4630
3	0.0222	0.0675	0.1380	0.2880	0.0218	0.0666	0.1363	0.2853
4	0.0153	0.0467	0.0957	0.2003	0.0150	0.0458	0.0940	0.1974
5	0.0113	0.0345	0.0707	0.1483	0.0110	0.0336	0.0690	0.1454
6	0.0086	0.0264	0.0543	0.1142	0.0084	0.0256	0.0527	0.1114
7	0.0068	0.0208	0.0428	0.0904	0.0065	0.0200	0.0413	0.0876
8	0.0054	0.0167	0.0344	0.0729	0.0052	0.0159	0.0330	0.0702
9	0.0044	0.0136	0.0280	0.0596	0.0042	0.0129	0.0267	0.0571
10	0.0036	0.0112	0.0231	0.0493	0.0034	0.0105	0.0219	0.0469
11	0.0030	0.0093	0.0192	0.0411	0.0028	0.0087	0.0180	0.0389
12	0.0025	0.0077	0.0161	0.0345	0.0023	0.0072	0.0150	0.0324
13	0.0021	0.0065	0.0135	0.0291	0.0019	0.0060	0.0125	0.0272
14	0.0018	0.0055	0.0114	0.0247	0.0016	0.0050	0.0105	0.0229
15	0.0015	0.0046	0.0097	0.0210	0.0014	0.0042	0.0088	0.0194
16	0.0013	0.0039	0.0082	0.0179	0.0011	0.0035	0.0075	0.0164
17	0.0011	0.0033	0.0070	0.0154	0.0010	0.0030	0.0063	0.0140
18	0.0009	0.0028	0.0060	0.0132	0.0008	0.0025	0.0053	0.0119
19	0.0008	0.0024	0.0051	0.0113	0.0007	0.0021	0.0045	0.0101
20	0.0007	0.0021	0.0044	0.0098	0.0006	0.0018	0.0039	0.0087
21	0.0006	0.0018	0.0038	0.0084	0.0005	0.0015	0.0033	0.0074
22	0.0005	0.0015	0.0032	0.0073	0.0004	0.0013	0.0028	0.0064
23	0.0004	0.0013	0.0028	0.0063	0.0004	0.0011	0.0024	0.0054
24	0.0004	0.0011	0.0024	0.0054	0.0003	0.0009	0.0020	0.0047
25	0.0003	0.0010	0.0021	0.0047	0.0003	0.0008	0.0017	0.0040
26	0.0003	0.0008	0.0018	0.0041	0.0002	0.0007	0.0015	0.0034
27	0.0002	0.0007	0.0015	0.0035	0.0002	0.0006	0.0013	0.0030
28	0.0002	0.0006	0.0013	0.0031	0.0002	0.0005	0.0011	0.0025
29	0.0002	0.0005	0.0011	0.0027	0.0001	0.0004	0.0009	0.0022
30	0.0001	0.0005	0.0010	0.0023	0.0001	0.0004	0.0008	0.0019
31	0.0001	0.0004	0.0009	0.0020	0.0001	0.0003	0.0007	0.0016
32	0.0001	0.0003	0.0007	0.0017	0.0001	0.0003	0.0006	0.0014
33	0.0001	0.0003	0.0006	0.0015	0.0001	0.0002	0.0005	0.0012
34	0.0001	0.0003	0.0006	0.0013	0.0001	0.0002	0.0004	0.0010
35	0.0001	0.0002	0.0005	0.0011	0.0001	0.0002	0.0004	0.0009
36	0.0001	0.0002	0.0004	0.0010	0.0000	0.0001	0.0003	0.0008
37	0.0001	0.0002	0.0004	0.0009	0.0000	0.0001	0.0003	0.0007
38	0.0000	0.0001	0.0003	0.0007	0.0000	0.0001	0.0002	0.0006
39	0.0000	0.0001	0.0003	0.0006	0.0000	0.0001	0.0002	0.0005
40	0.0000	0.0001	0.0002	0.0006	0.0000	0.0001	0.0002	0.0004
41	0.0000	0.0001	0.0002	0.0005	0.0000	0.0001	0.0001	0.0004
42	0.0000	0.0001	0.0002	0.0004	0.0000	0.0001	0.0001	0.0003
43	0.0000	0.0001	0.0001	0.0004	0.0000	0.0000	0.0001	0.0003
44	0.0000	0.0001	0.0001	0.0003	0.0000	0.0000	0.0001	0.0002
45	0.0000	0.0000	0.0001	0.0003	0.0000	0.0000	0.0001	0.0002
46	0.0000	0.0000	0.0001	0.0002	0.0000	0.0000	0.0001	0.0002
47	0.0000	0.0000	0.0001	0.0002	0.0000	0.0000	0.0001	0.0001
48	0.0000	0.0000	0.0001	0.0002	0.0000	0.0000	0.0000	0.0001
49	0.0000	0.0000	0.0001	0.0002	0.0000	0.0000	0.0000	0.0001
50	0.0000	0.0000	0.0001	0.0001	0.0000	0.0000	0.0000	0.0001

How much must be invested at the *end* of each period to accumulate $1

	At 17% Interest compounded and Deposits made				*At 18% Interest compounded and Deposits made*			
End of Year	*Monthly*	*Quarterly*	*Semi-Annually*	*Annually*	*Monthly*	*Quarterly*	*Semi-Annually*	*Annually*
1	0.0770	0.2346	0.4796	1.0000	0.0767	0.2337	0.4785	1.0000
2	0.0353	0.1076	0.2203	0.4608	0.0349	0.1066	0.2187	0.4587
3	0.0215	0.0656	0.1346	0.2826	0.0212	0.0647	0.1329	0.2799
4	0.0147	0.0449	0.0923	0.1945	0.0144	0.0440	0.0907	0.1917
5	0.0107	0.0327	0.0674	0.1426	0.0104	0.0319	0.0658	0.1398
6	0.0081	0.0248	0.0512	0.1086	0.0078	0.0240	0.0497	0.1059
7	0.0063	0.0193	0.0398	0.0849	0.0060	0.0185	0.0384	0.0824
8	0.0050	0.0152	0.0316	0.0677	0.0047	0.0146	0.0303	0.0652
9	0.0040	0.0122	0.0254	0.0547	0.0038	0.0116	0.0242	0.0524
10	0.0032	0.0099	0.0207	0.0447	0.0030	0.0093	0.0195	0.0425
11	0.0026	0.0081	0.0169	0.0368	0.0024	0.0076	0.0159	0.0348
12	0.0022	0.0067	0.0140	0.0305	0.0020	0.0062	0.0130	0.0286
13	0.0018	0.0055	0.0116	0.0254	0.0016	0.0051	0.0107	0.0237
14	0.0015	0.0046	0.0096	0.0212	0.0013	0.0042	0.0089	0.0197
15	0.0012	0.0038	0.0081	0.0178	0.0011	0.0035	0.0073	0.0164
16	0.0010	0.0032	0.0067	0.0150	0.0009	0.0029	0.0061	0.0137
17	0.0009	0.0027	0.0057	0.0127	0.0008	0.0024	0.0051	0.0115
18	0.0007	0.0022	0.0048	0.0107	0.0006	0.0020	0.0042	0.0096
19	0.0006	0.0019	0.0040	0.0091	0.0005	0.0016	0.0035	0.0081
20	0.0005	0.0016	0.0034	0.0077	0.0004	0.0014	0.0030	0.0068
21	0.0004	0.0013	0.0029	0.0065	0.0004	0.0011	0.0025	0.0057
22	0.0004	0.0011	0.0024	0.0056	0.0003	0.0010	0.0021	0.0048
23	0.0003	0.0009	0.0020	0.0047	0.0003	0.0008	0.0017	0.0041
24	0.0003	0.0008	0.0017	0.0040	0.0002	0.0007	0.0015	0.0035
25	0.0002	0.0007	0.0015	0.0034	0.0002	0.0006	0.0012	0.0029
26	0.0002	0.0006	0.0012	0.0029	0.0001	0.0005	0.0010	0.0025
27	0.0002	0.0005	0.0011	0.0025	0.0001	0.0004	0.0009	0.0021
28	0.0001	0.0004	0.0009	0.0021	0.0001	0.0003	0.0007	0.0018
29	0.0001	0.0003	0.0008	0.0018	0.0001	0.0003	0.0006	0.0015
30	0.0001	0.0003	0.0006	0.0015	0.0001	0.0002	0.0005	0.0013
31	0.0001	0.0002	0.0005	0.0013	0.0001	0.0002	0.0004	0.0011
32	0.0001	0.0002	0.0005	0.0011	0.0000	0.0002	0.0004	0.0009
33	0.0001	0.0002	0.0004	0.0010	0.0000	0.0001	0.0003	0.0008
34	0.0000	0.0001	0.0003	0.0008	0.0000	0.0001	0.0003	0.0006
35	0.0000	0.0001	0.0003	0.0007	0.0000	0.0001	0.0002	0.0006
36	0.0000	0.0001	0.0002	0.0006	0.0000	0.0001	0.0002	0.0005
37	0.0000	0.0001	0.0002	0.0005	0.0000	0.0001	0.0002	0.0004
38	0.0000	0.0001	0.0002	0.0004	0.0000	0.0001	0.0001	0.0003
39	0.0000	0.0001	0.0001	0.0004	0.0000	0.0000	0.0001	0.0003
40	0.0000	0.0001	0.0001	0.0003	0.0000	0.0000	0.0001	0.0002
41	0.0000	0.0000	0.0001	0.0003	0.0000	0.0000	0.0001	0.0002
42	0.0000	0.0000	0.0001	0.0002	0.0000	0.0000	0.0001	0.0002
43	0.0000	0.0000	0.0001	0.0002	0.0000	0.0000	0.0001	0.0001
44	0.0000	0.0000	0.0001	0.0002	0.0000	0.0000	0.0000	0.0001
45	0.0000	0.0000	0.0001	0.0001	0.0000	0.0000	0.0000	0.0001
46	0.0000	0.0000	0.0000	0.0001	0.0000	0.0000	0.0000	0.0001
47	0.0000	0.0000	0.0000	0.0001	0.0000	0.0000	0.0000	0.0001
48	0.0000	0.0000	0.0000	0.0001	0.0000	0.0000	0.0000	0.0001
49	0.0000	0.0000	0.0000	0.0001	0.0000	0.0000	0.0000	0.0001
50	0.0000	0.0000	0.0000	0.0001	0.0000	0.0000	0.0000	0.0000

TABLE 5

Periodic payments at the *end* of each period required to amortize a loan of $1 over time

Applications

Chapter Six

- What are the installment payments necessary to discharge a loan over a specific period of time?

Chapter Fifteen

- Calculating annuity yields.

Periodic payments at the *end* of each period required to amortize a loan of $1 over time

End of Year	At 5% Interest compounded and Payments made: Monthly	Quarterly	Semi-Annually	Annually	At 6% Interest compounded and Payments made: Monthly	Quarterly	Semi-Annually	Annually
1	0.0856	0.2579	0.5188	1.0500	0.0861	0.2594	0.5226	1.0600
2	0.0439	0.1321	0.2658	0.5378	0.0443	0.1336	0.2690	0.5454
3	0.0300	0.0903	0.1815	0.3672	0.0304	0.0917	0.1846	0.3741
4	0.0230	0.0693	0.1395	0.2820	0.0235	0.0708	0.1425	0.2886
5	0.0189	0.0568	0.1143	0.2310	0.0193	0.0582	0.1172	0.2374
6	0.0161	0.0485	0.0975	0.1970	0.0166	0.0499	0.1005	0.2034
7	0.0141	0.0425	0.0855	0.1728	0.0146	0.0440	0.0885	0.1791
8	0.0127	0.0381	0.0766	0.1547	0.0131	0.0396	0.0796	0.1610
9	0.0115	0.0347	0.0697	0.1407	0.0120	0.0362	0.0727	0.1470
10	0.0106	0.0319	0.0641	0.1295	0.0111	0.0334	0.0672	0.1359
11	0.0099	0.0297	0.0596	0.1204	0.0104	0.0312	0.0627	0.1268
12	0.0092	0.0278	0.0559	0.1128	0.0098	0.0294	0.0590	0.1193
13	0.0087	0.0263	0.0528	0.1065	0.0092	0.0278	0.0559	0.1130
14	0.0083	0.0249	0.0501	0.1010	0.0088	0.0265	0.0533	0.1076
15	0.0079	0.0238	0.0478	0.0963	0.0084	0.0254	0.0510	0.1030
16	0.0076	0.0228	0.0458	0.0923	0.0081	0.0244	0.0490	0.0990
17	0.0073	0.0219	0.0440	0.0887	0.0078	0.0236	0.0473	0.0954
18	0.0070	0.0211	0.0425	0.0855	0.0076	0.0228	0.0458	0.0924
19	0.0068	0.0205	0.0411	0.0827	0.0074	0.0221	0.0445	0.0896
20	0.0066	0.0198	0.0398	0.0802	0.0072	0.0215	0.0433	0.0872
21	0.0064	0.0193	0.0387	0.0780	0.0070	0.0210	0.0422	0.0850
22	0.0063	0.0188	0.0377	0.0760	0.0068	0.0205	0.0412	0.0830
23	0.0061	0.0184	0.0368	0.0741	0.0067	0.0201	0.0404	0.0813
24	0.0060	0.0179	0.0360	0.0725	0.0066	0.0197	0.0396	0.0797
25	0.0058	0.0176	0.0353	0.0710	0.0064	0.0194	0.0389	0.0782
26	0.0057	0.0172	0.0346	0.0696	0.0063	0.0190	0.0382	0.0769
27	0.0056	0.0169	0.0339	0.0683	0.0062	0.0188	0.0376	0.0757
28	0.0055	0.0166	0.0334	0.0671	0.0062	0.0185	0.0371	0.0746
29	0.0054	0.0164	0.0328	0.0660	0.0061	0.0182	0.0366	0.0736
30	0.0054	0.0161	0.0324	0.0651	0.0060	0.0180	0.0361	0.0726
31	0.0053	0.0159	0.0319	0.0641	0.0059	0.0178	0.0357	0.0718
32	0.0052	0.0157	0.0315	0.0633	0.0059	0.0176	0.0353	0.0710
33	0.0052	0.0155	0.0311	0.0625	0.0058	0.0174	0.0350	0.0703
34	0.0051	0.0153	0.0307	0.0618	0.0058	0.0173	0.0346	0.0696
35	0.0050	0.0152	0.0304	0.0611	0.0057	0.0171	0.0343	0.0690
36	0.0050	0.0150	0.0301	0.0604	0.0057	0.0170	0.0341	0.0684
37	0.0049	0.0149	0.0298	0.0598	0.0056	0.0169	0.0338	0.0679
38	0.0049	0.0147	0.0295	0.0593	0.0056	0.0167	0.0335	0.0674
39	0.0049	0.0146	0.0293	0.0588	0.0055	0.0166	0.0333	0.0669
40	0.0048	0.0145	0.0290	0.0583	0.0055	0.0165	0.0331	0.0665
41	0.0048	0.0144	0.0288	0.0578	0.0055	0.0164	0.0329	0.0661
42	0.0048	0.0143	0.0286	0.0574	0.0054	0.0163	0.0327	0.0657
43	0.0047	0.0142	0.0284	0.0570	0.0054	0.0163	0.0326	0.0653
44	0.0047	0.0141	0.0282	0.0566	0.0054	0.0162	0.0324	0.0650
45	0.0047	0.0140	0.0280	0.0563	0.0054	0.0161	0.0323	0.0647
46	0.0046	0.0139	0.0279	0.0559	0.0053	0.0160	0.0321	0.0644
47	0.0046	0.0138	0.0277	0.0556	0.0053	0.0160	0.0320	0.0641
48	0.0046	0.0138	0.0276	0.0553	0.0053	0.0159	0.0319	0.0639
49	0.0046	0.0137	0.0274	0.0550	0.0053	0.0159	0.0318	0.0637
50	0.0045	0.0136	0.0273	0.0548	0.0053	0.0158	0.0316	0.0634

Periodic payments at the *end* of each period required to amortize a loan of $1 over time

End of Year	At 7% Interest compounded and Payments made				At 8% Interest compounded and Payments made			
	Monthly	Quarterly	Semi-Annually	Annually	Monthly	Quarterly	Semi-Annually	Annually
1	0.0865	0.2610	0.5264	1.0700	0.0870	0.2626	0.5302	1.0800
2	0.0448	0.1350	0.2723	0.5531	0.0452	0.1365	0.2755	0.5608
3	0.0309	0.0931	0.1877	0.3811	0.0313	0.0946	0.1908	0.3880
4	0.0239	0.0722	0.1455	0.2952	0.0244	0.0737	0.1485	0.3019
5	0.0198	0.0597	0.1202	0.2439	0.0203	0.0612	0.1233	0.2505
6	0.0170	0.0514	0.1035	0.2098	0.0175	0.0529	0.1066	0.2163
7	0.0151	0.0455	0.0916	0.1856	0.0156	0.0470	0.0947	0.1921
8	0.0136	0.0411	0.0827	0.1675	0.0141	0.0426	0.0858	0.1740
9	0.0125	0.0377	0.0758	0.1535	0.0130	0.0392	0.0790	0.1601
10	0.0116	0.0350	0.0704	0.1424	0.0121	0.0366	0.0736	0.1490
11	0.0109	0.0328	0.0659	0.1334	0.0114	0.0344	0.0692	0.1401
12	0.0103	0.0310	0.0623	0.1259	0.0108	0.0326	0.0656	0.1327
13	0.0098	0.0294	0.0592	0.1197	0.0103	0.0311	0.0626	0.1265
14	0.0094	0.0282	0.0566	0.1143	0.0099	0.0298	0.0600	0.1213
15	0.0090	0.0271	0.0544	0.1098	0.0096	0.0288	0.0578	0.1168
16	0.0087	0.0261	0.0524	0.1059	0.0092	0.0278	0.0559	0.1130
17	0.0084	0.0253	0.0508	0.1024	0.0090	0.0270	0.0543	0.1096
18	0.0082	0.0245	0.0493	0.0994	0.0087	0.0263	0.0529	0.1067
19	0.0079	0.0239	0.0480	0.0968	0.0085	0.0257	0.0516	0.1041
20	0.0078	0.0233	0.0468	0.0944	0.0084	0.0252	0.0505	0.1019
21	0.0076	0.0228	0.0458	0.0923	0.0082	0.0247	0.0495	0.0998
22	0.0074	0.0224	0.0449	0.0904	0.0081	0.0242	0.0487	0.0980
23	0.0073	0.0219	0.0441	0.0887	0.0079	0.0239	0.0479	0.0964
24	0.0072	0.0216	0.0433	0.0872	0.0078	0.0235	0.0472	0.0950
25	0.0071	0.0212	0.0426	0.0858	0.0077	0.0232	0.0466	0.0937
26	0.0070	0.0209	0.0420	0.0846	0.0076	0.0229	0.0460	0.0925
27	0.0069	0.0207	0.0415	0.0834	0.0075	0.0227	0.0455	0.0914
28	0.0068	0.0204	0.0410	0.0824	0.0075	0.0224	0.0450	0.0905
29	0.0067	0.0202	0.0405	0.0814	0.0074	0.0222	0.0446	0.0896
30	0.0067	0.0200	0.0401	0.0806	0.0073	0.0220	0.0442	0.0888
31	0.0066	0.0198	0.0397	0.0798	0.0073	0.0219	0.0439	0.0881
32	0.0065	0.0196	0.0394	0.0791	0.0072	0.0217	0.0435	0.0875
33	0.0065	0.0195	0.0390	0.0784	0.0072	0.0216	0.0432	0.0869
34	0.0064	0.0193	0.0387	0.0778	0.0071	0.0215	0.0430	0.0863
35	0.0064	0.0192	0.0385	0.0772	0.0071	0.0213	0.0427	0.0858
36	0.0063	0.0191	0.0382	0.0767	0.0071	0.0212	0.0425	0.0853
37	0.0063	0.0190	0.0380	0.0762	0.0070	0.0211	0.0423	0.0849
38	0.0063	0.0188	0.0378	0.0758	0.0070	0.0210	0.0421	0.0845
39	0.0062	0.0188	0.0376	0.0754	0.0070	0.0210	0.0420	0.0842
40	0.0062	0.0187	0.0374	0.0750	0.0070	0.0209	0.0418	0.0839
41	0.0062	0.0186	0.0372	0.0747	0.0069	0.0208	0.0417	0.0836
42	0.0062	0.0185	0.0371	0.0743	0.0069	0.0207	0.0415	0.0833
43	0.0061	0.0184	0.0369	0.0740	0.0069	0.0207	0.0414	0.0830
44	0.0061	0.0184	0.0368	0.0738	0.0069	0.0206	0.0413	0.0828
45	0.0061	0.0183	0.0367	0.0735	0.0069	0.0206	0.0412	0.0826
46	0.0061	0.0182	0.0365	0.0733	0.0068	0.0205	0.0411	0.0824
47	0.0061	0.0182	0.0364	0.0730	0.0068	0.0205	0.0410	0.0822
48	0.0060	0.0181	0.0363	0.0728	0.0068	0.0205	0.0409	0.0820
49	0.0060	0.0181	0.0362	0.0726	0.0068	0.0204	0.0409	0.0819
50	0.0060	0.0181	0.0362	0.0725	0.0068	0.0204	0.0408	0.0817

Periodic payments at the *end* of each period required to amortize a loan of $1 over time

End of Year	At 9% Interest compounded and Payments made				At 10% Interest compounded and Payments made			
	Monthly	Quarterly	Semi-Annually	Annually	Monthly	Quarterly	Semi-Annually	Annually
1	0.0875	0.2642	0.5340	1.0900	0.0879	0.2658	0.5378	1.1000
2	0.0457	0.1380	0.2787	0.5685	0.0461	0.1395	0.2820	0.5762
3	0.0318	0.0960	0.1939	0.3951	0.0323	0.0975	0.1970	0.4021
4	0.0249	0.0751	0.1516	0.3087	0.0254	0.0766	0.1547	0.3155
5	0.0208	0.0626	0.1264	0.2571	0.0212	0.0641	0.1295	0.2638
6	0.0180	0.0544	0.1097	0.2229	0.0185	0.0559	0.1128	0.2296
7	0.0161	0.0485	0.0978	0.1987	0.0166	0.0501	0.1010	0.2054
8	0.0147	0.0442	0.0890	0.1807	0.0152	0.0458	0.0923	0.1874
9	0.0135	0.0408	0.0822	0.1668	0.0141	0.0425	0.0855	0.1736
10	0.0127	0.0382	0.0769	0.1558	0.0132	0.0398	0.0802	0.1627
11	0.0120	0.0360	0.0725	0.1469	0.0125	0.0377	0.0760	0.1540
12	0.0114	0.0343	0.0690	0.1397	0.0120	0.0360	0.0725	0.1468
13	0.0109	0.0328	0.0660	0.1336	0.0115	0.0346	0.0696	0.1408
14	0.0105	0.0316	0.0635	0.1284	0.0111	0.0334	0.0671	0.1357
15	0.0101	0.0305	0.0614	0.1241	0.0107	0.0324	0.0651	0.1315
16	0.0098	0.0296	0.0596	0.1203	0.0105	0.0315	0.0633	0.1278
17	0.0096	0.0289	0.0580	0.1170	0.0102	0.0307	0.0618	0.1247
18	0.0094	0.0282	0.0566	0.1142	0.0100	0.0301	0.0604	0.1219
19	0.0092	0.0276	0.0554	0.1117	0.0098	0.0295	0.0593	0.1195
20	0.0090	0.0271	0.0543	0.1095	0.0097	0.0290	0.0583	0.1175
21	0.0088	0.0266	0.0534	0.1076	0.0095	0.0286	0.0574	0.1156
22	0.0087	0.0262	0.0526	0.1059	0.0094	0.0282	0.0566	0.1140
23	0.0086	0.0258	0.0518	0.1044	0.0093	0.0279	0.0559	0.1126
24	0.0085	0.0255	0.0512	0.1030	0.0092	0.0276	0.0553	0.1113
25	0.0084	0.0252	0.0506	0.1018	0.0091	0.0273	0.0548	0.1102
26	0.0083	0.0250	0.0501	0.1007	0.0090	0.0271	0.0543	0.1092
27	0.0082	0.0247	0.0496	0.0997	0.0089	0.0269	0.0539	0.1083
28	0.0082	0.0245	0.0492	0.0989	0.0089	0.0267	0.0535	0.1075
29	0.0081	0.0243	0.0488	0.0981	0.0088	0.0265	0.0531	0.1067
30	0.0080	0.0242	0.0485	0.0973	0.0088	0.0264	0.0528	0.1061
31	0.0080	0.0240	0.0481	0.0967	0.0087	0.0262	0.0526	0.1055
32	0.0080	0.0239	0.0479	0.0961	0.0087	0.0261	0.0523	0.1050
33	0.0079	0.0238	0.0476	0.0956	0.0087	0.0260	0.0521	0.1045
34	0.0079	0.0236	0.0474	0.0951	0.0086	0.0259	0.0519	0.1041
35	0.0078	0.0235	0.0472	0.0946	0.0086	0.0258	0.0517	0.1037
36	0.0078	0.0235	0.0470	0.0942	0.0086	0.0257	0.0515	0.1033
37	0.0078	0.0234	0.0468	0.0939	0.0085	0.0257	0.0514	0.1030
38	0.0078	0.0233	0.0466	0.0935	0.0085	0.0256	0.0513	0.1027
39	0.0077	0.0232	0.0465	0.0932	0.0085	0.0255	0.0511	0.1025
40	0.0077	0.0232	0.0464	0.0930	0.0085	0.0255	0.0510	0.1023
41	0.0077	0.0231	0.0463	0.0927	0.0085	0.0254	0.0509	0.1020
42	0.0077	0.0230	0.0461	0.0925	0.0085	0.0254	0.0508	0.1019
43	0.0077	0.0230	0.0460	0.0923	0.0085	0.0254	0.0508	0.1017
44	0.0076	0.0230	0.0460	0.0921	0.0084	0.0253	0.0507	0.1015
45	0.0076	0.0229	0.0459	0.0919	0.0084	0.0253	0.0506	0.1014
46	0.0076	0.0229	0.0458	0.0917	0.0084	0.0253	0.0506	0.1013
47	0.0076	0.0228	0.0457	0.0916	0.0084	0.0252	0.0505	0.1011
48	0.0076	0.0228	0.0457	0.0915	0.0084	0.0252	0.0505	0.1010
49	0.0076	0.0228	0.0456	0.0913	0.0084	0.0252	0.0504	0.1009
50	0.0076	0.0228	0.0456	0.0912	0.0084	0.0252	0.0504	0.1009

Periodic payments at the *end* of each period required to amortize a loan of $1 over time

End of Year	At 11% Interest compounded and Payments made				At 12% Interest compounded and Payments made			
	Monthly	Quarterly	Semi-Annually	Annually	Monthly	Quarterly	Semi-Annually	Annually
1	0.0884	0.2674	0.5416	1.1100	0.0888	0.2690	0.5454	1.1200
2	0.0466	0.1410	0.2853	0.5839	0.0471	0.1425	0.2886	0.5917
3	0.0327	0.0990	0.2002	0.4092	0.0332	0.1005	0.2034	0.4163
4	0.0258	0.0781	0.1579	0.3223	0.0263	0.0796	0.1610	0.3292
5	0.0217	0.0657	0.1327	0.2706	0.0222	0.0672	0.1359	0.2774
6	0.0190	0.0575	0.1160	0.2364	0.0196	0.0590	0.1193	0.2432
7	0.0171	0.0517	0.1043	0.2122	0.0177	0.0533	0.1076	0.2191
8	0.0157	0.0474	0.0956	0.1943	0.0163	0.0490	0.0990	0.2013
9	0.0146	0.0441	0.0889	0.1806	0.0152	0.0458	0.0924	0.1877
10	0.0138	0.0415	0.0837	0.1698	0.0143	0.0433	0.0872	0.1770
11	0.0131	0.0395	0.0795	0.1611	0.0137	0.0412	0.0830	0.1684
12	0.0125	0.0378	0.0760	0.1540	0.0131	0.0396	0.0797	0.1614
13	0.0121	0.0364	0.0732	0.1482	0.0127	0.0382	0.0769	0.1557
14	0.0117	0.0352	0.0708	0.1432	0.0123	0.0371	0.0746	0.1509
15	0.0114	0.0342	0.0688	0.1391	0.0120	0.0361	0.0726	0.1468
16	0.0111	0.0334	0.0671	0.1355	0.0117	0.0353	0.0710	0.1434
17	0.0109	0.0327	0.0656	0.1325	0.0115	0.0346	0.0696	0.1405
18	0.0107	0.0320	0.0644	0.1298	0.0113	0.0341	0.0684	0.1379
19	0.0105	0.0315	0.0633	0.1276	0.0112	0.0335	0.0674	0.1358
20	0.0103	0.0310	0.0623	0.1256	0.0110	0.0331	0.0665	0.1339
21	0.0102	0.0306	0.0615	0.1238	0.0109	0.0327	0.0657	0.1322
22	0.0101	0.0303	0.0608	0.1223	0.0108	0.0324	0.0650	0.1308
23	0.0100	0.0300	0.0601	0.1210	0.0107	0.0321	0.0644	0.1296
24	0.0099	0.0297	0.0596	0.1198	0.0106	0.0319	0.0639	0.1285
25	0.0098	0.0295	0.0591	0.1187	0.0105	0.0316	0.0634	0.1275
26	0.0097	0.0292	0.0586	0.1178	0.0105	0.0315	0.0630	0.1267
27	0.0097	0.0291	0.0582	0.1170	0.0104	0.0313	0.0627	0.1259
28	0.0096	0.0289	0.0579	0.1163	0.0104	0.0311	0.0624	0.1252
29	0.0096	0.0287	0.0576	0.1156	0.0103	0.0310	0.0621	0.1247
30	0.0095	0.0286	0.0573	0.1150	0.0103	0.0309	0.0619	0.1241
31	0.0095	0.0285	0.0571	0.1145	0.0103	0.0308	0.0617	0.1237
32	0.0095	0.0284	0.0568	0.1140	0.0102	0.0307	0.0615	0.1233
33	0.0094	0.0283	0.0567	0.1136	0.0102	0.0306	0.0613	0.1229
34	0.0094	0.0282	0.0565	0.1133	0.0102	0.0305	0.0612	0.1226
35	0.0094	0.0281	0.0563	0.1129	0.0102	0.0305	0.0610	0.1223
36	0.0093	0.0281	0.0562	0.1126	0.0101	0.0304	0.0609	0.1221
37	0.0093	0.0280	0.0561	0.1124	0.0101	0.0304	0.0608	0.1218
38	0.0093	0.0280	0.0560	0.1121	0.0101	0.0303	0.0607	0.1216
39	0.0093	0.0279	0.0559	0.1119	0.0101	0.0303	0.0606	0.1215
40	0.0093	0.0279	0.0558	0.1117	0.0101	0.0303	0.0606	0.1213
41	0.0093	0.0278	0.0557	0.1115	0.0101	0.0302	0.0605	0.1212
42	0.0093	0.0278	0.0556	0.1114	0.0101	0.0302	0.0605	0.1210
43	0.0093	0.0278	0.0556	0.1113	0.0101	0.0302	0.0604	0.1209
44	0.0092	0.0277	0.0555	0.1111	0.0101	0.0302	0.0604	0.1208
45	0.0092	0.0277	0.0554	0.1110	0.0100	0.0301	0.0603	0.1207
46	0.0092	0.0277	0.0554	0.1109	0.0100	0.0301	0.0603	0.1207
47	0.0092	0.0277	0.0554	0.1108	0.0100	0.0301	0.0603	0.1206
48	0.0092	0.0277	0.0553	0.1107	0.0100	0.0301	0.0602	0.1205
49	0.0092	0.0276	0.0553	0.1107	0.0100	0.0301	0.0602	0.1205
50	0.0092	0.0276	0.0553	0.1106	0.0100	0.0301	0.0602	0.1204

Periodic payments at the *end* of each period required to amortize a loan of $1 over time

End of Year	At 13% Interest compounded and Payments made				At 14% Interest compounded and Payments made			
	Monthly	Quarterly	Semi-Annually	Annually	Monthly	Quarterly	Semi-Annually	Annually
1	0.0893	0.2706	0.5493	1.1300	0.0898	0.2723	0.5531	1.1400
2	0.0475	0.1440	0.2919	0.5995	0.0480	0.1455	0.2952	0.6073
3	0.0337	0.1020	0.2066	0.4235	0.0342	0.1035	0.2098	0.4307
4	0.0268	0.0811	0.1642	0.3362	0.0273	0.0827	0.1675	0.3432
5	0.0228	0.0688	0.1391	0.2843	0.0233	0.0704	0.1424	0.2913
6	0.0201	0.0606	0.1226	0.2502	0.0206	0.0623	0.1259	0.2572
7	0.0182	0.0549	0.1109	0.2261	0.0187	0.0566	0.1143	0.2332
8	0.0168	0.0507	0.1024	0.2084	0.0174	0.0524	0.1059	0.2156
9	0.0158	0.0475	0.0959	0.1949	0.0163	0.0493	0.0994	0.2022
10	0.0149	0.0450	0.0908	0.1843	0.0155	0.0468	0.0944	0.1917
11	0.0143	0.0430	0.0867	0.1758	0.0149	0.0449	0.0904	0.1834
12	0.0137	0.0414	0.0834	0.1690	0.0144	0.0433	0.0872	0.1767
13	0.0133	0.0401	0.0807	0.1634	0.0140	0.0420	0.0846	0.1712
14	0.0130	0.0390	0.0785	0.1587	0.0136	0.0410	0.0824	0.1666
15	0.0127	0.0381	0.0766	0.1547	0.0133	0.0401	0.0806	0.1628
16	0.0124	0.0373	0.0750	0.1514	0.0131	0.0394	0.0791	0.1596
17	0.0122	0.0367	0.0737	0.1486	0.0129	0.0387	0.0778	0.1569
18	0.0120	0.0361	0.0725	0.1462	0.0127	0.0382	0.0767	0.1546
19	0.0118	0.0356	0.0715	0.1441	0.0126	0.0378	0.0758	0.1527
20	0.0117	0.0352	0.0707	0.1424	0.0124	0.0374	0.0750	0.1510
21	0.0116	0.0349	0.0700	0.1408	0.0123	0.0371	0.0743	0.1495
22	0.0115	0.0346	0.0693	0.1395	0.0122	0.0368	0.0738	0.1483
23	0.0114	0.0343	0.0688	0.1383	0.0122	0.0365	0.0733	0.1472
24	0.0113	0.0341	0.0683	0.1373	0.0121	0.0363	0.0728	0.1463
25	0.0113	0.0339	0.0679	0.1364	0.0120	0.0362	0.0725	0.1455
26	0.0112	0.0337	0.0676	0.1357	0.0120	0.0360	0.0721	0.1448
27	0.0112	0.0336	0.0672	0.1350	0.0119	0.0359	0.0719	0.1442
28	0.0111	0.0334	0.0670	0.1344	0.0119	0.0358	0.0716	0.1437
29	0.0111	0.0333	0.0667	0.1339	0.0119	0.0357	0.0714	0.1432
30	0.0111	0.0332	0.0665	0.1334	0.0118	0.0356	0.0712	0.1428
31	0.0110	0.0331	0.0663	0.1330	0.0118	0.0355	0.0711	0.1425
32	0.0110	0.0331	0.0662	0.1327	0.0118	0.0354	0.0709	0.1421
33	0.0110	0.0330	0.0660	0.1323	0.0118	0.0354	0.0708	0.1419
34	0.0110	0.0329	0.0659	0.1321	0.0118	0.0353	0.0707	0.1416
35	0.0110	0.0329	0.0658	0.1318	0.0118	0.0353	0.0706	0.1414
36	0.0109	0.0328	0.0657	0.1316	0.0117	0.0352	0.0705	0.1413
37	0.0109	0.0328	0.0656	0.1314	0.0117	0.0352	0.0705	0.1411
38	0.0109	0.0328	0.0655	0.1313	0.0117	0.0352	0.0704	0.1410
39	0.0109	0.0327	0.0655	0.1311	0.0117	0.0352	0.0704	0.1409
40	0.0109	0.0327	0.0654	0.1310	0.0117	0.0351	0.0703	0.1407
41	0.0109	0.0327	0.0654	0.1309	0.0117	0.0351	0.0703	0.1407
42	0.0109	0.0327	0.0653	0.1308	0.0117	0.0351	0.0702	0.1406
43	0.0109	0.0326	0.0653	0.1307	0.0117	0.0351	0.0702	0.1405
44	0.0109	0.0326	0.0653	0.1306	0.0117	0.0351	0.0702	0.1404
45	0.0109	0.0326	0.0652	0.1305	0.0117	0.0351	0.0702	0.1404
46	0.0109	0.0326	0.0652	0.1305	0.0117	0.0351	0.0701	0.1403
47	0.0109	0.0326	0.0652	0.1304	0.0117	0.0351	0.0701	0.1403
48	0.0109	0.0326	0.0652	0.1304	0.0117	0.0350	0.0701	0.1403
49	0.0109	0.0326	0.0651	0.1303	0.0117	0.0350	0.0701	0.1402
50	0.0109	0.0326	0.0651	0.1303	0.0117	0.0350	0.0701	0.1402

Periodic payments at the *end* of each period required to amortize a loan of $1 over time

End of Year	At 15% Interest compounded and Payments made: Monthly	Quarterly	Semi-Annually	Annually	At 16% Interest compounded and Payments made: Monthly	Quarterly	Semi-Annually	Annually
1	0.0903	0.2739	0.5569	1.1500	0.0907	0.2755	0.5608	1.1600
2	0.0485	0.1470	0.2986	0.6151	0.0490	0.1485	0.3019	0.6230
3	0.0347	0.1050	0.2130	0.4380	0.0352	0.1066	0.2163	0.4453
4	0.0278	0.0842	0.1707	0.3503	0.0283	0.0858	0.1740	0.3574
5	0.0238	0.0720	0.1457	0.2983	0.0243	0.0736	0.1490	0.3054
6	0.0211	0.0639	0.1293	0.2642	0.0217	0.0656	0.1327	0.2714
7	0.0193	0.0583	0.1178	0.2404	0.0199	0.0600	0.1213	0.2476
8	0.0179	0.0542	0.1094	0.2229	0.0185	0.0559	0.1130	0.2302
9	0.0169	0.0511	0.1030	0.2096	0.0175	0.0529	0.1067	0.2171
10	0.0161	0.0487	0.0981	0.1993	0.0168	0.0505	0.1019	0.2069
11	0.0155	0.0468	0.0942	0.1911	0.0161	0.0487	0.0980	0.1989
12	0.0150	0.0452	0.0911	0.1845	0.0157	0.0472	0.0950	0.1924
13	0.0146	0.0440	0.0885	0.1791	0.0153	0.0460	0.0925	0.1872
14	0.0143	0.0430	0.0864	0.1747	0.0149	0.0450	0.0905	0.1829
15	0.0140	0.0421	0.0847	0.1710	0.0147	0.0442	0.0888	0.1794
16	0.0138	0.0414	0.0832	0.1679	0.0145	0.0435	0.0875	0.1764
17	0.0136	0.0408	0.0820	0.1654	0.0143	0.0430	0.0863	0.1740
18	0.0134	0.0403	0.0810	0.1632	0.0141	0.0425	0.0853	0.1719
19	0.0133	0.0399	0.0801	0.1613	0.0140	0.0421	0.0845	0.1701
20	0.0132	0.0396	0.0794	0.1598	0.0139	0.0418	0.0839	0.1687
21	0.0131	0.0393	0.0788	0.1584	0.0138	0.0415	0.0833	0.1674
22	0.0130	0.0390	0.0782	0.1573	0.0137	0.0413	0.0828	0.1664
23	0.0129	0.0388	0.0778	0.1563	0.0137	0.0411	0.0824	0.1654
24	0.0129	0.0386	0.0774	0.1554	0.0136	0.0409	0.0820	0.1647
25	0.0128	0.0385	0.0771	0.1547	0.0136	0.0408	0.0817	0.1640
26	0.0128	0.0383	0.0768	0.1541	0.0136	0.0407	0.0815	0.1634
27	0.0127	0.0382	0.0765	0.1535	0.0135	0.0406	0.0813	0.1630
28	0.0127	0.0381	0.0763	0.1531	0.0135	0.0405	0.0811	0.1625
29	0.0127	0.0380	0.0761	0.1527	0.0135	0.0404	0.0809	0.1622
30	0.0126	0.0380	0.0760	0.1523	0.0134	0.0404	0.0808	0.1619
31	0.0126	0.0379	0.0759	0.1520	0.0134	0.0403	0.0807	0.1616
32	0.0126	0.0378	0.0757	0.1517	0.0134	0.0403	0.0806	0.1614
33	0.0126	0.0378	0.0756	0.1515	0.0134	0.0402	0.0805	0.1612
34	0.0126	0.0378	0.0756	0.1513	0.0134	0.0402	0.0804	0.1610
35	0.0126	0.0377	0.0755	0.1511	0.0134	0.0402	0.0804	0.1609
36	0.0126	0.0377	0.0754	0.1510	0.0134	0.0401	0.0803	0.1608
37	0.0126	0.0377	0.0754	0.1509	0.0134	0.0401	0.0803	0.1607
38	0.0125	0.0376	0.0753	0.1507	0.0134	0.0401	0.0802	0.1606
39	0.0125	0.0376	0.0753	0.1506	0.0134	0.0401	0.0802	0.1605
40	0.0125	0.0376	0.0752	0.1506	0.0134	0.0401	0.0802	0.1604
41	0.0125	0.0376	0.0752	0.1505	0.0134	0.0401	0.0801	0.1604
42	0.0125	0.0376	0.0752	0.1504	0.0134	0.0401	0.0801	0.1603
43	0.0125	0.0376	0.0751	0.1504	0.0133	0.0400	0.0801	0.1603
44	0.0125	0.0376	0.0751	0.1503	0.0133	0.0400	0.0801	0.1602
45	0.0125	0.0375	0.0751	0.1503	0.0133	0.0400	0.0801	0.1602
46	0.0125	0.0375	0.0751	0.1502	0.0133	0.0400	0.0801	0.1602
47	0.0125	0.0375	0.0751	0.1502	0.0133	0.0400	0.0801	0.1601
48	0.0125	0.0375	0.0751	0.1502	0.0133	0.0400	0.0800	0.1601
49	0.0125	0.0375	0.0751	0.1502	0.0133	0.0400	0.0800	0.1601
50	0.0125	0.0375	0.0751	0.1501	0.0133	0.0400	0.0800	0.1601

Periodic payments at the *end* of each period required to amortize a loan of $1 over time

End of Year	At 17% Interest compounded and Payments made				At 18% Interest compounded and Payments made			
	Monthly	*Quarterly*	*Semi-Annually*	*Annually*	*Monthly*	*Quarterly*	*Semi-Annually*	*Annually*
1	0.0912	0.2771	0.5646	1.1700	0.0917	0.2787	0.5685	1.1800
2	0.0494	0.1501	0.3053	0.6308	0.0499	0.1516	0.3087	0.6387
3	0.0357	0.1081	0.2196	0.4526	0.0362	0.1097	0.2229	0.4599
4	0.0289	0.0874	0.1773	0.3645	0.0294	0.0890	0.1807	0.3717
5	0.0249	0.0752	0.1524	0.3126	0.0254	0.0769	0.1558	0.3198
6	0.0222	0.0673	0.1362	0.2786	0.0228	0.0690	0.1397	0.2859
7	0.0204	0.0618	0.1248	0.2549	0.0210	0.0635	0.1284	0.2624
8	0.0191	0.0577	0.1166	0.2377	0.0197	0.0596	0.1203	0.2452
9	0.0181	0.0547	0.1104	0.2247	0.0188	0.0566	0.1142	0.2324
10	0.0174	0.0524	0.1057	0.2147	0.0180	0.0543	0.1095	0.2225
11	0.0168	0.0506	0.1019	0.2068	0.0174	0.0526	0.1059	0.2148
12	0.0163	0.0492	0.0990	0.2005	0.0170	0.0512	0.1030	0.2086
13	0.0159	0.0480	0.0966	0.1954	0.0166	0.0501	0.1007	0.2037
14	0.0156	0.0471	0.0946	0.1912	0.0163	0.0492	0.0989	0.1997
15	0.0154	0.0463	0.0931	0.1878	0.0161	0.0485	0.0973	0.1964
16	0.0152	0.0457	0.0917	0.1850	0.0159	0.0479	0.0961	0.1937
17	0.0150	0.0452	0.0907	0.1827	0.0158	0.0474	0.0951	0.1915
18	0.0149	0.0447	0.0898	0.1807	0.0156	0.0470	0.0942	0.1896
19	0.0148	0.0444	0.0890	0.1791	0.0155	0.0466	0.0935	0.1881
20	0.0147	0.0441	0.0884	0.1777	0.0154	0.0464	0.0930	0.1868
21	0.0146	0.0438	0.0879	0.1765	0.0154	0.0461	0.0925	0.1857
22	0.0145	0.0436	0.0874	0.1756	0.0153	0.0460	0.0921	0.1848
23	0.0145	0.0434	0.0870	0.1747	0.0153	0.0458	0.0917	0.1841
24	0.0144	0.0433	0.0867	0.1740	0.0152	0.0457	0.0915	0.1835
25	0.0144	0.0432	0.0865	0.1734	0.0152	0.0456	0.0912	0.1829
26	0.0143	0.0431	0.0862	0.1729	0.0151	0.0455	0.0910	0.1825
27	0.0143	0.0430	0.0861	0.1725	0.0151	0.0454	0.0909	0.1821
28	0.0143	0.0429	0.0859	0.1721	0.0151	0.0453	0.0907	0.1818
29	0.0143	0.0428	0.0858	0.1718	0.0151	0.0453	0.0906	0.1815
30	0.0143	0.0428	0.0856	0.1715	0.0151	0.0452	0.0905	0.1813
31	0.0142	0.0427	0.0855	0.1713	0.0151	0.0452	0.0904	0.1811
32	0.0142	0.0427	0.0855	0.1711	0.0150	0.0452	0.0904	0.1809
33	0.0142	0.0427	0.0854	0.1710	0.0150	0.0451	0.0903	0.1808
34	0.0142	0.0426	0.0853	0.1708	0.0150	0.0451	0.0903	0.1806
35	0.0142	0.0426	0.0853	0.1707	0.0150	0.0451	0.0902	0.1806
36	0.0142	0.0426	0.0852	0.1706	0.0150	0.0451	0.0902	0.1805
37	0.0142	0.0426	0.0852	0.1705	0.0150	0.0451	0.0902	0.1804
38	0.0142	0.0426	0.0852	0.1704	0.0150	0.0451	0.0901	0.1803
39	0.0142	0.0426	0.0851	0.1704	0.0150	0.0450	0.0901	0.1803
40	0.0142	0.0426	0.0851	0.1703	0.0150	0.0450	0.0901	0.1802
41	0.0142	0.0425	0.0851	0.1703	0.0150	0.0450	0.0901	0.1802
42	0.0142	0.0425	0.0851	0.1702	0.0150	0.0450	0.0901	0.1802
43	0.0142	0.0425	0.0851	0.1702	0.0150	0.0450	0.0901	0.1801
44	0.0142	0.0425	0.0851	0.1702	0.0150	0.0450	0.0900	0.1801
45	0.0142	0.0425	0.0851	0.1701	0.0150	0.0450	0.0900	0.1801
46	0.0142	0.0425	0.0850	0.1701	0.0150	0.0450	0.0900	0.1801
47	0.0142	0.0425	0.0850	0.1701	0.0150	0.0450	0.0900	0.1801
48	0.0142	0.0425	0.0850	0.1701	0.0150	0.0450	0.0900	0.1801
49	0.0142	0.0425	0.0850	0.1701	0.0150	0.0450	0.0900	0.1801
50	0.0142	0.0425	0.0850	0.1701	0.0150	0.0450	0.0900	0.1800

Periodic payments at the *end* of each period required to amortize a loan of $1 over time

End of Year	At 19% Interest compounded and Payments made: Monthly	Quarterly	Semi-Annually	Annually	At 20% Interest compounded and Payments made: Monthly	Quarterly	Semi-Annually	Annually
1	0.0922	0.2804	0.5723	1.1900	0.0926	0.2820	0.5762	1.2000
2	0.0504	0.1532	0.3121	0.6466	0.0509	0.1547	0.3155	0.6545
3	0.0367	0.1112	0.2263	0.4673	0.0372	0.1128	0.2296	0.4747
4	0.0299	0.0906	0.1840	0.3790	0.0304	0.0923	0.1874	0.3863
5	0.0259	0.0786	0.1593	0.3271	0.0265	0.0802	0.1627	0.3344
6	0.0234	0.0707	0.1432	0.2933	0.0240	0.0725	0.1468	0.3007
7	0.0216	0.0653	0.1321	0.2699	0.0222	0.0671	0.1357	0.2774
8	0.0203	0.0614	0.1240	0.2529	0.0210	0.0633	0.1278	0.2606
9	0.0194	0.0585	0.1180	0.2402	0.0200	0.0604	0.1219	0.2481
10	0.0187	0.0563	0.1135	0.2305	0.0193	0.0583	0.1175	0.2385
11	0.0181	0.0546	0.1099	0.2229	0.0188	0.0566	0.1140	0.2311
12	0.0177	0.0532	0.1071	0.2169	0.0184	0.0553	0.1113	0.2253
13	0.0173	0.0522	0.1049	0.2121	0.0180	0.0543	0.1092	0.2206
14	0.0171	0.0513	0.1031	0.2082	0.0178	0.0535	0.1075	0.2169
15	0.0168	0.0506	0.1017	0.2051	0.0176	0.0528	0.1061	0.2139
16	0.0166	0.0501	0.1005	0.2025	0.0174	0.0523	0.1050	0.2114
17	0.0165	0.0496	0.0995	0.2004	0.0173	0.0519	0.1041	0.2094
18	0.0164	0.0492	0.0988	0.1987	0.0171	0.0515	0.1033	0.2078
19	0.0163	0.0489	0.0981	0.1972	0.0171	0.0513	0.1027	0.2065
20	0.0162	0.0487	0.0976	0.1960	0.0170	0.0510	0.1023	0.2054
21	0.0161	0.0485	0.0971	0.1951	0.0169	0.0508	0.1019	0.2044
22	0.0161	0.0483	0.0968	0.1942	0.0169	0.0507	0.1015	0.2037
23	0.0160	0.0482	0.0965	0.1935	0.0168	0.0506	0.1013	0.2031
24	0.0160	0.0481	0.0962	0.1930	0.0168	0.0505	0.1010	0.2025
25	0.0160	0.0480	0.0960	0.1925	0.0168	0.0504	0.1009	0.2021
26	0.0160	0.0479	0.0959	0.1921	0.0168	0.0503	0.1007	0.2018
27	0.0159	0.0478	0.0957	0.1917	0.0167	0.0503	0.1006	0.2015
28	0.0159	0.0478	0.0956	0.1915	0.0167	0.0502	0.1005	0.2012
29	0.0159	0.0477	0.0955	0.1912	0.0167	0.0502	0.1004	0.2010
30	0.0159	0.0477	0.0954	0.1910	0.0167	0.0501	0.1003	0.2008
31	0.0159	0.0477	0.0953	0.1909	0.0167	0.0501	0.1003	0.2007
32	0.0159	0.0476	0.0953	0.1907	0.0167	0.0501	0.1002	0.2006
33	0.0159	0.0476	0.0952	0.1906	0.0167	0.0501	0.1002	0.2005
34	0.0159	0.0476	0.0952	0.1905	0.0167	0.0501	0.1002	0.2004
35	0.0159	0.0476	0.0952	0.1904	0.0167	0.0501	0.1001	0.2003
36	0.0159	0.0476	0.0951	0.1904	0.0167	0.0500	0.1001	0.2003
37	0.0158	0.0475	0.0951	0.1903	0.0167	0.0500	0.1001	0.2002
38	0.0158	0.0475	0.0951	0.1903	0.0167	0.0500	0.1001	0.2002
39	0.0158	0.0475	0.0951	0.1902	0.0167	0.0500	0.1001	0.2002
40	0.0158	0.0475	0.0951	0.1902	0.0167	0.0500	0.1000	0.2001
41	0.0158	0.0475	0.0951	0.1902	0.0167	0.0500	0.1000	0.2001
42	0.0158	0.0475	0.0950	0.1901	0.0167	0.0500	0.1000	0.2001
43	0.0158	0.0475	0.0950	0.1901	0.0167	0.0500	0.1000	0.2001
44	0.0158	0.0475	0.0950	0.1901	0.0167	0.0500	0.1000	0.2001
45	0.0158	0.0475	0.0950	0.1901	0.0167	0.0500	0.1000	0.2001
46	0.0158	0.0475	0.0950	0.1901	0.0167	0.0500	0.1000	0.2000
47	0.0158	0.0475	0.0950	0.1901	0.0167	0.0500	0.1000	0.2000
48	0.0158	0.0475	0.0950	0.1900	0.0167	0.0500	0.1000	0.2000
49	0.0158	0.0475	0.0950	0.1900	0.0167	0.0500	0.1000	0.2000
50	0.0158	0.0475	0.0950	0.1900	0.0167	0.0500	0.1000	0.2000

TABLE 6

Monthly payments required to repay a Canadian mortgage loan of $1000 over various periods of time with interest compounded semi-annually

Applications

Chapter Seven

- Canadian mortgage loans.

Monthly payments required to repay a mortgage loan of $1000 over various periods of time with interest compounded semi-annually

% Interest

End of Year	*5.000*	*5.125*	*5.250*	*5.375*	*5.500*	*5.625*	*5.750*	*5.875*
1	85.584	85.640	85.696	85.752	85.808	85.864	85.920	85.977
2	43.848	43.903	43.958	44.013	44.068	44.123	44.178	44.233
3	29.948	30.003	30.058	30.113	30.168	30.223	30.278	30.333
4	23.006	23.062	23.117	23.173	23.228	23.284	23.340	23.395
5	18.848	18.904	18.960	19.016	19.073	19.129	19.185	19.242
6	16.081	16.138	16.195	16.252	16.309	16.366	16.423	16.481
7	14.110	14.167	14.225	14.283	14.341	14.399	14.457	14.515
8	12.636	12.694	12.752	12.811	12.869	12.928	12.987	13.046
9	11.493	11.552	11.611	11.670	11.730	11.789	11.849	11.909
10	10.581	10.641	10.701	10.762	10.822	10.882	10.943	11.004
11	9.839	9.900	9.961	10.022	10.083	10.144	10.206	10.268
12	9.223	9.285	9.346	9.408	9.470	9.532	9.595	9.658
13	8.705	8.767	8.829	8.892	8.955	9.018	9.081	9.145
14	8.262	8.325	8.389	8.452	8.516	8.580	8.644	8.708
15	7.881	7.945	8.009	8.073	8.138	8.203	8.268	8.333
16	7.550	7.614	7.679	7.744	7.810	7.875	7.941	8.008
17	7.259	7.325	7.390	7.456	7.522	7.589	7.656	7.723
18	7.003	7.069	7.135	7.202	7.269	7.336	7.404	7.472
19	6.775	6.842	6.909	6.976	7.044	7.112	7.181	7.250
20	6.571	6.639	6.707	6.775	6.844	6.913	6.982	7.052
21	6.389	6.457	6.526	6.595	6.664	6.734	6.804	6.875
22	6.224	6.293	6.363	6.432	6.503	6.573	6.644	6.716
23	6.075	6.145	6.215	6.286	6.357	6.428	6.500	6.572
24	5.939	6.010	6.081	6.153	6.224	6.297	6.369	6.442
25	5.816	5.887	5.959	6.031	6.104	6.177	6.250	6.324
26	5.703	5.775	5.848	5.921	5.994	6.068	6.142	6.216
27	5.600	5.673	5.746	5.820	5.894	5.968	6.043	6.118
28	5.505	5.578	5.652	5.727	5.802	5.877	5.952	6.028
29	5.418	5.492	5.566	5.641	5.717	5.793	5.869	5.946
30	5.337	5.412	5.487	5.563	5.639	5.716	5.793	5.870
31	5.262	5.338	5.414	5.490	5.567	5.645	5.722	5.801
32	5.193	5.269	5.346	5.423	5.501	5.579	5.657	5.736
33	5.129	5.206	5.283	5.361	5.439	5.518	5.597	5.677
34	5.070	5.147	5.225	5.304	5.382	5.462	5.542	5.622
35	5.014	5.092	5.171	5.250	5.330	5.410	5.490	5.571
36	4.963	5.041	5.121	5.200	5.281	5.361	5.442	5.524
37	4.914	4.994	5.074	5.154	5.235	5.316	5.398	5.480
38	4.869	4.949	5.030	5.111	5.192	5.274	5.357	5.439
39	4.827	4.908	4.989	5.071	5.153	5.235	5.318	5.402
40	4.788	4.869	4.951	5.033	5.116	5.199	5.282	5.366

Monthly payments required to repay a mortgage loan of $1000 over various periods of time with interest compounded semi-annually

% Interest

End of Year	*6.000*	*6.125*	*6.250*	*6.375*	*6.500*	*6.625*	*6.750*	*6.875*
1	86.033	86.089	86.145	86.201	86.257	86.313	86.369	86.425
2	44.287	44.342	44.397	44.452	44.507	44.562	44.617	44.672
3	30.389	30.444	30.499	30.554	30.610	30.665	30.721	30.776
4	23.451	23.507	23.563	23.619	23.675	23.731	23.787	23.844
5	19.299	19.355	19.412	19.469	19.526	19.583	19.640	19.697
6	16.538	16.596	16.653	16.711	16.769	16.827	16.885	16.943
7	14.573	14.632	14.690	14.749	14.808	14.867	14.926	14.985
8	13.106	13.165	13.224	13.284	13.344	13.404	13.464	13.524
9	11.969	12.030	12.090	12.151	12.211	12.272	12.333	12.394
10	11.065	11.126	11.188	11.249	11.311	11.373	11.435	11.497
11	10.330	10.392	10.454	10.516	10.579	10.642	10.705	10.768
12	9.720	9.784	9.847	9.910	9.974	10.038	10.102	10.166
13	9.209	9.273	9.337	9.401	9.466	9.531	9.596	9.661
14	8.773	8.838	8.903	8.969	9.034	9.100	9.166	9.233
15	8.399	8.465	8.531	8.597	8.664	8.731	8.798	8.865
16	8.074	8.141	8.208	8.275	8.343	8.410	8.479	8.547
17	7.790	7.858	7.926	7.994	8.062	8.131	8.200	8.270
18	7.540	7.609	7.678	7.747	7.816	7.886	7.956	8.026
19	7.319	7.388	7.458	7.528	7.598	7.669	7.740	7.811
20	7.122	7.192	7.263	7.334	7.405	7.477	7.548	7.621
21	6.946	7.017	7.088	7.160	7.232	7.305	7.378	7.451
22	6.787	6.859	6.932	7.004	7.077	7.151	7.224	7.298
23	6.645	6.717	6.791	6.864	6.938	7.012	7.087	7.162
24	6.515	6.589	6.663	6.737	6.812	6.887	6.963	7.039
25	6.398	6.473	6.547	6.623	6.698	6.774	6.850	6.927
26	6.291	6.367	6.442	6.518	6.595	6.672	6.749	6.826
27	6.194	6.270	6.346	6.423	6.501	6.578	6.656	6.734
28	6.105	6.182	6.259	6.337	6.415	6.493	6.572	6.651
29	6.023	6.101	6.179	6.257	6.336	6.415	6.495	6.575
30	5.948	6.027	6.105	6.184	6.264	6.344	6.424	6.505
31	5.879	5.958	6.038	6.118	6.198	6.279	6.360	6.441
32	5.816	5.895	5.976	6.056	6.137	6.219	6.300	6.383
33	5.757	5.837	5.918	6.000	6.081	6.164	6.246	6.329
34	5.703	5.784	5.865	5.947	6.030	6.113	6.196	6.279
35	5.653	5.734	5.817	5.899	5.982	6.066	6.150	6.234
36	5.606	5.688	5.771	5.855	5.938	6.023	6.107	6.192
37	5.563	5.646	5.730	5.813	5.898	5.983	6.068	6.153
38	5.523	5.607	5.691	5.775	5.860	5.946	6.031	6.118
39	5.486	5.570	5.655	5.740	5.825	5.911	5.998	6.085
40	5.451	5.536	5.621	5.707	5.793	5.880	5.967	6.054

Monthly payments required to repay a mortgage loan of $1000 over various periods of time with interest compounded semi-annually

% Interest

End of Year	*7.000*	*7.125*	*7.250*	*7.375*	*7.500*	*7.625*	*7.750*	*7.875*
1	86.481	86.537	86.593	86.649	86.705	86.760	86.816	86.872
2	44.727	44.782	44.837	44.892	44.948	45.003	45.058	45.113
3	30.831	30.887	30.942	30.998	31.054	31.109	31.165	31.221
4	23.900	23.956	24.013	24.069	24.125	24.182	24.239	24.295
5	19.754	19.811	19.869	19.926	19.984	20.041	20.099	20.156
6	17.001	17.059	17.118	17.176	17.235	17.293	17.352	17.411
7	15.044	15.103	15.163	15.222	15.282	15.342	15.401	15.461
8	13.584	13.644	13.705	13.766	13.826	13.887	13.948	14.009
9	12.456	12.517	12.579	12.640	12.702	12.764	12.827	12.889
10	11.559	11.622	11.685	11.747	11.810	11.874	11.937	12.000
11	10.832	10.895	10.959	11.023	11.087	11.152	11.216	11.281
12	10.231	10.295	10.360	10.425	10.490	10.556	10.621	10.687
13	9.727	9.792	9.858	9.924	9.991	10.057	10.124	10.191
14	9.299	9.366	9.433	9.500	9.567	9.635	9.703	9.771
15	8.932	9.000	9.068	9.137	9.205	9.274	9.343	9.412
16	8.615	8.684	8.753	8.823	8.892	8.962	9.032	9.102
17	8.339	8.409	8.479	8.549	8.620	8.691	8.762	8.834
18	8.097	8.168	8.239	8.310	8.382	8.454	8.526	8.598
19	7.883	7.955	8.027	8.099	8.172	8.245	8.318	8.392
20	7.693	7.766	7.839	7.912	7.986	8.060	8.134	8.209
21	7.524	7.598	7.672	7.746	7.821	7.896	7.971	8.047
22	7.373	7.447	7.522	7.598	7.673	7.749	7.825	7.902
23	7.237	7.313	7.388	7.465	7.541	7.618	7.695	7.773
24	7.115	7.191	7.268	7.345	7.423	7.500	7.578	7.657
25	7.004	7.082	7.159	7.237	7.316	7.394	7.473	7.553
26	6.904	6.982	7.061	7.140	7.219	7.298	7.378	7.458
27	6.813	6.892	6.972	7.051	7.131	7.212	7.292	7.374
28	6.730	6.810	6.890	6.971	7.052	7.133	7.215	7.297
29	6.655	6.736	6.817	6.898	6.980	7.062	7.144	7.227
30	6.586	6.667	6.749	6.831	6.914	6.997	7.080	7.163
31	6.523	6.605	6.688	6.771	6.854	6.937	7.021	7.106
32	6.465	6.548	6.631	6.715	6.799	6.883	6.968	7.053
33	6.412	6.496	6.580	6.664	6.749	6.834	6.919	7.005
34	6.363	6.448	6.532	6.618	6.703	6.789	6.875	6.961
35	6.319	6.404	6.489	6.575	6.661	6.747	6.834	6.921
36	6.277	6.363	6.449	6.535	6.622	6.709	6.797	6.884
37	6.239	6.326	6.412	6.499	6.587	6.674	6.762	6.851
38	6.204	6.291	6.378	6.466	6.554	6.642	6.731	6.820
39	6.172	6.259	6.347	6.435	6.524	6.613	6.702	6.791
40	6.142	6.230	6.318	6.407	6.496	6.586	6.675	6.765

Monthly payments required to repay a mortgage loan of $1000 over various periods of time with interest compounded semi-annually

% Interest

End of Year	8.000	8.125	8.250	8.375	8.500	8.625	8.750	8.875
1	86.928	86.984	87.040	87.096	87.152	87.208	87.264	87.319
2	45.168	45.223	45.278	45.333	45.389	45.444	45.499	45.554
3	31.276	31.332	31.388	31.444	31.500	31.555	31.611	31.667
4	24.352	24.409	24.465	24.522	24.579	24.636	24.693	24.750
5	20.214	20.272	20.330	20.388	20.446	20.504	20.562	20.620
6	17.470	17.529	17.588	17.647	17.706	17.766	17.825	17.885
7	15.521	15.582	15.642	15.702	15.763	15.823	15.884	15.945
8	14.071	14.132	14.194	14.255	14.317	14.379	14.441	14.503
9	12.951	13.014	13.077	13.140	13.203	13.266	13.329	13.392
10	12.064	12.128	12.192	12.256	12.320	12.385	12.449	12.514
11	11.345	11.410	11.476	11.541	11.607	11.672	11.738	11.804
12	10.753	10.819	10.886	10.952	11.019	11.086	11.153	11.221
13	10.258	10.326	10.393	10.461	10.529	10.597	10.665	10.734
14	9.839	9.908	9.977	10.046	10.115	10.184	10.254	10.324
15	9.482	9.551	9.621	9.691	9.762	9.832	9.903	9.974
16	9.173	9.244	9.315	9.386	9.458	9.529	9.601	9.674
17	8.905	8.977	9.049	9.122	9.194	9.267	9.340	9.414
18	8.671	8.744	8.817	8.891	8.965	9.039	9.113	9.187
19	8.465	8.539	8.614	8.688	8.763	8.838	8.914	8.989
20	8.284	8.359	8.434	8.510	8.586	8.662	8.738	8.815
21	8.122	8.198	8.275	8.352	8.428	8.506	8.583	8.661
22	7.979	8.056	8.133	8.211	8.289	8.367	8.446	8.524
23	7.850	7.929	8.007	8.086	8.165	8.244	8.323	8.403
24	7.735	7.815	7.894	7.973	8.053	8.133	8.214	8.295
25	7.632	7.712	7.792	7.873	7.954	8.035	8.116	8.198
26	7.539	7.620	7.701	7.782	7.864	7.946	8.028	8.111
27	7.455	7.537	7.619	7.701	7.783	7.866	7.949	8.033
28	7.379	7.461	7.544	7.627	7.711	7.794	7.878	7.963
29	7.310	7.393	7.477	7.561	7.645	7.729	7.814	7.899
30	7.247	7.331	7.416	7.500	7.585	7.671	7.756	7.842
31	7.190	7.275	7.360	7.446	7.531	7.618	7.704	7.790
32	7.138	7.224	7.310	7.396	7.482	7.569	7.656	7.744
33	7.091	7.177	7.264	7.351	7.438	7.525	7.613	7.701
34	7.048	7.135	7.222	7.310	7.397	7.486	7.574	7.663
35	7.008	7.096	7.184	7.272	7.361	7.449	7.538	7.628
36	6.972	7.060	7.149	7.238	7.327	7.416	7.506	7.596
37	6.939	7.028	7.117	7.207	7.296	7.386	7.477	7.567
38	6.909	6.998	7.088	7.178	7.268	7.359	7.450	7.541
39	6.881	6.971	7.061	7.152	7.243	7.334	7.425	7.517
40	6.856	6.946	7.037	7.128	7.220	7.311	7.403	7.495

Monthly payments required to repay a mortgage loan of $1000 over various periods of time with interest compounded semi-annually

% Interest

End of Year	*9.000*	*9.125*	*9.250*	*9.375*	*9.500*	*9.625*	*9.750*	*9.875*
1	87.375	87.431	87.487	87.543	87.599	87.654	87.710	87.766
2	45.609	45.665	45.720	45.775	45.830	45.886	45.941	45.996
3	31.723	31.779	31.835	31.891	31.948	32.004	32.060	32.116
4	24.807	24.864	24.921	24.979	25.036	25.093	25.151	25.208
5	20.679	20.737	20.796	20.854	20.913	20.971	21.030	21.089
6	17.944	18.004	18.064	18.123	18.183	18.243	18.304	18.364
7	16.006	16.067	16.128	16.189	16.251	16.312	16.374	16.435
8	14.565	14.627	14.690	14.753	14.815	14.878	14.941	15.004
9	13.456	13.520	13.584	13.648	13.712	13.776	13.840	13.905
10	12.579	12.644	12.709	12.774	12.840	12.906	12.971	13.037
11	11.870	11.937	12.003	12.070	12.137	12.204	12.271	12.338
12	11.288	11.356	11.424	11.492	11.560	11.628	11.697	11.765
13	10.803	10.872	10.941	11.010	11.080	11.149	11.219	11.289
14	10.394	10.464	10.534	10.605	10.676	10.747	10.818	10.889
15	10.045	10.117	10.188	10.260	10.332	10.405	10.477	10.550
16	9.746	9.819	9.892	9.965	10.038	10.112	10.185	10.259
17	9.487	9.561	9.635	9.710	9.784	9.859	9.934	10.009
18	9.262	9.337	9.412	9.488	9.564	9.640	9.716	9.792
19	9.065	9.141	9.218	9.294	9.371	9.448	9.526	9.603
20	8.892	8.969	9.047	9.124	9.202	9.281	9.359	9.438
21	8.739	8.817	8.896	8.975	9.054	9.133	9.213	9.292
22	8.604	8.683	8.762	8.842	8.922	9.003	9.083	9.164
23	8.483	8.563	8.644	8.725	8.806	8.887	8.969	9.051
24	8.376	8.457	8.539	8.620	8.702	8.785	8.867	8.950
25	8.280	8.362	8.444	8.527	8.610	8.694	8.777	8.861
26	8.194	8.277	8.360	8.444	8.528	8.612	8.697	8.781
27	8.117	8.201	8.285	8.369	8.454	8.539	8.625	8.710
28	8.047	8.132	8.217	8.303	8.388	8.474	8.560	8.647
29	7.985	8.070	8.156	8.242	8.329	8.416	8.502	8.590
30	7.928	8.015	8.101	8.188	8.276	8.363	8.451	8.539
31	7.877	7.965	8.052	8.140	8.228	8.316	8.404	8.493
32	7.831	7.919	8.007	8.096	8.184	8.273	8.362	8.451
33	7.790	7.878	7.967	8.056	8.145	8.235	8.324	8.414
34	7.752	7.841	7.930	8.020	8.110	8.200	8.290	8.381
35	7.717	7.807	7.897	7.988	8.078	8.169	8.260	8.351
36	7.686	7.777	7.867	7.958	8.049	8.141	8.232	8.324
37	7.658	7.749	7.840	7.932	8.023	8.115	8.207	8.299
38	7.632	7.724	7.815	7.907	8.000	8.092	8.184	8.277
39	7.609	7.701	7.793	7.885	7.978	8.071	8.164	8.257
40	7.587	7.680	7.773	7.866	7.959	8.052	8.145	8.239

Monthly payments required to repay a mortgage loan of $1000 over various periods of time with interest compounded semi-annually

% Interest

End of Year	*10.000*	*10.125*	*10.250*	*10.375*	*10.500*	*10.625*	*10.750*	*10.875*
1	87.822	87.878	87.933	87.989	88.045	88.101	88.156	88.212
2	46.052	46.107	46.162	46.218	46.273	46.328	46.384	46.439
3	32.172	32.229	32.285	32.341	32.398	32.454	32.510	32.567
4	25.266	25.323	25.381	25.438	25.496	25.554	25.612	25.669
5	21.148	21.207	21.266	21.325	21.384	21.443	21.502	21.562
6	18.424	18.484	18.545	18.605	18.666	18.727	18.788	18.848
7	16.497	16.559	16.621	16.683	16.745	16.807	16.869	16.932
8	15.067	15.131	15.194	15.258	15.321	15.385	15.449	15.513
9	13.969	14.034	14.099	14.164	14.229	14.295	14.360	14.426
10	13.103	13.170	13.236	13.303	13.369	13.436	13.503	13.570
11	12.406	12.473	12.541	12.609	12.677	12.746	12.814	12.883
12	11.834	11.903	11.973	12.042	12.112	12.181	12.251	12.321
13	11.360	11.430	11.501	11.572	11.643	11.714	11.785	11.857
14	10.961	11.033	11.105	11.177	11.249	11.322	11.395	11.468
15	10.623	10.696	10.769	10.843	10.916	10.990	11.064	11.139
16	10.333	10.408	10.483	10.557	10.632	10.708	10.783	10.859
17	10.084	10.160	10.236	10.312	10.388	10.465	10.542	10.619
18	9.869	9.946	10.023	10.100	10.178	10.255	10.333	10.411
19	9.681	9.759	9.837	9.916	9.994	10.073	10.153	10.232
20	9.517	9.596	9.675	9.755	9.835	9.915	9.995	10.076
21	9.372	9.453	9.533	9.614	9.695	9.776	9.857	9.939
22	9.245	9.327	9.408	9.490	9.572	9.654	9.737	9.819
23	9.133	9.215	9.298	9.381	9.464	9.547	9.630	9.714
24	9.033	9.117	9.200	9.284	9.368	9.452	9.537	9.621
25	8.945	9.029	9.114	9.198	9.283	9.368	9.454	9.539
26	8.866	8.951	9.037	9.122	9.208	9.294	9.380	9.467
27	8.796	8.882	8.968	9.055	9.141	9.228	9.315	9.403
28	8.733	8.820	8.907	8.994	9.082	9.170	9.257	9.346
29	8.677	8.765	8.852	8.940	9.029	9.117	9.206	9.295
30	8.627	8.715	8.804	8.892	8.981	9.071	9.160	9.250
31	8.582	8.671	8.760	8.849	8.939	9.029	9.119	9.209
32	8.541	8.631	8.721	8.811	8.901	8.992	9.082	9.173
33	8.505	8.595	8.686	8.776	8.867	8.958	9.050	9.141
34	8.472	8.563	8.654	8.745	8.837	8.929	9.021	9.113
35	8.442	8.534	8.626	8.718	8.810	8.902	8.994	9.087
36	8.416	8.508	8.600	8.693	8.785	8.878	8.971	9.064
37	8.392	8.484	8.577	8.670	8.763	8.857	8.950	9.044
38	8.370	8.463	8.556	8.650	8.743	8.837	8.931	9.025
39	8.351	8.444	8.538	8.632	8.726	8.820	8.914	9.009
40	8.333	8.427	8.521	8.615	8.710	8.804	8.899	8.994

Monthly payments required to repay a mortgage loan of $1000 over various periods of time with interest compounded semi-annually

% Interest

End of Year	*11.000*	*11.125*	*11.250*	*11.375*	*11.500*	*11.625*	*11.750*	*11.875*
1	88.268	88.324	88.379	88.435	88.491	88.546	88.602	88.658
2	46.495	46.550	46.606	46.661	46.716	46.772	46.827	46.883
3	32.623	32.680	32.736	32.793	32.850	32.906	32.963	33.020
4	25.727	25.785	25.843	25.901	25.959	26.017	26.075	26.134
5	21.621	21.680	21.740	21.800	21.859	21.919	21.979	22.039
6	18.909	18.970	19.032	19.093	19.154	19.215	19.277	19.338
7	16.994	17.057	17.120	17.183	17.246	17.309	17.372	17.435
8	15.577	15.641	15.706	15.770	15.835	15.899	15.964	16.029
9	14.491	14.557	14.623	14.689	14.755	14.822	14.888	14.955
10	13.637	13.705	13.772	13.840	13.908	13.976	14.044	14.112
11	12.951	13.020	13.089	13.159	13.228	13.298	13.367	13.437
12	12.392	12.462	12.533	12.603	12.674	12.745	12.817	12.888
13	11.928	12.000	12.072	12.145	12.217	12.289	12.362	12.435
14	11.541	11.614	11.687	11.761	11.835	11.909	11.983	12.058
15	11.213	11.288	11.363	11.438	11.513	11.589	11.664	11.740
16	10.935	11.011	11.087	11.163	11.240	11.317	11.394	11.471
17	10.696	10.773	10.851	10.928	11.006	11.084	11.163	11.241
18	10.490	10.568	10.647	10.726	10.805	10.885	10.964	11.044
19	10.312	10.391	10.471	10.552	10.632	10.713	10.793	10.874
20	10.156	10.237	10.319	10.400	10.481	10.563	10.645	10.727
21	10.021	10.103	10.185	10.268	10.350	10.433	10.516	10.600
22	9.902	9.985	10.069	10.152	10.236	10.320	10.404	10.488
23	9.798	9.882	9.967	10.051	10.136	10.221	10.306	10.391
24	9.706	9.791	9.877	9.962	10.048	10.134	10.220	10.306
25	9.625	9.711	9.798	9.884	9.971	10.057	10.144	10.232
26	9.554	9.641	9.728	9.815	9.902	9.990	10.078	10.166
27	9.490	9.578	9.666	9.754	9.842	9.931	10.019	10.108
28	9.434	9.522	9.611	9.700	9.789	9.878	9.968	10.057
29	9.384	9.473	9.563	9.652	9.742	9.832	9.922	10.012
30	9.339	9.429	9.519	9.610	9.700	9.791	9.882	9.973
31	9.300	9.390	9.481	9.572	9.663	9.755	9.846	9.938
32	9.264	9.356	9.447	9.539	9.630	9.722	9.814	9.907
33	9.233	9.325	9.417	9.509	9.601	9.694	9.786	9.879
34	9.205	9.297	9.390	9.482	9.575	9.668	9.761	9.855
35	9.180	9.273	9.366	9.459	9.552	9.646	9.739	9.833
36	9.157	9.251	9.344	9.438	9.532	9.626	9.720	9.814
37	9.137	9.231	9.325	9.419	9.513	9.608	9.702	9.797
38	9.119	9.214	9.308	9.402	9.497	9.592	9.687	9.782
39	9.103	9.198	9.293	9.388	9.483	9.578	9.673	9.768
40	9.089	9.184	9.279	9.374	9.470	9.565	9.661	9.756

Monthly payments required to repay a mortgage loan of $1000 over various periods of time with interest compounded semi-annually

% Interest

End of Year	*12.000*	*12.125*	*12.250*	*12.375*	*12.500*	*12.625*	*12.750*	*12.875*
1	88.713	88.769	88.825	88.880	88.936	88.992	89.047	89.103
2	46.938	46.994	47.049	47.105	47.161	47.216	47.272	47.327
3	33.076	33.133	33.190	33.247	33.303	33.360	33.417	33.474
4	26.192	26.250	26.309	26.367	26.425	26.484	26.542	26.601
5	22.098	22.158	22.218	22.279	22.339	22.399	22.459	22.520
6	19.400	19.462	19.523	19.585	19.647	19.709	19.771	19.834
7	17.498	17.562	17.625	17.689	17.753	17.816	17.880	17.944
8	16.094	16.159	16.225	16.290	16.355	16.421	16.487	16.552
9	15.021	15.088	15.155	15.222	15.290	15.357	15.424	15.492
10	14.180	14.249	14.317	14.386	14.455	14.524	14.593	14.663
11	13.507	13.577	13.647	13.718	13.788	13.859	13.930	14.001
12	12.960	13.031	13.103	13.175	13.247	13.320	13.392	13.465
13	12.508	12.581	12.655	12.728	12.802	12.876	12.950	13.024
14	12.132	12.207	12.282	12.357	12.432	12.508	12.583	12.659
15	11.816	11.892	11.969	12.045	12.122	12.199	12.276	12.353
16	11.548	11.626	11.704	11.782	11.860	11.938	12.016	12.095
17	11.320	11.399	11.478	11.557	11.637	11.716	11.796	11.876
18	11.124	11.204	11.285	11.365	11.446	11.527	11.608	11.689
19	10.956	11.037	11.119	11.200	11.282	11.364	11.447	11.529
20	10.810	10.892	10.975	11.058	11.141	11.224	11.308	11.391
21	10.683	10.767	10.851	10.935	11.019	11.103	11.188	11.273
22	10.573	10.658	10.743	10.828	10.913	10.998	11.084	11.170
23	10.477	10.563	10.648	10.735	10.821	10.907	10.994	11.081
24	10.393	10.479	10.566	10.653	10.740	10.828	10.915	11.003
25	10.319	10.407	10.494	10.582	10.670	10.758	10.847	10.935
26	10.254	10.343	10.431	10.520	10.609	10.698	10.787	10.876
27	10.197	10.286	10.376	10.465	10.555	10.645	10.735	10.825
28	10.147	10.237	10.327	10.417	10.508	10.598	10.689	10.780
29	10.103	10.194	10.284	10.375	10.466	10.557	10.649	10.740
30	10.064	10.155	10.247	10.338	10.430	10.522	10.614	10.706
31	10.029	10.121	10.213	10.305	10.398	10.490	10.583	10.675
32	9.999	10.091	10.184	10.277	10.369	10.462	10.555	10.649
33	9.972	10.065	10.158	10.251	10.345	10.438	10.532	10.625
34	9.948	10.041	10.135	10.229	10.323	10.417	10.511	10.605
35	9.927	10.021	10.115	10.209	10.303	10.398	10.492	10.587
36	9.908	10.002	10.097	10.191	10.286	10.381	10.476	10.571
37	9.891	9.986	10.081	10.176	10.271	10.366	10.461	10.557
38	9.877	9.972	10.067	10.162	10.258	10.353	10.449	10.544
39	9.864	9.959	10.055	10.150	10.246	10.342	10.437	10.533
40	9.852	9.948	10.044	10.139	10.235	10.331	10.428	10.524

Monthly payments required to repay a mortgage loan of $1000 over various periods of time with interest compounded semi-annually

% Interest

End of Year	*13.000*	*13.125*	*13.250*	*13.375*	*13.500*	*13.625*	*13.750*	*13.875*
1	89.158	89.214	89.270	89.325	89.381	89.436	89.492	89.547
2	47.383	47.438	47.494	47.550	47.605	47.661	47.717	47.772
3	33.531	33.588	33.645	33.702	33.759	33.816	33.873	33.931
4	26.660	26.718	26.777	26.836	26.895	26.954	27.012	27.071
5	22.580	22.641	22.701	22.762	22.822	22.883	22.944	23.005
6	19.896	19.958	20.021	20.083	20.146	20.208	20.271	20.334
7	18.008	18.073	18.137	18.201	18.266	18.330	18.395	18.459
8	16.618	16.684	16.750	16.817	16.883	16.949	17.016	17.083
9	15.560	15.627	15.695	15.763	15.831	15.900	15.968	16.037
10	14.732	14.802	14.871	14.941	15.011	15.081	15.151	15.222
11	14.072	14.143	14.215	14.286	14.358	14.430	14.502	14.574
12	13.537	13.610	13.683	13.757	13.830	13.904	13.977	14.051
13	13.099	13.173	13.248	13.323	13.398	13.473	13.548	13.624
14	12.735	12.811	12.887	12.964	13.040	13.117	13.194	13.271
15	12.430	12.508	12.586	12.664	12.742	12.820	12.898	12.977
16	12.174	12.253	12.332	12.411	12.491	12.570	12.650	12.730
17	11.956	12.036	12.117	12.198	12.278	12.359	12.441	12.522
18	11.771	11.852	11.934	12.016	12.098	12.180	12.263	12.345
19	11.612	11.695	11.778	11.861	11.944	12.028	12.111	12.195
20	11.475	11.559	11.643	11.728	11.812	11.897	11.982	12.067
21	11.358	11.443	11.528	11.613	11.699	11.785	11.870	11.957
22	11.256	11.342	11.428	11.515	11.601	11.688	11.775	11.862
23	11.167	11.255	11.342	11.429	11.517	11.604	11.692	11.780
24	11.091	11.179	11.267	11.355	11.444	11.532	11.621	11.710
25	11.024	11.113	11.202	11.291	11.380	11.470	11.559	11.649
26	10.966	11.056	11.145	11.235	11.325	11.415	11.506	11.596
27	10.915	11.005	11.096	11.187	11.277	11.368	11.459	11.551
28	10.871	10.962	11.053	11.144	11.236	11.327	11.419	11.511
29	10.832	10.924	11.015	11.107	11.199	11.292	11.384	11.476
30	10.798	10.890	10.983	11.075	11.168	11.261	11.353	11.446
31	10.768	10.861	10.954	11.047	11.140	11.233	11.327	11.420
32	10.742	10.835	10.929	11.022	11.116	11.210	11.304	11.398
33	10.719	10.813	10.907	11.001	11.095	11.189	11.283	11.378
34	10.699	10.793	10.887	10.982	11.076	11.171	11.266	11.361
35	10.681	10.776	10.871	10.965	11.060	11.155	11.250	11.345
36	10.666	10.761	10.856	10.951	11.046	11.142	11.237	11.332
37	10.652	10.747	10.843	10.938	11.034	11.129	11.225	11.321
38	10.640	10.736	10.831	10.927	11.023	11.119	11.215	11.311
39	10.629	10.725	10.821	10.917	11.014	11.110	11.206	11.302
40	10.620	10.716	10.813	10.909	11.005	11.102	11.198	11.295

Monthly payments required to repay a mortgage loan of $1000 over various periods of time with interest compounded semi-annually

% Interest

End of Year	*14.000*	*14.125*	*14.250*	*14.375*	*14.500*	*14.625*	*14.750*	*14.875*
1	89.603	89.658	89.714	89.769	89.825	89.880	89.936	89.991
2	47.828	47.884	47.939	47.995	48.051	48.107	48.162	48.218
3	33.988	34.045	34.102	34.159	34.217	34.274	34.331	34.389
4	27.130	27.189	27.249	27.308	27.367	27.426	27.485	27.545
5	23.066	23.127	23.188	23.249	23.310	23.371	23.432	23.494
6	20.397	20.460	20.523	20.586	20.649	20.712	20.775	20.839
7	18.524	18.589	18.654	18.719	18.784	18.850	18.915	18.981
8	17.149	17.216	17.283	17.350	17.417	17.485	17.552	17.619
9	16.105	16.174	16.243	16.312	16.381	16.450	16.519	16.589
10	15.292	15.363	15.433	15.504	15.575	15.646	15.717	15.789
11	14.646	14.718	14.791	14.864	14.936	15.009	15.082	15.155
12	14.125	14.199	14.273	14.348	14.422	14.497	14.571	14.646
13	13.699	13.775	13.851	13.927	14.003	14.079	14.156	14.232
14	13.348	13.425	13.503	13.580	13.658	13.736	13.814	13.892
15	13.055	13.134	13.213	13.292	13.372	13.451	13.530	13.610
16	12.810	12.890	12.971	13.051	13.132	13.213	13.294	13.375
17	12.603	12.685	12.767	12.849	12.931	13.013	13.095	13.178
18	12.428	12.511	12.594	12.677	12.761	12.844	12.928	13.012
19	12.279	12.363	12.447	12.532	12.616	12.701	12.786	12.871
20	12.152	12.237	12.322	12.408	12.494	12.580	12.665	12.752
21	12.043	12.129	12.215	12.302	12.389	12.476	12.563	12.650
22	11.949	12.036	12.124	12.211	12.299	12.387	12.475	12.563
23	11.868	11.957	12.045	12.134	12.222	12.311	12.400	12.489
24	11.799	11.888	11.977	12.067	12.156	12.246	12.335	12.425
25	11.739	11.829	11.919	12.009	12.099	12.190	12.280	12.371
26	11.687	11.777	11.868	11.959	12.050	12.141	12.233	12.324
27	11.642	11.733	11.825	11.916	12.008	12.100	12.192	12.283
28	11.603	11.695	11.787	11.879	11.971	12.064	12.156	12.249
29	11.569	11.661	11.754	11.847	11.940	12.033	12.126	12.219
30	11.539	11.633	11.726	11.819	11.912	12.006	12.099	12.193
31	11.514	11.607	11.701	11.795	11.889	11.983	12.077	12.171
32	11.492	11.586	11.680	11.774	11.868	11.963	12.057	12.151
33	11.472	11.567	11.661	11.756	11.851	11.945	12.040	12.135
34	11.455	11.550	11.645	11.740	11.835	11.930	12.025	12.121
35	11.441	11.536	11.631	11.726	11.822	11.917	12.013	12.108
36	11.428	11.523	11.619	11.715	11.810	11.906	12.002	12.097
37	11.417	11.512	11.608	11.704	11.800	11.896	11.992	12.088
38	11.407	11.503	11.599	11.695	11.791	11.888	11.984	12.080
39	11.398	11.495	11.591	11.687	11.784	11.880	11.977	12.073
40	11.391	11.488	11.584	11.681	11.777	11.874	11.970	12.067

Monthly payments required to repay a mortgage loan of $1000 over various periods of time with interest compounded semi-annually

End of Year	15.000	15.125	15.250	15.375	15.500	15.625	15.750	15.875
	% Interest							
1	90.047	90.102	90.158	90.213	90.269	90.324	90.380	90.435
2	48.274	48.330	48.385	48.441	48.497	48.553	48.609	48.665
3	34.446	34.504	34.561	34.619	34.676	34.734	34.791	34.849
4	27.604	27.663	27.723	27.782	27.842	27.901	27.961	28.021
5	23.555	23.617	23.678	23.740	23.801	23.863	23.925	23.987
6	20.902	20.966	21.029	21.093	21.157	21.221	21.285	21.349
7	19.046	19.112	19.177	19.243	19.309	19.375	19.441	19.507
8	17.687	17.755	17.822	17.890	17.958	18.026	18.094	18.163
9	16.658	16.728	16.798	16.867	16.937	17.007	17.078	17.148
10	15.860	15.932	16.003	16.075	16.147	16.219	16.291	16.363
11	15.229	15.302	15.376	15.449	15.523	15.597	15.671	15.745
12	14.721	14.797	14.872	14.947	15.023	15.099	15.174	15.250
13	14.309	14.386	14.463	14.540	14.617	14.695	14.772	14.850
14	13.970	14.049	14.128	14.206	14.285	14.364	14.443	14.523
15	13.690	13.770	13.850	13.930	14.011	14.091	14.172	14.253
16	13.456	13.538	13.619	13.701	13.783	13.865	13.947	14.029
17	13.261	13.343	13.426	13.509	13.593	13.676	13.759	13.843
18	13.096	13.180	13.264	13.348	13.433	13.517	13.602	13.687
19	12.956	13.041	13.127	13.212	13.298	13.384	13.470	13.556
20	12.838	12.924	13.011	13.097	13.184	13.271	13.358	13.445
21	12.737	12.825	12.912	13.000	13.088	13.175	13.263	13.352
22	12.651	12.740	12.828	12.917	13.006	13.094	13.183	13.272
23	12.578	12.667	12.757	12.846	12.936	13.025	13.115	13.205
24	12.515	12.605	12.696	12.786	12.876	12.967	13.057	13.148
25	12.461	12.552	12.643	12.734	12.825	12.917	13.008	13.099
26	12.415	12.507	12.598	12.690	12.782	12.874	12.966	13.058
27	12.376	12.468	12.560	12.652	12.745	12.837	12.930	13.022
28	12.341	12.434	12.527	12.620	12.713	12.806	12.899	12.992
29	12.312	12.405	12.499	12.592	12.685	12.779	12.873	12.966
30	12.287	12.380	12.474	12.568	12.662	12.756	12.850	12.944
31	12.265	12.359	12.453	12.548	12.642	12.736	12.831	12.925
32	12.246	12.341	12.435	12.530	12.625	12.719	12.814	12.909
33	12.230	12.325	12.420	12.515	12.610	12.705	12.800	12.895
34	12.216	12.311	12.406	12.502	12.597	12.692	12.788	12.883
35	12.204	12.299	12.395	12.490	12.586	12.682	12.777	12.873
36	12.193	12.289	12.385	12.481	12.577	12.672	12.768	12.864
37	12.184	12.280	12.376	12.472	12.568	12.665	12.761	12.857
38	12.176	12.273	12.369	12.465	12.561	12.658	12.754	12.850
39	12.170	12.266	12.363	12.459	12.555	12.652	12.748	12.845
40	12.164	12.260	12.357	12.454	12.550	12.647	12.744	12.840

Monthly payments required to repay a mortgage loan of $1000 over various periods of time with interest compounded semi-annually

% Interest

End of Year	*16.000*	*16.125*	*16.250*	*16.375*	*16.500*	*16.625*	*16.750*	*16.875*
1	90.490	90.546	90.601	90.656	90.712	90.767	90.823	90.878
2	48.720	48.776	48.832	48.888	48.944	49.000	49.056	49.112
3	34.906	34.964	35.022	35.079	35.137	35.195	35.253	35.311
4	28.080	28.140	28.200	28.260	28.320	28.380	28.440	28.500
5	24.049	24.111	24.173	24.235	24.297	24.359	24.421	24.483
6	21.413	21.477	21.541	21.605	21.670	21.734	21.799	21.863
7	19.573	19.640	19.706	19.773	19.839	19.906	19.973	20.039
8	18.231	18.299	18.368	18.436	18.505	18.574	18.643	18.712
9	17.218	17.289	17.359	17.430	17.501	17.572	17.643	17.714
10	16.436	16.508	16.581	16.653	16.726	16.799	16.872	16.945
11	15.819	15.894	15.968	16.043	16.117	16.192	16.267	16.342
12	15.326	15.403	15.479	15.555	15.632	15.709	15.785	15.862
13	14.928	15.006	15.084	15.162	15.240	15.319	15.397	15.476
14	14.602	14.682	14.761	14.841	14.921	15.001	15.081	15.162
15	14.334	14.415	14.496	14.578	14.659	14.741	14.822	14.904
16	14.112	14.194	14.277	14.360	14.443	14.526	14.609	14.692
17	13.927	14.011	14.095	14.179	14.263	14.347	14.432	14.516
18	13.772	13.857	13.942	14.028	14.113	14.199	14.284	14.370
19	13.642	13.728	13.815	13.901	13.988	14.074	14.161	14.248
20	13.532	13.620	13.707	13.795	13.882	13.970	14.058	14.146
21	13.440	13.528	13.617	13.705	13.794	13.883	13.971	14.060
22	13.362	13.451	13.540	13.630	13.719	13.809	13.899	13.988
23	13.295	13.385	13.475	13.566	13.656	13.746	13.837	13.928
24	13.239	13.330	13.420	13.512	13.603	13.694	13.785	13.876
25	13.191	13.282	13.374	13.466	13.557	13.649	13.741	13.833
26	13.150	13.242	13.334	13.427	13.519	13.611	13.704	13.797
27	13.115	13.208	13.301	13.393	13.486	13.579	13.672	13.766
28	13.085	13.179	13.272	13.365	13.459	13.552	13.646	13.739
29	13.060	13.154	13.247	13.341	13.435	13.529	13.623	13.717
30	13.038	13.132	13.227	13.321	13.415	13.510	13.604	13.698
31	13.020	13.114	13.209	13.303	13.398	13.493	13.588	13.682
32	13.004	13.099	13.194	13.289	13.384	13.479	13.574	13.669
33	12.990	13.086	13.181	13.276	13.371	13.467	13.562	13.657
34	12.979	13.074	13.170	13.265	13.361	13.456	13.552	13.647
35	12.969	13.065	13.160	13.256	13.352	13.448	13.543	13.639
36	12.960	13.056	13.152	13.248	13.344	13.440	13.536	13.632
37	12.953	13.049	13.145	13.241	13.338	13.434	13.530	13.626
38	12.947	13.043	13.139	13.236	13.332	13.428	13.525	13.621
39	12.941	13.038	13.134	13.231	13.327	13.424	13.520	13.617
40	12.937	13.033	13.130	13.227	13.323	13.420	13.516	13.613

TABLE 7

Balance outstanding on a Canadian mortgage loan of $1000 for 25 years at various rates of interest with interest compounded semi-annually

Applications

Chapter Seven

- Canadian mortgage loans.

Balance outstanding on a mortgage loan of $1000 for 25 years at various rates of interest compounded semi-annually

End of Year	5.00%	5.25%	5.50%	5.75%	6.00%	6.25%	6.50%	6.75%
1	979	980	981	981	982	983	983	984
2	957	959	960	962	963	964	965	967
3	934	937	939	941	943	945	946	948
4	910	913	916	919	921	924	926	929
5	885	889	892	895	898	901	905	908
6	858	863	867	870	874	878	882	885
7	831	835	840	844	849	853	857	861
8	801	806	811	816	821	826	831	835
9	770	776	782	787	792	798	803	808
10	738	744	750	756	762	768	773	779
11	704	710	717	723	729	735	741	747
12	668	675	682	688	695	701	708	714
13	631	638	645	651	658	665	672	678
14	591	598	605	612	619	626	633	640
15	550	557	564	571	578	585	592	599
16	506	513	520	527	535	542	549	555
17	460	467	474	481	488	495	502	509
18	412	419	426	432	439	446	452	459
19	362	368	374	381	387	393	399	406
20	309	314	320	326	332	337	343	349
21	253	258	263	268	273	278	283	288
22	194	198	202	206	211	215	219	223
23	133	136	139	141	144	147	150	150
24	68	70	71	73	74	76	78	79
25	0	0	0	0	0	0	0	0

Balance outstanding on a mortgage loan of $1000 for 25 years at various rates of interest compounded semi-annually

End of Year	*7.00%*	*7.25%*	*7.50%*	*7.75%*	*8.00%*	*8.25%*	*8.50%*	*8.75%*
1	984	985	986	986	987	987	988	988
2	968	969	970	971	972	973	974	975
3	950	952	953	955	957	958	960	961
4	931	933	935	938	940	942	944	946
5	910	913	916	919	921	924	926	929
6	889	892	895	898	902	905	908	911
7	865	869	873	877	880	884	887	891
8	840	844	849	853	857	861	865	869
9	813	818	823	827	832	837	841	845
10	784	789	795	800	805	810	815	820
11	753	759	765	770	776	781	786	792
12	720	726	732	738	744	750	755	761
13	685	691	697	704	710	716	722	728
14	647	653	660	666	673	679	685	691
15	606	613	619	626	633	639	646	652
16	562	569	576	583	589	596	602	609
17	516	522	529	536	542	549	556	552
18	466	472	479	485	492	498	505	511
19	412	418	424	431	437	443	449	455
20	355	360	366	372	378	383	389	395
21	293	289	303	308	313	319	324	329
22	227	231	236	240	244	248	252	257
23	157	160	163	166	169	172	175	178
24	81	83	84	86	88	90	91	93
25	0	0	0	0	0	0	0	0

Balance outstanding on a mortgage loan of $1000 for 25 years at various rates of interest compounded semi-annually

End of Year	*9.00%*	*9.25%*	*9.50%*	*9.75%*	*10.00%*	*10.25%*	*10.50%*	*10.75%*
1	989	989	989	990	990	991	991	991
2	976	977	978	979	979	980	981	982
3	962	964	965	966	968	969	970	971
4	947	949	951	953	954	956	958	959
5	931	933	936	938	940	942	944	946
6	913	916	919	921	924	926	929	931
7	894	897	900	903	906	909	912	915
8	873	876	880	884	887	890	894	897
9	850	854	858	862	866	869	873	877
10	824	829	833	838	842	846	850	854
11	797	802	807	811	816	821	825	830
12	766	772	777	782	787	792	797	802
13	734	739	745	750	756	761	766	772
14	698	704	709	715	721	727	732	738
15	658	664	671	677	683	689	694	700
16	615	622	628	634	640	646	652	658
17	568	575	581	587	594	600	606	612
18	568	575	581	587	542	548	554	560
19	461	467	474	480	485	491	497	503
20	400	406	412	417	423	429	434	440
21	334	339	344	349	354	359	364	369
22	261	265	270	274	278	282	287	291
23	182	185	188	191	194	197	201	204
24	95	97	98	100	102	104	105	107
25	0	0	0	0	0	0	0	0

Balance outstanding on a mortgage loan of $1000 for 25 years at various rates of interest compounded semi-annually

End of Year	*11.00%*	*11.25%*	*11.50%*	*11.75%*	*12.00%*	*12.25%*	*12.50%*	*12.75%*
1	992	992	992	993	993	993	993	994
2	982	983	984	984	985	986	986	987
3	972	973	974	975	976	977	978	979
4	961	962	963	965	966	967	968	970
5	948	950	951	953	955	956	958	959
6	933	936	938	940	942	944	946	948
7	918	920	923	925	928	930	932	934
8	900	903	906	909	912	914	917	920
9	880	884	887	890	894	897	900	903
10	858	862	866	870	873	877	880	884
11	834	838	842	847	851	854	858	862
12	807	812	816	821	825	829	833	838
13	777	782	787	792	796	801	805	810
14	743	749	754	759	764	769	774	779
15	706	711	717	722	728	733	738	743
16	664	670	676	681	687	692	698	703
17	618	624	630	635	641	647	652	658
18	566	572	578	584	590	595	601	607
19	509	515	521	526	532	538	543	549
20	445	451	456	462	467	472	478	483
21	374	379	384	389	394	399	404	409
22	295	299	304	308	312	316	320	325
23	207	210	213	217	220	223	226	229
24	109	111	113	114	116	118	120	122
25	0	0	0	0	0	0	0	0

Balance outstanding on a mortgage loan of $1000 for 25 years at various rates of interest compounded semi-annually

End of Year	*13.00%*	*13.25%*	*13.50%*	*13.75%*	*14.00%*	*14.25%*	*14.50%*	*14.75%*
1	994	994	994	995	995	995	995	996
2	987	988	988	989	989	990	990	990
3	979	980	981	982	982	983	984	984
4	971	972	973	974	975	976	977	978
5	961	962	963	965	966	967	968	970
6	949	951	953	954	956	958	959	960
7	937	939	941	943	945	946	948	950
8	922	924	927	929	931	934	936	938
9	906	908	911	914	916	919	921	924
10	887	890	893	896	899	902	905	908
11	866	869	873	876	879	883	886	889
12	842	846	849	853	857	861	864	868
13	814	819	823	827	831	835	839	843
14	783	788	793	797	801	806	810	814
15	748	753	758	763	768	772	777	781
16	709	714	719	724	729	734	739	743
17	663	669	674	679	685	690	695	700
18	612	618	623	628	634	639	644	649
19	554	560	565	570	576	581	586	591
20	488	493	499	504	509	514	519	524
21	414	418	423	428	433	437	442	447
22	329	333	337	341	345	350	354	358
23	233	236	239	242	245	249	252	255
24	124	125	127	129	131	133	135	137
25	0	0	0	0	0	0	0	0

Balance outstanding on a mortgage loan of $1000 for 25 years at various rates of interest compounded semi-annually

End of Year	*15.00%*	*15.25%*	*15.50%*	*15.75%*	*16.00%*	*16.25%*	*16.50%*	*16.75%*
1	996	996	996	996	996	997	997	997
2	991	991	991	992	992	992	993	993
3	985	986	986	987	987	988	988	989
4	978	979	980	981	981	982	983	984
5	971	972	973	974	975	976	977	977
6	962	963	964	966	967	968	969	970
7	952	953	955	956	958	959	961	962
8	940	942	944	945	947	949	951	952
9	926	928	931	933	935	937	939	941
10	910	913	915	918	920	923	925	927
11	892	895	898	901	903	906	909	911
12	871	874	877	881	884	887	890	892
13	846	850	854	857	861	864	867	870
14	818	822	826	830	834	838	841	845
15	786	790	794	798	803	807	811	814
16	748	753	757	762	766	770	775	779
17	705	709	714	719	724	728	733	737
18	654	659	664	669	674	679	683	688
19	596	601	606	611	616	621	626	630
20	529	534	539	544	549	553	558	563
21	451	456	461	465	470	474	479	483
22	362	366	370	374	378	382	386	390
23	258	261	264	268	271	274	277	280
24	138	140	142	144	146	148	149	151
25	0	0	0	0	0	0	0	0

TABLE 8

The present value of $1 per period payable at the *end* of each period (a $1 "ordinary" annuity)

What is $1 payable at the end of each period worth
today at various interest rates?

How much must be invested today in order for one to be able to draw $1 at the end of each period for a given number of periods?

Applications

Chapter Six

- What is the value today of the right to receive periodic payments at the end of various time periods?

Chapter Eight

- How much can one afford to borrow given the ability to make specific monthly payments?

Chapter Fifteen

- Proving annuity yields.

The present value of a $1 annuity at the *end* of each period

End of Year	At 3% Interest compounded and Payments or Withdrawals made				At 4% Interest compounded and Payments or Withdrawals made			
	Monthly	*Quarterly*	*Semi-Annually*	*Annually*	*Monthly*	*Quarterly*	*Semi-Annually*	*Annually*
1	11.807	3.926	1.956	0.971	11.744	3.902	1.942	0.962
2	23.266	7.737	3.854	1.913	23.028	7.652	3.808	1.886
3	34.386	11.435	5.697	2.829	33.871	11.255	5.601	2.775
4	45.179	15.024	7.486	3.717	44.289	14.718	7.325	3.630
5	55.652	18.508	9.222	4.580	54.299	18.046	8.983	4.452
6	65.817	21.889	10.908	5.417	63.917	21.243	10.575	5.242
7	75.681	25.171	12.543	6.230	73.159	24.316	12.106	6.002
8	85.255	28.356	14.131	7.020	82.039	27.270	13.578	6.733
9	94.545	31.447	15.673	7.786	90.572	30.108	14.992	7.435
10	103.562	34.447	17.169	8.530	98.770	32.835	16.351	8.111
11	112.312	37.359	18.621	9.253	106.648	35.455	17.658	8.760
12	120.804	40.185	20.030	9.954	114.217	37.974	18.914	9.385
13	129.045	42.928	21.399	10.635	121.490	40.394	20.121	9.986
14	137.043	45.590	22.727	11.296	128.478	42.720	21.281	10.563
15	144.805	48.173	24.016	11.938	135.192	44.955	22.396	11.118
16	152.338	50.681	25.267	12.561	141.644	47.103	23.468	11.652
17	159.649	53.115	26.482	13.166	147.843	49.167	24.499	12.166
18	166.744	55.477	27.661	13.754	153.799	51.150	25.489	12.659
19	173.629	57.769	28.805	14.324	159.523	53.056	26.441	13.134
20	180.311	59.994	29.916	14.877	165.022	54.888	27.355	13.590
21	186.796	62.154	30.994	15.415	170.306	56.648	28.235	14.029
22	193.089	64.250	32.041	15.937	175.383	58.340	29.080	14.451
23	199.197	66.284	33.056	16.444	180.261	59.966	29.892	14.857
24	205.124	68.258	34.043	16.936	184.949	61.528	30.673	15.247
25	210.876	70.175	35.000	17.413	189.452	63.029	31.424	15.622
26	216.459	72.034	35.929	17.877	193.780	64.471	32.145	15.983
27	221.877	73.839	36.831	18.327	197.938	65.858	32.838	16.330
28	227.135	75.591	37.706	18.764	201.934	67.190	33.505	16.663
29	232.237	77.291	38.556	19.188	205.773	68.470	34.145	16.984
30	237.189	78.942	39.380	19.600	209.461	69.701	34.761	17.292
31	241.995	80.543	40.181	20.000	213.006	70.883	35.353	17.588
32	246.659	82.098	40.958	20.389	216.411	72.019	35.921	17.874
33	251.186	83.606	41.712	20.766	219.683	73.111	36.468	18.148
34	255.578	85.071	42.444	21.132	222.827	74.160	36.994	18.411
35	259.841	86.492	43.155	21.487	225.848	75.168	37.499	18.665
36	263.979	87.871	43.845	21.832	228.751	76.137	37.984	18.908
37	267.994	89.210	44.514	22.167	231.540	77.068	38.451	19.143
38	271.890	90.509	45.164	22.492	234.220	77.963	38.899	19.368
39	275.672	91.770	45.795	22.808	236.795	78.823	39.330	19.584
40	279.342	92.994	46.407	23.115	239.270	79.649	39.745	19.793
41	282.903	94.182	47.002	23.412	241.647	80.443	40.143	19.993
42	286.360	95.335	47.579	23.701	243.931	81.206	40.526	20.186
43	289.714	96.453	48.139	23.982	246.126	81.940	40.893	20.371
44	292.970	97.539	48.682	24.254	248.235	82.644	41.247	20.549
45	296.129	98.593	49.210	24.519	250.262	83.322	41.587	20.720
46	299.195	99.616	49.722	24.775	252.209	83.972	41.914	20.885
47	302.171	100.609	50.219	25.025	254.080	84.598	42.228	21.043
48	305.058	101.573	50.702	25.267	255.877	85.199	42.529	21.195
49	307.861	102.508	51.170	25.502	257.605	85.776	42.820	21.341
50	310.581	103.416	51.625	25.730	259.264	86.331	43.098	21.482

The present value of a $1 annuity at the *end* of each period

End of Year	At 5% Interest compounded and Payments or Withdrawals made: Monthly	Quarterly	Semi-Annually	Annually	At 6% Interest compounded and Payments or Withdrawals made: Monthly	Quarterly	Semi-Annually	Annually
1	11.681	3.878	1.927	0.952	11.619	3.854	1.913	0.943
2	22.794	7.568	3.762	1.859	22.563	7.486	3.717	1.833
3	33.366	11.079	5.508	2.723	32.871	10.908	5.417	2.673
4	43.423	14.420	7.170	3.546	42.580	14.131	7.020	3.465
5	52.991	17.599	8.752	4.329	51.726	17.169	8.530	4.212
6	62.093	20.624	10.258	5.076	60.340	20.030	9.954	4.917
7	70.752	23.503	11.691	5.786	68.453	22.727	11.296	5.582
8	78.989	26.241	13.055	6.463	76.095	25.267	12.561	6.210
9	86.826	28.847	14.353	7.108	83.293	27.661	13.754	6.802
10	94.281	31.327	15.589	7.722	90.073	29.916	14.877	7.360
11	101.374	33.686	16.765	8.306	96.460	32.041	15.937	7.887
12	108.121	35.931	17.885	8.863	102.475	34.043	16.936	8.384
13	114.540	38.068	18.951	9.394	108.140	35.929	17.877	8.853
14	120.646	40.100	19.965	9.899	113.477	37.706	18.764	9.295
15	126.455	42.035	20.930	10.380	118.504	39.380	19.600	9.712
16	131.982	43.875	21.849	10.838	123.238	40.958	20.389	10.106
17	137.239	45.626	22.724	11.274	127.697	42.444	21.132	10.477
18	142.241	47.292	23.556	11.690	131.898	43.845	21.832	10.828
19	146.999	48.878	24.349	12.085	135.854	45.164	22.492	11.158
20	151.525	50.387	25.103	12.462	139.581	46.407	23.115	11.470
21	155.832	51.822	25.821	12.821	143.091	47.579	23.701	11.764
22	159.928	53.188	26.504	13.163	146.397	48.682	24.254	12.042
23	163.825	54.488	27.154	13.489	149.511	49.722	24.775	12.303
24	167.533	55.725	27.773	13.799	152.444	50.702	25.267	12.550
25	171.060	56.901	28.362	14.094	155.207	51.625	25.730	12.783
26	174.415	58.021	28.923	14.375	157.809	52.494	26.166	13.003
27	177.608	59.087	29.457	14.643	160.260	53.314	26.578	13.211
28	180.644	60.100	29.965	14.898	162.569	54.086	26.965	13.406
29	183.533	61.065	30.448	15.141	164.743	54.813	27.331	13.591
30	186.282	61.983	30.909	15.372	166.792	55.498	27.676	13.765
31	188.896	62.856	31.347	15.593	168.721	56.144	28.000	13.929
32	191.383	63.687	31.764	15.803	170.538	56.753	28.306	14.084
33	193.750	64.478	32.161	16.003	172.250	57.326	28.595	14.230
34	196.001	65.231	32.538	16.193	173.862	57.866	28.867	14.368
35	198.142	65.946	32.898	16.374	175.380	58.375	29.123	14.498
36	200.180	66.628	33.240	16.547	176.811	58.854	29.365	14.621
37	202.118	67.276	33.566	16.711	178.158	59.306	29.593	14.737
38	203.962	67.893	33.876	16.868	179.427	59.731	29.808	14.846
39	205.716	68.480	34.171	17.017	180.622	60.132	30.010	14.949
40	207.384	69.038	34.452	17.159	181.748	60.510	30.201	15.046
41	208.972	69.570	34.719	17.294	182.808	60.866	30.381	15.138
42	210.482	70.075	34.974	17.423	183.807	61.201	30.550	15.225
43	211.919	70.556	35.216	17.546	184.747	61.517	30.710	15.306
44	213.285	71.014	35.446	17.663	185.634	61.815	30.860	15.383
45	214.586	71.450	35.666	17.774	186.468	62.096	31.002	15.456
46	215.823	71.864	35.875	17.880	187.254	62.360	31.136	15.524
47	216.999	72.259	36.073	17.981	187.995	62.609	31.262	15.589
48	218.119	72.634	36.263	18.077	188.692	62.843	31.381	15.650
49	219.184	72.991	36.443	18.169	189.349	63.064	31.493	15.708
50	220.197	73.331	36.614	18.256	189.968	63.273	31.599	15.762

The present value of a $1 annuity at the *end* of each period

End of Year	At 7% Interest compounded and Payments or Withdrawals made: Monthly	Quarterly	Semi-Annually	Annually	At 8% Interest compounded and Payments or Withdrawals made: Monthly	Quarterly	Semi-Annually	Annually
1	11.557	3.831	1.900	0.935	11.496	3.808	1.886	0.926
2	22.335	7.405	3.673	1.808	22.111	7.325	3.630	1.783
3	32.386	10.740	5.329	2.624	31.912	10.575	5.242	2.577
4	41.760	13.850	6.874	3.387	40.962	13.578	6.733	3.312
5	50.502	16.753	8.317	4.100	49.318	16.351	8.111	3.993
6	58.654	19.461	9.663	4.767	57.035	18.914	9.385	4.623
7	66.257	21.987	10.921	5.389	64.159	21.281	10.563	5.206
8	73.348	24.344	12.094	5.971	70.738	23.468	11.652	5.747
9	79.960	26.543	13.190	6.515	76.812	25.489	12.659	6.247
10	86.126	28.594	14.212	7.024	82.421	27.355	13.590	6.710
11	91.877	30.508	15.167	7.499	87.601	29.080	14.451	7.139
12	97.240	32.294	16.058	7.943	92.383	30.673	15.247	7.536
13	102.242	33.960	16.890	8.358	96.798	32.145	15.983	7.904
14	106.906	35.514	17.667	8.745	100.876	33.505	16.663	8.244
15	111.256	36.964	18.392	9.108	104.641	34.761	17.292	8.559
16	115.313	38.317	19.069	9.447	108.117	35.921	17.874	8.851
17	119.096	39.579	19.701	9.763	111.327	36.994	18.411	9.122
18	122.624	40.756	20.290	10.059	114.291	37.984	18.908	9.372
19	125.914	41.855	20.841	10.336	117.027	38.899	19.368	9.604
20	128.983	42.880	21.355	10.594	119.554	39.745	19.793	9.818
21	131.844	43.836	21.835	10.836	121.888	40.526	20.186	10.017
22	134.513	44.728	22.283	11.061	124.042	41.247	20.549	10.201
23	137.001	45.561	22.701	11.272	126.031	41.914	20.885	10.371
24	139.322	46.337	23.091	11.469	127.868	42.529	21.195	10.529
25	141.487	47.061	23.456	11.654	129.565	43.098	21.482	10.675
26	143.505	47.737	23.796	11.826	131.131	43.624	21.748	10.810
27	145.388	48.368	24.113	11.987	132.577	44.110	21.993	10.935
28	147.144	48.956	24.410	12.137	133.912	44.558	22.220	11.051
29	148.781	49.505	24.686	12.278	135.145	44.973	22.430	11.158
30	150.308	50.017	24.945	12.409	136.283	45.355	22.623	11.258
31	151.731	50.495	25.186	12.532	137.335	45.709	22.803	11.350
32	153.059	50.941	25.411	12.647	138.305	46.036	22.969	11.435
33	154.298	51.356	25.621	12.754	139.202	46.338	23.122	11.514
34	155.453	51.744	25.817	12.854	140.029	46.617	23.264	11.587
35	156.530	52.106	26.000	12.948	140.793	46.874	23.395	11.655
36	157.534	52.444	26.171	13.035	141.499	47.112	23.516	11.717
37	158.471	52.759	26.331	13.117	142.150	47.332	23.628	11.775
38	159.344	53.053	26.480	13.193	142.752	47.535	23.731	11.829
39	160.159	53.327	26.619	13.265	143.307	47.723	23.827	11.879
40	160.919	53.583	26.749	13.332	143.820	47.896	23.915	11.925
41	161.627	53.821	26.870	13.394	144.294	48.057	23.997	11.967
42	162.288	54.044	26.983	13.452	144.731	48.205	24.073	12.007
43	162.904	54.252	27.089	13.507	145.135	48.341	24.143	12.043
44	163.479	54.446	27.187	13.558	145.508	48.468	24.207	12.077
45	164.015	54.627	27.279	13.606	145.852	48.584	24.267	12.108
46	164.515	54.795	27.365	13.650	146.170	48.692	24.323	12.137
47	164.981	54.953	27.445	13.692	146.464	48.792	24.374	12.164
48	165.416	55.099	27.520	13.730	146.735	48.884	24.421	12.189
49	165.821	55.236	27.590	13.767	146.985	48.969	24.465	12.212
50	166.199	55.364	27.655	13.801	147.216	49.047	24.505	12.233

The present value of a $1 annuity at the *end* of each period

End of Year	At 9% Interest compounded and Payments or Withdrawals made: Monthly	Quarterly	Semi-Annually	Annually	At 10% Interest compounded and Payments or Withdrawals made: Monthly	Quarterly	Semi-Annually	Annually
1	11.435	3.785	1.873	0.917	11.375	3.762	1.859	0.909
2	21.889	7.247	3.588	1.759	21.671	7.170	3.546	1.736
3	31.447	10.415	5.158	2.531	30.991	10.258	5.076	2.487
4	40.185	13.313	6.596	3.240	39.428	13.055	6.463	3.170
5	48.173	15.964	7.913	3.890	47.065	15.589	7.722	3.791
6	55.477	18.389	9.119	4.486	53.979	17.885	8.863	4.355
7	62.154	20.608	10.223	5.033	60.237	19.965	9.899	4.868
8	68.258	22.638	11.234	5.535	65.901	21.849	10.838	5.335
9	73.839	24.495	12.160	5.995	71.029	23.556	11.690	5.759
10	78.942	26.194	13.008	6.418	75.671	25.103	12.462	6.145
11	83.606	27.748	13.784	6.805	79.873	26.504	13.163	6.495
12	87.871	29.170	14.495	7.161	83.677	27.773	13.799	6.814
13	91.770	30.470	15.147	7.487	87.120	28.923	14.375	7.103
14	95.335	31.660	15.743	7.786	90.236	29.965	14.898	7.367
15	98.593	32.749	16.289	8.061	93.057	30.909	15.372	7.606
16	101.573	33.745	16.789	8.313	95.611	31.764	15.803	7.824
17	104.297	34.656	17.247	8.544	97.923	32.538	16.193	8.022
18	106.787	35.490	17.666	8.756	100.016	33.240	16.547	8.201
19	109.064	36.252	18.050	8.950	101.910	33.876	16.868	8.365
20	111.145	36.950	18.402	9.129	103.625	34.452	17.159	8.514
21	113.048	37.588	18.724	9.292	105.177	34.974	17.423	8.649
22	114.788	38.172	19.018	9.442	106.582	35.446	17.663	8.772
23	116.378	38.706	19.288	9.580	107.854	35.875	17.880	8.883
24	117.832	39.195	19.536	9.707	109.005	36.263	18.077	8.985
25	119.162	39.642	19.762	9.823	110.047	36.614	18.256	9.077
26	120.377	40.051	19.969	9.929	110.991	36.933	18.418	9.161
27	121.488	40.425	20.159	10.027	111.845	37.221	18.565	9.237
28	122.504	40.767	20.333	10.116	112.618	37.482	18.699	9.307
29	123.433	41.080	20.492	10.198	113.317	37.719	18.820	9.370
30	124.282	41.367	20.638	10.274	113.951	37.934	18.929	9.427
31	125.058	41.629	20.772	10.343	114.524	38.128	19.029	9.479
32	125.768	41.869	20.894	10.406	115.043	38.304	19.119	9.526
33	126.417	42.088	21.006	10.464	115.513	38.464	19.201	9.569
34	127.010	42.289	21.108	10.518	115.938	38.608	19.275	9.609
35	127.552	42.472	21.202	10.567	116.323	38.739	19.343	9.644
36	128.048	42.640	21.288	10.612	116.672	38.858	19.404	9.677
37	128.501	42.794	21.367	10.653	116.987	38.965	19.459	9.706
38	128.916	42.934	21.439	10.691	117.273	39.062	19.509	9.733
39	129.295	43.063	21.505	10.726	117.531	39.151	19.555	9.757
40	129.641	43.181	21.565	10.757	117.765	39.230	19.596	9.779
41	129.958	43.288	21.621	10.787	117.977	39.303	19.634	9.799
42	130.247	43.387	21.671	10.813	118.169	39.368	19.668	9.817
43	130.512	43.477	21.718	10.838	118.343	39.428	19.699	9.834
44	130.754	43.559	21.760	10.861	118.500	39.482	19.727	9.849
45	130.975	43.635	21.799	10.881	118.642	39.530	19.752	9.863
46	131.177	43.704	21.835	10.900	118.771	39.575	19.775	9.875
47	131.362	43.767	21.868	10.918	118.887	39.615	19.796	9.887
48	131.531	43.824	21.897	10.934	118.993	39.651	19.815	9.897
49	131.686	43.877	21.925	10.948	119.088	39.684	19.832	9.906
50	131.827	43.925	21.950	10.962	119.175	39.713	19.848	9.915

The present value of a $1 annuity at the *end* of each period

End of Year	At 11% Interest compounded and Payments or Withdrawals made: Monthly	Quarterly	Semi-Annually	Annually	At 12% Interest compounded and Payments or Withdrawals made: Monthly	Quarterly	Semi-Annually	Annually
1	11.315	3.739	1.846	0.901	11.255	3.717	1.833	0.893
2	21.456	7.094	3.505	1.713	21.243	7.020	3.465	1.690
3	30.545	10.104	4.996	2.444	30.108	9.954	4.917	2.402
4	38.691	12.805	6.335	3.102	37.974	12.561	6.210	3.037
5	45.993	15.227	7.538	3.696	44.955	14.877	7.360	3.605
6	52.537	17.401	8.619	4.231	51.150	16.936	8.384	4.111
7	58.403	19.351	9.590	4.712	56.648	18.764	9.295	4.564
8	63.660	21.100	10.462	5.146	61.528	20.389	10.106	4.968
9	68.372	22.670	11.246	5.537	65.858	21.832	10.828	5.328
10	72.595	24.078	11.950	5.889	69.701	23.115	11.470	5.650
11	76.380	25.341	12.583	6.207	73.111	24.254	12.042	5.938
12	79.773	26.475	13.152	6.492	76.137	25.267	12.550	6.194
13	82.814	27.492	13.662	6.750	78.823	26.166	13.003	6.424
14	85.539	28.404	14.121	6.982	81.206	26.965	13.406	6.628
15	87.982	29.223	14.534	7.191	83.322	27.676	13.765	6.811
16	90.171	29.957	14.904	7.379	85.199	28.306	14.084	6.974
17	92.134	30.616	15.237	7.549	86.865	28.867	14.368	7.120
18	93.892	31.207	15.536	7.702	88.343	29.365	14.621	7.250
19	95.469	31.737	15.805	7.839	89.655	29.808	14.846	7.366
20	96.882	32.213	16.046	7.963	90.819	30.201	15.046	7.469
21	98.148	32.640	16.263	8.075	91.853	30.550	15.225	7.562
22	99.283	33.023	16.458	8.176	92.770	30.860	15.383	7.645
23	100.300	33.366	16.633	8.266	93.583	31.136	15.524	7.718
24	101.212	33.675	16.790	8.348	94.306	31.381	15.650	7.784
25	102.029	33.951	16.932	8.422	94.947	31.599	15.762	7.843
26	102.761	34.199	17.058	8.488	95.515	31.792	15.861	7.896
27	103.418	34.422	17.173	8.548	96.020	31.964	15.950	7.943
28	104.006	34.621	17.275	8.602	96.468	32.117	16.029	7.984
29	104.534	34.801	17.367	8.650	96.866	32.252	16.099	8.022
30	105.006	34.961	17.450	8.694	97.218	32.373	16.161	8.055
31	105.430	35.106	17.524	8.733	97.531	32.480	16.217	8.085
32	105.810	35.235	17.591	8.769	97.809	32.575	16.266	8.112
33	106.150	35.351	17.651	8.801	98.056	32.660	16.310	8.135
34	106.455	35.455	17.705	8.829	98.275	32.735	16.350	8.157
35	106.728	35.549	17.753	8.855	98.469	32.802	16.385	8.176
36	106.973	35.632	17.797	8.879	98.641	32.861	16.416	8.192
37	107.193	35.708	17.836	8.900	98.794	32.914	16.443	8.208
38	107.390	35.775	17.871	8.919	98.930	32.960	16.468	8.221
39	107.566	35.836	17.903	8.936	99.050	33.002	16.490	8.233
40	107.724	35.890	17.931	8.951	99.157	33.039	16.509	8.244
41	107.866	35.939	17.956	8.965	99.252	33.072	16.526	8.253
42	107.993	35.982	17.979	8.977	99.336	33.101	16.542	8.262
43	108.107	36.022	18.000	8.989	99.411	33.127	16.556	8.270
44	108.209	36.057	18.018	8.999	99.477	33.150	16.568	8.276
45	108.301	36.088	18.035	9.008	99.536	33.170	16.579	8.283
46	108.383	36.117	18.050	9.016	99.588	33.189	16.588	8.288
47	108.456	36.142	18.063	9.024	99.635	33.205	16.597	8.293
48	108.522	36.165	18.075	9.030	99.676	33.219	16.605	8.297
49	108.581	36.185	18.086	9.036	99.712	33.232	16.611	8.301
50	108.634	36.204	18.096	9.042	99.745	33.243	16.618	8.304

The present value of a $1 annuity at the *end* of each period

End of Year	At 13% Interest compounded and Payments or Withdrawals made				At 14% Interest compounded and Payments or Withdrawls made			
	Monthly	Quarterly	Semi-Annually	Annually	Monthly	Quarterly	Semi-Annually	Annually
1	11.196	3.695	1.821	0.885	11.137	3.673	1.808	0.877
2	21.034	6.946	3.426	1.668	20.828	6.874	3.387	1.647
3	29.679	9.807	4.841	2.361	29.259	9.663	4.767	2.322
4	37.275	12.324	6.089	2.974	36.595	12.094	5.971	2.914
5	43.950	14.539	7.189	3.517	42.977	14.212	7.024	3.433
6	49.815	16.488	8.159	3.998	48.530	16.058	7.943	3.889
7	54.969	18.203	9.014	4.423	53.362	17.667	8.745	4.288
8	59.498	19.712	9.768	4.799	57.566	19.069	9.447	4.639
9	63.478	21.040	10.432	5.132	61.223	20.290	10.059	4.946
10	66.974	22.208	11.019	5.426	64.405	21.355	10.594	5.216
11	70.047	23.236	11.535	5.687	67.174	22.283	11.061	5.453
12	72.747	24.141	11.991	5.918	69.583	23.091	11.469	5.660
13	75.120	24.937	12.392	6.122	71.679	23.796	11.826	5.842
14	77.204	25.637	12.746	6.302	73.503	24.410	12.137	6.002
15	79.036	26.254	13.059	6.462	75.090	24.945	12.409	6.142
16	80.646	26.796	13.334	6.604	76.470	25.411	12.647	6.265
17	82.060	27.273	13.577	6.729	77.671	25.817	12.854	6.373
18	83.303	27.693	13.791	6.840	78.716	26.171	13.035	6.467
19	84.395	28.062	13.979	6.938	79.626	26.480	13.193	6.550
20	85.355	28.387	14.146	7.025	80.417	26.749	13.332	6.623
21	86.198	28.673	14.292	7.102	81.105	26.983	13.452	6.687
22	86.939	28.925	14.421	7.170	81.704	27.187	13.558	6.743
23	87.591	29.147	14.535	7.230	82.225	27.365	13.650	6.792
24	88.163	29.341	14.636	7.283	82.679	27.520	13.730	6.835
25	88.665	29.513	14.725	7.330	83.073	27.655	13.801	6.873
26	89.107	29.664	14.803	7.372	83.416	27.773	13.862	6.906
27	89.495	29.797	14.872	7.409	83.715	27.876	13.916	6.935
28	89.836	29.913	14.932	7.441	83.975	27.965	13.963	6.961
29	90.136	30.016	14.986	7.470	84.201	28.043	14.003	6.983
30	90.400	30.107	15.033	7.496	84.397	28.111	14.039	7.003
31	90.631	30.186	15.075	7.518	84.568	28.170	14.070	7.020
32	90.834	30.256	15.111	7.538	84.717	28.222	14.098	7.035
33	91.013	30.318	15.144	7.556	84.847	28.267	14.121	7.048
34	91.170	30.372	15.172	7.572	84.960	28.306	14.142	7.060
35	91.308	30.420	15.197	7.586	85.058	28.340	14.160	7.070
36	91.429	30.462	15.219	7.598	85.143	28.370	14.176	7.079
37	91.536	30.499	15.239	7.609	85.217	28.396	14.190	7.087
38	91.629	30.531	15.256	7.618	85.282	28.418	14.202	7.094
39	91.712	30.560	15.271	7.627	85.338	28.438	14.213	7.100
40	91.784	30.585	15.285	7.634	85.387	28.455	14.222	7.105
41	91.848	30.607	15.297	7.641	85.429	28.470	14.230	7.110
42	91.903	30.626	15.307	7.647	85.466	28.483	14.237	7.114
43	91.952	30.644	15.316	7.652	85.499	28.494	14.243	7.117
44	91.995	30.659	15.324	7.657	85.527	28.504	14.249	7.120
45	92.033	30.672	15.331	7.661	85.551	28.513	14.253	7.123
46	92.067	30.684	15.338	7.664	85.572	28.521	14.257	7.126
47	92.096	30.694	15.343	7.668	85.591	28.527	14.261	7.128
48	92.122	30.703	15.348	7.671	85.607	28.533	14.264	7.130
49	92.144	30.711	15.352	7.673	85.621	28.538	14.267	7.131
50	92.164	30.718	15.356	7.675	85.633	28.542	14.269	7.133

The present value of a $1 annuity at the *end* of each period

End of Year	At 15% Interest compounded and Payments or Withdrawals made: Monthly	Quarterly	Semi-Annually	Annually	At 16% Interest compounded and Payments or Withdrawals made: Monthly	Quarterly	Semi-Annually	Annually
1	11.079	3.651	1.796	0.870	11.022	3.630	1.783	0.862
2	20.624	6.803	3.349	1.626	20.424	6.733	3.312	1.605
3	28.847	9.523	4.694	2.283	28.444	9.385	4.623	2.246
4	35.931	11.870	5.857	2.855	35.285	11.652	5.747	2.798
5	42.035	13.896	6.864	3.352	41.122	13.590	6.710	3.274
6	47.292	15.645	7.735	3.784	46.100	15.247	7.536	3.685
7	51.822	17.154	8.489	4.160	50.347	16.663	8.244	4.039
8	55.725	18.457	9.142	4.487	53.970	17.874	8.851	4.344
9	59.087	19.581	9.706	4.772	57.061	18.908	9.372	4.607
10	61.983	20.551	10.194	5.019	59.697	19.793	9.818	4.833
11	64.478	21.388	10.617	5.234	61.946	20.549	10.201	5.029
12	66.628	22.111	10.983	5.421	63.864	21.195	10.529	5.197
13	68.480	22.735	11.299	5.583	65.501	21.748	10.810	5.342
14	70.075	23.273	11.573	5.724	66.897	22.220	11.051	5.468
15	71.450	23.738	11.810	5.847	68.087	22.623	11.258	5.575
16	72.634	24.139	12.015	5.954	69.103	22.969	11.435	5.668
17	73.654	24.485	12.193	6.047	69.970	23.264	11.587	5.749
18	74.533	24.784	12.347	6.128	70.709	23.516	11.717	5.818
19	75.290	25.042	12.479	6.198	71.340	23.731	11.829	5.877
20	75.942	25.264	12.594	6.259	71.878	23.915	11.925	5.929
21	76.504	25.456	12.694	6.312	72.336	24.073	12.007	5.973
22	76.988	25.622	12.780	6.359	72.728	24.207	12.077	6.011
23	77.405	25.765	12.855	6.399	73.062	24.323	12.137	6.044
24	77.765	25.888	12.919	6.434	73.347	24.421	12.189	6.073
25	78.074	25.995	12.975	6.464	73.590	24.505	12.233	6.097
26	78.341	26.087	13.023	6.491	73.797	24.577	12.272	6.118
27	78.571	26.166	13.065	6.514	73.974	24.638	12.304	6.136
28	78.769	26.235	13.101	6.534	74.124	24.691	12.332	6.152
29	78.939	26.294	13.132	6.551	74.253	24.736	12.356	6.166
30	79.086	26.345	13.159	6.566	74.363	24.774	12.377	6.177
31	79.213	26.389	13.183	6.579	74.457	24.807	12.394	6.187
32	79.322	26.427	13.203	6.591	74.536	24.835	12.409	6.196
33	79.416	26.460	13.221	6.600	74.605	24.859	12.422	6.203
34	79.497	26.488	13.236	6.609	74.663	24.879	12.433	6.210
35	79.566	26.513	13.249	6.617	74.712	24.897	12.443	6.215
36	79.626	26.534	13.260	6.623	74.754	24.912	12.451	6.220
37	79.678	26.552	13.270	6.629	74.791	24.925	12.458	6.224
38	79.723	26.568	13.279	6.634	74.821	24.936	12.464	6.228
39	79.761	26.581	13.286	6.638	74.848	24.945	12.469	6.231
40	79.794	26.593	13.292	6.642	74.870	24.953	12.474	6.233
41	79.823	26.603	13.298	6.645	74.889	24.960	12.477	6.236
42	79.847	26.612	13.303	6.648	74.905	24.966	12.481	6.238
43	79.868	26.619	13.307	6.650	74.919	24.971	12.483	6.239
44	79.887	26.626	13.310	6.652	74.931	24.975	12.486	6.241
45	79.902	26.631	13.313	6.654	74.941	24.979	12.488	6.242
46	79.916	26.636	13.316	6.656	74.950	24.982	12.489	6.243
47	79.928	26.640	13.318	6.657	74.957	24.984	12.491	6.244
48	79.938	26.644	13.320	6.659	74.964	24.987	12.492	6.245
49	79.946	26.647	13.322	6.660	74.969	24.989	12.493	6.246
50	79.954	26.650	13.324	6.661	74.973	24.990	12.494	6.246

The present value of a $1 annuity at the *end* of each period

End of Year	At 17% Interest compounded and Payments or Withdrawals made: Monthly	Quarterly	Semi-Annually	Annually	At 18% Interest compounded and Payments or Withdrawals made: Monthly	Quarterly	Semi-Annually	Annually
1	10.964	3.609	1.771	0.855	10.908	3.588	1.759	0.847
2	20.226	6.664	3.276	1.585	20.030	6.596	3.240	1.566
3	28.048	9.250	4.554	2.210	27.661	9.119	4.486	2.174
4	34.656	11.440	5.639	2.743	34.043	11.234	5.535	2.690
5	40.237	13.294	6.561	3.199	39.380	13.008	6.418	3.127
6	44.952	14.864	7.345	3.589	43.845	14.495	7.161	3.498
7	48.934	16.193	8.010	3.922	47.579	15.743	7.786	3.812
8	52.297	17.318	8.575	4.207	50.702	16.789	8.313	4.078
9	55.138	18.271	9.055	4.451	53.314	17.666	8.756	4.303
10	57.538	19.077	9.463	4.659	55.498	18.402	9.129	4.494
11	59.565	19.760	9.810	4.836	57.326	19.018	9.442	4.656
12	61.277	20.338	10.104	4.988	58.854	19.536	9.707	4.793
13	62.724	20.828	10.354	5.118	60.132	19.969	9.929	4.910
14	63.945	21.242	10.566	5.229	61.201	20.333	10.116	5.008
15	64.977	21.593	10.747	5.324	62.096	20.638	10.274	5.092
16	65.849	21.890	10.900	5.405	62.843	20.894	10.406	5.162
17	66.585	22.141	11.030	5.475	63.469	21.108	10.518	5.222
18	67.207	22.354	11.141	5.534	63.992	21.288	10.612	5.273
19	67.732	22.534	11.235	5.584	64.430	21.439	10.691	5.316
20	68.176	22.687	11.315	5.628	64.796	21.565	10.757	5.353
21	68.550	22.816	11.382	5.665	65.102	21.671	10.813	5.384
22	68.867	22.926	11.440	5.696	65.358	21.760	10.861	5.410
23	69.134	23.018	11.489	5.723	65.572	21.835	10.900	5.432
24	69.360	23.097	11.530	5.746	65.751	21.897	10.934	5.451
25	69.551	23.163	11.566	5.766	65.901	21.950	10.962	5.467
26	69.712	23.219	11.596	5.783	66.026	21.994	10.985	5.480
27	69.848	23.267	11.621	5.798	66.131	22.031	11.005	5.492
28	69.963	23.307	11.643	5.810	66.219	22.062	11.022	5.502
29	70.060	23.341	11.661	5.820	66.292	22.088	11.036	5.510
30	70.142	23.370	11.677	5.829	66.353	22.109	11.048	5.517
31	70.211	23.394	11.690	5.837	66.405	22.128	11.058	5.523
32	70.270	23.415	11.701	5.844	66.447	22.143	11.066	5.528
33	70.319	23.433	11.711	5.849	66.483	22.156	11.073	5.532
34	70.361	23.448	11.719	5.854	66.513	22.166	11.079	5.536
35	70.396	23.460	11.726	5.858	66.538	22.175	11.084	5.539
36	70.426	23.471	11.732	5.862	66.559	22.183	11.089	5.541
37	70.451	23.480	11.737	5.865	66.577	22.189	11.092	5.543
38	70.473	23.487	11.741	5.867	66.592	22.195	11.095	5.545
39	70.491	23.494	11.744	5.869	66.604	22.199	11.098	5.547
40	70.506	23.499	11.747	5.871	66.614	22.203	11.100	5.548
41	70.519	23.504	11.750	5.873	66.623	22.206	11.102	5.549
42	70.529	23.508	11.752	5.874	66.630	22.209	11.103	5.550
43	70.539	23.511	11.754	5.875	66.636	22.211	11.104	5.551
44	70.546	23.514	11.756	5.876	66.641	22.213	11.105	5.552
45	70.553	23.516	11.757	5.877	66.645	22.214	11.106	5.552
46	70.558	23.518	11.758	5.878	66.649	22.215	11.107	5.553
47	70.563	23.520	11.759	5.879	66.652	22.217	11.108	5.553
48	70.567	23.521	11.760	5.879	66.654	22.217	11.108	5.554
49	70.570	23.523	11.761	5.880	66.656	22.218	11.109	5.554
50	70.573	23.524	11.761	5.880	66.658	22.219	11.109	5.554

TABLE 9

The future value of $1 invested at the *beginning* of each period

The future value of "an annuity due" assuming deposits are made monthly, quarterly, semi-annually or annually at various interest rates

Applications

Chapter Nine

- How much will $1 invested at the beginning of each period amount to at some time in the future?

Chapter Sixteen

- The future value of a series of life insurance premiums.

The future value of $1 invested at the *beginning* of each period

End of Year	3% Interest compounded and Deposits made				4% Interest compounded and Deposits made			
	Monthly	*Quarterly*	*Semi-Annually*	*Annually*	*Monthly*	*Quarterly*	*Semi-Annually*	*Annually*
1	12.197	4.076	2.045	1.030	12.263	4.101	2.060	1.040
2	24.765	8.275	4.152	2.091	25.026	8.369	4.204	2.122
3	37.715	12.601	6.323	3.184	38.309	12.809	6.434	3.246
4	51.059	17.059	8.559	4.309	52.133	17.430	8.755	4.416
5	64.808	21.652	10.863	5.468	66.520	22.239	11.169	5.633
6	78.976	26.385	13.237	6.662	81.493	27.243	13.680	6.898
7	93.575	31.261	15.682	7.892	97.077	32.450	16.293	8.214
8	108.618	36.285	18.201	9.159	113.295	37.869	19.012	9.583
9	124.119	41.461	20.797	10.464	130.174	43.508	21.841	11.006
10	140.091	46.795	23.471	11.808	147.741	49.375	24.783	12.486
11	156.549	52.290	26.225	13.192	166.023	55.481	27.845	14.026
12	173.507	57.952	29.063	14.618	185.050	61.835	31.030	15.627
13	190.981	63.786	31.987	16.086	204.853	68.447	34.344	17.292
14	208.987	69.797	34.999	17.599	225.462	75.327	37.792	19.024
15	227.540	75.990	38.102	19.157	246.911	82.486	41.379	20.825
16	246.658	82.371	41.299	20.762	269.234	89.937	45.112	22.698
17	266.357	88.945	44.592	22.414	292.466	97.689	48.994	24.645
18	286.655	95.720	47.985	24.117	316.644	105.757	53.034	26.671
19	307.571	102.699	51.481	25.870	341.808	114.152	57.237	28.778
20	329.123	109.891	55.082	27.676	367.997	122.888	61.610	30.969
21	351.330	117.300	58.792	29.537	395.253	131.979	66.159	33.248
22	374.213	124.934	62.614	31.453	423.620	141.439	70.893	35.618
23	397.792	132.800	66.552	33.426	453.142	151.283	75.817	38.083
24	422.088	140.905	70.609	35.459	483.867	161.527	80.941	40.646
25	447.123	149.256	74.788	37.553	515.843	172.186	86.271	43.312
26	472.919	157.859	79.094	39.710	549.123	183.279	91.817	46.084
27	499.500	166.724	83.530	41.931	583.758	194.822	97.587	48.968
28	526.890	175.858	88.100	44.219	619.804	206.833	103.589	51.966
29	555.113	185.269	92.808	46.575	657.319	219.332	109.835	55.085
30	584.194	194.966	97.658	49.003	696.363	232.339	116.333	58.328
31	614.159	204.956	102.655	51.503	736.997	245.874	123.093	61.701
32	645.036	215.250	107.803	54.078	779.287	259.958	130.126	65.210
33	676.853	225.856	113.106	56.730	823.299	274.615	137.444	68.858
34	709.636	236.784	118.570	59.462	869.105	289.866	145.057	72.652
35	743.418	248.043	124.199	62.276	916.777	305.737	152.977	76.598
36	778.226	259.644	129.998	65.174	966.391	322.252	161.218	80.702
37	814.093	271.597	135.973	68.159	1018.026	339.438	169.792	84.970
38	851.052	283.913	142.128	71.234	1071.765	357.321	178.712	89.409
39	889.134	296.602	148.469	74.401	1127.694	375.931	187.992	94.026
40	928.375	309.676	155.002	77.663	1185.901	395.296	197.647	98.827
41	968.809	323.147	161.732	81.023	1246.480	415.448	207.693	103.820
42	1010.473	337.027	168.665	84.484	1309.527	436.418	218.144	109.012
43	1053.404	351.328	175.808	88.048	1375.142	458.239	229.017	114.413
44	1097.641	366.062	183.167	91.720	1443.431	480.947	240.330	120.029
45	1143.224	381.244	190.749	95.501	1514.501	504.576	252.100	125.871
46	1190.193	396.886	198.559	99.397	1588.468	529.165	264.345	131.945
47	1238.591	413.003	206.606	103.408	1665.447	554.752	277.085	138.263
48	1288.460	429.609	214.896	107.541	1745.564	581.378	290.340	144.834
49	1339.847	446.718	223.436	111.797	1828.944	609.085	304.130	151.667
50	1392.796	464.347	232.235	116.181	1915.721	637.918	318.477	158.774

The future value of $1 invested at the *beginning* of each period

End of Year	5% Interest compounded and Deposits made				6% Interest compounded and Deposits made			
	Monthly	*Quarterly*	*Semi-Annually*	*Annually*	*Monthly*	*Quarterly*	*Semi-Annually*	*Annually*
1	12.330	4.127	2.076	1.050	12.397	4.152	2.091	1.060
2	25.291	8.463	4.256	2.153	25.559	8.559	4.309	2.184
3	38.915	13.021	6.547	3.310	39.533	13.237	6.662	3.375
4	53.236	17.811	8.955	4.526	54.368	18.201	9.159	4.637
5	68.289	22.845	11.483	5.802	70.119	23.471	11.808	5.975
6	84.113	28.135	14.140	7.142	86.841	29.063	14.618	7.394
7	100.747	33.695	16.932	8.549	104.594	34.999	17.599	8.897
8	118.231	39.539	19.865	10.027	123.443	41.299	20.762	10.491
9	136.610	45.679	22.946	11.578	143.454	47.985	24.117	12.181
10	155.929	52.133	26.183	13.207	164.699	55.082	27.676	13.972
11	176.237	58.916	29.584	14.917	187.254	62.614	31.453	15.870
12	197.584	66.044	33.158	16.713	211.201	70.609	35.459	17.882
13	220.022	73.535	36.912	18.599	236.625	79.094	39.710	20.015
14	243.609	81.408	40.856	20.579	263.616	88.100	44.219	22.276
15	268.403	89.682	45.000	22.657	292.273	97.658	49.003	24.673
16	294.465	98.377	49.354	24.840	322.697	107.803	54.078	27.213
17	321.860	107.516	53.928	27.132	354.997	118.570	59.462	29.906
18	350.657	117.120	58.734	29.539	389.290	129.998	65.174	32.760
19	380.927	127.213	63.783	32.066	425.698	142.128	71.234	35.786
20	412.746	137.820	69.088	34.719	464.351	155.002	77.663	38.993
21	446.193	148.968	74.661	37.505	505.388	168.665	84.484	42.392
22	481.351	160.684	80.516	40.430	548.957	183.167	91.720	45.996
23	518.308	172.997	86.668	43.502	595.213	198.559	99.397	49.816
24	557.156	185.937	93.131	46.727	644.321	214.896	107.541	53.865
25	597.991	199.536	99.921	50.113	696.459	232.235	116.181	58.156
26	640.915	213.828	107.056	53.669	751.812	250.638	125.347	62.706
27	686.036	228.848	114.551	57.403	810.580	270.170	135.072	67.528
28	733.465	244.633	122.426	61.323	872.972	290.901	145.388	72.640
29	783.320	261.223	130.699	65.439	939.212	312.904	156.333	78.058
30	835.726	278.657	139.391	69.761	1009.538	336.258	167.945	83.802
31	890.814	296.980	148.524	74.299	1084.201	361.044	180.264	89.890
32	948.719	316.236	158.118	79.064	1163.469	387.351	193.333	96.343
33	1009.588	336.474	168.199	84.067	1247.627	415.272	207.198	103.184
34	1073.570	357.742	178.789	89.320	1336.975	444.907	221.907	110.435
35	1140.826	380.094	189.916	94.836	1431.834	476.361	237.512	118.121
36	1211.523	403.585	201.606	100.628	1532.543	509.744	254.067	126.268
37	1285.837	428.272	213.888	106.710	1639.465	545.176	271.631	134.904
38	1363.953	454.217	226.792	113.095	1752.980	582.782	290.264	144.058
39	1446.065	481.484	240.349	119.800	1873.498	622.696	310.032	153.762
40	1532.379	510.140	254.592	126.840	2001.448	665.059	331.004	164.048
41	1623.108	540.256	269.557	134.232	2137.290	710.022	353.253	174.951
42	1718.479	571.906	285.279	141.993	2281.511	757.744	376.857	186.508
43	1818.730	605.168	301.796	150.143	2434.627	808.394	401.898	198.758
44	1924.110	640.125	319.150	158.700	2597.187	862.152	428.465	211.744
45	2034.881	676.863	337.383	167.685	2769.773	919.209	456.649	225.508
46	2151.319	715.473	356.539	177.119	2953.003	979.767	486.550	240.099
47	2273.715	756.049	376.664	187.025	3147.535	1044.041	518.272	255.565
48	2402.372	798.693	397.808	197.427	3354.066	1112.260	551.926	271.958
49	2537.612	843.509	420.023	208.348	3573.334	1184.664	587.629	289.336
50	2679.771	890.609	443.362	219.815	3806.127	1261.512	625.506	307.756

The future value of $1 invested at the *beginning* of each period

End of Year	7% Monthly	7% Quarterly	7% Semi-Annually	7% Annually	8% Monthly	8% Quarterly	8% Semi-Annually	8% Annually
	7% Interest compounded and Deposits made				*8% Interest compounded and Deposits made*			
1	12.465	4.178	2.106	1.070	12.533	4.204	2.122	1.080
2	25.831	8.656	4.362	2.215	26.106	8.755	4.416	2.246
3	40.163	13.457	6.779	3.440	40.806	13.680	6.898	3.506
4	55.531	18.602	9.368	4.751	56.726	19.012	9.583	4.867
5	72.011	24.116	12.142	6.153	73.967	24.783	12.486	6.336
6	89.681	30.027	15.113	7.654	92.639	31.030	15.627	7.923
7	108.629	36.363	18.296	9.260	112.861	37.792	19.024	9.637
8	128.947	43.154	21.705	10.978	134.761	45.112	22.698	11.488
9	150.733	50.434	25.357	12.816	158.479	53.034	26.671	13.487
10	174.094	58.236	29.269	14.784	184.166	61.610	30.969	15.645
11	199.145	66.599	33.460	16.888	211.984	70.893	35.618	17.977
12	226.006	75.562	37.950	19.141	242.112	80.941	40.646	20.495
13	254.809	85.170	42.759	21.550	274.740	91.817	46.084	23.215
14	285.694	95.469	47.911	24.129	310.076	103.589	51.966	26.152
15	318.811	106.507	53.429	26.888	348.345	116.333	58.328	29.324
16	354.323	118.339	59.341	29.840	389.791	130.126	65.210	32.750
17	392.402	131.020	65.674	32.999	434.676	145.057	72.652	36.450
18	433.234	144.613	72.458	36.379	483.287	161.218	80.702	40.446
19	477.017	159.183	79.725	39.995	535.932	178.712	89.409	44.762
20	523.965	174.800	87.510	43.865	592.947	197.647	98.827	49.423
21	574.308	191.539	95.849	48.006	654.694	218.144	109.012	54.457
22	628.289	209.481	104.782	52.436	721.567	240.330	120.029	59.893
23	686.173	228.712	114.351	57.177	793.989	264.345	131.945	65.765
24	748.242	249.326	124.602	62.249	872.423	290.340	144.834	72.106
25	814.797	271.420	135.583	67.676	957.367	318.477	158.774	78.954
26	886.164	295.102	147.346	73.484	1049.360	348.934	173.851	86.351
27	962.689	320.486	159.947	79.698	1148.990	381.901	190.159	94.339
28	1044.747	347.694	173.445	86.347	1256.888	417.586	207.798	102.966
29	1132.737	376.857	187.905	93.461	1373.742	456.213	226.876	112.283
30	1227.087	408.115	203.395	101.073	1500.295	498.023	247.510	122.346
31	1328.259	441.620	219.988	109.218	1637.352	543.280	269.829	133.214
32	1436.743	477.533	237.763	117.933	1785.784	592.268	293.968	144.951
33	1553.071	516.026	256.804	127.259	1946.536	645.294	320.078	157.627
34	1677.807	557.285	277.201	137.237	2120.631	702.691	348.318	171.317
35	1811.561	601.509	299.051	147.913	2309.175	764.820	378.862	186.102
36	1954.984	648.911	322.457	159.337	2513.368	832.070	411.899	202.070
37	2108.774	699.719	347.530	171.561	2734.510	904.863	447.631	219.316
38	2273.683	754.179	374.389	184.640	2974.005	983.657	486.280	237.941
39	2450.512	812.551	403.161	198.635	3233.379	1068.946	528.082	258.057
40	2640.125	875.118	433.983	213.610	3514.281	1161.265	573.295	279.781
41	2843.445	942.182	466.999	229.632	3818.498	1261.195	622.197	303.244
42	3061.462	1014.064	502.367	246.776	4147.964	1369.362	675.090	328.583
43	3295.240	1091.112	540.255	265.121	4504.776	1486.445	732.299	355.950
44	3545.919	1173.696	580.841	284.749	4891.203	1613.180	794.176	385.506
45	3814.718	1262.215	624.317	305.752	5309.703	1750.362	861.103	417.426
46	4102.949	1357.094	670.890	328.224	5762.939	1898.853	933.490	451.900
47	4412.017	1458.792	720.781	352.270	6253.793	2059.583	1011.785	489.132
48	4743.427	1567.797	774.225	377.999	6785.388	2233.563	1096.468	529.343
49	5098.794	1684.636	831.475	405.529	7361.105	2421.885	1188.061	572.770
50	5479.851	1809.870	892.803	434.986	7984.606	2625.730	1287.129	619.672

The future value of $1 invested at the *beginning* of each period

End of Year	9% Monthly	9% Quarterly	9% Semi-Annually	9% Annually	10% Monthly	10% Quarterly	10% Semi-Annually	10% Annually
	9% Interest compounded and Deposits made				*10% Interest compounded and Deposits made*			
1	12.601	4.230	2.137	1.090	12.670	4.256	2.153	1.100
2	26.385	8.854	4.471	2.278	26.667	8.955	4.526	2.310
3	41.461	13.908	7.019	3.573	42.130	14.140	7.142	3.641
4	57.952	19.433	9.802	4.985	59.212	19.865	10.027	5.105
5	75.990	25.472	12.841	6.523	78.082	26.183	13.207	6.716
6	95.720	32.073	16.160	8.200	98.929	33.158	16.713	8.487
7	117.300	39.289	19.784	10.028	121.958	40.856	20.579	10.436
8	140.905	47.176	23.742	12.021	147.399	49.354	24.840	12.579
9	166.724	55.797	28.064	14.193	175.504	58.734	29.539	14.937
10	194.966	65.221	32.783	16.560	206.552	69.088	34.719	17.531
11	225.856	75.523	37.937	19.141	240.851	80.516	40.430	20.384
12	259.644	86.783	43.565	21.953	278.742	93.131	46.727	23.523
13	296.602	99.091	49.711	25.019	320.600	107.056	53.669	26.975
14	337.027	112.544	56.423	28.361	366.841	122.426	61.323	30.772
15	381.244	127.251	63.752	32.003	417.924	139.391	69.761	34.950
16	429.609	143.326	71.756	35.974	474.357	158.118	79.064	39.545
17	482.510	160.897	80.497	40.301	536.698	178.789	89.320	44.599
18	540.374	180.104	90.041	45.018	605.568	201.606	100.628	50.159
19	603.667	201.099	100.464	50.160	681.649	226.792	113.095	56.275
20	672.896	224.048	111.847	55.765	765.697	254.592	126.840	63.002
21	748.620	249.133	124.276	61.873	858.546	285.279	141.993	70.403
22	831.447	276.553	137.850	68.532	961.117	319.150	158.700	78.543
23	922.044	306.526	152.673	75.790	1074.429	356.539	177.119	87.497
24	1021.139	339.288	168.859	83.701	1199.606	397.808	197.427	97.347
25	1129.530	375.101	186.536	92.324	1337.890	443.362	219.815	108.182
26	1248.089	414.246	205.839	101.723	1490.655	493.645	244.499	120.100
27	1377.770	457.036	226.918	111.968	1659.417	549.149	271.713	133.210
28	1519.616	503.808	249.937	123.135	1845.849	610.414	301.716	147.631
29	1674.768	554.935	275.075	135.308	2051.804	678.039	334.794	163.494
30	1844.474	610.820	302.525	148.575	2279.325	752.684	371.263	180.943
31	2030.100	671.907	332.502	163.037	2530.671	835.079	411.470	200.138
32	2233.139	738.681	365.238	178.800	2808.335	926.027	455.798	221.252
33	2455.224	811.670	400.986	195.982	3115.075	1026.417	504.670	244.477
34	2698.142	891.453	440.024	214.711	3453.934	1137.229	558.551	270.024
35	2963.848	978.662	482.654	235.125	3828.277	1259.544	617.955	298.127
36	3254.479	1073.989	529.207	257.376	4241.818	1394.557	683.448	329.039
37	3572.373	1178.190	580.044	281.630	4698.662	1543.586	755.654	363.043
38	3920.087	1292.090	635.560	308.066	5203.343	1708.087	835.261	400.448
39	4300.420	1416.592	696.184	336.882	5760.871	1889.665	923.027	441.593
40	4716.430	1552.683	762.388	368.292	6376.780	2090.093	1019.790	486.852
41	5171.465	1701.442	834.684	402.528	7057.183	2311.327	1126.471	536.637
42	5669.186	1864.048	913.632	439.846	7808.832	2555.529	1244.087	591.401
43	6213.596	2041.790	999.846	480.522	8639.189	2825.083	1373.758	651.641
44	6809.075	2236.077	1093.994	524.859	9556.496	3122.619	1516.721	717.905
45	7460.415	2448.448	1196.806	573.186	10569.856	3451.043	1674.338	790.795
46	8172.855	2680.588	1309.079	625.863	11689.328	3813.562	1848.110	870.975
47	8952.126	2934.336	1431.684	683.280	12926.024	4213.716	2039.694	959.172
48	9804.499	3211.704	1565.572	745.866	14292.218	4655.410	2250.915	1056.190
49	10736.830	3514.891	1711.781	814.084	15801.470	5142.958	2483.786	1162.909
50	11756.620	3846.298	1871.444	888.441	17468.761	5681.120	2740.526	1280.299

The future value of $1 invested at the *beginning* of each period

End of Year	*11% Interest compounded and Deposits made* Monthly	Quarterly	Semi-Annually	Annually	*12% Interest compounded and Deposits made* Monthly	Quarterly	Semi-Annually	Annually
1	12.740	4.283	2.168	1.110	12.809	4.309	2.184	1.120
2	26.953	9.056	4.581	2.342	27.243	9.159	4.637	2.374
3	42.812	14.377	7.267	3.710	43.508	14.618	7.394	3.779
4	60.506	20.307	10.256	5.228	61.835	20.762	10.491	5.353
5	80.247	26.918	13.583	6.913	82.486	27.676	13.972	7.115
6	102.273	34.286	17.287	8.783	105.757	35.459	17.882	9.089
7	126.847	42.498	21.409	10.859	131.979	44.219	22.276	11.300
8	154.265	51.652	25.996	13.164	161.527	54.078	27.213	13.776
9	184.856	61.855	31.103	15.722	194.822	65.174	32.760	16.549
10	218.987	73.228	36.786	18.561	232.339	77.663	38.993	19.655
11	257.068	85.904	43.112	21.713	274.615	91.720	45.996	23.133
12	299.555	100.033	50.153	25.212	322.252	107.541	53.865	27.029
13	346.959	115.782	57.989	29.095	375.931	125.347	62.706	31.393
14	399.848	133.336	66.711	33.405	436.418	145.388	72.640	36.280
15	458.858	152.901	76.419	38.190	504.576	167.945	83.802	41.753
16	524.696	174.710	87.225	43.501	581.378	193.333	96.343	47.884
17	598.152	199.018	99.251	49.396	667.921	221.907	110.435	54.750
18	680.109	226.112	112.637	55.939	765.439	254.067	126.268	62.440
19	771.551	256.312	127.536	63.203	875.325	290.264	144.058	71.052
20	873.573	289.974	144.119	71.265	999.148	331.004	164.048	80.699
21	987.402	327.494	162.576	80.214	1138.674	376.857	186.508	91.503
22	1114.402	369.314	183.119	90.148	1295.896	428.465	211.744	103.603
23	1256.099	415.928	205.984	101.174	1473.057	486.550	240.099	117.155
24	1414.193	467.885	231.434	113.413	1672.687	551.926	271.958	132.334
25	1590.581	525.797	259.759	126.999	1897.635	625.506	307.756	149.334
26	1787.381	590.347	291.287	142.079	2151.112	708.322	347.978	168.374
27	2006.954	662.296	326.377	158.817	2436.736	801.532	393.172	189.699
28	2251.936	742.492	365.434	177.397	2758.585	906.440	443.952	213.583
29	2525.267	831.880	408.906	198.021	3121.252	1024.516	501.008	240.333
30	2830.228	931.514	457.290	220.913	3529.914	1157.411	565.116	270.293
31	3170.478	1042.568	511.143	246.324	3990.405	1306.985	637.148	303.848
32	3550.102	1166.351	571.083	274.529	4509.297	1475.332	718.083	341.429
33	3973.655	1304.322	637.798	305.837	5093.998	1664.808	809.022	383.521
34	4446.221	1458.108	712.053	340.590	5752.854	1878.066	911.200	430.663
35	4973.472	1629.520	794.701	379.164	6495.269	2118.089	1026.008	483.463
36	5561.736	1820.581	886.690	421.982	7331.841	2388.237	1155.006	542.599
37	6218.074	2033.541	989.076	469.511	8274.511	2692.290	1299.949	608.831
38	6950.362	2270.910	1103.035	522.267	9336.736	3034.506	1462.806	683.010
39	7767.389	2535.488	1229.873	580.826	10533.677	3419.672	1645.792	766.091
40	8678.962	2830.391	1371.048	645.827	11882.420	3853.180	1851.396	859.142
41	9696.021	3159.097	1528.179	717.978	13402.218	4341.097	2082.412	963.359
42	10830.772	3525.479	1703.069	798.065	15114.764	4890.253	2341.982	1080.083
43	12096.836	3933.857	1897.726	886.963	17044.504	5508.332	2633.634	1210.813
44	13509.408	4389.043	2114.385	985.639	19218.983	6203.985	2961.335	1357.230
45	15085.440	4896.403	2355.531	1095.169	21669.240	6986.949	3329.540	1521.218
46	16843.850	5461.918	2623.933	1216.747	24430.251	7868.181	3743.254	1704.884
47	18805.740	6092.253	2922.671	1351.700	27541.428	8860.017	4208.104	1910.590
48	20994.658	6794.837	3255.174	1501.497	31047.180	9976.336	4730.410	2140.981
49	23436.875	7577.952	3625.258	1667.771	34997.549	11232.763	5317.272	2399.018
50	26161.702	8450.829	4037.171	1852.336	39448.923	12646.883	5976.670	2688.020

The future value of $1 invested at the *beginning* of each period

End of Year	*13% Interest compounded and Deposits made* Monthly	Quarterly	Semi-Annually	Annually	*14% Interest compounded and Deposits made* Monthly	Quarterly	Semi-Annually	Annually
1	12.879	4.336	2.199	1.130	12.950	4.362	2.215	1.140
2	27.537	9.263	4.694	2.407	27.834	9.368	4.751	2.440
3	44.217	14.863	7.523	3.850	44.941	15.113	7.654	3.921
4	63.200	21.227	10.732	5.480	64.603	21.705	10.978	5.610
5	84.803	28.460	14.372	7.323	87.201	29.269	14.784	7.536
6	109.388	36.680	18.500	9.405	113.174	37.950	19.141	9.730
7	137.367	46.022	23.182	11.757	143.025	47.911	24.129	12.233
8	169.208	56.638	28.493	14.416	177.335	59.341	29.840	15.085
9	205.443	68.704	34.517	17.420	216.769	72.458	36.379	18.337
10	246.681	82.416	41.349	20.814	262.091	87.510	43.865	22.045
11	293.610	97.999	49.098	24.650	314.183	104.782	52.436	26.271
12	347.017	115.710	57.888	28.985	374.054	124.602	62.249	31.089
13	407.796	135.837	67.857	33.883	442.865	147.346	73.484	36.581
14	476.965	158.711	79.164	39.417	521.954	173.445	86.347	42.842
15	555.681	184.707	91.989	45.672	612.854	203.395	101.073	49.980
16	645.263	214.251	106.536	52.739	717.329	237.763	117.933	58.118
17	747.210	247.827	123.035	60.725	837.406	277.201	137.237	67.394
18	863.228	285.985	141.748	69.749	975.416	322.457	159.337	77.969
19	995.261	329.351	162.974	79.947	1134.037	374.389	184.640	90.025
20	1145.519	378.635	187.048	91.470	1316.346	433.983	213.610	103.768
21	1316.517	434.645	214.354	104.491	1525.882	502.367	246.776	119.436
22	1511.119	498.299	245.325	119.205	1766.711	580.841	284.749	137.297
23	1732.582	570.641	280.453	135.831	2043.505	670.890	328.224	157.659
24	1984.614	652.855	320.295	154.620	2361.636	774.225	377.999	180.871
25	2271.435	746.290	365.486	175.850	2727.278	892.803	434.986	207.333
26	2597.846	852.477	416.743	199.841	3147.525	1028.875	500.230	237.499
27	2969.313	973.155	474.880	226.950	3630.533	1185.020	574.929	271.889
28	3392.054	1110.303	540.819	257.583	4185.674	1364.200	660.451	311.094
29	3873.147	1266.168	615.610	292.199	4823.721	1569.813	758.365	355.787
30	4420.647	1443.305	700.440	331.315	5557.056	1805.759	870.467	406.737
31	5043.719	1644.617	796.655	375.516	6399.908	2076.513	998.812	464.820
32	5752.796	1873.404	905.786	425.463	7368.633	2387.208	1145.755	531.035
33	6559.748	2133.414	1029.564	481.903	8482.030	2743.739	1313.990	606.520
34	7478.086	2428.909	1169.956	545.681	9761.703	3152.866	1506.602	692.573
35	8523.184	2764.733	1329.193	617.749	11232.486	3622.349	1727.124	790.673
36	9712.540	3146.388	1509.803	699.187	12922.918	4161.091	1979.599	902.507
37	11066.065	3580.130	1714.656	791.211	14865.803	4779.310	2268.657	1029.998
38	12606.421	4073.067	1947.005	895.198	17098.842	5488.731	2599.601	1175.338
39	14359.396	4633.279	2210.541	1012.704	19665.368	6302.807	2978.498	1341.025
40	16354.339	5269.945	2509.450	1145.486	22615.184	7236.979	3412.297	1529.909
41	18624.648	5993.502	2848.480	1295.529	26005.532	8308.962	3908.954	1745.236
42	21208.334	6815.806	3233.016	1465.078	29902.201	9539.087	4477.576	1990.709
43	24148.653	7750.336	3669.167	1656.668	34380.807	10950.685	5128.592	2270.548
44	27494.831	8812.406	4163.860	1873.165	39528.256	12570.525	5873.940	2589.565
45	31302.890	10019.423	4724.954	2117.806	45444.436	14429.329	6727.288	2953.244
46	35636.585	11391.168	5361.360	2394.251	52244.151	16562.349	7704.287	3367.838
47	40568.470	12950.124	6083.188	2706.633	60059.348	19010.039	8822.854	3840.475
48	46181.117	14721.840	6901.903	3059.626	69041.683	21818.820	10103.500	4379.282
49	52568.490	16735.353	7830.510	3458.507	79365.458	25041.960	11569.712	4993.521
50	59837.529	19023.661	8883.759	3909.243	91231.007	28740.588	13248.378	5693.754

The future value of $1 invested at the *beginning* of each period

End of Year	15% Interest compounded and Deposits made: Monthly	Quarterly	Semi-Annually	Annually	16% Interest compounded and Deposits made: Monthly	Quarterly	Semi-Annually	Annually
1	13.021	4.389	2.231	1.150	13.093	4.416	2.246	1.160
2	28.135	9.475	4.808	2.473	28.441	9.583	4.867	2.506
3	45.679	15.368	7.787	3.993	46.433	15.627	7.923	4.066
4	66.044	22.195	11.230	5.742	67.524	22.698	11.488	5.877
5	89.682	30.106	15.208	7.754	92.249	30.969	15.645	7.977
6	117.120	39.271	19.806	10.067	121.234	40.646	20.495	10.414
7	148.968	49.891	25.118	12.727	155.211	51.966	26.152	13.240
8	185.937	62.195	31.258	15.786	195.042	65.210	32.750	16.519
9	228.848	76.452	38.353	19.304	241.735	80.702	40.446	20.321
10	278.657	92.970	46.553	23.349	296.472	98.827	49.423	24.733
11	336.474	112.110	56.028	28.002	360.637	120.029	59.893	29.850
12	403.585	134.285	66.978	33.352	435.857	144.834	72.106	35.786
13	481.484	159.979	79.632	39.505	524.035	173.851	86.351	42.672
14	571.906	189.749	94.255	46.580	627.404	207.798	102.966	50.660
15	676.863	224.242	111.154	54.717	748.580	247.510	122.346	59.925
16	798.693	264.207	130.683	64.075	890.631	293.968	144.951	70.673
17	940.108	310.513	153.252	74.836	1057.153	348.318	171.317	83.141
18	1104.255	364.166	179.332	87.212	1252.363	411.899	202.070	97.603
19	1294.790	426.330	209.471	101.444	1481.201	486.280	237.941	114.380
20	1515.955	498.357	244.301	117.810	1749.461	573.295	279.781	133.841
21	1772.673	581.811	284.551	136.632	2063.934	675.090	328.583	156.415
22	2070.659	678.505	331.065	158.276	2432.583	794.176	385.506	182.601
23	2416.548	790.539	384.817	183.168	2864.738	933.490	451.900	212.978
24	2818.040	920.348	446.935	211.793	3371.342	1096.468	529.343	248.214
25	3284.074	1070.751	518.720	244.712	3965.218	1287.129	619.672	289.088
26	3825.025	1245.015	601.676	282.569	4661.402	1510.175	725.032	336.502
27	4452.936	1446.927	697.543	326.104	5477.518	1771.107	847.923	391.503
28	5181.786	1680.871	808.328	376.170	6434.227	2076.361	991.264	455.303
29	6027.803	1951.932	936.355	433.745	7555.748	2433.465	1158.457	529.312
30	7009.821	2265.996	1084.306	499.957	8870.476	2851.227	1353.470	615.162
31	8149.702	2629.886	1255.281	576.100	10411.692	3339.948	1580.934	714.747
32	9472.825	3051.508	1452.865	663.666	12218.415	3911.683	1846.248	830.267
33	11008.645	3540.020	1681.198	764.365	14336.384	4580.532	2155.710	964.270
34	12791.356	4106.035	1945.065	880.170	16819.217	5362.991	2516.667	1119.713
35	14860.645	4761.849	2249.997	1013.346	19729.770	6278.358	2937.686	1300.027
36	17262.582	5521.708	2602.383	1166.498	23141.726	7349.207	3428.764	1509.191
37	20050.641	6402.118	3009.609	1342.622	27141.462	8601.949	4001.557	1751.822
38	23286.893	7422.206	3480.210	1545.165	31830.235	10067.480	4669.662	2033.273
39	27043.388	8604.132	4024.049	1778.090	37326.748	11781.944	5448.940	2359.757
40	31403.755	9973.570	4652.522	2045.954	43770.149	13787.624	6357.890	2738.478
41	36465.072	11560.270	5378.801	2353.997	51323.561	16133.986	7418.090	3177.795
42	42340.018	13398.701	6218.108	2708.246	60178.204	18878.899	8654.706	3687.402
43	49159.389	15528.800	7188.032	3115.633	70558.244	22090.057	10097.096	4278.546
44	57075.004	17996.840	8308.900	3584.128	82726.461	25846.659	11779.499	4964.274
45	66263.089	20856.435	9604.203	4122.898	96990.907	30241.352	13741.854	5759.718
46	76928.202	24169.707	11101.088	4742.482	113712.701	35382.520	16030.745	6682.433
47	89307.779	28008.630	12830.925	5455.005	133315.171	41396.961	18700.507	7752.782
48	103677.429	32456.600	14829.968	6274.405	156294.575	48433.005	21814.518	8994.387
49	120357.065	37610.243	17140.113	7216.716	183232.658	56664.182	25446.700	10434.649
50	139718.028	43581.513	19809.773	8300.374	214811.387	66293.495	29683.277	12105.353

The future value of $1 invested at the *beginning* of each period

End of Year	17% Interest compounded and Deposits made				18% Interest compounded and Deposits made			
	Monthly	Quarterly	Semi-Annually	Annually	Monthly	Quarterly	Semi-Annually	Annually
1	13.164	4.443	2.262	1.170	13.237	4.471	2.278	1.180
2	28.750	9.692	4.925	2.539	29.063	9.802	4.985	2.572
3	47.201	15.891	8.060	4.141	47.985	16.160	8.200	4.215
4	69.046	23.213	11.751	6.014	70.609	23.742	12.021	6.154
5	94.907	31.861	16.096	8.207	97.658	32.783	16.560	8.442
6	125.524	42.076	21.211	10.772	129.998	43.565	21.953	11.142
7	161.771	54.142	27.232	13.773	168.665	56.423	28.361	14.327
8	204.684	68.393	34.321	17.285	214.896	71.756	35.974	18.086
9	255.488	85.226	42.665	21.393	270.170	90.041	45.018	22.521
10	315.635	105.108	52.489	26.200	336.258	111.847	55.765	27.755
11	386.842	128.591	64.054	31.824	415.272	137.850	68.532	33.931
12	471.144	156.329	77.668	38.404	509.744	168.859	83.701	41.219
13	570.948	189.091	93.695	46.103	622.696	205.839	101.723	49.818
14	689.105	227.788	112.562	55.110	757.744	249.937	123.135	59.965
15	828.990	273.494	134.773	65.649	919.209	302.525	148.575	71.939
16	994.599	327.481	160.920	77.979	1112.260	365.238	178.800	86.068
17	1190.662	391.247	191.702	92.406	1343.075	440.024	214.711	102.740
18	1422.779	466.564	227.938	109.285	1619.041	529.207	257.376	122.414
19	1697.581	555.524	270.597	129.033	1948.992	635.560	308.066	145.628
20	2022.917	660.599	320.816	152.139	2343.487	762.388	368.292	173.021
21	2408.079	784.709	379.934	179.172	2815.153	913.632	439.846	205.345
22	2864.069	931.301	449.530	210.801	3379.085	1093.994	524.859	243.487
23	3403.912	1104.447	531.461	247.808	4053.332	1309.079	625.863	288.494
24	4043.028	1308.959	627.911	291.105	4859.474	1565.572	745.866	341.603
25	4799.672	1550.518	741.455	341.763	5823.312	1871.444	888.441	404.272
26	5695.456	1835.834	875.121	401.032	6975.695	2236.203	1057.835	478.221
27	6755.968	2172.835	1032.477	470.378	8353.504	2671.184	1259.092	565.481
28	8011.499	2570.882	1217.720	551.512	10000.838	3189.908	1498.205	668.447
29	9497.912	3041.035	1435.792	646.439	11970.421	3808.495	1782.296	789.948
30	11257.664	3596.356	1692.513	757.504	14325.289	4546.172	2119.823	933.319
31	13341.020	4252.271	1994.731	887.449	17140.813	5425.865	2520.840	1102.496
32	15807.487	5027.005	2350.509	1039.486	20507.104	6474.916	2997.288	1302.125
33	18727.518	5942.079	2769.340	1217.368	24531.903	7725.929	3563.357	1537.688
34	22184.518	7022.917	3262.399	1425.491	29344.026	9217.784	4235.902	1815.652
35	26277.232	8299.547	3842.840	1668.994	35097.488	10996.850	5034.953	2143.649
36	31122.562	9807.435	4526.149	1953.894	41976.431	13118.419	5984.306	2530.686
37	36858.908	11588.474	5330.558	2287.225	50201.020	15648.429	7112.232	2987.389
38	43650.121	13692.144	6277.529	2677.224	60034.489	18665.514	8452.321	3526.299
39	51690.182	16176.890	7392.326	3133.522	71791.563	22263.443	10044.481	4162.213
40	61208.743	19111.742	8704.693	3667.391	85848.534	26554.040	11936.126	4912.591
41	72477.689	22578.236	10249.645	4292.017	102655.304	31670.658	14183.589	5798.038
42	85818.901	26672.677	12068.400	5022.830	122749.784	37772.319	16853.800	6842.865
43	101613.452	31508.818	14209.485	5877.881	146775.109	45048.664	20026.278	8075.760
44	120312.489	37221.016	16730.023	6878.291	175500.224	53725.840	23795.499	9530.577
45	142450.125	43967.965	19697.264	8048.770	209844.493	64073.535	28273.711	11247.261
46	168658.690	51937.110	23190.373	9418.231	250907.126	76413.353	33594.274	13272.948
47	199686.792	61349.848	27302.550	11020.500	300002.356	91128.815	39915.635	15663.259
48	236420.706	72467.683	32143.506	12895.155	358701.506	108677.278	47426.044	18483.825
49	279909.682	85599.489	37842.401	15088.502	428883.275	129604.146	56349.161	21812.094
50	331395.922	101110.094	44551.283	17654.717	512793.874	154559.826	66950.716	25739.451

TABLE 10

How much must be invested at the *beginning* of each period to accumulate $1 by some future date, assuming deposits are made monthly, quarterly, semi-annually or annually at various interest rates?

Applications

Chapter Nine

- Periodic payments at the beginning of each period required to attain a certain savings level by the end of a given time period.

How much must be invested at the *beginning* of each period to accumulate $1

End of Year	At 3% Interest compounded and Deposits made				At 4% Interest compounded and Deposits made			
	Monthly	*Quarterly*	*Semi-Annually*	*Annually*	*Monthly*	*Quarterly*	*Semi-Annually*	*Annually*
1	0.0820	0.2454	0.4889	0.9709	0.0815	0.2438	0.4853	0.9615
2	0.0405	0.1218	0.2444	0.4926	0.0401	0.1207	0.2426	0.4902
3	0.0266	0.0800	0.1605	0.3235	0.0262	0.0788	0.1585	0.3203
4	0.0196	0.0591	0.1186	0.2390	0.0192	0.0579	0.1165	0.2355
5	0.0155	0.0465	0.0934	0.1884	0.0151	0.0454	0.0913	0.1846
6	0.0127	0.0382	0.0767	0.1546	0.0123	0.0371	0.0746	0.1508
7	0.0107	0.0322	0.0647	0.1305	0.0103	0.0311	0.0626	0.1266
8	0.0092	0.0278	0.0558	0.1125	0.0089	0.0267	0.0537	0.1085
9	0.0081	0.0243	0.0488	0.0984	0.0077	0.0232	0.0467	0.0945
10	0.0072	0.0215	0.0432	0.0872	0.0068	0.0205	0.0412	0.0833
11	0.0064	0.0193	0.0387	0.0781	0.0060	0.0182	0.0366	0.0741
12	0.0058	0.0174	0.0349	0.0705	0.0054	0.0163	0.0329	0.0666
13	0.0052	0.0158	0.0317	0.0640	0.0049	0.0148	0.0297	0.0601
14	0.0048	0.0144	0.0290	0.0585	0.0045	0.0134	0.0270	0.0547
15	0.0044	0.0133	0.0266	0.0538	0.0041	0.0122	0.0246	0.0499
16	0.0041	0.0122	0.0246	0.0496	0.0037	0.0112	0.0226	0.0458
17	0.0038	0.0113	0.0228	0.0460	0.0034	0.0103	0.0208	0.0422
18	0.0035	0.0105	0.0212	0.0427	0.0032	0.0096	0.0192	0.0390
19	0.0033	0.0098	0.0197	0.0398	0.0029	0.0088	0.0178	0.0361
20	0.0030	0.0092	0.0184	0.0372	0.0027	0.0082	0.0166	0.0336
21	0.0029	0.0086	0.0173	0.0349	0.0025	0.0077	0.0154	0.0313
22	0.0027	0.0081	0.0162	0.0327	0.0024	0.0071	0.0144	0.0292
23	0.0025	0.0076	0.0153	0.0308	0.0022	0.0067	0.0135	0.0273
24	0.0024	0.0072	0.0144	0.0290	0.0021	0.0063	0.0126	0.0256
25	0.0022	0.0068	0.0136	0.0274	0.0019	0.0059	0.0118	0.0240
26	0.0021	0.0064	0.0128	0.0259	0.0018	0.0055	0.0111	0.0226
27	0.0020	0.0060	0.0122	0.0246	0.0017	0.0052	0.0105	0.0212
28	0.0019	0.0057	0.0115	0.0233	0.0016	0.0049	0.0098	0.0200
29	0.0018	0.0054	0.0109	0.0221	0.0015	0.0046	0.0093	0.0189
30	0.0017	0.0052	0.0104	0.0210	0.0014	0.0043	0.0088	0.0178
31	0.0016	0.0049	0.0099	0.0200	0.0014	0.0041	0.0083	0.0169
32	0.0016	0.0047	0.0094	0.0190	0.0013	0.0039	0.0078	0.0159
33	0.0015	0.0045	0.0090	0.0182	0.0012	0.0037	0.0074	0.0151
34	0.0014	0.0043	0.0086	0.0173	0.0012	0.0035	0.0070	0.0143
35	0.0013	0.0041	0.0082	0.0165	0.0011	0.0033	0.0067	0.0136
36	0.0013	0.0039	0.0078	0.0158	0.0010	0.0031	0.0063	0.0129
37	0.0012	0.0037	0.0075	0.0151	0.0010	0.0030	0.0060	0.0122
38	0.0012	0.0035	0.0071	0.0145	0.0009	0.0028	0.0057	0.0116
39	0.0011	0.0034	0.0068	0.0138	0.0009	0.0027	0.0054	0.0111
40	0.0011	0.0033	0.0065	0.0133	0.0008	0.0026	0.0052	0.0105
41	0.0010	0.0031	0.0063	0.0127	0.0008	0.0024	0.0049	0.0100
42	0.0010	0.0030	0.0060	0.0122	0.0008	0.0023	0.0047	0.0095
43	0.0010	0.0029	0.0058	0.0117	0.0007	0.0022	0.0045	0.0091
44	0.0009	0.0028	0.0055	0.0112	0.0007	0.0021	0.0042	0.0087
45	0.0009	0.0026	0.0053	0.0108	0.0007	0.0020	0.0040	0.0083
46	0.0008	0.0025	0.0051	0.0104	0.0006	0.0019	0.0039	0.0079
47	0.0008	0.0024	0.0049	0.0100	0.0006	0.0018	0.0037	0.0075
48	0.0008	0.0023	0.0047	0.0096	0.0006	0.0017	0.0035	0.0072
49	0.0007	0.0023	0.0045	0.0092	0.0005	0.0017	0.0034	0.0069
50	0.0007	0.0022	0.0044	0.0089	0.0005	0.0016	0.0032	0.0066

How much must be invested at the *beginning* of each period to accumulate $1

End of Year	At 5% Interest compounded and Deposits made				At 6% Interest compounded and Deposits made			
	Monthly	Quarterly	Semi-Annually	Annually	Monthly	Quarterly	Semi-Annually	Annually
1	0.0811	0.2423	0.4818	0.9524	0.0807	0.2408	0.4783	0.9434
2	0.0395	0.1182	0.2349	0.4646	0.0391	0.1168	0.2321	0.4580
3	0.0257	0.0768	0.1527	0.3021	0.0253	0.0755	0.1501	0.2963
4	0.0188	0.0561	0.1117	0.2210	0.0184	0.0549	0.1092	0.2157
5	0.0146	0.0438	0.0871	0.1724	0.0143	0.0426	0.0847	0.1674
6	0.0119	0.0355	0.0707	0.1400	0.0115	0.0344	0.0684	0.1352
7	0.0099	0.0297	0.0591	0.1170	0.0096	0.0286	0.0568	0.1124
8	0.0085	0.0253	0.0503	0.0997	0.0081	0.0242	0.0482	0.0953
9	0.0073	0.0219	0.0436	0.0864	0.0070	0.0208	0.0415	0.0821
10	0.0064	0.0192	0.0382	0.0757	0.0061	0.0182	0.0361	0.0716
11	0.0057	0.0170	0.0338	0.0670	0.0053	0.0160	0.0318	0.0630
12	0.0051	0.0151	0.0302	0.0598	0.0047	0.0142	0.0282	0.0559
13	0.0045	0.0136	0.0271	0.0538	0.0042	0.0126	0.0252	0.0500
14	0.0041	0.0123	0.0245	0.0486	0.0038	0.0114	0.0226	0.0449
15	0.0037	0.0112	0.0222	0.0441	0.0034	0.0102	0.0204	0.0405
16	0.0034	0.0102	0.0203	0.0403	0.0031	0.0093	0.0185	0.0367
17	0.0031	0.0093	0.0185	0.0369	0.0028	0.0084	0.0168	0.0334
18	0.0029	0.0085	0.0170	0.0339	0.0026	0.0077	0.0153	0.0305
19	0.0026	0.0079	0.0157	0.0312	0.0023	0.0070	0.0140	0.0279
20	0.0024	0.0073	0.0145	0.0288	0.0022	0.0065	0.0129	0.0256
21	0.0022	0.0067	0.0134	0.0267	0.0020	0.0059	0.0118	0.0236
22	0.0021	0.0062	0.0124	0.0247	0.0018	0.0055	0.0109	0.0217
23	0.0019	0.0058	0.0115	0.0230	0.0017	0.0050	0.0101	0.0201
24	0.0018	0.0054	0.0107	0.0214	0.0016	0.0047	0.0093	0.0186
25	0.0017	0.0050	0.0100	0.0200	0.0014	0.0043	0.0086	0.0172
26	0.0016	0.0047	0.0093	0.0186	0.0013	0.0040	0.0080	0.0159
27	0.0015	0.0044	0.0087	0.0174	0.0012	0.0037	0.0074	0.0148
28	0.0014	0.0041	0.0082	0.0163	0.0011	0.0034	0.0069	0.0138
29	0.0013	0.0038	0.0077	0.0153	0.0011	0.0032	0.0064	0.0128
30	0.0012	0.0036	0.0072	0.0143	0.0010	0.0030	0.0060	0.0119
31	0.0011	0.0034	0.0067	0.0135	0.0009	0.0028	0.0055	0.0111
32	0.0011	0.0032	0.0063	0.0126	0.0009	0.0026	0.0052	0.0104
33	0.0010	0.0030	0.0059	0.0119	0.0008	0.0024	0.0048	0.0097
34	0.0009	0.0028	0.0056	0.0112	0.0007	0.0022	0.0045	0.0091
35	0.0009	0.0026	0.0053	0.0105	0.0007	0.0021	0.0042	0.0085
36	0.0008	0.0025	0.0050	0.0099	0.0007	0.0020	0.0039	0.0079
37	0.0008	0.0023	0.0047	0.0094	0.0006	0.0018	0.0037	0.0074
38	0.0007	0.0022	0.0044	0.0088	0.0006	0.0017	0.0034	0.0069
39	0.0007	0.0021	0.0042	0.0083	0.0005	0.0016	0.0032	0.0065
40	0.0007	0.0020	0.0039	0.0079	0.0005	0.0015	0.0030	0.0061
41	0.0006	0.0019	0.0037	0.0074	0.0005	0.0014	0.0028	0.0057
42	0.0006	0.0017	0.0035	0.0070	0.0004	0.0013	0.0027	0.0054
43	0.0005	0.0017	0.0033	0.0067	0.0004	0.0012	0.0025	0.0050
44	0.0005	0.0016	0.0031	0.0063	0.0004	0.0012	0.0023	0.0047
45	0.0005	0.0015	0.0030	0.0060	0.0004	0.0011	0.0022	0.0044
46	0.0005	0.0014	0.0028	0.0056	0.0003	0.0010	0.0021	0.0042
47	0.0004	0.0013	0.0027	0.0053	0.0003	0.0010	0.0019	0.0039
48	0.0004	0.0013	0.0025	0.0051	0.0003	0.0009	0.0018	0.0037
49	0.0004	0.0012	0.0024	0.0048	0.0003	0.0008	0.0017	0.0035
50	0.0004	0.0011	0.0023	0.0045	0.0003	0.0008	0.0016	0.0032

How much must be invested at the *beginning* of each period to accumulate $1

End of Year	At 7% Interest compounded and Deposits made: Monthly	Quarterly	Semi-Annually	Annually	At 8% Interest compounded and Deposits made: Monthly	Quarterly	Semi-Annually	Annually
1	0.0802	0.2393	0.4748	0.9346	0.0798	0.2379	0.4713	0.9259
2	0.0387	0.1155	0.2292	0.4515	0.0383	0.1142	0.2264	0.4452
3	0.0249	0.0743	0.1475	0.2907	0.0245	0.0731	0.1450	0.2852
4	0.0180	0.0538	0.1067	0.2105	0.0176	0.0526	0.1044	0.2055
5	0.0139	0.0415	0.0824	0.1625	0.0135	0.0403	0.0801	0.1578
6	0.0112	0.0333	0.0662	0.1307	0.0108	0.0322	0.0640	0.1262
7	0.0092	0.0275	0.0547	0.1080	0.0089	0.0265	0.0526	0.1038
8	0.0078	0.0232	0.0461	0.0911	0.0074	0.0222	0.0441	0.0871
9	0.0066	0.0198	0.0394	0.0780	0.0063	0.0189	0.0375	0.0741
10	0.0057	0.0172	0.0342	0.0676	0.0054	0.0162	0.0323	0.0639
11	0.0050	0.0150	0.0299	0.0592	0.0047	0.0141	0.0281	0.0556
12	0.0044	0.0132	0.0264	0.0522	0.0041	0.0124	0.0246	0.0488
13	0.0039	0.0117	0.0234	0.0464	0.0036	0.0109	0.0217	0.0431
14	0.0035	0.0105	0.0209	0.0414	0.0032	0.0097	0.0192	0.0382
15	0.0031	0.0094	0.0187	0.0372	0.0029	0.0086	0.0171	0.0341
16	0.0028	0.0085	0.0169	0.0335	0.0026	0.0077	0.0153	0.0305
17	0.0025	0.0076	0.0152	0.0303	0.0023	0.0069	0.0138	0.0274
18	0.0023	0.0069	0.0138	0.0275	0.0021	0.0062	0.0124	0.0247
19	0.0021	0.0063	0.0125	0.0250	0.0019	0.0056	0.0112	0.0223
20	0.0019	0.0057	0.0114	0.0228	0.0017	0.0051	0.0101	0.0202
21	0.0017	0.0052	0.0104	0.0208	0.0015	0.0046	0.0092	0.0184
22	0.0016	0.0048	0.0095	0.0191	0.0014	0.0042	0.0083	0.0167
23	0.0015	0.0044	0.0087	0.0175	0.0013	0.0038	0.0076	0.0152
24	0.0013	0.0040	0.0080	0.0161	0.0011	0.0034	0.0069	0.0139
25	0.0012	0.0037	0.0074	0.0148	0.0010	0.0031	0.0063	0.0127
26	0.0011	0.0034	0.0068	0.0136	0.0010	0.0029	0.0058	0.0116
27	0.0010	0.0031	0.0063	0.0125	0.0009	0.0026	0.0053	0.0106
28	0.0010	0.0029	0.0058	0.0116	0.0008	0.0024	0.0048	0.0097
29	0.0009	0.0027	0.0053	0.0107	0.0007	0.0022	0.0044	0.0089
30	0.0008	0.0025	0.0049	0.0099	0.0007	0.0020	0.0040	0.0082
31	0.0008	0.0023	0.0045	0.0092	0.0006	0.0018	0.0037	0.0075
32	0.0007	0.0021	0.0042	0.0085	0.0006	0.0017	0.0034	0.0069
33	0.0006	0.0019	0.0039	0.0079	0.0005	0.0015	0.0031	0.0063
34	0.0006	0.0018	0.0036	0.0073	0.0005	0.0014	0.0029	0.0058
35	0.0006	0.0017	0.0033	0.0068	0.0004	0.0013	0.0026	0.0054
36	0.0005	0.0015	0.0031	0.0063	0.0004	0.0012	0.0024	0.0049
37	0.0005	0.0014	0.0029	0.0058	0.0004	0.0011	0.0022	0.0046
38	0.0004	0.0013	0.0027	0.0054	0.0003	0.0010	0.0021	0.0042
39	0.0004	0.0012	0.0025	0.0050	0.0003	0.0009	0.0019	0.0039
40	0.0004	0.0011	0.0023	0.0047	0.0003	0.0009	0.0017	0.0036
41	0.0004	0.0011	0.0021	0.0044	0.0003	0.0008	0.0016	0.0033
42	0.0003	0.0010	0.0020	0.0041	0.0002	0.0007	0.0015	0.0030
43	0.0003	0.0009	0.0019	0.0038	0.0002	0.0007	0.0014	0.0028
44	0.0003	0.0009	0.0017	0.0035	0.0002	0.0006	0.0013	0.0026
45	0.0003	0.0008	0.0016	0.0033	0.0002	0.0006	0.0012	0.0024
46	0.0002	0.0007	0.0015	0.0030	0.0002	0.0005	0.0011	0.0022
47	0.0002	0.0007	0.0014	0.0028	0.0002	0.0005	0.0010	0.0020
48	0.0002	0.0006	0.0013	0.0026	0.0001	0.0004	0.0009	0.0019
49	0.0002	0.0006	0.0012	0.0025	0.0001	0.0004	0.0008	0.0017
50	0.0002	0.0006	0.0011	0.0023	0.0001	0.0004	0.0008	0.0016

How much must be invested at the *beginning* of each period to accumulate $1

End of Year	At 9% Interest compounded and Deposits made				At 10% Interest compounded and Deposits made			
	Monthly	Quarterly	Semi-Annually	Annually	Monthly	Quarterly	Semi-Annually	Annually
1	0.0794	0.2364	0.4679	0.9174	0.0789	0.2349	0.4646	0.9091
2	0.0379	0.1129	0.2237	0.4390	0.0375	0.1117	0.2210	0.4329
3	0.0241	0.0719	0.1425	0.2799	0.0237	0.0707	0.1400	0.2746
4	0.0173	0.0515	0.1020	0.2006	0.0169	0.0503	0.0997	0.1959
5	0.0132	0.0393	0.0779	0.1533	0.0128	0.0382	0.0757	0.1489
6	0.0104	0.0312	0.0619	0.1219	0.0101	0.0302	0.0598	0.1178
7	0.0085	0.0255	0.0505	0.0997	0.0082	0.0245	0.0486	0.0958
8	0.0071	0.0212	0.0421	0.0832	0.0068	0.0203	0.0403	0.0795
9	0.0060	0.0179	0.0356	0.0705	0.0057	0.0170	0.0339	0.0669
10	0.0051	0.0153	0.0305	0.0604	0.0048	0.0145	0.0288	0.0570
11	0.0044	0.0132	0.0264	0.0522	0.0042	0.0124	0.0247	0.0491
12	0.0039	0.0115	0.0230	0.0456	0.0036	0.0107	0.0214	0.0425
13	0.0034	0.0101	0.0201	0.0400	0.0031	0.0093	0.0186	0.0371
14	0.0030	0.0089	0.0177	0.0353	0.0027	0.0082	0.0163	0.0325
15	0.0026	0.0079	0.0157	0.0312	0.0024	0.0072	0.0143	0.0286
16	0.0023	0.0070	0.0139	0.0278	0.0021	0.0063	0.0126	0.0253
17	0.0021	0.0062	0.0124	0.0248	0.0019	0.0056	0.0112	0.0224
18	0.0019	0.0056	0.0111	0.0222	0.0017	0.0050	0.0099	0.0199
19	0.0017	0.0050	0.0100	0.0199	0.0015	0.0044	0.0088	0.0178
20	0.0015	0.0045	0.0089	0.0179	0.0013	0.0039	0.0079	0.0159
21	0.0013	0.0040	0.0080	0.0162	0.0012	0.0035	0.0070	0.0142
22	0.0012	0.0036	0.0073	0.0146	0.0010	0.0031	0.0063	0.0127
23	0.0011	0.0033	0.0065	0.0132	0.0009	0.0028	0.0056	0.0114
24	0.0010	0.0029	0.0059	0.0119	0.0008	0.0025	0.0051	0.0103
25	0.0009	0.0027	0.0054	0.0108	0.0007	0.0023	0.0045	0.0092
26	0.0008	0.0024	0.0049	0.0098	0.0007	0.0020	0.0041	0.0083
27	0.0007	0.0022	0.0044	0.0089	0.0006	0.0018	0.0037	0.0075
28	0.0007	0.0020	0.0040	0.0081	0.0005	0.0016	0.0033	0.0068
29	0.0006	0.0018	0.0036	0.0074	0.0005	0.0015	0.0030	0.0061
30	0.0005	0.0016	0.0033	0.0067	0.0004	0.0013	0.0027	0.0055
31	0.0005	0.0015	0.0030	0.0061	0.0004	0.0012	0.0024	0.0050
32	0.0004	0.0014	0.0027	0.0056	0.0004	0.0011	0.0022	0.0045
33	0.0004	0.0012	0.0025	0.0051	0.0003	0.0010	0.0020	0.0041
34	0.0004	0.0011	0.0023	0.0047	0.0003	0.0009	0.0018	0.0037
35	0.0003	0.0010	0.0021	0.0043	0.0003	0.0008	0.0016	0.0034
36	0.0003	0.0009	0.0019	0.0039	0.0002	0.0007	0.0015	0.0030
37	0.0003	0.0008	0.0017	0.0036	0.0002	0.0006	0.0013	0.0028
38	0.0003	0.0008	0.0016	0.0032	0.0002	0.0006	0.0012	0.0025
39	0.0002	0.0007	0.0014	0.0030	0.0002	0.0005	0.0011	0.0023
40	0.0002	0.0006	0.0013	0.0027	0.0002	0.0005	0.0010	0.0021
41	0.0002	0.0006	0.0012	0.0025	0.0001	0.0004	0.0009	0.0019
42	0.0002	0.0005	0.0011	0.0023	0.0001	0.0004	0.0008	0.0017
43	0.0002	0.0005	0.0010	0.0021	0.0001	0.0004	0.0007	0.0015
44	0.0001	0.0004	0.0009	0.0019	0.0001	0.0003	0.0007	0.0014
45	0.0001	0.0004	0.0008	0.0017	0.0001	0.0003	0.0006	0.0013
46	0.0001	0.0004	0.0008	0.0016	0.0001	0.0003	0.0005	0.0011
47	0.0001	0.0003	0.0007	0.0015	0.0001	0.0002	0.0005	0.0010
48	0.0001	0.0003	0.0006	0.0013	0.0001	0.0002	0.0004	0.0009
49	0.0001	0.0003	0.0006	0.0012	0.0001	0.0002	0.0004	0.0009
50	0.0001	0.0003	0.0005	0.0011	0.0001	0.0002	0.0004	0.0008

How much must be invested at the *beginning* of each period to accumulate $1

End of Year	At 11% Interest compounded and Deposits made: Monthly	Quarterly	Semi-Annually	Annually	At 12% Interest compounded and Deposits made: Monthly	Quarterly	Semi-Annually	Annually
1	0.0785	0.2335	0.4612	0.9009	0.0781	0.2321	0.4580	0.8929
2	0.0371	0.1104	0.2183	0.4270	0.0367	0.1092	0.2157	0.4212
3	0.0234	0.0696	0.1376	0.2696	0.0230	0.0684	0.1352	0.2646
4	0.0165	0.0492	0.0975	0.1913	0.0162	0.0482	0.0953	0.1868
5	0.0125	0.0372	0.0736	0.1447	0.0121	0.0361	0.0716	0.1405
6	0.0098	0.0292	0.0578	0.1139	0.0095	0.0282	0.0559	0.1100
7	0.0079	0.0235	0.0467	0.0921	0.0076	0.0226	0.0449	0.0885
8	0.0065	0.0194	0.0385	0.0760	0.0062	0.0185	0.0367	0.0726
9	0.0054	0.0162	0.0322	0.0636	0.0051	0.0153	0.0305	0.0604
10	0.0046	0.0137	0.0272	0.0539	0.0043	0.0129	0.0256	0.0509
11	0.0039	0.0116	0.0232	0.0461	0.0036	0.0109	0.0217	0.0432
12	0.0033	0.0100	0.0199	0.0397	0.0031	0.0093	0.0186	0.0370
13	0.0029	0.0086	0.0172	0.0344	0.0027	0.0080	0.0159	0.0319
14	0.0025	0.0075	0.0150	0.0299	0.0023	0.0069	0.0138	0.0276
15	0.0022	0.0065	0.0131	0.0262	0.0020	0.0060	0.0119	0.0240
16	0.0019	0.0057	0.0115	0.0230	0.0017	0.0052	0.0104	0.0209
17	0.0017	0.0050	0.0101	0.0202	0.0015	0.0045	0.0091	0.0183
18	0.0015	0.0044	0.0089	0.0179	0.0013	0.0039	0.0079	0.0160
19	0.0013	0.0039	0.0078	0.0158	0.0011	0.0034	0.0069	0.0141
20	0.0011	0.0034	0.0069	0.0140	0.0010	0.0030	0.0061	0.0124
21	0.0010	0.0031	0.0062	0.0125	0.0009	0.0027	0.0054	0.0109
22	0.0009	0.0027	0.0055	0.0111	0.0008	0.0023	0.0047	0.0097
23	0.0008	0.0024	0.0049	0.0099	0.0007	0.0021	0.0042	0.0085
24	0.0007	0.0021	0.0043	0.0088	0.0006	0.0018	0.0037	0.0076
25	0.0006	0.0019	0.0038	0.0079	0.0005	0.0016	0.0032	0.0067
26	0.0006	0.0017	0.0034	0.0070	0.0005	0.0014	0.0029	0.0059
27	0.0005	0.0015	0.0031	0.0063	0.0004	0.0012	0.0025	0.0053
28	0.0004	0.0013	0.0027	0.0056	0.0004	0.0011	0.0023	0.0047
29	0.0004	0.0012	0.0024	0.0050	0.0003	0.0010	0.0020	0.0042
30	0.0004	0.0011	0.0022	0.0045	0.0003	0.0009	0.0018	0.0037
31	0.0003	0.0010	0.0020	0.0041	0.0003	0.0008	0.0016	0.0033
32	0.0003	0.0009	0.0018	0.0036	0.0002	0.0007	0.0014	0.0029
33	0.0003	0.0008	0.0016	0.0033	0.0002	0.0006	0.0012	0.0026
34	0.0002	0.0007	0.0014	0.0029	0.0002	0.0005	0.0011	0.0023
35	0.0002	0.0006	0.0013	0.0026	0.0002	0.0005	0.0010	0.0021
36	0.0002	0.0005	0.0011	0.0024	0.0001	0.0004	0.0009	0.0018
37	0.0002	0.0005	0.0010	0.0021	0.0001	0.0004	0.0008	0.0016
38	0.0001	0.0004	0.0009	0.0019	0.0001	0.0003	0.0007	0.0015
39	0.0001	0.0004	0.0008	0.0017	0.0001	0.0003	0.0006	0.0013
40	0.0001	0.0004	0.0007	0.0015	0.0001	0.0003	0.0005	0.0012
41	0.0001	0.0003	0.0007	0.0014	0.0001	0.0002	0.0005	0.0010
42	0.0001	0.0003	0.0006	0.0013	0.0001	0.0002	0.0004	0.0009
43	0.0001	0.0003	0.0005	0.0011	0.0001	0.0002	0.0004	0.0008
44	0.0001	0.0002	0.0005	0.0010	0.0001	0.0002	0.0003	0.0007
45	0.0001	0.0002	0.0004	0.0009	0.0000	0.0001	0.0003	0.0007
46	0.0001	0.0002	0.0004	0.0008	0.0000	0.0001	0.0003	0.0006
47	0.0001	0.0002	0.0003	0.0007	0.0000	0.0001	0.0002	0.0005
48	0.0000	0.0001	0.0003	0.0007	0.0000	0.0001	0.0002	0.0005
49	0.0000	0.0001	0.0003	0.0006	0.0000	0.0001	0.0002	0.0004
50	0.0000	0.0001	0.0002	0.0005	0.0000	0.0001	0.0002	0.0004

How much must be invested at the *beginning* of each period to accumulate $1

End of Year	At 13% Interest compounded and Deposits made				At 14% Interest compounded and Deposits made			
	Monthly	Quarterly	Semi-Annually	Annually	Monthly	Quarterly	Semi-Annually	Annually
1	0.0776	0.2306	0.4547	0.8850	0.0772	0.2292	0.4515	0.8772
2	0.0363	0.1080	0.2131	0.4155	0.0359	0.1067	0.2105	0.4099
3	0.0226	0.0673	0.1329	0.2598	0.0223	0.0662	0.1307	0.2550
4	0.0158	0.0471	0.0932	0.1825	0.0155	0.0461	0.0911	0.1782
5	0.0118	0.0351	0.0696	0.1366	0.0115	0.0342	0.0676	0.1327
6	0.0091	0.0273	0.0541	0.1063	0.0088	0.0264	0.0522	0.1028
7	0.0073	0.0217	0.0431	0.0851	0.0070	0.0209	0.0414	0.0817
8	0.0059	0.0177	0.0351	0.0694	0.0056	0.0169	0.0335	0.0663
9	0.0049	0.0146	0.0290	0.0574	0.0046	0.0138	0.0275	0.0545
10	0.0041	0.0121	0.0242	0.0480	0.0038	0.0114	0.0228	0.0454
11	0.0034	0.0102	0.0204	0.0406	0.0032	0.0095	0.0191	0.0381
12	0.0029	0.0086	0.0173	0.0345	0.0027	0.0080	0.0161	0.0322
13	0.0025	0.0074	0.0147	0.0295	0.0023	0.0068	0.0136	0.0273
14	0.0021	0.0063	0.0126	0.0254	0.0019	0.0058	0.0116	0.0233
15	0.0018	0.0054	0.0109	0.0219	0.0016	0.0049	0.0099	0.0200
16	0.0015	0.0047	0.0094	0.0190	0.0014	0.0042	0.0085	0.0172
17	0.0013	0.0040	0.0081	0.0165	0.0012	0.0036	0.0073	0.0148
18	0.0012	0.0035	0.0071	0.0143	0.0010	0.0031	0.0063	0.0128
19	0.0010	0.0030	0.0061	0.0125	0.0009	0.0027	0.0054	0.0111
20	0.0009	0.0026	0.0053	0.0109	0.0008	0.0023	0.0047	0.0096
21	0.0008	0.0023	0.0047	0.0096	0.0007	0.0020	0.0041	0.0084
22	0.0007	0.0020	0.0041	0.0084	0.0006	0.0017	0.0035	0.0073
23	0.0006	0.0018	0.0036	0.0074	0.0005	0.0015	0.0030	0.0063
24	0.0005	0.0015	0.0031	0.0065	0.0004	0.0013	0.0026	0.0055
25	0.0004	0.0013	0.0027	0.0057	0.0004	0.0011	0.0023	0.0048
26	0.0004	0.0012	0.0024	0.0050	0.0003	0.0010	0.0020	0.0042
27	0.0003	0.0010	0.0021	0.0044	0.0003	0.0008	0.0017	0.0037
28	0.0003	0.0009	0.0018	0.0039	0.0002	0.0007	0.0015	0.0032
29	0.0003	0.0008	0.0016	0.0034	0.0002	0.0006	0.0013	0.0028
30	0.0002	0.0007	0.0014	0.0030	0.0002	0.0006	0.0011	0.0025
31	0.0002	0.0006	0.0013	0.0027	0.0002	0.0005	0.0010	0.0022
32	0.0002	0.0005	0.0011	0.0024	0.0001	0.0004	0.0009	0.0019
33	0.0002	0.0005	0.0010	0.0021	0.0001	0.0004	0.0008	0.0016
34	0.0001	0.0004	0.0009	0.0018	0.0001	0.0003	0.0007	0.0014
35	0.0001	0.0004	0.0008	0.0016	0.0001	0.0003	0.0006	0.0013
36	0.0001	0.0003	0.0007	0.0014	0.0001	0.0002	0.0005	0.0011
37	0.0001	0.0003	0.0006	0.0013	0.0001	0.0002	0.0004	0.0010
38	0.0001	0.0002	0.0005	0.0011	0.0001	0.0002	0.0004	0.0009
39	0.0001	0.0002	0.0005	0.0010	0.0001	0.0002	0.0003	0.0007
40	0.0001	0.0002	0.0004	0.0009	0.0000	0.0001	0.0003	0.0007
41	0.0001	0.0002	0.0004	0.0008	0.0000	0.0001	0.0003	0.0006
42	0.0000	0.0001	0.0003	0.0007	0.0000	0.0001	0.0002	0.0005
43	0.0000	0.0001	0.0003	0.0006	0.0000	0.0001	0.0002	0.0004
44	0.0000	0.0001	0.0002	0.0005	0.0000	0.0001	0.0002	0.0004
45	0.0000	0.0001	0.0002	0.0005	0.0000	0.0001	0.0001	0.0003
46	0.0000	0.0001	0.0002	0.0004	0.0000	0.0001	0.0001	0.0003
47	0.0000	0.0001	0.0002	0.0004	0.0000	0.0001	0.0001	0.0003
48	0.0000	0.0001	0.0001	0.0003	0.0000	0.0000	0.0001	0.0002
49	0.0000	0.0001	0.0001	0.0003	0.0000	0.0000	0.0001	0.0002
50	0.0000	0.0001	0.0001	0.0003	0.0000	0.0000	0.0001	0.0002

How much must be invested at the *beginning* of each period to accumulate $1

End of Year	At 15% Interest compounded and Deposits made Monthly	Quarterly	Semi-Annually	Annually	At 16% interest compounded and deposits made Monthly	Quarterly	Semi-Annually	Annually
1	0.0768	0.2278	0.4483	0.8696	0.0764	0.2264	0.4452	0.8621
2	0.0355	0.1055	0.2080	0.4044	0.0352	0.1044	0.2055	0.3991
3	0.0219	0.0651	0.1284	0.2504	0.0215	0.0640	0.1262	0.2459
4	0.0151	0.0451	0.0890	0.1741	0.0148	0.0441	0.0871	0.1702
5	0.0112	0.0332	0.0658	0.1290	0.0108	0.0323	0.0639	0.1254
6	0.0085	0.0255	0.0505	0.0993	0.0082	0.0246	0.0488	0.0960
7	0.0067	0.0200	0.0398	0.0786	0.0064	0.0192	0.0382	0.0755
8	0.0054	0.0161	0.0320	0.0633	0.0051	0.0153	0.0305	0.0605
9	0.0044	0.0131	0.0261	0.0518	0.0041	0.0124	0.0247	0.0492
10	0.0036	0.0108	0.0215	0.0428	0.0034	0.0101	0.0202	0.0404
11	0.0030	0.0089	0.0178	0.0357	0.0028	0.0083	0.0167	0.0335
12	0.0025	0.0074	0.0149	0.0300	0.0023	0.0069	0.0139	0.0279
13	0.0021	0.0063	0.0126	0.0253	0.0019	0.0058	0.0116	0.0234
14	0.0017	0.0053	0.0106	0.0215	0.0016	0.0048	0.0097	0.0197
15	0.0015	0.0045	0.0090	0.0183	0.0013	0.0040	0.0082	0.0167
16	0.0013	0.0038	0.0077	0.0156	0.0011	0.0034	0.0069	0.0141
17	0.0011	0.0032	0.0065	0.0134	0.0009	0.0029	0.0058	0.0120
18	0.0009	0.0027	0.0056	0.0115	0.0008	0.0024	0.0049	0.0102
19	0.0008	0.0023	0.0048	0.0099	0.0007	0.0021	0.0042	0.0087
20	0.0007	0.0020	0.0041	0.0085	0.0006	0.0017	0.0036	0.0075
21	0.0006	0.0017	0.0035	0.0073	0.0005	0.0015	0.0030	0.0064
22	0.0005	0.0015	0.0030	0.0063	0.0004	0.0013	0.0026	0.0055
23	0.0004	0.0013	0.0026	0.0055	0.0003	0.0011	0.0022	0.0047
24	0.0004	0.0011	0.0022	0.0047	0.0003	0.0009	0.0019	0.0040
25	0.0003	0.0009	0.0019	0.0041	0.0003	0.0008	0.0016	0.0035
26	0.0003	0.0008	0.0017	0.0035	0.0002	0.0007	0.0014	0.0030
27	0.0002	0.0007	0.0014	0.0031	0.0002	0.0006	0.0012	0.0026
28	0.0002	0.0006	0.0012	0.0027	0.0002	0.0005	0.0010	0.0022
29	0.0002	0.0005	0.0011	0.0023	0.0001	0.0004	0.0009	0.0019
30	0.0001	0.0004	0.0009	0.0020	0.0001	0.0004	0.0007	0.0016
31	0.0001	0.0004	0.0008	0.0017	0.0001	0.0003	0.0006	0.0014
32	0.0001	0.0003	0.0007	0.0015	0.0001	0.0003	0.0005	0.0012
33	0.0001	0.0003	0.0006	0.0013	0.0001	0.0002	0.0005	0.0010
34	0.0001	0.0002	0.0005	0.0011	0.0001	0.0002	0.0004	0.0009
35	0.0001	0.0002	0.0004	0.0010	0.0001	0.0002	0.0003	0.0008
36	0.0001	0.0002	0.0004	0.0009	0.0000	0.0001	0.0003	0.0007
37	0.0000	0.0002	0.0003	0.0007	0.0000	0.0001	0.0002	0.0006
38	0.0000	0.0001	0.0003	0.0006	0.0000	0.0001	0.0002	0.0005
39	0.0000	0.0001	0.0002	0.0006	0.0000	0.0001	0.0002	0.0004
40	0.0000	0.0001	0.0002	0.0005	0.0000	0.0001	0.0002	0.0004
41	0.0000	0.0001	0.0002	0.0004	0.0000	0.0001	0.0001	0.0003
42	0.0000	0.0001	0.0002	0.0004	0.0000	0.0001	0.0001	0.0003
43	0.0000	0.0001	0.0001	0.0003	0.0000	0.0000	0.0001	0.0002
44	0.0000	0.0001	0.0001	0.0003	0.0000	0.0000	0.0001	0.0002
45	0.0000	0.0000	0.0001	0.0002	0.0000	0.0000	0.0001	0.0002
46	0.0000	0.0000	0.0001	0.0002	0.0000	0.0000	0.0001	0.0001
47	0.0000	0.0000	0.0001	0.0002	0.0000	0.0000	0.0001	0.0001
48	0.0000	0.0000	0.0001	0.0002	0.0000	0.0000	0.0000	0.0001
49	0.0000	0.0000	0.0001	0.0001	0.0000	0.0000	0.0000	0.0001
50	0.0000	0.0000	0.0001	0.0001	0.0000	0.0000	0.0000	0.0001

How much must be invested at the *beginning* of each period to accumulate $1

End of Year	At 17% Interest compounded and Deposits made				At 18% Interest compounded and Deposits made			
	Monthly	Quarterly	Semi-Annually	Annually	Monthly	Quarterly	Semi-Annually	Annually
1	0.0760	0.2251	0.4420	0.8547	0.0755	0.2237	0.4390	0.8475
2	0.0348	0.1032	0.2030	0.3939	0.0344	0.1020	0.2006	0.3887
3	0.0212	0.0629	0.1241	0.2415	0.0208	0.0619	0.1219	0.2372
4	0.0145	0.0431	0.0851	0.1663	0.0142	0.0421	0.0832	0.1625
5	0.0105	0.0314	0.0621	0.1218	0.0102	0.0305	0.0604	0.1185
6	0.0080	0.0238	0.0471	0.0928	0.0077	0.0230	0.0456	0.0898
7	0.0062	0.0185	0.0367	0.0726	0.0059	0.0177	0.0353	0.0698
8	0.0049	0.0146	0.0291	0.0579	0.0047	0.0139	0.0278	0.0553
9	0.0039	0.0117	0.0234	0.0467	0.0037	0.0111	0.0222	0.0444
10	0.0032	0.0095	0.0191	0.0382	0.0030	0.0089	0.0179	0.0360
11	0.0026	0.0078	0.0156	0.0314	0.0024	0.0073	0.0146	0.0295
12	0.0021	0.0064	0.0129	0.0260	0.0020	0.0059	0.0119	0.0243
13	0.0018	0.0053	0.0107	0.0217	0.0016	0.0049	0.0098	0.0201
14	0.0015	0.0044	0.0089	0.0181	0.0013	0.0040	0.0081	0.0167
15	0.0012	0.0037	0.0074	0.0152	0.0011	0.0033	0.0067	0.0139
16	0.0010	0.0031	0.0062	0.0128	0.0009	0.0027	0.0056	0.0116
17	0.0008	0.0026	0.0052	0.0108	0.0007	0.0023	0.0047	0.0097
18	0.0007	0.0021	0.0044	0.0092	0.0006	0.0019	0.0039	0.0082
19	0.0006	0.0018	0.0037	0.0077	0.0005	0.0016	0.0032	0.0069
20	0.0005	0.0015	0.0031	0.0066	0.0004	0.0013	0.0027	0.0058
21	0.0004	0.0013	0.0026	0.0056	0.0004	0.0011	0.0023	0.0049
22	0.0003	0.0011	0.0022	0.0047	0.0003	0.0009	0.0019	0.0041
23	0.0003	0.0009	0.0019	0.0040	0.0002	0.0008	0.0016	0.0035
24	0.0002	0.0008	0.0016	0.0034	0.0002	0.0006	0.0013	0.0029
25	0.0002	0.0006	0.0013	0.0029	0.0002	0.0005	0.0011	0.0025
26	0.0002	0.0005	0.0011	0.0025	0.0001	0.0004	0.0009	0.0021
27	0.0001	0.0005	0.0010	0.0021	0.0001	0.0004	0.0008	0.0018
28	0.0001	0.0004	0.0008	0.0018	0.0001	0.0003	0.0007	0.0015
29	0.0001	0.0003	0.0007	0.0015	0.0001	0.0003	0.0006	0.0013
30	0.0001	0.0003	0.0006	0.0013	0.0001	0.0002	0.0005	0.0011
31	0.0001	0.0002	0.0005	0.0011	0.0001	0.0002	0.0004	0.0009
32	0.0001	0.0002	0.0004	0.0010	0.0000	0.0002	0.0003	0.0008
33	0.0001	0.0002	0.0004	0.0008	0.0000	0.0001	0.0003	0.0007
34	0.0000	0.0001	0.0003	0.0007	0.0000	0.0001	0.0002	0.0006
35	0.0000	0.0001	0.0003	0.0006	0.0000	0.0001	0.0002	0.0005
36	0.0000	0.0001	0.0002	0.0005	0.0000	0.0001	0.0002	0.0004
37	0.0000	0.0001	0.0002	0.0004	0.0000	0.0001	0.0001	0.0003
38	0.0000	0.0001	0.0002	0.0004	0.0000	0.0001	0.0001	0.0003
39	0.0000	0.0001	0.0001	0.0003	0.0000	0.0000	0.0001	0.0002
40	0.0000	0.0001	0.0001	0.0003	0.0000	0.0000	0.0001	0.0002
41	0.0000	0.0000	0.0001	0.0002	0.0000	0.0000	0.0001	0.0002
42	0.0000	0.0000	0.0001	0.0002	0.0000	0.0000	0.0001	0.0001
43	0.0000	0.0000	0.0001	0.0002	0.0000	0.0000	0.0000	0.0001
44	0.0000	0.0000	0.0001	0.0001	0.0000	0.0000	0.0000	0.0001
45	0.0000	0.0000	0.0001	0.0001	0.0000	0.0000	0.0000	0.0001
46	0.0000	0.0000	0.0000	0.0001	0.0000	0.0000	0.0000	0.0001
47	0.0000	0.0000	0.0000	0.0001	0.0000	0.0000	0.0000	0.0001
48	0.0000	0.0000	0.0000	0.0001	0.0000	0.0000	0.0000	0.0001
49	0.0000	0.0000	0.0000	0.0001	0.0000	0.0000	0.0000	0.0000
50	0.0000	0.0000	0.0000	0.0001	0.0000	0.0000	0.0000	0.0000

TABLE 11

Periodic payments at the *beginning* of each period required to amortize a loan of $1 over time

Applications

Chapters Nine and Seventeen

- What are the installment (lease) payments necessary to recover the cost of an investment over a specific period of time along with a desired return on investment?

Periodic payments at the *beginning* of each period required to amortize a loan of $1 over time

	At 5% Interest compounded and Payments made				At 6% Interest compounded and Payments made			
End of Year	Monthly	Quarterly	Semi-Annually	Annually	Monthly	Quarterly	Semi-Annually	Annually
1	0.0853	0.2547	0.5062	1.0000	0.0856	0.2556	0.5074	1.0000
2	0.0437	0.1305	0.2593	0.5122	0.0441	0.1316	0.2612	0.5146
3	0.0298	0.0891	0.1771	0.3497	0.0303	0.0903	0.1792	0.3529
4	0.0229	0.0685	0.1361	0.2686	0.0234	0.0697	0.1383	0.2723
5	0.0188	0.0561	0.1115	0.2200	0.0192	0.0574	0.1138	0.2240
6	0.0160	0.0479	0.0951	0.1876	0.0165	0.0492	0.0975	0.1919
7	0.0141	0.0420	0.0835	0.1646	0.0145	0.0434	0.0859	0.1690
8	0.0126	0.0376	0.0747	0.1474	0.0131	0.0390	0.0773	0.1519
9	0.0115	0.0342	0.0680	0.1340	0.0119	0.0356	0.0706	0.1387
10	0.0106	0.0315	0.0626	0.1233	0.0110	0.0329	0.0653	0.1282
11	0.0098	0.0293	0.0582	0.1147	0.0103	0.0307	0.0609	0.1196
12	0.0092	0.0275	0.0545	0.1075	0.0097	0.0289	0.0573	0.1125
13	0.0087	0.0259	0.0515	0.1014	0.0092	0.0274	0.0543	0.1066
14	0.0083	0.0246	0.0489	0.0962	0.0088	0.0261	0.0517	0.1015
15	0.0079	0.0235	0.0466	0.0918	0.0084	0.0250	0.0495	0.0971
16	0.0075	0.0225	0.0447	0.0879	0.0081	0.0241	0.0476	0.0934
17	0.0073	0.0216	0.0429	0.0845	0.0078	0.0232	0.0459	0.0900
18	0.0070	0.0209	0.0414	0.0815	0.0075	0.0225	0.0445	0.0871
19	0.0068	0.0202	0.0401	0.0788	0.0073	0.0218	0.0432	0.0845
20	0.0066	0.0196	0.0389	0.0764	0.0071	0.0212	0.0420	0.0822
21	0.0064	0.0191	0.0378	0.0743	0.0070	0.0207	0.0410	0.0802
22	0.0062	0.0186	0.0368	0.0724	0.0068	0.0202	0.0400	0.0783
23	0.0061	0.0181	0.0359	0.0706	0.0067	0.0198	0.0392	0.0767
24	0.0059	0.0177	0.0351	0.0690	0.0065	0.0194	0.0384	0.0752
25	0.0058	0.0174	0.0344	0.0676	0.0064	0.0191	0.0377	0.0738
26	0.0057	0.0170	0.0337	0.0663	0.0063	0.0188	0.0371	0.0726
27	0.0056	0.0167	0.0331	0.0650	0.0062	0.0185	0.0365	0.0714
28	0.0055	0.0164	0.0326	0.0639	0.0061	0.0182	0.0360	0.0704
29	0.0054	0.0162	0.0320	0.0629	0.0060	0.0180	0.0355	0.0694
30	0.0053	0.0159	0.0316	0.0620	0.0060	0.0178	0.0351	0.0685
31	0.0053	0.0157	0.0311	0.0611	0.0059	0.0175	0.0347	0.0677
32	0.0052	0.0155	0.0307	0.0603	0.0058	0.0174	0.0343	0.0670
33	0.0051	0.0153	0.0303	0.0595	0.0058	0.0172	0.0340	0.0663
34	0.0051	0.0151	0.0300	0.0588	0.0057	0.0170	0.0336	0.0657
35	0.0050	0.0150	0.0297	0.0582	0.0057	0.0169	0.0333	0.0651
36	0.0050	0.0148	0.0294	0.0576	0.0056	0.0167	0.0331	0.0645
37	0.0049	0.0147	0.0291	0.0570	0.0056	0.0166	0.0328	0.0640
38	0.0049	0.0145	0.0288	0.0565	0.0055	0.0165	0.0326	0.0635
39	0.0048	0.0144	0.0286	0.0560	0.0055	0.0164	0.0324	0.0631
40	0.0048	0.0143	0.0283	0.0555	0.0055	0.0163	0.0321	0.0627
41	0.0048	0.0142	0.0281	0.0551	0.0054	0.0162	0.0320	0.0623
42	0.0047	0.0141	0.0279	0.0547	0.0054	0.0161	0.0318	0.0620
43	0.0047	0.0140	0.0277	0.0543	0.0054	0.0160	0.0316	0.0616
44	0.0047	0.0139	0.0275	0.0539	0.0054	0.0159	0.0315	0.0613
45	0.0046	0.0138	0.0274	0.0536	0.0053	0.0159	0.0313	0.0610
46	0.0046	0.0137	0.0272	0.0533	0.0053	0.0158	0.0312	0.0608
47	0.0046	0.0137	0.0270	0.0530	0.0053	0.0157	0.0311	0.0605
48	0.0046	0.0136	0.0269	0.0527	0.0053	0.0157	0.0309	0.0603
49	0.0045	0.0135	0.0268	0.0524	0.0053	0.0156	0.0308	0.0601
50	0.0045	0.0135	0.0266	0.0522	0.0052	0.0156	0.0307	0.0599

Periodic payments at the *beginning* of each period required to amortize a loan of $1 over time

End of Year	At 7% Interest compounded and Payments made				At 8% Interest compounded and Payments made			
	Monthly	*Quarterly*	*Semi-Annually*	*Annually*	*Monthly*	*Quarterly*	*Semi-Annually*	*Annually*
1	0.0860	0.2565	0.5086	1.0000	0.0864	0.2575	0.5098	1.0000
2	0.0445	0.1327	0.2630	0.5169	0.0449	0.1338	0.2649	0.5192
3	0.0307	0.0915	0.1813	0.3561	0.0311	0.0927	0.1834	0.3593
4	0.0238	0.0710	0.1406	0.2759	0.0243	0.0722	0.1428	0.2796
5	0.0197	0.0587	0.1162	0.2279	0.0201	0.0600	0.1185	0.2319
6	0.0170	0.0505	0.1000	0.1961	0.0174	0.0518	0.1025	0.2003
7	0.0150	0.0447	0.0885	0.1734	0.0155	0.0461	0.0910	0.1778
8	0.0136	0.0404	0.0799	0.1565	0.0140	0.0418	0.0825	0.1611
9	0.0124	0.0370	0.0733	0.1434	0.0129	0.0385	0.0760	0.1482
10	0.0115	0.0344	0.0680	0.1331	0.0121	0.0358	0.0708	0.1380
11	0.0108	0.0322	0.0637	0.1246	0.0113	0.0337	0.0665	0.1297
12	0.0102	0.0304	0.0602	0.1177	0.0108	0.0320	0.0631	0.1229
13	0.0097	0.0289	0.0572	0.1118	0.0103	0.0305	0.0602	0.1171
14	0.0093	0.0277	0.0547	0.1069	0.0098	0.0293	0.0577	0.1123
15	0.0089	0.0266	0.0525	0.1026	0.0095	0.0282	0.0556	0.1082
16	0.0086	0.0256	0.0507	0.0989	0.0092	0.0273	0.0538	0.1046
17	0.0083	0.0248	0.0490	0.0957	0.0089	0.0265	0.0522	0.1015
18	0.0081	0.0241	0.0476	0.0929	0.0087	0.0258	0.0509	0.0988
19	0.0079	0.0235	0.0464	0.0904	0.0085	0.0252	0.0496	0.0964
20	0.0077	0.0229	0.0452	0.0882	0.0083	0.0247	0.0486	0.0943
21	0.0075	0.0224	0.0442	0.0863	0.0081	0.0242	0.0476	0.0924
22	0.0074	0.0220	0.0434	0.0845	0.0080	0.0238	0.0468	0.0908
23	0.0073	0.0216	0.0426	0.0829	0.0079	0.0234	0.0460	0.0893
24	0.0071	0.0212	0.0418	0.0815	0.0078	0.0231	0.0454	0.0879
25	0.0070	0.0209	0.0412	0.0802	0.0077	0.0227	0.0448	0.0867
26	0.0069	0.0206	0.0406	0.0790	0.0076	0.0225	0.0442	0.0857
27	0.0068	0.0203	0.0401	0.0780	0.0075	0.0222	0.0437	0.0847
28	0.0068	0.0201	0.0396	0.0770	0.0074	0.0220	0.0433	0.0838
29	0.0067	0.0199	0.0391	0.0761	0.0074	0.0218	0.0429	0.0830
30	0.0066	0.0196	0.0387	0.0753	0.0073	0.0216	0.0425	0.0822
31	0.0066	0.0195	0.0384	0.0746	0.0072	0.0214	0.0422	0.0816
32	0.0065	0.0193	0.0380	0.0739	0.0072	0.0213	0.0419	0.0810
33	0.0064	0.0191	0.0377	0.0733	0.0071	0.0212	0.0416	0.0804
34	0.0064	0.0190	0.0374	0.0727	0.0071	0.0210	0.0413	0.0799
35	0.0064	0.0189	0.0372	0.0722	0.0071	0.0209	0.0411	0.0794
36	0.0063	0.0187	0.0369	0.0717	0.0070	0.0208	0.0409	0.0790
37	0.0063	0.0186	0.0367	0.0712	0.0070	0.0207	0.0407	0.0786
38	0.0062	0.0185	0.0365	0.0708	0.0070	0.0206	0.0405	0.0783
39	0.0062	0.0184	0.0363	0.0705	0.0069	0.0205	0.0404	0.0779
40	0.0062	0.0183	0.0361	0.0701	0.0069	0.0205	0.0402	0.0776
41	0.0062	0.0183	0.0360	0.0698	0.0069	0.0204	0.0401	0.0774
42	0.0061	0.0182	0.0358	0.0695	0.0069	0.0203	0.0399	0.0771
43	0.0061	0.0181	0.0357	0.0692	0.0068	0.0203	0.0398	0.0769
44	0.0061	0.0181	0.0355	0.0689	0.0068	0.0202	0.0397	0.0767
45	0.0061	0.0180	0.0354	0.0687	0.0068	0.0202	0.0396	0.0765
46	0.0060	0.0179	0.0353	0.0685	0.0068	0.0201	0.0395	0.0763
47	0.0060	0.0179	0.0352	0.0683	0.0068	0.0201	0.0394	0.0761
48	0.0060	0.0178	0.0351	0.0681	0.0068	0.0201	0.0394	0.0760
49	0.0060	0.0178	0.0350	0.0679	0.0068	0.0200	0.0393	0.0758
50	0.0060	0.0178	0.0349	0.0677	0.0067	0.0200	0.0392	0.0757

Periodic payments at the *beginning* of each period required to amortize a loan of $1 over time

End of Year	At 9% Interest compounded and Payments made				At 10% Interest compounded and Payments made			
	Monthly	Quarterly	Semi-Annually	Annually	Monthly	Quarterly	Semi-Annually	Annually
1	0.0868	0.2584	0.5110	1.0000	0.0872	0.2593	0.5122	1.0000
2	0.0453	0.1349	0.2667	0.5215	0.0458	0.1361	0.2686	0.5238
3	0.0316	0.0939	0.1855	0.3624	0.0320	0.0951	0.1876	0.3656
4	0.0247	0.0735	0.1451	0.2832	0.0252	0.0747	0.1474	0.2868
5	0.0206	0.0613	0.1209	0.2359	0.0211	0.0626	0.1233	0.2398
6	0.0179	0.0532	0.1049	0.2045	0.0184	0.0545	0.1075	0.2087
7	0.0160	0.0475	0.0936	0.1823	0.0165	0.0489	0.0962	0.1867
8	0.0145	0.0432	0.0852	0.1658	0.0150	0.0447	0.0879	0.1704
9	0.0134	0.0399	0.0787	0.1530	0.0140	0.0414	0.0815	0.1579
10	0.0126	0.0373	0.0736	0.1430	0.0131	0.0389	0.0764	0.1480
11	0.0119	0.0352	0.0694	0.1348	0.0124	0.0368	0.0724	0.1400
12	0.0113	0.0335	0.0660	0.1281	0.0119	0.0351	0.0690	0.1334
13	0.0108	0.0321	0.0632	0.1225	0.0114	0.0337	0.0663	0.1280
14	0.0104	0.0309	0.0608	0.1178	0.0110	0.0326	0.0639	0.1234
15	0.0101	0.0299	0.0587	0.1138	0.0107	0.0316	0.0620	0.1195
16	0.0098	0.0290	0.0570	0.1104	0.0104	0.0307	0.0603	0.1162
17	0.0095	0.0282	0.0555	0.1074	0.0101	0.0300	0.0588	0.1133
18	0.0093	0.0276	0.0542	0.1048	0.0099	0.0294	0.0576	0.1108
19	0.0091	0.0270	0.0530	0.1025	0.0097	0.0288	0.0565	0.1087
20	0.0089	0.0265	0.0520	0.1005	0.0096	0.0283	0.0555	0.1068
21	0.0088	0.0260	0.0511	0.0987	0.0094	0.0279	0.0547	0.1051
22	0.0086	0.0256	0.0503	0.0972	0.0093	0.0275	0.0539	0.1036
23	0.0085	0.0253	0.0496	0.0958	0.0092	0.0272	0.0533	0.1023
24	0.0084	0.0250	0.0490	0.0945	0.0091	0.0269	0.0527	0.1012
25	0.0083	0.0247	0.0484	0.0934	0.0090	0.0266	0.0522	0.1002
26	0.0082	0.0244	0.0479	0.0924	0.0089	0.0264	0.0517	0.0992
27	0.0082	0.0242	0.0475	0.0915	0.0089	0.0262	0.0513	0.0984
28	0.0081	0.0240	0.0471	0.0907	0.0088	0.0260	0.0509	0.0977
29	0.0080	0.0238	0.0467	0.0900	0.0088	0.0259	0.0506	0.0970
30	0.0080	0.0236	0.0464	0.0893	0.0087	0.0257	0.0503	0.0964
31	0.0079	0.0235	0.0461	0.0887	0.0087	0.0256	0.0500	0.0959
32	0.0079	0.0234	0.0458	0.0882	0.0086	0.0255	0.0498	0.0954
33	0.0079	0.0232	0.0456	0.0877	0.0086	0.0254	0.0496	0.0950
34	0.0078	0.0231	0.0453	0.0872	0.0086	0.0253	0.0494	0.0946
35	0.0078	0.0230	0.0451	0.0868	0.0085	0.0252	0.0492	0.0943
36	0.0078	0.0229	0.0450	0.0865	0.0085	0.0251	0.0491	0.0939
37	0.0077	0.0229	0.0448	0.0861	0.0085	0.0250	0.0489	0.0937
38	0.0077	0.0228	0.0446	0.0858	0.0085	0.0250	0.0488	0.0934
39	0.0077	0.0227	0.0445	0.0855	0.0084	0.0249	0.0487	0.0932
40	0.0077	0.0226	0.0444	0.0853	0.0084	0.0249	0.0486	0.0930
41	0.0076	0.0226	0.0443	0.0851	0.0084	0.0248	0.0485	0.0928
42	0.0076	0.0225	0.0442	0.0848	0.0084	0.0248	0.0484	0.0926
43	0.0076	0.0225	0.0441	0.0846	0.0084	0.0247	0.0483	0.0924
44	0.0076	0.0225	0.0440	0.0845	0.0084	0.0247	0.0483	0.0923
45	0.0076	0.0224	0.0439	0.0843	0.0084	0.0247	0.0482	0.0922
46	0.0076	0.0224	0.0438	0.0842	0.0084	0.0247	0.0482	0.0921
47	0.0076	0.0223	0.0438	0.0840	0.0083	0.0246	0.0481	0.0920
48	0.0075	0.0223	0.0437	0.0839	0.0083	0.0246	0.0481	0.0919
49	0.0075	0.0223	0.0436	0.0838	0.0083	0.0246	0.0480	0.0918
50	0.0075	0.0223	0.0436	0.0837	0.0083	0.0246	0.0480	0.0917

Periodic payments at the *beginning* of each period required to amortize a loan of $1 over time

End of Year	At 11% Monthly	At 11% Quarterly	At 11% Semi-Annually	At 11% Annually	At 12% Monthly	At 12% Quarterly	At 12% Semi-Annually	At 12% Annually
1	0.0876	0.2603	0.5134	1.0000	0.0880	0.2612	0.5146	1.0000
2	0.0462	0.1372	0.2704	0.5261	0.0466	0.1383	0.2723	0.5283
3	0.0324	0.0963	0.1897	0.3687	0.0329	0.0975	0.1919	0.3717
4	0.0256	0.0760	0.1496	0.2904	0.0261	0.0773	0.1519	0.2940
5	0.0215	0.0639	0.1258	0.2438	0.0220	0.0653	0.1282	0.2477
6	0.0189	0.0559	0.1100	0.2130	0.0194	0.0573	0.1125	0.2172
7	0.0170	0.0503	0.0988	0.1912	0.0175	0.0517	0.1015	0.1956
8	0.0156	0.0461	0.0906	0.1751	0.0161	0.0476	0.0934	0.1797
9	0.0145	0.0429	0.0843	0.1627	0.0150	0.0445	0.0871	0.1676
10	0.0136	0.0404	0.0793	0.1530	0.0142	0.0420	0.0822	0.1580
11	0.0130	0.0384	0.0753	0.1452	0.0135	0.0400	0.0783	0.1504
12	0.0124	0.0368	0.0721	0.1388	0.0130	0.0384	0.0752	0.1441
13	0.0120	0.0354	0.0694	0.1335	0.0126	0.0371	0.0726	0.1390
14	0.0116	0.0343	0.0671	0.1290	0.0122	0.0360	0.0704	0.1347
15	0.0113	0.0333	0.0652	0.1253	0.0119	0.0351	0.0685	0.1311
16	0.0110	0.0325	0.0636	0.1221	0.0116	0.0343	0.0670	0.1280
17	0.0108	0.0318	0.0622	0.1193	0.0114	0.0336	0.0657	0.1254
18	0.0106	0.0312	0.0610	0.1170	0.0112	0.0331	0.0645	0.1232
19	0.0104	0.0307	0.0600	0.1149	0.0110	0.0326	0.0635	0.1212
20	0.0102	0.0302	0.0591	0.1131	0.0109	0.0321	0.0627	0.1195
21	0.0101	0.0298	0.0583	0.1116	0.0108	0.0318	0.0620	0.1181
22	0.0100	0.0295	0.0576	0.1102	0.0107	0.0315	0.0613	0.1168
23	0.0099	0.0292	0.0570	0.1090	0.0106	0.0312	0.0608	0.1157
24	0.0098	0.0289	0.0565	0.1079	0.0105	0.0309	0.0603	0.1147
25	0.0097	0.0287	0.0560	0.1070	0.0104	0.0307	0.0599	0.1138
26	0.0096	0.0285	0.0556	0.1061	0.0104	0.0305	0.0595	0.1131
27	0.0096	0.0283	0.0552	0.1054	0.0103	0.0304	0.0591	0.1124
28	0.0095	0.0281	0.0549	0.1047	0.0103	0.0302	0.0589	0.1118
29	0.0095	0.0280	0.0546	0.1041	0.0102	0.0301	0.0586	0.1113
30	0.0094	0.0278	0.0543	0.1036	0.0102	0.0300	0.0584	0.1108
31	0.0094	0.0277	0.0541	0.1032	0.0102	0.0299	0.0582	0.1104
32	0.0094	0.0276	0.0539	0.1027	0.0101	0.0298	0.0580	0.1101
33	0.0093	0.0275	0.0537	0.1024	0.0101	0.0297	0.0578	0.1098
34	0.0093	0.0274	0.0535	0.1020	0.0101	0.0297	0.0577	0.1095
35	0.0093	0.0274	0.0534	0.1017	0.0101	0.0296	0.0576	0.1092
36	0.0093	0.0273	0.0533	0.1015	0.0100	0.0295	0.0575	0.1090
37	0.0092	0.0273	0.0531	0.1012	0.0100	0.0295	0.0574	0.1088
38	0.0092	0.0272	0.0530	0.1010	0.0100	0.0295	0.0573	0.1086
39	0.0092	0.0272	0.0529	0.1008	0.0100	0.0294	0.0572	0.1084
40	0.0092	0.0271	0.0529	0.1006	0.0100	0.0294	0.0571	0.1083
41	0.0092	0.0271	0.0528	0.1005	0.0100	0.0294	0.0571	0.1082
42	0.0092	0.0270	0.0527	0.1004	0.0100	0.0293	0.0570	0.1081
43	0.0092	0.0270	0.0527	0.1002	0.0100	0.0293	0.0570	0.1080
44	0.0092	0.0270	0.0526	0.1001	0.0100	0.0293	0.0569	0.1079
45	0.0091	0.0270	0.0526	0.1000	0.0099	0.0293	0.0569	0.1078
46	0.0091	0.0269	0.0525	0.0999	0.0099	0.0293	0.0569	0.1077
47	0.0091	0.0269	0.0525	0.0998	0.0099	0.0292	0.0568	0.1077
48	0.0091	0.0269	0.0524	0.0998	0.0099	0.0292	0.0568	0.1076
49	0.0091	0.0269	0.0524	0.0997	0.0099	0.0292	0.0568	0.1076
50	0.0091	0.0269	0.0524	0.0996	0.0099	0.0292	0.0568	0.1075

Column groups: At 11% Interest compounded and Payments made; At 12% Interest compounded and Payments made

Periodic payments at the *beginning* of each period required to amortize a loan of $1 over time

End of Year	At 13% Interest compounded and Payments made: Monthly	Quarterly	Semi-Annually	Annually	At 14% Interest compounded and Payments made: Monthly	Quarterly	Semi-Annually	Annually
1	0.0884	0.2621	0.5157	1.0000	0.0888	0.2630	0.5169	1.0000
2	0.0470	0.1394	0.2741	0.5305	0.0475	0.1406	0.2759	0.5327
3	0.0333	0.0988	0.1940	0.3748	0.0338	0.1000	0.1961	0.3778
4	0.0265	0.0786	0.1542	0.2975	0.0270	0.0799	0.1565	0.3011
5	0.0225	0.0666	0.1306	0.2516	0.0230	0.0680	0.1331	0.2555
6	0.0199	0.0587	0.1151	0.2214	0.0204	0.0602	0.1177	0.2256
7	0.0180	0.0532	0.1042	0.2001	0.0185	0.0547	0.1069	0.2046
8	0.0166	0.0491	0.0961	0.1844	0.0172	0.0507	0.0989	0.1891
9	0.0156	0.0460	0.0900	0.1725	0.0161	0.0476	0.0929	0.1773
10	0.0148	0.0436	0.0852	0.1631	0.0153	0.0452	0.0882	0.1682
11	0.0141	0.0417	0.0814	0.1556	0.0147	0.0434	0.0845	0.1609
12	0.0136	0.0401	0.0783	0.1495	0.0142	0.0418	0.0815	0.1550
13	0.0132	0.0388	0.0758	0.1446	0.0138	0.0406	0.0790	0.1501
14	0.0128	0.0378	0.0737	0.1404	0.0134	0.0396	0.0770	0.1461
15	0.0125	0.0369	0.0719	0.1369	0.0132	0.0387	0.0753	0.1428
16	0.0123	0.0361	0.0704	0.1340	0.0129	0.0380	0.0739	0.1400
17	0.0121	0.0355	0.0692	0.1315	0.0127	0.0374	0.0727	0.1376
18	0.0119	0.0350	0.0681	0.1294	0.0126	0.0369	0.0717	0.1356
19	0.0117	0.0345	0.0672	0.1276	0.0124	0.0365	0.0708	0.1339
20	0.0116	0.0341	0.0664	0.1260	0.0123	0.0361	0.0701	0.1324
21	0.0115	0.0338	0.0657	0.1246	0.0122	0.0358	0.0695	0.1312
22	0.0114	0.0335	0.0651	0.1234	0.0121	0.0355	0.0689	0.1301
23	0.0113	0.0332	0.0646	0.1224	0.0120	0.0353	0.0685	0.1291
24	0.0112	0.0330	0.0642	0.1215	0.0120	0.0351	0.0681	0.1283
25	0.0112	0.0328	0.0638	0.1207	0.0119	0.0349	0.0677	0.1276
26	0.0111	0.0327	0.0634	0.1200	0.0118	0.0348	0.0674	0.1270
27	0.0111	0.0325	0.0631	0.1195	0.0118	0.0347	0.0672	0.1265
28	0.0110	0.0324	0.0629	0.1189	0.0118	0.0345	0.0669	0.1260
29	0.0110	0.0323	0.0627	0.1185	0.0117	0.0345	0.0667	0.1256
30	0.0109	0.0322	0.0625	0.1181	0.0117	0.0344	0.0666	0.1253
31	0.0109	0.0321	0.0623	0.1177	0.0117	0.0343	0.0664	0.1250
32	0.0109	0.0320	0.0621	0.1174	0.0117	0.0342	0.0663	0.1247
33	0.0109	0.0319	0.0620	0.1171	0.0117	0.0342	0.0662	0.1245
34	0.0109	0.0319	0.0619	0.1169	0.0116	0.0341	0.0661	0.1243
35	0.0108	0.0318	0.0618	0.1167	0.0116	0.0341	0.0660	0.1241
36	0.0108	0.0318	0.0617	0.1165	0.0116	0.0341	0.0659	0.1239
37	0.0108	0.0318	0.0616	0.1163	0.0116	0.0340	0.0659	0.1238
38	0.0108	0.0317	0.0615	0.1162	0.0116	0.0340	0.0658	0.1237
39	0.0108	0.0317	0.0615	0.1160	0.0116	0.0340	0.0658	0.1236
40	0.0108	0.0317	0.0614	0.1159	0.0116	0.0340	0.0657	0.1235
41	0.0108	0.0316	0.0614	0.1158	0.0116	0.0339	0.0657	0.1234
42	0.0108	0.0316	0.0613	0.1157	0.0116	0.0339	0.0656	0.1233
43	0.0108	0.0316	0.0613	0.1156	0.0116	0.0339	0.0656	0.1232
44	0.0108	0.0316	0.0613	0.1156	0.0116	0.0339	0.0656	0.1232
45	0.0107	0.0316	0.0612	0.1155	0.0116	0.0339	0.0656	0.1231
46	0.0107	0.0316	0.0612	0.1155	0.0116	0.0339	0.0656	0.1231
47	0.0107	0.0316	0.0612	0.1154	0.0115	0.0339	0.0655	0.1231
48	0.0107	0.0315	0.0612	0.1154	0.0115	0.0339	0.0655	0.1230
49	0.0107	0.0315	0.0612	0.1153	0.0115	0.0339	0.0655	0.1230
50	0.0107	0.0315	0.0611	0.1153	0.0115	0.0339	0.0655	0.1230

Periodic payments at the *beginning* of each period required to amortize a loan of $1 over time

End of Year	At 15% Interest compounded and Payments made: Monthly	Quarterly	Semi-Annually	Annually	At 16% Interest compounded and Payments made: Monthly	Quarterly	Semi-Annually	Annually
1	0.0891	0.2640	0.5181	1.0000	0.0895	0.2649	0.5192	1.0000
2	0.0479	0.1417	0.2777	0.5349	0.0483	0.1428	0.2796	0.5370
3	0.0342	0.1012	0.1982	0.3808	0.0347	0.1025	0.2003	0.3838
4	0.0275	0.0812	0.1588	0.3046	0.0280	0.0825	0.1611	0.3081
5	0.0235	0.0694	0.1355	0.2594	0.0240	0.0708	0.1380	0.2633
6	0.0209	0.0616	0.1203	0.2298	0.0214	0.0631	0.1229	0.2340
7	0.0191	0.0562	0.1096	0.2090	0.0196	0.0577	0.1123	0.2135
8	0.0177	0.0522	0.1018	0.1938	0.0183	0.0538	0.1046	0.1985
9	0.0167	0.0492	0.0958	0.1822	0.0173	0.0509	0.0988	0.1871
10	0.0159	0.0469	0.0912	0.1733	0.0165	0.0486	0.0943	0.1784
11	0.0153	0.0451	0.0876	0.1661	0.0159	0.0468	0.0908	0.1714
12	0.0148	0.0436	0.0847	0.1604	0.0155	0.0454	0.0879	0.1659
13	0.0144	0.0424	0.0823	0.1557	0.0151	0.0442	0.0857	0.1614
14	0.0141	0.0414	0.0804	0.1519	0.0148	0.0433	0.0838	0.1577
15	0.0138	0.0406	0.0788	0.1487	0.0145	0.0425	0.0822	0.1546
16	0.0136	0.0399	0.0774	0.1460	0.0143	0.0419	0.0810	0.1521
17	0.0134	0.0394	0.0763	0.1438	0.0141	0.0413	0.0799	0.1500
18	0.0133	0.0389	0.0753	0.1419	0.0140	0.0409	0.0790	0.1482
19	0.0131	0.0385	0.0745	0.1403	0.0138	0.0405	0.0783	0.1467
20	0.0130	0.0382	0.0739	0.1389	0.0137	0.0402	0.0776	0.1454
21	0.0129	0.0379	0.0733	0.1378	0.0136	0.0399	0.0771	0.1443
22	0.0128	0.0376	0.0728	0.1368	0.0136	0.0397	0.0767	0.1434
23	0.0128	0.0374	0.0724	0.1359	0.0135	0.0395	0.0763	0.1426
24	0.0127	0.0372	0.0720	0.1352	0.0135	0.0394	0.0760	0.1420
25	0.0127	0.0371	0.0717	0.1345	0.0134	0.0392	0.0757	0.1414
26	0.0126	0.0369	0.0714	0.1340	0.0134	0.0391	0.0755	0.1409
27	0.0126	0.0368	0.0712	0.1335	0.0133	0.0390	0.0753	0.1405
28	0.0125	0.0367	0.0710	0.1331	0.0133	0.0389	0.0751	0.1401
29	0.0125	0.0367	0.0708	0.1327	0.0133	0.0389	0.0749	0.1398
30	0.0125	0.0366	0.0707	0.1324	0.0133	0.0388	0.0748	0.1396
31	0.0125	0.0365	0.0706	0.1322	0.0133	0.0388	0.0747	0.1393
32	0.0125	0.0365	0.0705	0.1319	0.0132	0.0387	0.0746	0.1391
33	0.0124	0.0364	0.0704	0.1317	0.0132	0.0387	0.0745	0.1390
34	0.0124	0.0364	0.0703	0.1316	0.0132	0.0386	0.0745	0.1388
35	0.0124	0.0364	0.0702	0.1314	0.0132	0.0386	0.0744	0.1387
36	0.0124	0.0363	0.0702	0.1313	0.0132	0.0386	0.0744	0.1386
37	0.0124	0.0363	0.0701	0.1312	0.0132	0.0386	0.0743	0.1385
38	0.0124	0.0363	0.0701	0.1311	0.0132	0.0386	0.0743	0.1384
39	0.0124	0.0363	0.0700	0.1310	0.0132	0.0385	0.0743	0.1384
40	0.0124	0.0362	0.0700	0.1309	0.0132	0.0385	0.0742	0.1383
41	0.0124	0.0362	0.0700	0.1309	0.0132	0.0385	0.0742	0.1382
42	0.0124	0.0362	0.0699	0.1308	0.0132	0.0385	0.0742	0.1382
43	0.0124	0.0362	0.0699	0.1308	0.0132	0.0385	0.0742	0.1382
44	0.0124	0.0362	0.0699	0.1307	0.0132	0.0385	0.0742	0.1381
45	0.0124	0.0362	0.0699	0.1307	0.0132	0.0385	0.0741	0.1381
46	0.0124	0.0362	0.0699	0.1306	0.0132	0.0385	0.0741	0.1381
47	0.0124	0.0362	0.0698	0.1306	0.0132	0.0385	0.0741	0.1381
48	0.0124	0.0362	0.0698	0.1306	0.0132	0.0385	0.0741	0.1380
49	0.0124	0.0362	0.0698	0.1306	0.0132	0.0385	0.0741	0.1380
50	0.0124	0.0362	0.0698	0.1306	0.0132	0.0385	0.0741	0.1380

Periodic payments at the *beginning* of each period required to amortize a loan of $1 over time

End of Year	At 17% Interest compounded and Payments made				At 18% Interest compounded and Payments made			
	Monthly	*Quarterly*	*Semi-Annually*	*Annually*	*Monthly*	*Quarterly*	*Semi-Annually*	*Annually*
1	0.0899	0.2658	0.5204	1.0000	0.0903	0.2667	0.5215	1.0000
2	0.0488	0.1439	0.2814	0.5392	0.0492	0.1451	0.2832	0.5413
3	0.0352	0.1037	0.2024	0.3868	0.0356	0.1049	0.2045	0.3898
4	0.0285	0.0838	0.1634	0.3116	0.0289	0.0852	0.1658	0.3150
5	0.0245	0.0722	0.1405	0.2671	0.0250	0.0736	0.1430	0.2710
6	0.0219	0.0645	0.1255	0.2381	0.0225	0.0660	0.1281	0.2423
7	0.0202	0.0592	0.1151	0.2179	0.0207	0.0608	0.1178	0.2223
8	0.0189	0.0554	0.1075	0.2032	0.0194	0.0570	0.1104	0.2078
9	0.0179	0.0525	0.1018	0.1920	0.0185	0.0542	0.1048	0.1969
10	0.0171	0.0503	0.0974	0.1835	0.0178	0.0520	0.1005	0.1886
11	0.0166	0.0485	0.0940	0.1767	0.0172	0.0503	0.0972	0.1820
12	0.0161	0.0472	0.0912	0.1713	0.0167	0.0490	0.0945	0.1768
13	0.0157	0.0461	0.0890	0.1670	0.0164	0.0479	0.0924	0.1726
14	0.0154	0.0452	0.0872	0.1634	0.0161	0.0471	0.0907	0.1692
15	0.0152	0.0444	0.0858	0.1605	0.0159	0.0464	0.0893	0.1664
16	0.0150	0.0438	0.0846	0.1581	0.0157	0.0458	0.0882	0.1642
17	0.0148	0.0433	0.0836	0.1561	0.0155	0.0453	0.0872	0.1623
18	0.0147	0.0429	0.0827	0.1544	0.0154	0.0450	0.0865	0.1607
19	0.0146	0.0426	0.0820	0.1530	0.0153	0.0446	0.0858	0.1594
20	0.0145	0.0423	0.0815	0.1519	0.0152	0.0444	0.0853	0.1583
21	0.0144	0.0420	0.0810	0.1509	0.0151	0.0442	0.0848	0.1574
22	0.0143	0.0418	0.0806	0.1500	0.0151	0.0440	0.0845	0.1566
23	0.0143	0.0417	0.0802	0.1493	0.0150	0.0438	0.0842	0.1560
24	0.0142	0.0415	0.0799	0.1487	0.0150	0.0437	0.0839	0.1555
25	0.0142	0.0414	0.0797	0.1482	0.0150	0.0436	0.0837	0.1550
26	0.0141	0.0413	0.0795	0.1478	0.0149	0.0435	0.0835	0.1546
27	0.0141	0.0412	0.0793	0.1474	0.0149	0.0434	0.0834	0.1543
28	0.0141	0.0412	0.0792	0.1471	0.0149	0.0434	0.0832	0.1540
29	0.0141	0.0411	0.0790	0.1468	0.0149	0.0433	0.0831	0.1538
30	0.0141	0.0410	0.0789	0.1466	0.0148	0.0433	0.0830	0.1536
31	0.0140	0.0410	0.0788	0.1464	0.0148	0.0432	0.0830	0.1534
32	0.0140	0.0410	0.0788	0.1463	0.0148	0.0432	0.0829	0.1533
33	0.0140	0.0409	0.0787	0.1461	0.0148	0.0432	0.0828	0.1532
34	0.0140	0.0409	0.0786	0.1460	0.0148	0.0432	0.0828	0.1531
35	0.0140	0.0409	0.0786	0.1459	0.0148	0.0432	0.0828	0.1530
36	0.0140	0.0409	0.0786	0.1458	0.0148	0.0431	0.0827	0.1529
37	0.0140	0.0409	0.0785	0.1457	0.0148	0.0431	0.0827	0.1529
38	0.0140	0.0408	0.0785	0.1457	0.0148	0.0431	0.0827	0.1528
39	0.0140	0.0408	0.0785	0.1456	0.0148	0.0431	0.0827	0.1528
40	0.0140	0.0408	0.0785	0.1456	0.0148	0.0431	0.0827	0.1527
41	0.0140	0.0408	0.0784	0.1455	0.0148	0.0431	0.0826	0.1527
42	0.0140	0.0408	0.0784	0.1455	0.0148	0.0431	0.0826	0.1527
43	0.0140	0.0408	0.0784	0.1455	0.0148	0.0431	0.0826	0.1527
44	0.0140	0.0408	0.0784	0.1454	0.0148	0.0431	0.0826	0.1526
45	0.0140	0.0408	0.0784	0.1454	0.0148	0.0431	0.0826	0.1526
46	0.0140	0.0408	0.0784	0.1454	0.0148	0.0431	0.0826	0.1526
47	0.0140	0.0408	0.0784	0.1454	0.0148	0.0431	0.0826	0.1526
48	0.0140	0.0408	0.0784	0.1454	0.0148	0.0431	0.0826	0.1526
49	0.0140	0.0408	0.0784	0.1454	0.0148	0.0431	0.0826	0.1526
50	0.0140	0.0408	0.0784	0.1454	0.0148	0.0431	0.0826	0.1526

Periodic payments at the *beginning* of each period required to amortize a loan of $1 over time

End of Year	At 19% Interest compounded and Payments made				At 20% Interest compounded and Payments made			
	Monthly	*Quarterly*	*Semi-Annually*	*Annually*	*Monthly*	*Quarterly*	*Semi-Annually*	*Annually*
1	0.0907	0.2677	0.5227	1.0000	0.0911	0.2686	0.5238	1.0000
2	0.0496	0.1462	0.2850	0.5434	0.0501	0.1474	0.2868	0.5455
3	0.0361	0.1062	0.2066	0.3927	0.0366	0.1075	0.2087	0.3956
4	0.0294	0.0865	0.1681	0.3185	0.0299	0.0879	0.1704	0.3219
5	0.0255	0.0750	0.1454	0.2748	0.0261	0.0764	0.1480	0.2786
6	0.0230	0.0675	0.1308	0.2464	0.0236	0.0690	0.1334	0.2506
7	0.0213	0.0623	0.1206	0.2268	0.0218	0.0639	0.1234	0.2312
8	0.0200	0.0586	0.1133	0.2125	0.0206	0.0603	0.1162	0.2172
9	0.0191	0.0559	0.1078	0.2018	0.0197	0.0576	0.1108	0.2067
10	0.0184	0.0537	0.1036	0.1937	0.0190	0.0555	0.1068	0.1988
11	0.0178	0.0521	0.1004	0.1873	0.0185	0.0539	0.1036	0.1926
12	0.0174	0.0508	0.0978	0.1823	0.0181	0.0527	0.1012	0.1877
13	0.0171	0.0498	0.0958	0.1782	0.0177	0.0517	0.0992	0.1839
14	0.0168	0.0490	0.0942	0.1750	0.0175	0.0509	0.0977	0.1807
15	0.0166	0.0483	0.0929	0.1723	0.0173	0.0503	0.0964	0.1782
16	0.0164	0.0478	0.0918	0.1702	0.0171	0.0498	0.0954	0.1762
17	0.0162	0.0474	0.0909	0.1684	0.0170	0.0494	0.0946	0.1745
18	0.0161	0.0470	0.0902	0.1670	0.0169	0.0491	0.0939	0.1732
19	0.0160	0.0467	0.0896	0.1657	0.0168	0.0488	0.0934	0.1721
20	0.0160	0.0465	0.0891	0.1647	0.0167	0.0486	0.0930	0.1711
21	0.0159	0.0463	0.0887	0.1639	0.0167	0.0484	0.0926	0.1704
22	0.0158	0.0461	0.0884	0.1632	0.0166	0.0483	0.0923	0.1697
23	0.0158	0.0460	0.0881	0.1626	0.0166	0.0482	0.0921	0.1692
24	0.0158	0.0459	0.0879	0.1622	0.0165	0.0481	0.0919	0.1688
25	0.0157	0.0458	0.0877	0.1618	0.0165	0.0480	0.0917	0.1684
26	0.0157	0.0457	0.0875	0.1614	0.0165	0.0479	0.0916	0.1681
27	0.0157	0.0457	0.0874	0.1611	0.0165	0.0479	0.0914	0.1679
28	0.0157	0.0456	0.0873	0.1609	0.0165	0.0478	0.0913	0.1677
29	0.0157	0.0456	0.0872	0.1607	0.0164	0.0478	0.0913	0.1675
30	0.0156	0.0455	0.0871	0.1605	0.0164	0.0478	0.0912	0.1674
31	0.0156	0.0455	0.0871	0.1604	0.0164	0.0477	0.0912	0.1673
32	0.0156	0.0455	0.0870	0.1603	0.0164	0.0477	0.0911	0.1672
33	0.0156	0.0454	0.0870	0.1602	0.0164	0.0477	0.0911	0.1671
34	0.0156	0.0454	0.0869	0.1601	0.0164	0.0477	0.0910	0.1670
35	0.0156	0.0454	0.0869	0.1600	0.0164	0.0477	0.0910	0.1669
36	0.0156	0.0454	0.0869	0.1600	0.0164	0.0477	0.0910	0.1669
37	0.0156	0.0454	0.0869	0.1599	0.0164	0.0477	0.0910	0.1669
38	0.0156	0.0454	0.0868	0.1599	0.0164	0.0476	0.0910	0.1668
39	0.0156	0.0454	0.0868	0.1598	0.0164	0.0476	0.0910	0.1668
40	0.0156	0.0454	0.0868	0.1598	0.0164	0.0476	0.0910	0.1668
41	0.0156	0.0454	0.0868	0.1598	0.0164	0.0476	0.0909	0.1668
42	0.0156	0.0454	0.0868	0.1598	0.0164	0.0476	0.0909	0.1667
43	0.0156	0.0454	0.0868	0.1598	0.0164	0.0476	0.0909	0.1667
44	0.0156	0.0454	0.0868	0.1597	0.0164	0.0476	0.0909	0.1667
45	0.0156	0.0454	0.0868	0.1597	0.0164	0.0476	0.0909	0.1667
46	0.0156	0.0454	0.0868	0.1597	0.0164	0.0476	0.0909	0.1667
47	0.0156	0.0454	0.0868	0.1597	0.0164	0.0476	0.0909	0.1667
48	0.0156	0.0454	0.0868	0.1597	0.0164	0.0476	0.0909	0.1667
49	0.0156	0.0454	0.0868	0.1597	0.0164	0.0476	0.0909	0.1667
50	0.0156	0.0454	0.0868	0.1597	0.0164	0.0476	0.0909	0.1667

TABLE 12

The present value of $1 per period payable at the *beginning* of each period (a $1 "annuity due")

What is $1 payable at the beginning of each period worth today at various interest rates?

How much must be invested today to be able to draw $1 at the beginning of each period for a given number of periods?

Applications

Chapter Nine

- What is the value today of the right to receive periodic payments at the beginning of various time periods?

Chapter Sixteen

- What is the present value of a series of insurance premiums?

Chapter Seventeen

- What is the present value of a series of lease payments?

The present value of a $1 annuity due at the *beginning* of each period

End of Year	At 3% Interest compounded Monthly	Quarterly	Semi-Annually	Annually	At 4% Interest compounded Monthly	Quarterly	Semi-Annually	Annually
1	11.837	3.956	1.985	1.000	11.783	3.941	1.980	1.000
2	23.324	7.795	3.912	1.971	23.105	7.728	3.884	1.962
3	34.472	11.521	5.783	2.913	33.984	11.368	5.713	2.886
4	45.292	15.137	7.598	3.829	44.436	14.865	7.472	3.775
5	55.791	18.647	9.361	4.717	54.480	18.226	9.162	4.630
6	65.981	22.053	11.071	5.580	64.130	21.456	10.787	5.452
7	75.871	25.359	12.732	6.417	73.403	24.560	12.348	6.242
8	85.468	28.568	14.343	7.230	82.313	27.542	13.849	7.002
9	94.782	31.683	15.908	8.020	90.874	30.409	15.292	7.733
10	103.821	34.705	17.426	8.786	99.099	33.163	16.678	8.435
11	112.593	37.639	18.900	9.530	107.003	35.810	18.011	9.111
12	121.106	40.486	20.331	10.253	114.597	38.354	19.292	9.760
13	129.368	43.250	21.720	10.954	121.895	40.798	20.523	10.385
14	137.386	45.932	23.068	11.635	128.906	43.147	21.707	10.986
15	145.167	48.535	24.376	12.296	135.643	45.405	22.844	11.563
16	152.719	51.061	25.646	12.938	142.116	47.574	23.938	12.118
17	160.048	53.513	26.879	13.561	148.336	49.659	24.989	12.652
18	167.160	55.893	28.076	14.166	154.312	51.662	25.999	13.166
19	174.063	58.203	29.237	14.754	160.054	53.587	26.969	13.659
20	180.762	60.444	30.365	15.324	165.572	55.437	27.903	14.134
21	187.263	62.620	31.459	15.877	170.873	57.215	28.799	14.590
22	193.572	64.732	32.521	16.415	175.968	58.923	29.662	15.029
23	199.695	66.781	33.552	16.937	180.862	60.565	30.490	15.451
24	205.637	68.770	34.553	17.444	185.565	62.143	31.287	15.857
25	211.404	70.701	35.525	17.936	190.084	63.659	32.052	16.247
26	217.000	72.575	36.468	18.413	194.426	65.116	32.788	16.622
27	222.432	74.393	37.383	18.877	198.598	66.516	33.495	16.983
28	227.703	76.158	38.271	19.327	202.607	67.862	34.175	17.330
29	232.818	77.871	39.134	19.764	206.458	69.155	34.828	17.663
30	237.782	79.534	39.971	20.188	210.159	70.398	35.456	17.984
31	242.600	81.147	40.784	20.600	213.716	71.592	36.060	18.292
32	247.276	82.713	41.572	21.000	217.132	72.739	36.640	18.588
33	251.814	84.233	42.338	21.389	220.416	73.842	37.197	18.874
34	256.217	85.709	43.081	21.766	223.570	74.902	37.733	19.148
35	260.491	87.140	43.802	22.132	226.601	75.920	38.249	19.411
36	264.639	88.530	44.502	22.487	229.514	76.899	38.744	19.665
37	268.664	89.879	45.182	22.832	232.312	77.839	39.220	19.908
38	272.570	91.188	45.842	23.167	235.001	78.743	39.677	20.143
39	276.361	92.458	46.482	23.492	237.585	79.611	40.117	20.368
40	280.040	93.691	47.103	23.808	240.067	80.446	40.539	20.584
41	283.611	94.888	47.707	24.115	242.453	81.248	40.946	20.793
42	287.076	96.050	48.292	24.412	244.744	82.018	41.336	20.993
43	290.439	97.177	48.861	24.701	246.947	82.759	41.711	21.186
44	293.702	98.271	49.412	24.982	249.063	83.471	42.072	21.371
45	296.869	99.333	49.948	25.254	251.096	84.155	42.419	21.549
46	299.943	100.363	50.468	25.519	253.049	84.812	42.752	21.720
47	302.926	101.364	50.972	25.775	254.927	85.444	43.072	21.885
48	305.821	102.335	51.462	26.025	256.730	86.051	43.380	22.043
49	308.631	103.277	51.938	26.267	258.463	86.634	43.676	22.195
50	311.357	104.191	52.399	26.502	260.128	87.195	43.960	22.341

The present value of a $1 annuity due at the *beginning* of each period

	At 5% Interest compounded				*At 6% Interest compounded*			
End of Year	*Monthly*	*Quarterly*	*Semi-Annually*	*Annually*	*Monthly*	*Quarterly*	*Semi-Annually*	*Annually*
1	11.730	3.927	1.976	1.000	11.677	3.912	1.971	1.000
2	22.889	7.663	3.856	1.952	22.676	7.598	3.829	1.943
3	33.505	11.218	5.646	2.859	33.035	11.071	5.580	2.833
4	43.604	14.601	7.349	3.723	42.793	14.343	7.230	3.673
5	53.212	17.819	8.971	4.546	51.984	17.426	8.786	4.465
6	62.351	20.882	10.514	5.329	60.641	20.331	10.253	5.212
7	71.047	23.796	11.983	6.076	68.795	23.068	11.635	5.917
8	79.319	26.569	13.381	6.786	76.476	25.646	12.938	6.582
9	87.188	29.208	14.712	7.463	83.710	28.076	14.166	7.210
10	94.674	31.719	15.979	8.108	90.524	30.365	15.324	7.802
11	101.796	34.107	17.185	8.722	96.942	32.521	16.415	8.360
12	108.571	36.381	18.332	9.306	102.987	34.553	17.444	8.887
13	115.017	38.544	19.424	9.863	108.681	36.468	18.413	9.384
14	121.149	40.602	20.464	10.394	114.044	38.271	19.327	9.853
15	126.982	42.560	21.454	10.899	119.096	39.971	20.188	10.295
16	132.532	44.423	22.395	11.380	123.854	41.572	21.000	10.712
17	137.811	46.197	23.292	11.838	128.336	43.081	21.766	11.106
18	142.833	47.884	24.145	12.274	132.557	44.502	22.487	11.477
19	147.611	49.489	24.957	12.690	136.534	45.842	23.167	11.828
20	152.157	51.016	25.730	13.085	140.279	47.103	23.808	12.158
21	156.481	52.470	26.466	13.462	143.806	48.292	24.412	12.470
22	160.595	53.853	27.166	13.821	147.129	49.412	24.982	12.764
23	164.508	55.169	27.833	14.163	150.259	50.468	25.519	13.042
24	168.231	56.421	28.467	14.489	153.206	51.462	26.025	13.303
25	171.773	57.613	29.071	14.799	155.983	52.399	26.502	13.550
26	175.142	58.746	29.646	15.094	158.598	53.282	26.951	13.783
27	178.348	59.825	30.193	15.375	161.061	54.113	27.375	14.003
28	181.397	60.852	30.714	15.643	163.382	54.897	27.774	14.211
29	184.298	61.828	31.210	15.898	165.567	55.635	28.151	14.406
30	187.058	62.758	31.681	16.141	167.626	56.331	28.506	14.591
31	189.683	63.642	32.130	16.372	169.564	56.986	28.840	14.765
32	192.181	64.483	32.558	16.593	171.391	57.604	29.156	14.929
33	194.557	65.284	32.965	16.803	173.111	58.186	29.453	15.084
34	196.817	66.046	33.352	17.003	174.731	58.734	29.733	15.230
35	198.968	66.771	33.720	17.193	176.257	59.250	29.997	15.368
36	201.014	67.461	34.071	17.374	177.695	59.737	30.246	15.498
37	202.960	68.117	34.405	17.547	179.048	60.195	30.481	15.621
38	204.811	68.741	34.723	17.711	180.324	60.627	30.702	15.737
39	206.573	69.336	35.025	17.868	181.525	61.034	30.910	15.846
40	208.248	69.901	35.313	18.017	182.656	61.418	31.107	15.949
41	209.842	70.439	35.587	18.159	183.722	61.779	31.292	16.046
42	211.359	70.951	35.848	18.294	184.726	62.119	31.467	16.138
43	212.802	71.438	36.096	18.423	185.671	62.440	31.631	16.225
44	214.174	71.902	36.333	18.546	186.562	62.742	31.786	16.306
45	215.480	72.343	36.557	18.663	187.401	63.027	31.932	16.383
46	216.722	72.762	36.771	18.774	188.191	63.295	32.070	16.456
47	217.904	73.162	36.975	18.880	188.935	63.548	32.200	16.524
48	219.028	73.542	37.169	18.981	189.636	63.786	32.323	16.589
49	220.097	73.903	37.354	19.077	190.296	64.010	32.438	16.650
50	221.114	74.247	37.529	19.169	190.918	64.222	32.547	16.708

The present value of a $1 annuity due at the *beginning* of each period

End of Year	At 7% Interest compounded Monthly	Quarterly	Semi-Annually	Annually	At 8% Interest compounded Monthly	Quarterly	Semi-Annually	Annually
1	11.625	3.898	1.966	1.000	11.572	3.884	1.962	1.000
2	22.465	7.535	3.802	1.935	22.258	7.472	3.775	1.926
3	32.575	10.927	5.515	2.808	32.125	10.787	5.452	2.783
4	42.004	14.093	7.115	3.624	41.235	13.849	7.002	3.577
5	50.797	17.046	8.608	4.387	49.647	16.678	8.435	4.312
6	58.997	19.801	10.002	5.100	57.415	19.292	9.760	4.993
7	66.644	22.372	11.303	5.767	64.587	21.707	10.986	5.623
8	73.775	24.770	12.517	6.389	71.210	23.938	12.118	6.206
9	80.426	27.007	13.651	6.971	77.325	25.999	13.166	6.747
10	86.629	29.095	14.710	7.515	82.971	27.903	14.134	7.247
11	92.413	31.042	15.698	8.024	88.185	29.662	15.029	7.710
12	97.807	32.859	16.620	8.499	92.999	31.287	15.857	8.139
13	102.838	34.554	17.482	8.943	97.444	32.788	16.622	8.536
14	107.530	36.135	18.285	9.358	101.548	34.175	17.330	8.904
15	111.905	37.611	19.036	9.745	105.338	35.456	17.984	9.244
16	115.985	38.987	19.736	10.108	108.838	36.640	18.588	9.559
17	119.790	40.272	20.390	10.447	112.069	37.733	19.148	9.851
18	123.339	41.470	21.001	10.763	115.053	38.744	19.665	10.122
19	126.649	42.587	21.571	11.059	117.807	39.677	20.143	10.372
20	129.735	43.630	22.102	11.336	120.351	40.539	20.584	10.604
21	132.613	44.603	22.599	11.594	122.700	41.336	20.993	10.818
22	135.297	45.511	23.063	11.836	124.869	42.072	21.371	11.017
23	137.801	46.358	23.495	12.061	126.872	42.752	21.720	11.201
24	140.135	47.148	23.899	12.272	128.721	43.380	22.043	11.371
25	142.312	47.885	24.277	12.469	130.428	43.960	22.341	11.529
26	144.343	48.573	24.629	12.654	132.005	44.496	22.617	11.675
27	146.236	49.214	24.957	12.826	133.461	44.992	22.873	11.810
28	148.002	49.813	25.264	12.987	134.805	45.449	23.109	11.935
29	149.649	50.371	25.550	13.137	136.046	45.872	23.327	12.051
30	151.184	50.892	25.818	13.278	137.192	46.262	23.528	12.158
31	152.617	51.378	26.067	13.409	138.250	46.623	23.715	12.258
32	153.952	51.832	26.300	13.532	139.227	46.957	23.887	12.350
33	155.198	52.255	26.518	13.647	140.130	47.265	24.047	12.435
34	156.359	52.650	26.721	13.754	140.963	47.549	24.194	12.514
35	157.443	53.018	26.910	13.854	141.732	47.812	24.330	12.587
36	158.453	53.362	27.087	13.948	142.442	48.055	24.456	12.655
37	159.395	53.682	27.253	14.035	143.098	48.279	24.573	12.717
38	160.274	53.981	27.407	14.117	143.704	48.486	24.680	12.775
39	161.093	54.260	27.551	14.193	144.263	48.678	24.780	12.829
40	161.858	54.521	27.685	14.265	144.779	48.854	24.872	12.879
41	162.570	54.763	27.810	14.332	145.256	49.018	24.957	12.925
42	163.235	54.990	27.928	14.394	145.696	49.169	25.036	12.967
43	163.855	55.201	28.037	14.452	146.103	49.308	25.109	13.007
44	164.433	55.399	28.139	14.507	146.478	49.437	25.176	13.043
45	164.972	55.582	28.234	14.558	146.825	49.556	25.238	13.077
46	165.474	55.754	28.323	14.606	147.145	49.666	25.295	13.108
47	165.943	55.914	28.406	14.650	147.440	49.768	25.349	13.137
48	166.380	56.064	28.484	14.692	147.713	49.861	25.398	13.164
49	166.788	56.203	28.556	14.730	147.965	49.948	25.443	13.189
50	167.168	56.333	28.623	14.767	148.197	50.028	25.485	13.212

The present value of a $1 annuity due at the *beginning* of each period

End of Year	At 9% Interest compounded Monthly	Quarterly	Semi-Annually	Annually	At 10% Interest compounded Monthly	Quarterly	Semi-Annually	Annually
1	11.521	3.870	1.957	1.000	11.469	3.856	1.952	1.000
2	22.053	7.410	3.749	1.917	21.851	7.349	3.723	1.909
3	31.683	10.649	5.390	2.759	31.249	10.514	5.329	2.736
4	40.486	13.612	6.893	3.531	39.757	13.381	6.786	3.487
5	48.535	16.323	8.269	4.240	47.458	15.979	8.108	4.170
6	55.893	18.803	9.529	4.890	54.428	18.332	9.306	4.791
7	62.620	21.072	10.683	5.486	60.739	20.464	10.394	5.355
8	68.770	23.147	11.740	6.033	66.451	22.395	11.380	5.868
9	74.393	25.046	12.707	6.535	71.621	24.145	12.274	6.335
10	79.534	26.783	13.593	6.995	76.302	25.730	13.085	6.759
11	84.233	28.372	14.405	7.418	80.539	27.166	13.821	7.145
12	88.530	29.826	15.148	7.805	84.374	28.467	14.489	7.495
13	92.458	31.156	15.828	8.161	87.846	29.646	15.094	7.814
14	96.050	32.373	16.451	8.487	90.988	30.714	15.643	8.103
15	99.333	33.486	17.022	8.786	93.833	31.681	16.141	8.367
16	102.335	34.504	17.544	9.061	96.408	32.558	16.593	8.606
17	105.079	35.436	18.023	9.313	98.739	33.352	17.003	8.824
18	107.588	36.288	18.461	9.544	100.849	34.071	17.374	9.022
19	109.882	37.068	18.862	9.756	102.759	34.723	17.711	9.201
20	111.979	37.781	19.230	9.950	104.488	35.313	18.017	9.365
21	113.896	38.434	19.566	10.129	106.053	35.848	18.294	9.514
22	115.648	39.031	19.874	10.292	107.470	36.333	18.546	9.649
23	117.251	39.577	20.156	10.442	108.753	36.771	18.774	9.772
24	118.716	40.077	20.415	10.580	109.913	37.169	18.981	9.883
25	120.055	40.534	20.651	10.707	110.964	37.529	19.169	9.985
26	121.280	40.952	20.868	10.823	111.916	37.856	19.339	10.077
27	122.399	41.334	21.066	10.929	112.777	38.152	19.493	10.161
28	123.423	41.684	21.248	11.027	113.556	38.419	19.633	10.237
29	124.359	42.005	21.414	11.116	114.262	38.662	19.761	10.307
30	125.214	42.298	21.567	11.198	114.900	38.882	19.876	10.370
31	125.996	42.566	21.706	11.274	115.479	39.081	19.980	10.427
32	126.711	42.811	21.834	11.343	116.002	39.262	20.075	10.479
33	127.365	43.035	21.951	11.406	116.476	39.425	20.161	10.526
34	127.962	43.240	22.058	11.464	116.905	39.573	20.239	10.569
35	128.509	43.428	22.156	11.518	117.293	39.707	20.310	10.609
36	129.008	43.600	22.246	11.567	117.644	39.829	20.374	10.644
37	129.465	43.757	22.328	11.612	117.962	39.939	20.432	10.677
38	129.883	43.900	22.404	11.653	118.250	40.039	20.485	10.706
39	130.264	44.032	22.473	11.691	118.511	40.129	20.533	10.733
40	130.613	44.152	22.536	11.726	118.747	40.211	20.576	10.757
41	130.932	44.262	22.594	11.757	118.960	40.285	20.616	10.779
42	131.224	44.363	22.647	11.787	119.154	40.353	20.651	10.799
43	131.491	44.455	22.695	11.813	119.329	40.413	20.684	10.817
44	131.734	44.539	22.740	11.838	119.487	40.469	20.713	10.834
45	131.957	44.616	22.780	11.861	119.631	40.519	20.740	10.849
46	132.161	44.687	22.817	11.881	119.760	40.564	20.764	10.863
47	132.347	44.751	22.852	11.900	119.878	40.605	20.786	10.875
48	132.518	44.810	22.883	11.918	119.984	40.642	20.806	10.887
49	132.673	44.864	22.911	11.934	120.080	40.676	20.824	10.897
50	132.816	44.914	22.938	11.948	120.168	40.706	20.840	10.906

The present value of a $1 annuity due at the *beginning* of each period

End of Year	*At 11% Interest compounded*				*At 12% Interest compounded*			
	Monthly	*Quarterly*	*Semi-Annually*	*Annually*	*Monthly*	*Quarterly*	*Semi-Annually*	*Annually*
1	11.418	3.842	1.948	1.000	11.368	3.829	1.943	1.000
2	21.652	7.289	3.698	1.901	21.456	7.230	3.673	1.893
3	30.825	10.382	5.270	2.713	30.409	10.253	5.212	2.690
4	39.046	13.157	6.683	3.444	38.354	12.938	6.582	3.402
5	46.415	15.646	7.952	4.102	45.405	15.324	7.802	4.037
6	53.019	17.879	9.093	4.696	51.662	17.444	8.887	4.605
7	58.938	19.883	10.117	5.231	57.215	19.327	9.853	5.111
8	64.244	21.681	11.038	5.712	62.143	21.000	10.712	5.564
9	68.999	23.293	11.865	6.146	66.516	22.487	11.477	5.968
10	73.261	24.740	12.608	6.537	70.398	23.808	12.158	6.328
11	77.081	26.038	13.275	6.889	73.842	24.982	12.764	6.650
12	80.504	27.203	13.875	7.207	76.899	26.025	13.303	6.938
13	83.573	28.248	14.414	7.492	79.611	26.951	13.783	7.194
14	86.323	29.185	14.898	7.750	82.018	27.774	14.211	7.424
15	88.788	30.026	15.333	7.982	84.155	28.506	14.591	7.628
16	90.998	30.781	15.724	8.191	86.051	29.156	14.929	7.811
17	92.978	31.458	16.075	8.379	87.733	29.733	15.230	7.974
18	94.753	32.065	16.391	8.549	89.227	30.246	15.498	8.120
19	96.344	32.610	16.674	8.702	90.552	30.702	15.737	8.250
20	97.770	33.099	16.929	8.839	91.728	31.107	15.949	8.366
21	99.048	33.537	17.157	8.963	92.771	31.467	16.138	8.469
22	100.193	33.931	17.363	9.075	93.697	31.786	16.306	8.562
23	101.220	34.284	17.548	9.176	94.519	32.070	16.456	8.645
24	102.140	34.601	17.714	9.266	95.249	32.323	16.589	8.718
25	102.964	34.885	17.863	9.348	95.896	32.547	16.708	8.784
26	103.703	35.140	17.997	9.422	96.470	32.746	16.813	8.843
27	104.366	35.368	18.117	9.488	96.980	32.923	16.907	8.896
28	104.960	35.574	18.225	9.548	97.433	33.080	16.991	8.943
29	105.492	35.758	18.322	9.602	97.834	33.220	17.065	8.984
30	105.969	35.923	18.410	9.650	98.191	33.344	17.131	9.022
31	106.396	36.071	18.488	9.694	98.507	33.455	17.190	9.055
32	106.780	36.204	18.558	9.733	98.787	33.553	17.242	9.085
33	107.123	36.323	18.622	9.769	99.036	33.640	17.289	9.112
34	107.431	36.430	18.679	9.801	99.257	33.717	17.331	9.135
35	107.707	36.526	18.730	9.829	99.454	33.786	17.368	9.157
36	107.954	36.612	18.776	9.855	99.628	33.847	17.401	9.176
37	108.176	36.690	18.817	9.879	99.782	33.901	17.430	9.192
38	108.374	36.759	18.854	9.900	99.919	33.949	17.456	9.208
39	108.552	36.821	18.887	9.919	100.041	33.992	17.479	9.221
40	108.712	36.877	18.917	9.936	100.149	34.030	17.500	9.233
41	108.855	36.927	18.944	9.951	100.245	34.064	17.518	9.244
42	108.983	36.972	18.968	9.965	100.330	34.094	17.534	9.253
43	109.098	37.012	18.990	9.977	100.405	34.121	17.549	9.262
44	109.201	37.048	19.009	9.989	100.472	34.144	17.562	9.270
45	109.293	37.081	19.027	9.999	100.531	34.165	17.573	9.276
46	109.376	37.110	19.043	10.008	100.584	34.184	17.584	9.283
47	109.450	37.136	19.057	10.016	100.631	34.201	17.593	9.288
48	109.517	37.159	19.069	10.024	100.673	34.216	17.601	9.293
49	109.576	37.180	19.081	10.030	100.709	34.229	17.608	9.297
50	109.630	37.199	19.091	10.036	100.742	34.240	17.615	9.301

The present value of a $1 annuity due at the *beginning* of each period

End of Year	*At 13% Interest compounded* Monthly	Quarterly	Semi-Annually	Annually	*At 14% Interest compounded* Monthly	Quarterly	Semi-Annually	Annually
1	11.317	3.815	1.939	1.000	11.267	3.802	1.935	1.000
2	21.262	7.172	3.648	1.885	21.071	7.115	3.624	1.877
3	30.000	10.126	5.156	2.668	29.600	10.002	5.100	2.647
4	37.679	12.725	6.485	3.361	37.021	12.517	6.389	3.322
5	44.426	15.012	7.656	3.974	43.478	14.710	7.515	3.914
6	50.355	17.024	8.689	4.517	49.096	16.620	8.499	4.433
7	55.565	18.795	9.600	4.998	53.984	18.285	9.358	4.889
8	60.143	20.353	10.403	5.423	58.237	19.736	10.108	5.288
9	64.165	21.724	11.111	5.799	61.937	21.001	10.763	5.639
10	67.700	22.930	11.735	6.132	65.157	22.102	11.336	5.946
11	70.806	23.992	12.285	6.426	67.958	23.063	11.836	6.216
12	73.535	24.926	12.770	6.687	70.395	23.899	12.272	6.453
13	75.933	25.747	13.198	6.918	72.516	24.629	12.654	6.660
14	78.041	26.471	13.575	7.122	74.360	25.264	12.987	6.842
15	79.892	27.107	13.907	7.302	75.966	25.818	13.278	7.002
16	81.520	27.667	14.201	7.462	77.362	26.300	13.532	7.142
17	82.949	28.159	14.459	7.604	78.578	26.721	13.754	7.265
18	84.206	28.593	14.687	7.729	79.635	27.087	13.948	7.373
19	85.310	28.974	14.888	7.840	80.555	27.407	14.117	7.467
20	86.280	29.310	15.065	7.938	81.355	27.685	14.265	7.550
21	87.132	29.605	15.221	8.025	82.051	27.928	14.394	7.623
22	87.881	29.865	15.359	8.102	82.657	28.139	14.507	7.687
23	88.539	30.094	15.480	8.170	83.184	28.323	14.606	7.743
24	89.118	30.295	15.587	8.230	83.643	28.484	14.692	7.792
25	89.626	30.472	15.682	8.283	84.042	28.623	14.767	7.835
26	90.073	30.628	15.765	8.330	84.389	28.745	14.832	7.873
27	90.465	30.765	15.838	8.372	84.691	28.851	14.890	7.906
28	90.810	30.886	15.903	8.409	84.954	28.944	14.940	7.935
29	91.113	30.992	15.960	8.441	85.183	29.025	14.984	7.961
30	91.379	31.085	16.010	8.470	85.382	29.095	15.022	7.983
31	91.613	31.167	16.054	8.496	85.555	29.156	15.055	8.003
32	91.818	31.239	16.094	8.518	85.706	29.210	15.084	8.020
33	91.999	31.303	16.128	8.538	85.837	29.256	15.110	8.035
34	92.158	31.359	16.158	8.556	85.951	29.297	15.132	8.048
35	92.297	31.408	16.185	8.572	86.050	29.332	15.152	8.060
36	92.420	31.452	16.209	8.586	86.136	29.363	15.169	8.070
37	92.528	31.490	16.230	8.598	86.211	29.390	15.183	8.079
38	92.622	31.523	16.248	8.609	86.277	29.413	15.196	8.087
39	92.705	31.553	16.264	8.618	86.334	29.433	15.208	8.094
40	92.778	31.579	16.278	8.627	86.383	29.451	15.218	8.100
41	92.843	31.602	16.291	8.634	86.426	29.467	15.226	8.105
42	92.899	31.622	16.302	8.641	86.464	29.480	15.234	8.110
43	92.949	31.640	16.312	8.647	86.496	29.492	15.240	8.114
44	92.992	31.655	16.320	8.652	86.524	29.502	15.246	8.117
45	93.030	31.669	16.328	8.657	86.549	29.511	15.251	8.120
46	93.064	31.681	16.335	8.661	86.571	29.519	15.255	8.123
47	93.094	31.691	16.341	8.664	86.589	29.525	15.259	8.126
48	93.120	31.701	16.346	8.668	86.606	29.531	15.263	8.128
49	93.142	31.709	16.350	8.671	86.620	29.537	15.266	8.130
50	93.162	31.716	16.354	8.673	86.632	29.541	15.268	8.131

The present value of a $1 annuity due at the *beginning* of each period

End of Year	At 15% Interest compounded Monthly	Quarterly	Semi-Annually	Annually	At 16% Interest compounded Monthly	Quarterly	Semi-Annually	Annually
1	11.218	3.788	1.930	1.000	11.169	3.775	1.926	1.000
2	20.882	7.058	3.601	1.870	20.696	7.002	3.577	1.862
3	29.208	9.880	5.046	2.626	28.823	9.760	4.993	2.605
4	36.381	12.315	6.297	3.283	35.756	12.118	6.206	3.246
5	42.560	14.417	7.379	3.855	41.670	14.134	7.247	3.798
6	47.884	16.232	8.315	4.352	46.715	15.857	8.139	4.274
7	52.470	17.797	9.126	4.784	51.019	17.330	8.904	4.685
8	56.421	19.149	9.827	5.160	54.690	18.588	9.559	5.039
9	59.825	20.315	10.434	5.487	57.821	19.665	10.122	5.344
10	62.758	21.322	10.959	5.772	60.493	20.584	10.604	5.607
11	65.284	22.190	11.413	6.019	62.772	21.371	11.017	5.833
12	67.461	22.940	11.807	6.234	64.716	22.043	11.371	6.029
13	69.336	23.587	12.147	6.421	66.374	22.617	11.675	6.197
14	70.951	24.146	12.441	6.583	67.789	23.109	11.935	6.342
15	72.343	24.628	12.696	6.724	68.995	23.528	12.158	6.468
16	73.542	25.044	12.917	6.847	70.025	23.887	12.350	6.575
17	74.575	25.403	13.107	6.954	70.903	24.194	12.514	6.668
18	75.464	25.713	13.273	7.047	71.652	24.456	12.655	6.749
19	76.231	25.981	13.415	7.128	72.291	24.680	12.775	6.818
20	76.892	26.212	13.539	7.198	72.836	24.872	12.879	6.877
21	77.461	26.411	13.646	7.259	73.301	25.036	12.967	6.929
22	77.951	26.583	13.739	7.312	73.698	25.176	13.043	6.973
23	78.373	26.731	13.819	7.359	74.036	25.295	13.108	7.011
24	78.737	26.859	13.888	7.399	74.325	25.398	13.164	7.044
25	79.050	26.970	13.948	7.434	74.571	25.485	13.212	7.073
26	79.320	27.065	14.000	7.464	74.781	25.560	13.253	7.097
27	79.553	27.148	14.045	7.491	74.960	25.624	13.288	7.118
28	79.753	27.219	14.084	7.514	75.113	25.678	13.319	7.136
29	79.926	27.280	14.117	7.534	75.243	25.725	13.344	7.152
30	80.075	27.333	14.146	7.551	75.354	25.765	13.367	7.166
31	80.203	27.379	14.172	7.566	75.449	25.799	13.386	7.177
32	80.313	27.418	14.193	7.579	75.530	25.828	13.402	7.187
33	80.408	27.452	14.212	7.591	75.599	25.853	13.416	7.196
34	80.490	27.481	14.228	7.600	75.658	25.875	13.428	7.203
35	80.561	27.507	14.243	7.609	75.708	25.893	13.438	7.210
36	80.622	27.529	14.255	7.617	75.751	25.908	13.447	7.215
37	80.674	27.548	14.265	7.623	75.788	25.922	13.455	7.220
38	80.719	27.564	14.275	7.629	75.819	25.933	13.461	7.224
39	80.758	27.578	14.282	7.634	75.846	25.943	13.467	7.228
40	80.792	27.590	14.289	7.638	75.868	25.951	13.471	7.231
41	80.820	27.601	14.295	7.642	75.888	25.958	13.475	7.233
42	80.845	27.610	14.300	7.645	75.904	25.964	13.479	7.236
43	80.867	27.617	14.305	7.648	75.918	25.969	13.482	7.238
44	80.885	27.624	14.309	7.650	75.930	25.974	13.485	7.239
45	80.901	27.630	14.312	7.652	75.940	25.978	13.487	7.241
46	80.915	27.635	14.315	7.654	75.949	25.981	13.489	7.242
47	80.927	27.639	14.317	7.656	75.957	25.984	13.490	7.243
48	80.937	27.643	14.319	7.657	75.963	25.986	13.492	7.244
49	80.946	27.646	14.321	7.659	75.968	25.988	13.493	7.245
50	80.953	27.649	14.323	7.660	75.973	25.990	13.494	7.246

The present value of a $1 annuity due at the *beginning* of each period

End of Year	At 17% Interest compounded Monthly	Quarterly	Semi-Annually	Annually	At 18% Interest compounded Monthly	Quarterly	Semi-Annually	Annually
1	11.120	3.762	1.922	1.000	11.071	3.749	1.917	1.000
2	20.512	6.947	3.554	1.855	20.331	6.893	3.531	1.847
3	28.446	9.644	4.941	2.585	28.076	9.529	4.890	2.566
4	35.147	11.927	6.119	3.210	34.553	11.740	6.033	3.174
5	40.807	13.859	7.119	3.743	39.971	13.593	6.995	3.690
6	45.588	15.496	7.969	4.199	44.502	15.148	7.805	4.127
7	49.627	16.881	8.691	4.589	48.292	16.451	8.487	4.498
8	53.038	18.054	9.304	4.922	51.462	17.544	9.061	4.812
9	55.920	19.047	9.825	5.207	54.113	18.461	9.544	5.078
10	58.353	19.888	10.268	5.451	56.331	19.230	9.950	5.303
11	60.409	20.600	10.644	5.659	58.186	19.874	10.292	5.494
12	62.145	21.203	10.963	5.836	59.737	20.415	10.580	5.656
13	63.612	21.713	11.234	5.988	61.034	20.868	10.823	5.793
14	64.851	22.145	11.465	6.118	62.119	21.248	11.027	5.910
15	65.898	22.510	11.660	6.229	63.027	21.567	11.198	6.008
16	66.782	22.820	11.827	6.324	63.786	21.834	11.343	6.092
17	67.528	23.082	11.968	6.405	64.421	22.058	11.464	6.162
18	68.159	23.304	12.088	6.475	64.952	22.246	11.567	6.222
19	68.691	23.492	12.190	6.534	65.396	22.404	11.653	6.273
20	69.141	23.651	12.276	6.584	65.768	22.536	11.726	6.316
21	69.521	23.786	12.350	6.628	66.078	22.647	11.787	6.353
22	69.843	23.900	12.412	6.665	66.338	22.740	11.838	6.384
23	70.114	23.996	12.465	6.696	66.556	22.817	11.881	6.410
24	70.343	24.078	12.510	6.723	66.737	22.883	11.918	6.432
25	70.536	24.147	12.549	6.746	66.889	22.938	11.948	6.451
26	70.700	24.206	12.581	6.766	67.017	22.984	11.974	6.467
27	70.838	24.256	12.609	6.783	67.123	23.022	11.996	6.480
28	70.954	24.298	12.632	6.798	67.212	23.054	12.014	6.492
29	71.053	24.333	12.652	6.810	67.286	23.081	12.029	6.502
30	71.136	24.363	12.669	6.820	67.349	23.104	12.042	6.510
31	71.206	24.389	12.684	6.829	67.401	23.123	12.053	6.517
32	71.265	24.410	12.696	6.837	67.444	23.139	12.062	6.523
33	71.316	24.429	12.706	6.844	67.481	23.153	12.070	6.528
34	71.358	24.444	12.715	6.849	67.511	23.164	12.077	6.532
35	71.394	24.457	12.722	6.854	67.536	23.173	12.082	6.536
36	71.424	24.468	12.729	6.858	67.558	23.181	12.087	6.539
37	71.449	24.478	12.734	6.862	67.576	23.188	12.091	6.541
38	71.471	24.486	12.739	6.865	67.590	23.193	12.094	6.543
39	71.489	24.492	12.743	6.867	67.603	23.198	12.097	6.545
40	71.505	24.498	12.746	6.869	67.613	23.202	12.099	6.547
41	71.518	24.503	12.749	6.871	67.622	23.205	12.101	6.548
42	71.529	24.507	12.751	6.873	67.629	23.208	12.102	6.549
43	71.538	24.510	12.753	6.874	67.635	23.210	12.104	6.550
44	71.546	24.513	12.755	6.875	67.641	23.212	12.105	6.551
45	71.552	24.516	12.756	6.876	67.645	23.214	12.106	6.552
46	71.558	24.518	12.758	6.877	67.648	23.215	12.107	6.552
47	71.563	24.520	12.759	6.878	67.651	23.216	12.107	6.553
48	71.567	24.521	12.760	6.879	67.654	23.217	12.108	6.553
49	71.570	24.522	12.760	6.879	67.656	23.218	12.109	6.554
50	71.573	24.523	12.761	6.880	67.658	23.219	12.109	6.554

TABLE 13

Evaluating annuity yields

Mortality table
Male and Female life tables, Canada 1970-1972
Expectation of life in years

Age	*Male*	*Female*	*Age*	*Male*	*Female*
10	61.17	67.91	50	24.52	29.86
11	60.19	66.93	51	23.71	28.98
12	59.22	65.95	52	22.91	28.11
13	58.24	64.97	53	22.11	27.24
14	57.28	63.99	54	21.34	26.38
15	56.33	63.02	55	20.57	25.53
16	55.39	62.05	56	19.82	24.68
17	54.46	61.08	57	19.08	23.85
18	53.53	60.11	58	8.35	23.02
19	52.62	59.15	59	17.64	22.20
20	51.71	58.18	60	16.95	21.39
21	50.80	57.21	61	16.27	20.58
22	49.89	56.25	62	15.61	19.79
23	48.98	55.28	63	14.96	19.01
24	46.07	54.31	64	14.33	18.25
25	47.16	53.34	65	13.72	17.47
26	46.23	52.37	66	13.12	16.72
27	45.30	51.40	67	12.54	15.98
28	44.37	50.44	68	11.98	15.26
29	43.44	49.47	69	11.43	14.55
30	42.50	48.51	70	10.90	13.85
31	41.56	47.54	71	10.38	13.17
32	40.63	46.58	72	9.88	12.51
33	39.69	45.62	73	9.39	11.86
34	38.76	44.67	74	8.92	11.24
35	37.83	43.71	75	8.47	10.63
36	36.90	42.76	76	8.02	10.03
37	35.97	41.81	77	7.60	9.46
38	35.05	40.87	78	7.19	8.91
39	34.13	39.92	79	6.79	8.38
40	33.22	38.99	80	6.41	7.88
41	32.32	38.05	81	6.05	7.39
42	31.42	37.13	82	5.70	6.93
43	30.53	36.20	83	5.36	6.48
44	29.65	35.28	84	5.04	6.06
45	28.77	34.37	85	4.74	5.67
46	27.90	33.45			
47	27.04	32.55			
48	26.19	31.65			
49	25.35	30.75			

The Springbank Wealthy Series
Order Now!

How do people with no greater advantages than you manage to achieve so much more success? In his highly-readable books on personal financial planning, Henry Zimmer gives the answers, outlining simple techniques for making your income work harder and helping your investments grow.

THE WEALTHY PROCRASTINATOR

Financial planning for those over forty!

Unlike David Chilton's The Wealthy Barber, Zimmer's new book, *The Wealthy Procrastinator,* is aimed at men and women over forty. This intriguing story spans a twenty-year period from 1995 to 2015, anticipating the kind of political, social and economic restructuring that might occur and its effect on the ordinary Canadian. Using Zimmer's commonsense principles, the book's fictional heroes progress from mid-life financial chaos to a successful retirement. *The Wealthy Procrastinator* goes beyond the basics of mortgage prepayment, mutual fund programs and life insurance protection to cover such issues as the wise use of severance payments, inheritances, wills, and specific criteria for buying or starting a business.

Now Available

"For people over forty who have neglected their financial planning, The Wealthy Procrastinator takes the mystery out of money management. If you want to spend less time worrying about your financial future and more time enjoying life, I strongly recommend it."

Dian Cohen, former Financial Editor,
CTV News

Quantity________ **$15.95**

THE MONEY MANAGER FOR CANADIANS

Henry Zimmer's 70,000 best-seller—updated and revised!

Already a stand-by for investment-minded Canadians, *The Money Manager* is a useful companion book to the Springbank Wealthy Series. In this new edition, Henry Zimmer has updated his popular guide to show that you don't need to be a mathematical genius to survive in an uncertain economy. This complete and easy-to-understand reference book includes simple tables for calculating investment yields, the costs of borrowing money and leasing, life insurance costs and benefits, current mortgage rates and terms, and other financial arrangements.

Now Available

Quantity________ **$15.95**

THE WEALTHY PAPER CARRIERS

For the first time—a motivational story on wealth accumulation for young adults!

The Wealthy Paper Carriers is an entertaining and motivational story that shows young adults how to gain more from life than low-paying, low-prestige jobs with no future. Written in the novel form, it tells the story of a brother and sister faced with various life choices over a twenty-year period. Henry Zimmer demonstrates how success is a matter of working intelligently rather than excessively. He shows how to set goals and priorities and suggests a step by step plan to achieve them. For young people—and anyone intimidated by the world of financial planning—*The Wealthy Paper Carriers* is easy to read and easy to understand. Written in collaboration with students and teachers, it is particularly recommended for educators.

Release November, 1993 in time for Christmas!

Quantity________ **$15.95**

THE WEALTHY WOMEN

A story of financial planning for women of all ages.

Destined to be a sure-fire best seller, Henry Zimmer's newest financial planning novel is aimed specifically at Canadian women of all ages and circumstances. Written with extensive input from successful women in various fields, *The Wealthy Women* reviews the standing of women in our changing society, spotlights exciting opportunities, and suggests practical ways of setting goals and achieving personal success.

Release: Spring, 1994

Quantity________ **$15.95**

TOTAL NUMBER OF COPIES OF ALL BOOKS

Quantity________ x $17.07 (GST Included) = $__________

Name

Firm IF APPLICABLE

Title IF APPLICABLE

Address

City Province Postal Code

Telephone ( ) Fax ( )

Please Mail or Fax your order to:

Springbank Publishing

5425 Elbow Drive S.W. Calgary, Alberta T2V 1H7
Fax: (403) 640-9138
Telephone: (403) 640-9137 for information only

For bulk orders and to arrange Mr. Zimmer's speaking engagements, please contact: Susan Blanchard, (403) 242-9769
Fax: (403) 686-0889

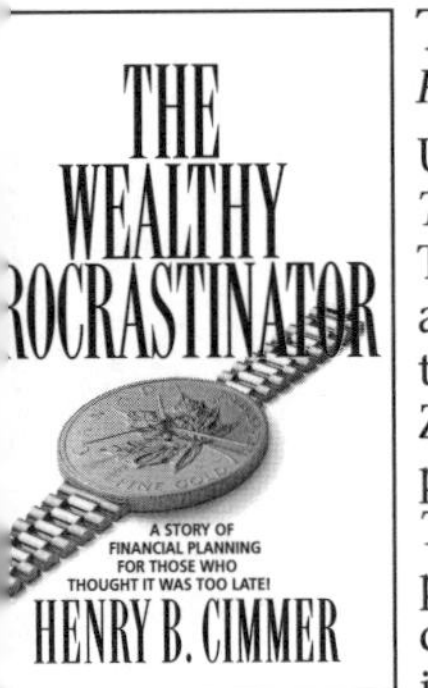